BEYOND RETRIBUTION

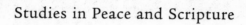

Studies in Peace and Scripture

BEYOND RETRIBUTION

*A New Testament Vision
for Justice, Crime, and Punishment*

CHRISTOPHER D. MARSHALL

*William B. Eerdmans Publishing Company
Grand Rapids, Michigan / Cambridge, U.K.*

*Lime Grove House Publishing
Auckland, New Zealand / Sydney, Australia*

Published jointly 2001 by
Wm. B. Eerdmans Publishing Co.
255 Jefferson Ave. S.E., Grand Rapids, Michigan 49503 /
P.O. Box 163, Cambridge CB3 9PU U.K.
www.eerdmans.com
and by
Lime Grove House Publishing Ltd
P.O. Box 37-955
Parnell, Auckland, N.Z. /
P.O. Box 1704
Rozelle, N.S.W.
Sydney, Australia

Printed in the United States of America

06 05 04 03 02   7 6 5 4 3 2

Library of Congress Cataloging-in-Publication Data

Marshall, Christopher D.
Beyond retribution: a New Testament vision for justice, crime, and punishment /
Christopher D. Marshall.
p.   cm.
Includes bibliographical references.
Eerdmans ISBN 0-8028-4797-8 (pbk.: alk. paper)
1. Criminal justice, Administration of. 2. Christianity and justice. I. Title.

HV7419.M36 2001
364 — dc21

2001023015

Lime Grove House ISBN 1-876798-30-0

For Margaret, Peter, and Andrew
and in memory of my father,
Tom Marshall (1921-1993),
with loving gratitude

ὧν δέδωκάς μοι ὅτι σοί εἰσιν
(JOHN 17:9)

CONTENTS

CONTENTS

Contents

Visions of peace abound in the Bible, whose pages are also filled with the language and the reality of war. In this respect, the Bible is thoroughly at home in the modern world, whether as a literary classic or as a unique sacred text. This is, perhaps, a part of the Bible's realism: bridging the distance between its world and our own is a history filled with visions of peace accompanying the reality of war. That alone would justify study of peace and war in the Bible. However, for those communities in which the Bible is sacred scripture, the matter is more urgent. For them, it is crucial to understand what the Bible says about peace — and about war. These issues have often divided Christians from each other, and the way Christians have understood them has had terrible consequences for Jews and, indeed, for the world. A series of scholarly investigations cannot hope to resolve these issues, but it can hope, as this one does, to aid our understanding of them.

Over the past century a substantial body of literature has grown up around the topic of the Bible and war. Studies in great abundance have been devoted to historical questions about ancient Israel's conception and conduct of war and about the position of the early church on participation in the Roman Empire and its military. It is not surprising that many of these studies have been motivated by theological and ethical concerns, which may themselves be attributed to the Bible's own seemingly disjunctive preoccupation with peace and, at the same time, with war. If not within the Bible itself, then at least from Aqiba and Tertullian, the question has been raised whether — and if so, then on what basis — those who worship God may legitimately participate in war. With the Reformation, the churches divided on this question. The division was unequal, with the majority of Christendom agreeing that, however regrettable war may be, Christians have biblical warrant for participating in it. A minority countered that, however necessary war may appear, Christians have a biblical mandate to avoid it. Modern historical studies have served to bolster one side of this division or the other.

Meanwhile, it has become clear that a narrow focus on participation in war is not the only way, and likely not the best way, to approach the Bible on the topic of peace. War and peace are not simply two sides of the same coin; each is broader than its contrast with the other. In spite of agreement on this point, the number of studies devoted to the Bible and peace is still very small, especially in English. Consequently, answers to the most basic questions remain to be settled. Among these questions is that of what the Bible means in speaking of *shalom* or *eirēnē*, the Hebrew and the Greek terms usually translated into English as "peace." By the same token, what the Bible has to say about peace is not limited to its use of these two terms. Questions remain about the relation of peace, in the Bible, to considerations of justice, integrity, and — in the broadest sense — salvation. And of course there still remains the question of the relation between peace and war. In fact, what the Bible says about peace is often framed in the language of war. The Bible very often uses martial imagery to portray God's own action, whether it be in creation, in judgment against or in defense of Israel, or in the cross and resurrection of Jesus Christ — actions aimed at achieving peace.

This close association of peace and war, to which we have already drawn attention, presents serious problems for the contemporary appropriation of the Bible. Are human freedom, justice, and liberation — and the liberation of creation — furthered or hindered by the martial, frequently royal, and pervasively masculine terms in which the Bible speaks of peace? These questions cannot be answered by the rigorous and critical exegesis of the biblical texts alone; they demand serious moral and theological reflection. But that reflection will be substantially aided by exegetical studies of the kind included in this series, even as these studies will be illumined by including just that kind of reflection within them.

SERIES PREFACE

"Studies in Peace and Scripture" is sponsored by the Institute of Mennonite Studies, the research agency of the Associated Mennonite Biblical Seminary. (The volumes in this series appear with various publishers.) The seminary and the tradition it represents have a particular interest in peace and, even more so, an abiding interest in the Bible. We hope that this ecumenical series will contribute to a deeper understanding of both.

BEN C. OLLENBURGER,
Old Testament Editor

WILLARD M. SWARTLEY,
New Testament Editor

PREFACE

During a visit to the offices of the Mennonite Central Committee in Akron, Pennsylvania, in 1991, I was given a copy of Howard Zehr's book *Changing Lenses: A New Focus for Crime and Justice*. I didn't get around to reading this remarkable book until I returned to New Zealand the following year, and even then did so primarily because I was interested in the chapter on biblical justice. The book made a deep impression on me. Here was an authoritative, well-researched, clearly written, and profoundly Christian analysis of the Western criminal-justice system, together with a proposal for an alternative "restorative" approach to dealing with criminal offending that would be more just, more humane, and more compatible with both Christian values and the social needs of our day. I was inspired to write a lengthy review of the book, which was published in the New Zealand journal *Stimulus* in May 1993, along with responses from lawyers, judges, and a prison chaplain.

The article engendered a good deal of interest from readers. Like other Western countries, New Zealand has experienced something of an epidemic in criminal offending over recent decades. One study found that almost one-third of New Zealanders claim to have been a victim of crime (usually minor) at some time in their lives. Such was the interest in the issue that the publishers of *Stimulus* decided to convene a conference on crime and to invite Dr. Zehr as the keynote speaker. The conference was held in June 1994. I was asked to be one of several contributors at the conference, and I presented a paper on the contribution of New Testament teaching to criminal justice issues. That paper was the embryo out of which this book has emerged.

Over recent decades, a growing number of Christians have become active in promoting the concept of "restorative" or "transformative" justice and in developing programs for dealing with criminal offenders based on restorative principles. They insist that this approach flows directly from the peace-making heart of the Christian gospel and is consistent with the teaching of the Scriptures. Yet to date comparatively little has been done to test or demonstrate this claim in detail from the teachings of the New Testament, which must be the primary reference point for Christian belief and practice. The available Christian literature on restorative justice, or on crime and punishment in general, contains comparatively little detailed reflection on what the New Testament has to say about such matters. Even Dr. Zehr's marvelous chapter on biblical justice makes limited reference to New Testament material. The same applies to other recent works on restorative justice. In Jim Consedine's *Restorative Justice: Healing the Effects of Crime,* the chapter on biblical justice has barely two pages on New Testament teaching. A. P. Boers devotes a chapter to New Testament teaching in *Justice that Heals: A Biblical Vision for Victims and Offenders,* while J. A. Hoyles's wider discussion of *Punishment in the Bible* has three chapters on New Testament material. Timothy Gorringe's illuminating historical and theological study *God's Just Vengeance* includes some examination of New Testament material but with a specific focus on the theme of atonement. All these books include useful insights, but their treatment of the New Testament data is relatively general, with little focused exegesis. My hope is that this extended survey of New Testament texts will go some way in serving as a supplement to Dr. Zehr's summary of Old Testament materials in furnishing the biblical foundations for the restorative justice movement.

In the first chapter I discuss some of the methodological problems entailed in applying to the public domain of mainstream society ethical teaching from the New Testament that is addressed primarily to the community of faith. Much more is required than identifying relevant texts, shuffling them into some convenient arrangement, and applying them directly to contemporary social problems. In Chapter 2, I make an attempt to understand the conception of "justice" that New Testament authors work with. Paul's teaching on the justice of God, especially as it emerges in his letter to the Romans, indicates that he understands divine justice in restorative more than retributive terms. The same is true of Jesus, who personally embodies the saving justice of God and who summons his followers to live consistently with the character of divine justice by practicing forgiveness and non-retaliation toward their enemies.

In Chapter 3, I review the long-standing debate over the ethics and purpose of punishment. The various theories of punishment that have emerged out of this debate all have something important to offer the attempt to understand the social institution of punishment, yet all have distinct limitations. Advocates of restorative justice are often reluctant to speak of punishment at all, although, as I suggest in this chapter, a reasonable case can be made for justifying punishment as a potentially restorative mechanism. In Chapter 4 I pursue further the theme of punishment, this time examining what the New Testament has to say about punishment, both human and divine. It is impossible to escape the conclusion that the New Testament writers see a valid place for punishment in the administration of justice, though in nearly every case it serves a predominantly redemptive rather than retributive purpose.

In light of this, there is good reason to expect Christians to oppose in principle the institution of capital punishment. Yet the extensive biblical materials appearing to sanction the death penalty compel many believers, including some Christian pacifists, to support its continuing use today. In Chapter 5, I offer a careful critique of the common biblical and moral arguments used in support of capital punishment. In the final chapter I draw together the threads of the discussion and affirm the pervasive New Testament challenge to imitate the justice of God by imitating the way of Christ in dealing with offenders and offending. Central to such imitation lies the practice of forgiveness, so in the concluding pages of the book I seek to understand the dynamics of the forgiveness process and its social relevance.

In writing this study, I have employed gender-inclusive language, which is itself a matter of restorative justice. I have not, of course, changed gender-exclusive language in sources I quote verbatim, which is a matter of historical respect. And while I have attempted to reduce the number of masculine possessive pronouns used for God, it has been beyond my stylistic ability to eliminate them entirely. (I use masculine pronouns, since this reflects the dominant practice of the ancient biblical authors.) I have also continued to refer to the Hebrew scriptures as the "Old Testament," since I believe there is nothing pejorative in this designation. Certainly at a theological level it signals belief that the Hebrew Bible bears witness to an earlier form of the covenant that has now been fulfilled and transformed by Christ. But it is "old" in the sense of being antecedent, not in the sense of being inferior or second-rate. The designation acknowledges the great antiquity of God's covenant dealings with the human race, without a record of which the "new thing" God has done in Christ would be impossible to understand. All quotations from the Bible are from the NRSV, except where noted otherwise.

I carried out the initial work on this book in the small snatches of time available to me in the midst of a busy academic job, where the urgent so easily crams out the important, and completed it during a period of study leave in 1999. I am grateful to Gill Philps-Townsley for her help in tracking down relevant literature, and to Mark Forman and Tim Meadowcroft for proofreading. Mark and Janelle Forman also assisted with preparing indexes. I am also very grateful for the advice of Willard Swartley, Ted Koontz, and Millard Lind of Associated Mennonite Biblical Seminary in Elkhart, Indiana, whom I got to know during a sabbatical leave at the seminary in 1991-92. Their scholarly insight and common commitment to the gospel of peace continues to inspire me. Thanks also to Mary Hietbrink of Eerdmans, whose editorial skill and care have added polish to the final product.

The great New Zealand poet James K. Baxter once described writing as robbery — "robbery from my employers, from my wife, from my children, and possibly from the Almighty."[1] Anyone who has undertaken serious writing knows what he means. I can only hope that all those from whom I have robbed time to write this book will count the outcome worth the loss. And there is something peculiarly appropriate about counting oneself a robber in an essay on crime and punishment!

CHRIS MARSHALL

1. In *Landfall* 53 (March 1960): 41-42.

ABBREVIATIONS

AB   Anchor Bible Commentary

ABD   *The Anchor Bible Dictionary.* Ed. D. N. Freedman. New York:
            Doubleday, 1992.

ABR   *Australian Biblical Review*

AJT   *Asia Journal of Theology*

ANRW   *Aufstieg und Niedergang der römischen Welt: Geschichte und Kul-
            tur Roms im Spiegel der neueren Forschung.* Ed. H. Temporini
            and W. Haase. Berlin/New York: Walter de Gruyter, 1971-.

Antiquities Flavius Josephus. *Jewish Antiquities.* Trans. H. St. J.
            Thackery, L. H. Feldman, R. Marcus, and A. Mikgren. Vols.
            5-13. Loeb Classical Library. London/Cambridge, Mass.:
            Heinemann/Harvard University Press, 1928-1965.

BBR   *Bulletin for Biblical Research*

BDCE   *Baker's Dictionary of Christian Ethics.* Ed. C. F. H. Henry.
            Grand Rapids: Baker, 1973.

BR   *Biblical Research*

BS   *Bibliotheca Sacra*

BTB   *Biblical Theology Bulletin*

b. 'Abod. Zar. Babylonian Talmud, tractate *'Abodah Zarah.* Trans. I. Ep-
            stein. In *The Baylonian Talmud, translated in English with Notes,
            Glossary, and Indices.* London: Soncino Press, 1935-52.

b. B. Qam.   Babylonian Talmud, tractate *Baba Qamma*

b. Sanh.   Babylonian Talmud, tractate *Sanhedrin*

CBQ   *Catholic Biblical Quarterly*

ABBREVIATIONS

CV	*The Christian Verdict*
DFTh	*Dictionary of Feminist Theologies.* Ed. L. M. Russell & J. S. Clarkson. Louisville: Westminster John Knox, 1996.
DJG	*Dictionary of Jesus and the Gospels.* Ed. J. B. Green, S. McKnight, and I. H. Marshall. Leicester: Inter-Varsity Press, 1992.
DPL	*Dictionary of Paul and His Letters.* Ed. G. F. Hawthorne, R. P. Martin, and D. G. Reid. Leicester: Inter-Varsity Press, 1993.
DSS	Dead Sea Scrolls
EBCE	*Encyclopedia of Biblical and Christian Ethics.* Ed. R. K. Harrison. Nashville: Nelson, 1989.
EDNT	*Exegetical Dictionary of the New Testament.* Ed. H. Balz and G. Schneider. Grand Rapids: William B. Eerdmans, 1991.
EDT	*Evangelical Dictionary of Theology.* Ed. W. A. Elwell. Grand Rapids: Baker, 1984.
ER	*The Encyclopedia of Religion.* Ed. M. Eliade. New York: MacMillan, 1987.
EuroJTh	*European Journal of Theology*
ERT	*Evangelical Review of Theology*
EvQ	*Evangelical Quarterly*
ExpT	*Expository Times*
F&F	*Faith and Freedom: A Journal of Christian Ethics*
HDB	*Hastings Dictionary of the Bible.* Ed. J. Hastings. Edinburgh: T. & T. Clark, 1919.
HDCG	*Dictionary of Christ and the Gospels.* Ed. J. Hastings. Edinburgh: T. & T. Clark, 1908.
Histories	Tacitus. *The Histories.* Trans. K. Wellesley. Harmondsworth: Penguin, 1964.
HTR	*Harvard Theological Review*
IDB	*Interpreter's Dictionary of the Bible.* Ed. G. A. Buttrick. Nashville: Abingdon, 1962.
IDB Supp	*Interpreter's Dictionary of the Bible, Supplementary Volume.* Ed. K. Crim. Nashville: Abingdon, 1976.
ISBE	*The International Standard Bible Encyclopedia.* Ed. G. W. Bromiley. Grand Rapids: William B. Eerdmans, 1979.
JAAR	*Journal of the American Academy of Religion*
JBL	*Journal of Biblical Literature*
JES	*Journal of Ecumenical Studies*

JESHO	*Journal of Economic and Social History of the Orient*
JETS	*Journal of the Evangelical Theological Society*
JR	*Journal of Religion*
JSNT	*Journal for the Study of the New Testament*
JTSA	*Journal of Theology for Southern Africa*
Laws	Plato. *The Laws.* Trans. T. J. Saunders. Harmondsworth: Penguin, 1970.
LTJ	*Lutheran Theological Journal*
LXX	Septuagint
MCC	Mennonite Central Committee
ME	*The Mennonite Encyclopedia.* Ed. C. J. Dyck and D. D. Martin. Scottdale, Pa.: Herald Press, 1990.
m. B. Qam.	Mishnah, tractate *Baba Qamma.* Trans. H. Danby. In *The Mishnah: Translated from the Hebrew with Introduction and Brief Explanatory Notes.* Oxford: Oxford University Press, 1933.
m. Mak.	Mishnah, tractate *Makkoth*
m. Sanh.	Mishnah, tractate *Sanhedrin*
NDCE	*A New Dictionary of Christian Ethics.* Ed. J. MacQuarrie and J. Childress. London: SCM, 1986.
NIDNTT	*New International Dictionary of New Testament Theology.* Ed. C. Brown. Grand Rapids: Zondervan, 1975.
NovT	*Novum Testamentum*
NPCJ	*New Perspectives on Crime and Justice.* Occasional Papers of MCC U.S. Office of Criminal Justice and MCC Canada Victim Offender Ministries Program.
NTS	*New Testament Studies*
RelSt	*Religious Studies*
Republic	Plato. *The Republic.* Trans. D. Lee. Rev. ed. Harmondsworth: Penguin, 1974.
RTR	*The Reformed Theological Review*
SBET	*Scottish Bulletin of Evangelical Theology*
SBL	Society of Biblical Literature
SBLDS	Society of Biblical Literature Dissertation Series
SJT	*Scottish Journal of Theology*
SNTSMS	Society for the Study of the New Testament Monograph Series
Special Laws	Philo. *The Special Laws.* Trans. F. H. Colson. Vols. 7-8. Loeb

	Classical Library. London/Cambridge, Mass.: Heinemann/ Harvard University Press, 1928-1965.
StChEth	*Studies in Christian Ethics*
Str-B	Strack, H. L., and P. Billerbeck. *Kommentar zum Neuen Testament aus Talmud und Midrash.* Vols. 1-6. Munich: C. H. Beck, 1926-61.
StTh	*Studia Theologica*
SWJT	*Southwestern Journal of Theology*
TBT	*The Bible Today*
TDNT	*Theological Dictionary of the New Testament.* Ed. G. Kittel and G. Friedrich. 1928-1973; ET: Grand Rapids: William B. Eerdmans, 1974.
ThTo	*Theology Today*
t. Sanh.	Tosefta tractate *Sanhedrin*
TWOT	*Theological Wordbook of the Old Testament.* Ed. R. L. Harris, G. L. Archer Jr., and B. K. Waltke. Chicago: Moody, 1980.
TynBul	*Tyndale Bulletin*
War	Flavius Josephus. *The Jewish War.* Trans. H. St. J. Thackery and L. H. Feldman. Vols. 2-4. Loeb Classical Library. London/Cambridge, Mass.: Heinemann/Harvard University Press, 1928-1965.
WBC	Word Biblical Commentary
WCC	World Council of Churches
WTJ	*Westminster Theological Journal*
ZAW	*Zeitschrift für die alttestamentliche Wissenschaft*
ZNW	*Zeitschrift für die neutestamentliche Wissenschaft*
ZTK	*Zeitschrift für Theologie und Kirche*
1QM	Qumran War Rule
1QS	Qumran Community Rule

CHAPTER 1

INTRODUCTION

Gaining a Perspective

Few issues evoke such powerful emotional responses today as crime and its consequences. For many people, fear of crime is second only to fear of death. Like death, crime can enter a person's life at any time, destroy forever a sense of safety and security, and leave a legacy of anxiety and mistrust. This legacy is bequeathed not only to the immediate victims of crime and their loved ones but also to the wider society. Where serious criminal offending is perceived to be increasing and to be largely random in its occurrence, even those who have never been directly victimized can feel their freedom restricted and their lives diminished by a constant worry that they may be next to suffer. Crime is also one of the most difficult areas of human behavior to deal with from a Christian perspective. When we are confronted with rape, murder, home invasions, and child abuse, familiar platitudes about hating the sin yet loving the sinner seem pitifully inadequate. Anger, resentment, and loathing rise up, and, whatever we may believe about love and forgiveness, what we really want is swift retribution. It is important to admit to these common human reactions and to resist giving them a premature Christian baptism. For, if Michael Ignatieff is correct, "the great moral weakness of our age . . . is not, as some people think, a general lack of moral principles, but on the contrary, indignant moral posturing by people too lazy to think through the consequences of strong emotions."[1] And for Christians, it is not just the hu-

---

1. Ignatieff, "Imprisonment and the Need for Justice," *Theology* 45, no. 764 (1992): 98.

man consequences that make it imperative to think beyond immediate emotional reactions to crime, though these are considerable, but also the consequences for our witness to the gospel of redemption through Jesus Christ.

In this chapter I consider what is entailed in thinking through a Christian position on crime and punishment, and I raise some initial questions about the extent to which the New Testament speaks to such issues. This is preparatory to my larger aim in this book of exploring whether and in what ways the teaching of the New Testament is compatible with, or may contribute to, the vision of "restorative justice." Several criminal-justice experts advocate restorative justice as a viable alternative to the increasingly dysfunctional Western system of criminal justice, which is based largely on the concept of retribution. Unlike retributive justice, which centers on the notions of law-breaking, guilt, and punishment, restorative justice focuses on relationships, reconciliation, and reparation of harm done. It understands crime less as a matter of law-breaking than as the infliction of injury or loss on another human being. "Restorative justice is a peacemaking response to crime, and a critique of criminology as a military science," suggests Wayne Northey. "It does not counter a harm done by a new harm, but with a healing response to victim, offender and the wider community. If restorative justice practice has educational and rehabilitative spin-offs, these are good but secondary goals to restoring the brokenness arising from the criminal act."[2] Such "peace-making justice," David Cayley explains, "insists on accountability, reparation and reform — but tries to avoid ostracization, stigmatization, and the compounding of old violence with new violence."[3]

Restorative justice (and its siblings, "relational" and "transformative" justice, all of which are expressions of the so-called "community justice" or "alternative dispute resolution" movement)[4] is not, according to its proponents, a minor variation of the current justice system, a way of helping it become more effective or more just. It is not rehabilitationism

2. Northey, "Restorative Justice: Rebirth of an Ancient Practice," *NPCJ* 14 (1994): 6.

3. Cayley, *The Expanding Prison: The Crisis in Crime and Punishment and the Search for Alternatives* (Toronto: Anansi Press, 1998), 11.

4. For a detailed theoretical analysis, see G. C. Pavlich, *Justice Fragmented: Mediating Community Disputes under Postmodern Conditions* (London: Routledge, 1996). See also Cayley, *The Expanding Prison*, 151-365.

in new guise.[5] It is an alternative model, a "third way" between the retributive and rehabilitative models that have dominated penal philosophy, a distinctive way of thinking about crime and punishment, a different paradigm, to use Howard Zehr's term, to conceptualize criminal justice. Not that the restorative paradigm is a modern innovation. Advocates of the approach argue that systems of restorative justice are typical of most traditional societies, including traditional Maori society in New Zealand,[6] and that a restorative approach to criminal offending prevailed in Western European society in the pre-modern period.[7] More recently, programs based on restorative principles have been introduced into or alongside the conventional justice systems of many jurisdictions. The Victim Offender Reconciliation Programme (VORP) is a case in point. Initiated on an experimental basis by Canadian Mennonites in 1974, VORP has since spread throughout the United States and to several countries in Europe. Another example is the entire New Zealand youth justice system, which was reorganized along restorative lines in 1989, resulting in a remarkable reduction in court appearances, custodial sentences, and recidivism by young offenders. The central concept of the new system — the transfer of power from the state to the "family group conference" — has been described as New Zealand's gift to the world.[8]

Christian advocates of restorative justice argue that the legal system of biblical Israel was also based on restorative principles. This might come as a surprise to many people. It is widely believed that Old Testament criminal law was harsh and merciless, "an eye for an eye and a tooth for a tooth" — "the law of the claw," as it has been called — and not a few theologians insist that divine justice is essentially retributive

5. There are, however, points of contact between "new rehabilitationism" and restorative justice. See B. A. Hudson, *Understanding Justice: An Introduction to Ideas, Perspectives, and Controversies in Modern Penal Theory* (Buckingham, U.K.: Open University Press, 1996), 63-67, 73-74, 150-51.

6. J. Consedine, *Restorative Justice: Healing the Effects of Crime* (Lyttelton, N. Z.: Ploughshares Publications, 1995), 81-97; and *Restorative Justice: Contemporary Themes and Practice*, ed. H. Bowen and J. Consedine (Lyttelton, N.Z.: Ploughshares Publications, 1999), 25-35, 90-94.

7. H. Zehr, *Changing Lenses: A New Focus for Crime and Justice* (Scottdale, Pa.: Herald Press, 1990), 97-124.

8. Consedine, *Restorative Justice*, 98-107. See also F. W. M. McElrea, "The New Zealand Model of Family Group Conferences," *European Journal of Criminal Policy and Research* 6 (1998): 527-43.

in character.[9] But Howard Zehr, drawing on the work of Old Testament scholars Millard Lind and Perry Yoder, argues cogently that in biblical notions of domestic justice the keynote is restitution rather than retribution. When wrongdoing occurred, Israel's law was more concerned with the restoration of *shalom* than the punishment of the offender.[10] Is this also true of the New Testament? What does the New Testament have to say about issues of crime and punishment? Does New Testament teaching articulate restorative or retributive conceptions of justice, or a mixture of both? This question is of interest both from a historical point of view, since the New Testament reflects rather different sociopolitical and cultural realities than the Old Testament, and from a moral and theological point of view, since Christian practice is more directly accountable to New Testament principles than to Old Testament ones. What then does the New Testament have to say about the matter, and how are its perspectives to be related to the other moral and public policy considerations pertaining to criminal justice?

My intention in this study is to survey New Testament texts that have a significant bearing on crime and punishment. In doing so, my assumption is that a Christian perspective on this, or on any other ethical question, ought to be deeply conditioned by the biblical witness. This is not to say that answers to the complex questions of crime and punishment can be read off the surface of the text or that the Bible is our *only* source of guidance on such matters. A variety of other resources must also be employed and held in some kind of balance.

Sources of Moral Guidance

Christian ethics is the attempt to understand and justify the moral obligations that guide human behavior in relation to the will and character of God, who is Creator, Redeemer, and Sustainer of all things. This makes Christian ethics a distinctive enterprise. Its distinctiveness lies not so much in the *content* of the moral values themselves (Christians

9. Typical is D. A. Kidner, *The Death Penalty: An Ethical and Biblical Exposition* (London: Falcon Booklets, 1963), 3-10.

10. Zehr, *Changing Lenses,* 126-57; see also P. B. Yoder, *Shalom: The Bible's Word for Salvation, Justice, and Peace* (Newton, Kans.: Faith and Life Press, 1987).

and non-Christians share many similar values)[11] but in its mode of *moral reasoning* — in other words, in the way Christians understand the origin, sanction, and achievement of these values. At the heart of Christian ethics lies an appeal to divine revelation. Christian ethical judgments are governed ultimately by belief in the self-disclosure of God's own moral character and purposes, preeminently in the person and work of Jesus Christ, not by the utilitarian dictates of human reason, affections, volition, or environmental conditioning. In the attempt to clarify the ethical corollaries of divine revelation, Christian ethics draws on five main sources of moral guidance.[12]

- *Scripture:* The Bible serves as the primary record of God's self-disclosure in the events of salvation history, as apprehended by the community of faith. Inasmuch as it presents God as a righteous Being who demands righteousness of human creatures, the Bible is profoundly concerned with ethics. According to the biblical tradition, ethical behavior stands in a twofold relationship to God's self-revelation. It is a response of gratitude for God's saving acts in history, while the saving acts themselves provide the pattern and standard for human conduct. The people of God are enjoined to model their behavior on the actions of God; the covenant requires nothing less than the "imitation of God" (Lev. 11:45; Deut. 10:17-19). The meaning of "justice," for instance, is arrived at not by contemplating some abstract norm of justice, but by remembering how God delivered his people from oppression, and then acting in a manner consistent with this (Mic. 6:3-5, 8; Exod. 20:1-17). For Christian ethics, the imitation of God centers on the imitation of

11. There are, of course, some significant differences as well. Christians feel themselves accountable to certain demands that go beyond natural human prudence or philosophically justifiable morality, such as preference for the outcast, service of others unto death, even loving one's enemies at cost to oneself.

12. See my fuller discussion in "The Use of the Bible in Ethics: Scripture, Ethics, and the Social Justice Statement," in *Voices for Justice: Church, Law, and State in New Zealand,* ed. J. Boston and A. Cameron (Palmerston North, N.Z.: Dunmore Press, 1994), esp. 108-11. For a related discussion, see R. B. Hays, *The Moral Vision of the New Testament: A Contemporary Introduction to New Testament Ethics* (Edinburgh: T. & T. Clark, 1996), esp. 209-11, 296-98.

Christ (1 Pet. 2:21), whose concrete manner of living and acting is known to us only through the biblical record.

- *Tradition:* Revelation, including biblical revelation, is received, reflected on, and interpreted by the people of God down through history. This interpretation and application of revelation constitutes the theological and moral tradition of Christianity, which serves as a second source for discerning God's will. It is not only the Roman Catholic Church that uses tradition in this way; all branches of Christianity have appealed to historical precedents and experience in formulating moral and doctrinal teaching. Such tradition is more than a collection of dogmatic and moral propositions transmitted from the past; it is also the story of a particular people, handed on and reappropriated by each generation, which continues the story. We cannot separate ourselves from our narrative traditions and heritage. We enter into life in the midst of tradition; we are fundamentally shaped by tradition; and even our ability to question and change tradition comes from the tradition itself.

- *Moral Philosophy:* The great moral traditions of Western philosophy, which have appealed principally to the exercise of human reason for the determination of right and wrong, have also had a profound impact on both the content and the methodology of Christian ethics. (The very word "ethics" is the legacy of Greek philosophy.) Of particular significance has been the concept of natural law, which has been very influential in Catholic moral theology. The extent to which natural-law considerations should shape Christian ethics is much contested, but some concept of a "natural" revelation of God's moral will accessible to all humanity by virtue of creation has played a role in most expressions of Christian ethics, including New Testament ethics (e.g., Matt. 5:46-47; Rom. 1:28; 2:14-16; Acts 17:16-34; 1 Cor. 11:13-15).

- *Empirical Data:* Christian ethics is more than a speculative exercise; it also requires attention to the full range of contextual and human factors that bear on each ethical situation. Indeed, the first task of moral analysis is to clarify the decision-making situation and identify the range of available options. The data furnished by the social sciences and by other empirical analyses thus plays an indispensable role in ethical discernment. The special contribution of such descriptive research is to keep ethical evaluation in touch with reality, where the rubber hits the road.[13] Nowhere is this more important than in issues of crime and punishment.

- *The Spirit-in-Community:* The New Testament places great emphasis on a twofold role for the Holy Spirit in Christian ethical life — that of bringing about inner moral renewal in believers so that they spontaneously manifest ethical virtues,[14] and that of guiding them in ethical decision-making.[15] Moral character-formation and moral decision-making are inseparably linked within the Spirit's orbit. It is crucial to recognize that in the New Testament the Spirit's work is expressed in the context of the church.[16] "There can be no solitary believer who lives the moral and ethical life isolated from or independent of the community of faith," explains Frank Matera. "The moral life is lived by, and in, the church."[17] The gathered community provides the necessary checks and balances that prevent the Spirit's direction from degenerating into individualistic subjectivism.

Now while these five components may be conceptually distinguished, they are in practice inseparable. Scripture, for example, cannot be entirely distinguished from tradition, since the Bible is both the product of tradition and the shaper of tradition. Similarly, empirical data does not exist in isolation from the moral values and ideological commitments that govern the gathering, classification, and interpretation of data. Again, the Spirit's guidance of the community is not merely intuitive but often employs the text of Scripture and the wisdom learned from ecclesiastical tradition or scientific discovery. All five sources, then, are intertwined, although there is still value in distinguishing between them, since in different Christian traditions different strands

---

13. See L. Sowle Cahill, *Between the Sexes: Foundations for a Christian Ethics of Sexuality* (Philadelphia: Fortress Press, 1985), 5-6, 145-48.

14. See, e.g., Gal. 5:16-26; 6:1; Rom. 8:13, 26-27; 9:1; 14:17; 15:13, 30; 2 Cor. 3:18; 6:6; Col. 1:8.

15. See, e.g., John 14:25-31; 15:21–16:15; Acts 15:28; Rom. 8:4-6, 14; Gal. 5:16, 18, 25; cf. Rom. 8:13; Gal. 6:8; 1 Cor. 2:12.

16. 1 Cor. 3:16; 6:19; 12:13; 14:26-37; 1 Thess. 5:19-22; 2 Thess. 2:2; 1 John 4:1.

17. Matera, *New Testament Ethics: The Legacies of Jesus and Paul* (Louisville, Ky.: Westminster John Knox, 1996), 252.

have the dominant role, while in all traditions ethical arguments gain in persuasiveness by employing all five in a coherent way.

It should also be clear from this delineation of the several sources of ethical guidance that the slogan *sola Scriptura* does not really apply in Christian ethics. By itself the Bible is not enough to tell us what to do. The Bible may be a necessary source for Christian ethical reflection, but it is not a sufficient resource on its own. Arriving at moral judgments on, for example, issues of crime and punishment entails a dialectic between scriptural and nonscriptural factors, between considerations that appeal to the the biblical witness, and those based on circumstance, experience, and rational inquiry. The challenge of Christian ethics is to achieve a judicious balance between these considerations in the task of moral deliberation. Yet it is still the case that most Christians, including those who do not subscribe to a "high" view of biblical inspiration, would agree that written Scripture possesses unique authority in Christian ethical reasoning. The essential test of validity for ethical judgments is whether they are demonstrably consistent with what is perceived to be both the spirit and the text of biblical teaching, even if our perception of these features changes over time. In attempting to think through a Christian position on criminal justice matters, then, our normative (though not exclusive) reference point should be the witness of Scripture, and in particular the New Testament.

But in turning to the New Testament we encounter two immediate problems — one of focus and the other of faith. The first problem is that New Testament writers do not focus on penal justice per se. They talk about sin and salvation more than crime and punishment, and while sin and crime are closely connected, they are not synonymous.[18] There is no corpus of criminal laws in the New Testament comparable to that of the Old Testament and only fleeting references to the judicial functions of the state. Can we therefore expect any substantial guid-

18. See T. J. Gorringe, *God's Just Vengeance: Crime, Violence, and the Rhetoric of Salvation* (Cambridge: Cambridge University Press, 1996), 17-22, 42. On the biblical "symbolism of sin," see J. Goldingay, "Your Iniquities Have Made a Separation between You and Your God," in *Atonement Today*, ed. J. Goldingay (London: SPCK, 1995), 39-53. Cf. also M. Grey ("Falling into Freedom: Searching for New Interpretations of Sin in a Secular Society," *SJT* 47, no. 2 [1994]: 223-43), who observes that today "we have lost a common grammar of sin . . . between secular and religious discourse" (223).

ance from the New Testament on our subject? Do we take the apparent silence of New Testament writers on criminal matters as an indication that Old Testament patterns continue unchanged? Or does the New Testament have something new to offer? If so, where do we look for it? The second problem is that the New Testament documents are addressed to Christian believers within the community of faith, not to secular rulers responsible for the administration of domestic justice. As W. D. Davies observes,

> In much of the New Testament and the practice of the Early Church, there is no clear indication of the relevance of the early Christian moral teaching to society and to the world at large. . . . There is no suggestion in the New Testament that the Church should in any way instruct the world as to how to carry on its business. The secular magistrates and judges, the rulers of this world are not directly addressed as if the Church had either any right to do so or any superior wisdom to offer. . . . It was not the primary concern of the Church to influence society and culture but to be itself in its moral life, as in other respects, the people of God, in the world but not of it.[19]

Put simply, the New Testament writers articulate the ethics of discipleship, not the ethics of public policy. So when Jesus calls his followers to turn the other cheek to the assailant, to surrender possessions freely to those who demand them, and to love even their enemies (Matt. 5:38-48; Luke 6:27-45), in what sense is this relevant to those outside the community of disciples? Is there any way in which this ethic of radical love can be realistically applied to the functions of government or the judiciary in a mixed society?

The Problem of Focus:
Criminal Justice from the Underside

In light of the first problem, there is a temptation — especially evident in conservative Christian circles — to appeal almost exclusively to se-

---

19. W. D. Davies, "The Relevance of the Moral Teaching of the Early Church," in *Neotestamentica et Semitica: Studies in Honour of Matthew Black,* ed. E. E. Ellis and M. Wilcox (Edinburgh: T. & T. Clark, 1969), 30-31.

lected Old Testament proof-texts on crime and punishment and extend this teaching to the Christian era by citing New Testament texts about the eternal validity of the law (Matt. 5:17-20; Luke 16:17). Certainly it is crucial to consider Old Testament teaching; it has much to teach us. It also provides the indispensable context for understanding New Testament teaching, as well as certain aspects of our modern legal system.[20] But any position that minimizes the discontinuity at the social-institutional level between Old Testament Israel and early Christianity, and that fails to assess the normative value of Old Testament material in light of the distinctive features of New Testament revelation, can hardly lay claim to being authentically Christian. And proof-texting is always dangerous. It is not only those texts that speak directly of wrongdoing and retribution that are relevant, but the whole sweep of biblical teaching on the nature of God and humankind, on covenant and community, on justice and peace, on honor and shame, on sin and redemption.

But the observation that New Testament writers do not discuss penal justice per se needs careful testing. The statement is true with respect to penal justice at a theoretical level. "The student who expects to find in the New Testament a blue-print to guide society in its quest for a satisfactory penal policy will surely be disappointed," J. A. Hoyles rightly observes. "The Christian Scriptures provide no infallible ready-reckoner for the guidance of a criminal court, no clear directions as to whether punishment is permissible in a Christian country, no precise advice as to what kinds of penalty are appropriate for particular offences."[21] This is not surprising. The New Testament authors are pastors and theologians, not legal or social theorists, and we cannot expect

20. According to M. Umbreit, "The law given to Moses contained the foundation for compensation, liability, responsibility, and other ethical principles that are quite common to us in our modern world" (*Crime and Reconciliation: Creative Options for Victims and Offenders* [Nashville: Abingdon, 1985], 72-73). Conversely, R. Westbrook notes, "The modern conception of crime as a wrong against society which is to be suppressed by impersonal punishment is derived ultimately from the jurisprudence of classical Greece." According to Westbrook, the influence of Greek conceptions on the understanding of biblical law is already discernible in post-biblical rabbinic jurisprudence, which entailed "a radical reinterpretation of the biblical texts" ("Punishments and Crimes," *ABD* V:555).

21. Hoyles, *Punishment in the Bible* (London: Epworth, 1986), 47.

them to write as such. But at another level there is a surprising wealth of detail in the New Testament on all the major components of a criminal justice system — laws, crime, criminals, courts, police, prisons, and punishments. Even a cursory review of this material provides a fascinating insight into the social location of the early Christian communities and their perspective on the surrounding social order. It also offers meager comfort for those who would want to base a strong "law and order" platform on the biblical text.

Take *law* to begin with. The New Testament writers have a great deal to say about law, none so extensively and reflectively as the apostle Paul. Paul's perspective on law is exceedingly complex and the subject of enormous debate in current New Testament scholarship, but it is noteworthy that he expresses extreme skepticism about the ability of an external law-code to control human wrongdoing. Law, even "holy and just and good" law (Rom. 7:12), stirs up sin and increases transgression, but can do nothing to make people good (Rom. 5:20; 7:7-12; Gal. 3:19-24). Something more potent than the rule of law is needed to deal with human wickedness. Significantly, God's redemptive justice is made known "apart from law," although the law bears witness to it (Rom. 3:21), and its recipients find themselves now able to fulfill the true purpose of the law (Rom. 8:1-4). They now live their lives under "the law of Christ" (Gal. 6:2; 1 Cor. 9:2), but this is the law of love, not a code of legislation. In all this, of course, Paul is not thinking primarily of what we would call criminal law. But given the social, moral, and civic function of the Mosaic law in first-century Judaism, Paul's perspective on the law cannot be limited to purely theological concerns.[22]

Criminals also figure prominently in the New Testament narratives. The parables and parabolic sayings of Jesus are populated by a veritable gallery of rogues — including thieves, bandits, fraudsters, murderers, child abusers, and corrupt judges — and Jesus himself is eventually classed with the criminals (Luke 22:37; Matt. 26:55; John 18:30) and suffers a criminal's fate. It has been said that the very first Christian community was formed by the three outlaws on Golgotha: Jesus and "the two *other* criminals *also*" who were crucified with him (*de kai heteroi kakouroi duo sun autō,* Luke 23:32).

---

22. See the provocative comments of D. Georgi, *Theocracy in Paul's Praxis and Theology* (Minneapolis: Fortress Press, 1991), 90-93.

Then there are the *courts*. Jesus advises his followers to avoid going to court in order to seek legal redress for wrongs suffered (Matt. 5:25, 40; Luke 12:57),[23] and forestalls any possibility of perjury by ruling out all oath-taking, judicial or otherwise (Matt. 5:33-37).[24] In 1 Corinthians 6, Paul sharply criticizes the litigious Corinthians for taking even their "trivial cases" (v. 2) before "unrighteous" magistrates (v. 1), who have "no standing" in the church (v. 4).[25] Paul is aware that the muckraking and character assassination that litigation invariably entailed in antiquity would do nothing to enhance relationships in the church, and that there was little chance of Roman judges and juries administering justice fairly to believers of lower social rank. In a similar vein, James reminds his readers how the law courts favor the rich at the expense of the poor (James 2:6; cf. Luke 18:1-8). Scenes of courtrooms in the New Testament often show them to be little more than kangaroo courts where justice is perverted and the innocent — like John the Baptist, Jesus, and the Apostles — are condemned.[26] "An hour is coming," Jesus warns his fol-

---

23. On the Jewish system of courts at the time of Jesus, see P. S. Alexander, "Jewish Law in the Time of Jesus: Towards a Clarification of the Problem," in *Law and Religion: Essays on the Place of Law in Israel and Early Christianity*, ed. B. Lindars (Cambridge: James Clarke, 1988), 47-56. More briefly, E. P. Sanders, "The Synoptic Jesus and the Law," in his book entitled *Jewish Law from Jesus to the Mishnah: Five Studies* (London: SCM, 1990), 16-19.

24. On the concept of perjury in the ancient Mediterranean world, see J. T. Fitzgerald, "The Problem of Perjury in Greek Context: Prolegomena to an Exegesis of Matthew 5:33; 1 Timothy 1:10; and *Didache* 2:3," in *The Social World of the First Christians,* ed. L. M. White and O. L. Yarbrough (Minneapolis: Augsburg Fortress, 1995), 156-77.

25. For a brief overview of the Roman court system, see B. Witherington, *Conflict and Community in Corinth: A Socio-Rhetorical Commentary on 1 and 2 Corinthians* (Grand Rapids: William B. Eerdmans, 1995), 162-64; J. Stambaugh and D. Balch, *The Social World of the First Christians* (London: SPCK, 1986), 32-34; A. A. Ruprecht, "Legal System, Roman," *DPL,* 546-50; and D. J. Williams, *Paul's Metaphors: Their Context and Character* (Peabody, Mass.: Hendrickson, 1999), 141-64.

26. Note especially Luke's emphasis on the miscarriage of justice in the trial of Jesus (Luke 23:4, 14-15, 22; 23:47; Acts 3:13-18; 4:10, 24-29; 7:51-53; cf. Mark 15:10). The innocence of John the Baptist is implied in Mark 6:24-28. While it is true that in Acts the Roman courts frequently vindicate the innocence of the apostles, this is not because of the intrinsic justness of the system (cf. Acts 16:19-40; 24:25) but because of Roman indifference to internal Jewish squabbles. On the role of courtroom scenes in Luke and Acts, see R. J. Cassidy, *Society and Politics in Acts of the Apostles* (Maryknoll, N.Y.: Orbis, 1987), esp. 147-70.

lowers of the Jewish legal authorities, "when those who kill you will think that by doing so they are offering worship to God" (John 16:2).

The *police* get even worse press. In the Roman provinces, the task of maintaining public order belonged both to the Roman governor, through the troops under his command, and to the indigenous authorities, who often had their own specially recruited police wardens. The Jewish high priest, for instance, had his own Temple Guard under the command of the captain of the Temple (John 18:3, 12; Matt. 27:65; Acts 5:24-26). After cataloguing the violence and brutality ascribed to the police authorities in the New Testament narratives, such as the massacre of innocent children (Matt. 2:16), the execution of John the Baptist (Matt. 14:10), the slaughter of the Galileans (Luke 13:1), the arrest, scourging, and crucifixion of Jesus (Matt. 26:50; 27:26, 31), the imprisonment and flogging of the apostles (Acts 4:3; 5:26, 40), the beheading of James and the arbitrary arrest of Peter (Acts 12:2-3), and the scourging (without trial) of Paul and Silas (Acts 16:22, 24), Jean Lasserre offers this comment:

> Admittedly most of these crimes were committed by the police on the orders of the king, the governor or the Sanhedrin, but the fact remains: the police referred to in the New Testament are often involved in very dirty work; the police of the temple and Pilate's police play an important part in the crucifixion of our Saviour. In the New Testament the police contribute more often to disorder than to order, and above all to the major disorder of executing the Son of God. . . . After this we should be very much on our guard against the optimistic benevolence with which so many theologians talk of the police.[27]

Another prop of the criminal justice system is *prison* — that most despicable and violent of all modern social institutions — and this too is mentioned remarkably often in the New Testament. In the ancient world, prisons functioned principally as holding tanks where offenders could be detained prior to trial or to the carrying out of the sentence of the court, such as execution, exile, or enslavement, or until debts or fines had been paid. Long-term incarceration was not itself commonly employed as a punishment, although it was not unknown for prisoners to spend lengthy periods in confinement. With few exceptions, prisons in the Roman period were dark, disease-ridden, overcrowded places. It

27. Lasserre, *War and the Gospel* (London: James Clarke, 1962), 194-95.

was common for prisoners to die in custody, either from disease or starvation (cf. Matt. 25:36), brutal torture (cf. Matt. 18:34), execution (cf. Mark 6:14-29), or suicide (cf. Phil. 1:19-24).[28] Imprisonment is commonly described by ancient authors as a fate worse than death; the very thought of it was appalling.[29] It is little wonder, then, that prison is viewed throughout the Bible, as Lee Griffith demonstrates, not merely as a social institution or a material entity but as the embodiment of "the spirit and the power of death." The Bible has nothing good to say about prisons, and anyone who listens carefully to what it does say should not be surprised at the "failure" of the prison system today:

> The Bible identifies the prison with the spirit and power of death. As such, the problem with prisons has nothing to do with the utilitarian criteria of deterrence. As such, the problem is not that prisons have failed to forestall violent criminality and murderous rampages; the problem is that prisons are *identical in spirit* to the violence and murder that they pretend to combat. The biblical discernment of the spirit of the prison demythologizes our pretenses. Whenever we cage people, we are in reality fueling and participating in the same spirit we claim to renounce. In the biblical understanding, the spirit of the prison is the spirit of death.[30]

Accordingly, as Mark Olson observes, "To think that slamming people behind bars, breaking their spirits, and destroying their souls could do anything other than lead to more evil is the ultimate naiveté."[31] The overwhelming emphasis of the Bible is that God's purpose is to break open prison cells and set the captives free.[32] Release of prisoners was an important element of messianic expectation (Isa. 42:6-7; 61:1; Zech. 9:9-

---

28. C. S. Wansink suggests that the imprisoned Paul's reference to voluntary death in Philippians 1:23-24 may be an allusion to suicide or to ensuring his own execution by failing to testify or cooperate with the authorities. See *Chained in Christ: The Experience and Rhetoric of Paul's Imprisonments* (Sheffield: Sheffield Academic Press, 1996), 96-125.

29. On prisons in the Roman world, see Wansink, *Chained in Christ*, 27-95.

30. Griffith, *The Fall of the Prison: Biblical Perspectives on Prison Abolition* (Grand Rapids: William B. Eerdmans, 1993), 106.

31. Olson, "The God Who Dared," *The Other Side* 26, no. 3 (1990): 15.

32. See, e.g., Deut. 7:8; 24:18; Lam. 3:34-36; Pss. 68:6; 79:11; 102:19-20; 107:10-16; 118:5; 146:7; Isa. 42:7; 45:13; 49:8-9; 61:1; Mic. 6:4; Zech. 9:11; Luke 4:18; Acts 5:19; 12:6-11; 16:25-26; Eph. 4:8; Col. 2:15; 1 Pet. 3:19; Rev. 2:10.

12), and Jesus expressly claims to fulfill this hope in his inaugural address at Nazareth (Luke 4:18). It is not coincidental, then, that in the book of Acts the apostles are repeatedly being broken out of prison by divine intervention (Acts 5:19, 22-23; 12:6-11; 16:25-26), perhaps demonstrating God's attitude toward the practice of incarcerating people.[33] The early church was led by a bunch of jailbirds, and God was the prime accomplice in their escape! So thoroughly does God identify with the imprisoned that Jesus nominates "caring" for the imprisoned as a criterion of eschatological judgment and one of the ways in which people may encounter his own presence after Easter (Matt. 25:31-46), something the early church took seriously (cf. Heb. 13:3).[34]

Prison is not the only criminal sanction cited in the New Testament. A whole variety of other judicial and extra-judicial *punishments* are also mentioned in passing — decapitation,[35] drowning,[36] hanging,[37] precipitation,[38] mutilation,[39] stoning,[40] excommunication,[41] exile,[42] chaining,[43] putting in stocks,[44] scourging,[45] sawing in two,[46] torture

---

33. It is striking that in Acts 16:25-26, the chains of all those in prison, not just the Christians, were loosened.

34. Wansink explains that visiting prisoners was no simple act of charity. Sometimes material and emotional support was necessary for the prisoner's survival (including bribing the guards). It was also a risky business for those who visited; it cast suspicion on them, often leading to their own imprisonment or death. Responding to the dominical tradition to visit prisoners (Matt. 25:36-44), the early Christians developed a reputation among pagans for their eagerness to serve their imprisoned. "Visitation apparently became so standard that church officers needed to encourage Christians to visit with moderation," Wansink says (*Chained in Christ*, 81). Cf. B. M. Rapske, "The Importance of Helpers to the Imprisoned Paul in the Book of Acts," *TynBul* 42, no. 1 (1991): 3-30.

35. Mark 6:27; Matt. 14:10; Acts 12:2; Heb. 11:37.

36. Mark 9:42; Matt. 18:6.

37. Matt. 27:5.

38. Luke 4:29.

39. Matt. 25:51; Luke 12:46; cf. Acts 13:11.

40. Luke 20:6; John 8:5; 10:31; cf. Matt. 21:44; 23:35; Acts 7:59-60.

41. Matt. 18:17; 1 Cor. 5:2-11.

42. Rev. 1:9.

43. Acts 12:6; 28:20; cf. 23:29; 26:31.

44. Acts 16:23-24.

45. Mark 10:34; 15:15; Matt. 10:17; 18:34; 23:34; 27:26; Luke 23:22; John 19:1; Acts 16:22; 22:24.

46. Heb. 11:37.

(which came in many forms),[47] and crucifixion.[48] Quite often the victims of such barbarities are not evildoers but those at the margins of mainstream Jewish and Greco-Roman society.

Clearly, then, there is more in the New Testament on our subject than first meets the eye. Moreover, it appears that the New Testament writers viewed the main elements of the criminal justice system of their day in a rather critical light. In one sense, they offer us an "underbelly perspective" on it, for they write as, to, and on behalf of the victims of abusive state power. This is not to say that they advocate political anarchy or the abolition of the judicial system. In principle the New Testament authors affirm the law-keeping functions of the state and counsel respect, submission, and cooperation.[49] At the same time, they bear eloquent testimony to the darker side of judicial power and violence, demonstrated most grimly in the conviction and execution of Jesus, the one who was classified with the criminals (Luke 22:37; Matt. 26:55; John 18:30). For believers, then, the effort to arrive at a Christian perspective on criminal justice can never rely solely on a cataloguing of biblical laws and penalties, or on some abstract theory of justice, or on pragmatic social-cost analyses of crime and punishment. It must reckon with the sobering fact that "the kings of the earth took their stand, and the rulers . . . gathered together against the Lord and against his Messiah," and employed the full force of arguably the two finest judicial systems in the ancient world to do away with him (Acts 4:26-27). The man who identified with lawbreakers in his ministry was finally counted among them on Golgotha, but not before calling those who would follow him to be prepared to meet a criminal's end as well (Mark 8:34-35).

The Problem of Faith:
Christian Ethics in the Public Arena

The way in which the "in-house" ethical teaching of the New Testament applies to the wider pluralist community is a persistent problem for

---

47. Matt. 18:34; 24:9; Heb. 11:35; 13:3; cf. Rev. 9:6.

48. Mark 15:22; Matt. 20:19; 26:2; 23:34; Luke 24:7; John 12:32, 33; 21:18; Gal. 3:10-23.

49. Mark 12:17; Rom. 13:1-6; 1 Pet. 2:13-17; 1 Tim. 2:1-4; Titus 3:1-2.

Christian ethicists. There is no simple answer to this dilemma, nor is there a single answer. Down through history different models have been proposed for bringing Christian values to bear in the non-Christian or semi-Christian public arena.[50] What is appropriate for one historical and cultural setting may not be appropriate for another, and a diversity of responses may be valid in the same setting. It is too big a task to examine this issue in detail here. It will be enough to identify some of the key questions that need to be wrestled with in any attempt to apply Christian insights to the criminal justice domain.

(1) *The Realism of Eschatological Ethics:* One such question concerns the extent to which the eschatological ethics of the New Testament are realistic. A dilemma is created by the fact that the Bible attests to both an ethics of creation and an ethics of redemption. The distinction between these two strands of moral teaching is by no means clear-cut, since redemption entails the affirmation, recovery, and eschatological transformation of creation. When, for example, Jesus appeals to creation in his teaching on anxiety (Matt. 6:25-34; Luke 12:22-32) or marriage (Mark 10:2-12; Matt. 19:3-9), it is creation as viewed from the perspective of eschatological redemption.[51] Similarly, when Paul cites the Genesis accounts of original creation to support his argument against "gender-bending" in Corinth, and appeals to the pattern of ongoing creation in the facts of human reproduction to rule out any implication of sexual inequality in the creation order (1 Cor. 11:7-12), he does so from the vantage point of those who are "in the Lord" (v. 11; cf. Gal. 3:28). In each case, the eschatological order stands in direct continuity with the created order.

That said, however, it is still possible to posit a distinction in the New Testament between ethical standards enjoined on all people by virtue of their being creatures made in God's image, and, on the other hand, standards that go beyond what is "naturally" human and are conditioned by the eschatological reality breaking redemptively into the present. Many of the so-called "hard sayings" of Jesus come into the latter category. He beckons his disciples not simply to love their neighbors

---

50. On classical answers to the problem, see J. H. Yoder, *The Christian Witness to the State* (Newton, Kans.: Faith & Life Press, 1964), esp. 60-73.

51. See B. D. Chilton and J. I. H. McDonald, *Jesus and the Ethics of the Kingdom* (London: SPCK, 1987), 38 and passim.

but to love even their enemies, not merely to avoid adultery and murder but to eschew lust and anger, not simply to forgive fellow believers who offend against them, and to do so repeatedly, but even to bless those who hate and persecute them. They are summoned to nothing less than divine perfection (Matt. 5:21-48). These radical demands, several of which concern dealing with offenders and offending, are best thought of not as new laws to be obeyed, but as new moral challenges to be pursued in response to the dawning kingdom. A. E. Harvey proposes that Jesus' moral teaching is better located in the Wisdom tradition than in the legal tradition of Israel. Jesus' "strenuous commands" are not new legislation but are wise sayings intended to raise his hearers' level of moral awareness to new heights, to challenge them to forms of conduct that transcend basic legal requirements, to call them to leave behind the commonsense, prudential morality that depends upon the stability and predictability of creation, because something unprecedented is taking place in his ministry that changes everything — the Kingdom of God is dawning.[52] Yet Jesus is still serious about these demands; they are not impossible ideals but realistic goals to strive after. They are *realistic* insofar as they are empowered by the new *reality* of God's redeeming power that has broken into the world. So when Jesus summons his followers to perfection (Matt. 5:48), he counts *genuine* attainment to be possible, but not necessarily *total* attainment, for God's kingdom is not yet here in its fullness. Paul exemplifies this tension. He identifies perfection *(teteleiōmai)* as the ultimate goal he reaches after, yet at the same time he concedes that he is not yet perfect (Phil. 3:12-16) and will not be so until he sees Christ face-to-face (1 Cor. 13:9-12).[53]

If the "not yet" of redemption limits the extent of Christian attainment to Jesus' high calling,[54] the overt resistance of an unbelieving world still saddled by sin and death will hinder even more its attain-

---

52. A. E. Harvey, *Strenuous Commands: The Ethic of Jesus* (London: SCM, 1990).

53. On the progressive nature of ethical attainment, see W. D. Davies and D. C. Allison Jr., "Reflections on the Sermon on the Mount," *SJT* 44, no. 3 (1991): 306-9.

54. To underline this point, Robin Gill suggests that Christian communities should be regarded as "harbingers and carriers" of Christian values more than as "exemplars" of them, since Christians often do not exemplify the values they espouse in theory. See *Moral Communities* (Exeter: University of Exeter Press, 1992), 54-55, 63. While this is a helpful insight, care is needed lest Jesus' ethical standards become reduced entirely to theoretical ideals that none can aspire to.

ment to similar values. The peculiar problem for Christian ethics, then, lies not in articulating a "creation ethic" that all people of goodwill can aspire to, but in deciding how the eschatological values of Christian existence are to be commended to, and worked out in the midst of, the wider fallen world. One common way of coming to terms with this dilemma is by positing a dualism in the moral will of God. In medieval Catholicism, for example, a distinction was drawn between standards that applied to saintly Christians and those that applied to everyone else. The lower-level ethic (or "precepts"), which included the double-love commandment (Mark 12:28-32) and the Golden Rule (Matt. 7:12), was incumbent on all who sought salvation. The political order also functioned at this lower level; its task was to satisfy society's need for justice. The higher-level ethic (or "evangelical counsels") was appropriate only for those seeking perfection and rewards in heaven; it required entering religious orders and taking vows of chastity (Matt. 19:12; 22:30), poverty (Matt. 19:21; Mark 6:7-9; 10:21), and obedience (John 14:15).

In the two-kingdom ethic of both classical Lutheranism and sectarian Protestantism, the dualism expresses itself as a distinction between two spheres of application rather than two classes of people.[55] In Lutheran tradition, every Christian belongs simultaneously to two realms. In the private, spiritual realm, he or she is accountable to the gospel's demand of radical love. In the public, temporal realm, though still under divine command, he or she operates according to natural law and civil justice, which will sometimes require the exercise of punitive — even lethal — judgment. As Ernst Troeltsch explains,

> The practice of government and the administration of justice are offices appointed by Divine command, and Luther describes with great vigour the contrast between the system of law which is carried out from the ruling prince down to the gaoler and hangman, in which the work of government, administration, and punishment, including hanging, breaking on the wheel, and beheading, is all a service to God, and the nonofficial purely personal morality, in which, on the other hand, the true service of God consists in loving one's enemies, in sacri-

55. Luther's position actually turned on three dualisms: a church/world dualism, a private/public dualism, and a reason/revelation dualism. On this point, see J. M. Stayer, *Anabaptists and the Sword*, 2d rev. ed. (Lawrence, Kans.: Coronado Press, 1976), 33-44.

fice, renunciation and endurance, in loving care for others and self-sacrifice.[56]

The Schleitheim Confession of sixteenth-century Anabaptism also posits different ethics for the spiritual and the temporal realms, but strips the latter of any pretense of being Christian. Political authorities are ordained by God to use lethal coercion, but they do so "outside the perfection of Christ." A complete separation is required between church and state. There is little hope of Christianizing the wider social order, apart from the conversion of individuals and their transfer out of the world and into the kingdom of God.[57] A similar, if less rigorous, church/world dualism has also characterized other sectarian groups.

Even those approaches that espouse a theocratic ideal and repudiate in principle any kind of dualism often end up with a de facto dualism. The most common expression of this is a sharp distinction between personal and social ethics. The lofty standards of Jesus' teaching are confined to the interpersonal sphere, while the corporate or social sphere is held accountable to a different set of social norms, typically validated by the Old Testament more than the New. The failure of the New Testament to elaborate an appropriate social ethic is sometimes seen as a virtue,[58] at other times as its greatest weakness. "From neither its christology, its eschatology, nor its ecclesiology has it developed a theology of justice for the historical, societal, and international systems," Rolf P. Knierim laments. "Where Christianity in its own history

56. Troeltsch, *The Social Teaching of the Christian Churches,* 2 vols. (New York: Macmillan, 1931), 2: 549; cf. 533.

57. On the Anabaptist dualism, see especially Stayer, *Anabaptists and the Sword;* J. H. Yoder, "Anabaptists and the Sword Revisited: Systematic Historiography and Undogmatic Nonresistants," *Sonderdruck aus 'Zweitschrift für Kirchengeschichte'* II:270-83; and Yoder, *Christian Attitudes to War, Peace, and Revolution: A Companion to Bainton* (Elkhart, Ind.: Goshen Biblical Seminary, 1983), 163-200. Recent Mennonite thought has questioned such a church/world dualism from a variety of perspectives. In addition to Yoder, see J. R. Burkholder, "Mennonite Peace Theology: Reconnaissance and Exploration," unpublished paper, Peace Theology Colloquium VI, Elkhart, Indiana, June 1991; Burkholder, "Nonresistance," *ME* V:637-38; *Mennonite Peace Theology: A Panorama of Types,* ed. J. R. Burkholder and B. N. Gingerich (Akron, Pa.: MCC, 1991); and T. Koontz, "Mennonites and the State: Preliminary Reflections," in *Essays on Peace Theology and Witness,* ed. W. M. Swartley (Elkhart, Ind.: Institute of Mennonite Studies, 1988), 35-60.

58. Cf. M. Hill, "The Victory of Personal Relationships: Paul and Social Ethics," in *Christians in Society,* ed. B. G. Webb (Homebush West, N.S.W.: Lancer, 1988), 131-44.

has attempted it, it has — considering its claims to superiority — fared worse than Israel."[59]

Whether or not this is a valid criticism, it underlines the fact that acceptance of a two-kingdom dualism, or even a rigid and simplistic distinction between personal and social ethics,[60] effectively renders most of New Testament teaching irrelevant to criminal justice issues. This is the case because the criminal justice system is today a function of the secular, corporate state, whereas New Testament teaching is addressed primarily to the faith community and advocates an ethic which presupposes religious conversion and empowerment by the eschatological Spirit. The latter is by definition inapplicable to the former. However, any model that imposes a sharp dualism in the moral will of God must finally be repudiated on both theological and moral grounds. Such an approach renders God double-minded, compromises Christ's claim to universal lordship, and marginalizes the moral voice of Jesus in the wider community. History also attests to how dangerous such a "solution" is. By sanctioning a sub-Christian ethic for the state, the church has often forfeited its prophetic witness and enabled the state literally to get away with murder. For the same reason, the contribution of mainstream churches to the reform and humanization of penal practice has been, at best, ambiguous, despite boasting a religion that centers on forgiveness, mercy, and redemption.[61]

59. Knierim, *The Task of Old Testament Theology: Substance, Method, and Cases* (Grand Rapids: William B. Eerdmans, 1995), 107.

60. To posit a hard-and-fast distinction between personal and social ethics is simplistic and misleading because the moral formation of individuals always takes place in communities. Personal ethics derive from the shared moral traditions of the wider communities that individuals belong to. This is especially true of biblical ethics, which are addressed in the first instance to the covenant community and to individuals insofar as they are part of that community. It is also wrong to suggest that Jesus taught only personal ethics. It is impossible to explain the crucifixion of Jesus if he merely called individuals to greater private holiness. This is not to say that there is no difference between the way ethical norms work out in group conduct and in individual conduct. But it is better to distinguish between "simple" morality, entailing virtues like honesty, self-control, compassion, faithfulness, and so on, over which an individual has considerable control, and "complex" morality, entailing such virtues as freedom, justice, and equality, which involve many lives simultaneously and cannot be exercised apart from complex social interactions, which necessarily bring conflict and require compromise. Cf. B. C. Birch & L. L. Rasmussen, *Bible and Ethics in the Christian Life* (Minneapolis: Augsburg, 1989), 212n.11.

61. It is true, on the one hand, that many prison reformers, like John Howard in the

Over against a two-sphere ethic, it must therefore be affirmed that God has only one moral will for human life. This will is expressed most clearly in the person, work, and teaching of Jesus Christ, and may be actualized most fully in the communities of disciples who follow him. Yet its relevance and authority must not be restricted to this community alone. Christians should never say that Christ's ethic of redemptive love does not apply to mainstream society. As John Redekop points out, "The unfaithfulness of Christians begins when we say that it is inappropriate to bring Christ's ethic to bear on certain of our problems and relationships. Christians should not be advocates in any situations or relationships for a sub-Christian culture or ethic."[62] On the other hand, the tragic reality of the Fall, the power and pervasiveness of sin, the "not yet" of the kingdom, and the religious and cultural pluralism of contemporary society cannot simply be ignored. The constraints they impose must be acknowledged. Such is the weight of sin and idolatry in the fallen world that God's redemptive will cannot be done to the same extent in unbelieving society as in the church. But rather than sanctifying a lower-level ethic for society at large, the Christian community should summon society to move in the direction of Jesus' teaching, to emulate as fully as possible within the constraints of its non-Christian setting the values and conduct appropriate to life under the reign of God, as proclaimed and embodied by Christ. Not only does a continuity exist between creation and redemption, with redemptive ethics being a recapitulation — that is, a deepening, enriching, and extending — of the moral obligations of creaturehood, but the ethical de-

---

eighteenth century, have been driven by Christian compassion, and that penal innovations — such as prison visitation, probation services, and the development of rehabilitation programs — have been undergirded by distinctively Christian theological beliefs. On the other hand, the very use of prolonged imprisonment, including solitary confinement, as an instrument of reformation and deserved punishment was itself a Christian innovation with roots in monasticism; cf. Cayley, *The Expanding Prison*, 123-50. Moreover, images of God as lawgiver and chastiser, together with punitive theologies of atonement, purgatory, and the afterlife, have been used historically to sanction and encourage harsh treatment of criminals, cf. T. J. Gorringe, *God's Just Vengeance*. In the judgment of W. Moberly, with the exception of the Quakers, "modern reforms in the practice and principles of punishment do not seem to have owed very much to Christian inspiration." See *The Ethics of Punishment* (London: Faber & Faber, 1968), 33-34.

62. Redekop, "An Analysis of Capital Punishment," in *On Capital Punishment*, ed. J. H. Redekop and E. A. Martens (Hillsboro, Kans.: Kindred Press, 1987), 16.

mands of Jesus point the way toward true liberty and humanization.[63] The fact that these demands are articulated in religious language and depend upon eschatological presuppositions does not thereby render them totally inapplicable to secular life and relationships. Certainly Jesus' standards cannot be adequately attained apart from the empowering of God's Spirit, but they can be approximated — and the wind of the Spirit often blows in unexpected places!

Accordingly, while it would be impossible, indeed wrong, for secular courts to require victims to love and forgive those who have wronged them, as Jesus summons his followers to aspire to, Christians should at least encourage the legal system to establish procedures that are consistent with and that move in the direction of the personal and relational values expressed in Jesus' call to forgiveness and love of the enemy. These procedures may be commended to government bodies on pragmatic, even financial grounds,[64] though for Christians they spring ultimately from the conviction that the values of God's kingdom are consonant with the nature of human creaturehood and consistent with the true direction of human history. This means that while we repudiate any dualism in God's will that sanctifies a sub-Christian ethic for one sphere in life, we must still recognize a fundamental *duality* between church and world. Failure to do so encourages a reduction of Jesus' radical demands to common sense and enlightened self-interest and a relinquishment of spiritual empowerment as the sine qua non of Christian existence. We must therefore allow a gap between what committed believers and nonbelievers will aspire to and achieve, as well as between the absolute standards Jesus sets and our partial attainment of them this side of the consummation of the kingdom. But it is a *gap*, not a gaping *chasm* dividing two unrelated realms.

(2) *Love and Justice:* Another key question, one not unrelated to the eschatological issues just considered, concerns the connection between love and justice. How are they related? Is it possible to be simultaneously

63. On this, see C. D. Marshall, "'Made a Little Lower than the Angels: Human Rights in the Biblical Tradition," in *Human Rights and the Common Good: Christian Perspectives,* ed. B. Atkin and K. Evans (Wellington, N. Z.: Victoria University Press, 1999), esp. 52-64.

64. Cayley's comment is apposite: "It remains to be seen whether crippling costs will finally force the United States into the rational discussion of prison policy that considerations of justice and prudence have so far failed to bring about" (*The Expanding Prison,* 58).

loving and just? Do love and justice pertain to different domains, with love being the norm for private life and justice the norm for public life? Or do both norms apply in all spheres of life? Is it possible to conceive of the state as an instrument of Christian love? Or does the essentially personal character of love preclude its expression through institutional forms and government bureaucracies? Such questions as these have particular pertinence to the area of criminal justice. Is the task of the judicial system solely to dispense justice, or should we expect it to show love as well? Can it do both? Is a judge summoned to love the criminal he or she is sentencing to punishment? Is penal retribution consistent with the imperative to love our neighbor, especially if, as Paul claims, "love does no wrong to a neighbor" (Rom. 13:10)?

These are complex questions, and there is no consensus among Christian ethicists on how they should be answered.[65] Some argue that love and justice are identical: justice is simply love distributed. Others see love and justice as standing in tension. Tolstoy, for instance, maintained that if we took seriously the commandment to love our neighbor, we would have to abandon the whole system of punitive justice.[66] Most ethicists, however, see love and justice as different yet compatible and inseparable norms. Love requires justice, and justice expresses love, though love is more than justice. In complex social relations or institutional contexts, love is mediated via justice since pure agape-love cannot be institutionalized or applied to the public realm. Some, like Helmut Thielicke, would consider military violence and penal justice to be the "alien work" of love, where love seeks to destroy what is against love. Others, like Reinhold Niebuhr, would see such military and penal coercion, insofar as they are demanded by justice, to be a partial expression of love that at the same time stands under the judgment of love.

In such discussion, much depends on how we understand justice and love. We all have an intuitive awareness of what each term means,

---

65. For much of this section, I am indebted to J. Boston, "Love, Justice, and the State," in *Voices for Justice: Church, Law, and State in New Zealand,* ed. J. Boston and A. Cameron (Palmerston North, N.Z.: Dunmore Press, 1994), 69-105 (which includes references to secondary literature). See also D. B. Forrester, *Christian Justice and Public Policy* (Cambridge: Cambridge University Press, 1997), 205-29.

66. See Tolstoy, *The Law of Love and the Law of Violence* (New York: Holt, Rinehart & Winston, 1970), and *The Kingdom of God and Peace Essays* (London: Oxford University Press, 1936).

but arriving at agreed-upon definitions is more difficult. Both are inclusive or generic terms that embrace a wide variety of specific senses and applications depending on the circumstances in which they are used. With respect to *justice,* for example, we find reference to natural justice and rough justice, distributive justice and retributive justice, commutative justice and remedial justice, poetic justice and practical justice, as well as to innumerable other categories.[67] Whether there is a single master concept underlying all uses of the term — such as fairness or equity or reasonableness or impartiality or respect or mutual advantage or power — and what justice requires in each context are matters that are sharply disputed. Indeed, such is the diversity of ways in which justice is understood and acted upon in postmodern pluralist society that some writers simply conclude that "nobody knows what justice is,"[68] or that the very quest for a singular conception of universal justice based on reason is not only impossible but illegitimate.[69] There is no agreed-upon, neutral, transcendent criterion against which ideas of justice can be measured, they claim; it all depends on a larger belief system about the meaning and direction of life and the world, and such belief systems are relative to particular communities and historical locations. There is therefore no such thing as "justice" singular, only "justices" plural, the justices of particular communities or of vested interest groups within those communities. Over against such postmodern skepticism, one might insist that, on theological grounds, a single universal justice that transcends all local diversity *must* exist since God is the source and arbiter of true justice. If God is just and God is one, then God's justice must stand apart from all cultural construals of justice. Yet even if we grant the universality of God's justice, the fact remains that every human attempt to give account of that justice and to apply it concretely to real-life situations is unavoidably particular, and hence partial and falli-

67. Contemporary ethicists stress that justice is a complex, many-sided reality depending on the types of relationships involved. E. C. Biesner, for example, distinguishes between voluntary, involuntary, and accidental relationships, and identifies five types of justice, each of which he illustrates from the Bible. See "Justice and Poverty: Two Views Contrasted," *Transformation* 10, no. 1 (1993): 18-19.

68. On this point, see D. B. Forrester, "Political Justice and Christian Theology," *StChEth* 3, no. 1 (1990): 1-13; and Forrester, *Christian Justice and Public Policy,* esp. 36-80.

69. See Pavlich, *Justice Fragmented,* 2-5, 16-41.

ble.[70] Divine justice itself may be absolute and pure, but our capacity to know, describe, and fulfill that justice most assuredly is not. (Much the same can be said of that other, most slippery of concepts, truth.)

Such disputes on the meaning and scope of justice obviously have a direct bearing on how we understand the role of love in the dispensation of criminal justice. If corrective justice is understood in essentially retributive terms, then acts of mercy or forgiveness will be seen as, at best, a foregoing of the legitimate claims of justice or, at worst, a distinct injustice. But if justice is understood in more relational and restorative terms — making things right and repairing relationships — then justice is actually consummated in forgiveness and reconciliation.[71] Significantly, there is no tension in Scripture between God's justice and God's love, suggesting that divine justice is understood fundamentally not in abstract, arithmetical terms but as God's attention to the demands of specific relationships grounded in his steadfast love.

But what does *love* mean? It is commonplace in Christian ethics to differentiate between one-way or "agape" love, which is a disinterested benevolence to all, regardless of their response, and two-way love, such as friendship love or erotic love, which is reciprocal. Because it does not seek reciprocation, agape-love is usually considered superior to other loves, a truer reflection of divine love. At minimum it requires us to love our neighbors as ourselves, which has affinities with notions of justice; at the extreme it requires us to love our neighbors, and even our enemies, at great expense to ourselves, which takes us well beyond the norms of justice. Paul Ricoeur's handling of the New Testament data exemplifies this distinction. He points to important differences between the notion of love affirmed by the "Golden Rule" (Matt. 7:12; Luke 6:31), which operates on the principle of reciprocity, and the form

70. See the useful discussion on this issue by M. Volf, *Exclusion and Embrace: A Theological Exploration of Identity, Otherness, and Reconciliation* (Nashville: Abingdon Press, 1996), 193-231.

71. So Boston, "Love, Justice, and the State," 95; and Volf, *Exclusion and Embrace*, 220-25. Unfortunately, Volf uses the term "restorative justice" anomalously to designate what I mean by retributive justice. "In the framework of restorative justice, no reconciliation is possible. On the contrary, the pursuit of such justice will deepen the conflict and reinstate the 'compulsion of evil deeds.' Hence the need for forgiveness" (123). Later he makes it clear, however, that there can be no genuine justice without the will to embrace the other (216ff).

of love expressed by "love your enemies" (Matt. 5:44; Luke 6:31) and the "new commandment" (John 13:34; cf. 1 John 2:7; 3:8), which operates on the principle of grace or "the logic of superabundance." Whereas the Golden Rule requires justice and equity, enemy-love transcends justice and leaves no place for coercion or punitive retribution. Ricoeur finds it significant that Jesus did not replace the Golden Rule with a new ethic of agape-love but complemented one with the other. He summoned his disciples to go beyond the minimal expression of reciprocal love to the fuller form of unrequited service and generosity.[72]

However, in a stimulating and insightful essay, Linda Woodhead challenges this common notion that the superiority of Christian agape-love lies in its gratuitous and nonreciprocal character, its volitional determination to show respect for others simply in recognition of their status as fellow human creatures and regardless of their individual virtue. Such an emotionally detached and abstract notion of love, Woodhead argues, is peculiarly masculine and falls well short of the kind of love that God demonstrates. Christian love is better understood, she proposes, as "an active desire for the well-being of the neighbour, and for communion with him or her, based on a recognition of the neighbour's unique worth." It involves the whole person — mind, will, *and* emotions — and it values the other person not merely because he or she belongs to the human family but because he or she is a particular and unique person and is loveable (even likeable) as such. While love is not conditional upon getting love in return, it still seeks after communion with the one loved and thus desires reciprocation. The fullest expression of Christian love is therefore found not in gratuitous, one-way relationships but in mutual two-way relationship, where both parties are wholly involved with each other. God models such love. God so loved the world (John 3:16), despite its estrangement from and hostility to God's self, that God spared no cost to be reconciled to humanity (Rom. 5:6-11; 2 Cor. 5:18-20). God was not content with displaying a superior one-way love toward humanity; God sought a wholehearted relationship of committed, covenant love from humankind in return.[73]

Woodhead's reflections on the nature of Christian love are ex-

---

72. Ricoeur, "The Golden Rule: Exegetical and Theological Perplexities," *NTS* 36 (1990): 392-97.

73. Woodhead, "Love and Justice," *StChEth* 5, no. 1 (1992): 44-63.

tremely valuable. Her treatment of love rings true to both the common human experience of love and to the scriptural witness to divine love, more so than the somewhat bloodless approach of mainstream theological ethics. Strangely, however, Woodhead does not subject conventional notions of justice to a similar feminist analysis. In her discussion of the relationship between love and justice, Woodhead accepts without critique the post-Enlightenment understanding of justice as that which seeks to regulate fairly the competing claims of individuals in society through positive law. On this understanding there is "a huge difference" between love and justice, Woodhead says, for love can never be legislated or enforced by compulsion. Love must come from the heart and goes beyond the limits of legal obligation.[74] True enough. But the difference between love and justice might not have seemed so huge had Woodhead, like other feminists, conceptualized justice in relational and liberationist terms, justice as the existence of right relationships, where there is no exploitation, and all parties exercise appropriate power. "For feminist theologians," Karen Lebacqz explains, "justice and liberation cannot be separated from love and reconciliation," for justice is "power-in-relation."[75] Moreover, Woodhead's own definition of love as that which seeks the well-being of others invites a closer connection between love and justice than does the more traditional formulation. As she herself observes, the traditional understanding of Christian love that stresses unconditional self-sacrifice on behalf of the needs of others has often been used to justify nonresistance to injustice and servile acceptance of abuse. By contrast, her new conception of love *requires* active resistance to oppression, abuse, and criminal offending, since to allow someone to commit acts of violence and violation without reply serves the well-being of no one, neither victim nor offender.

Enough has been said to show the complexities involved in bringing the demands of Christian love to bear on matters of public policy and state-administered justice. In general terms it may be true to say, along with Daryl Charles, that "maintaining justice and social order, not maintaining love, is the state's chief task."[76] But to remove the state from ac-

74. Woodhead, "Love and Justice," 59-61.

75. Lebacqz, "Justice," *DFTh*, 159. See also A. M. Isasi-Díaz, "Justice and Social Change," 159-62 in the same work.

76. Charles, "Pauline Ethics and Capital Justice: Proscription or Prescription (Rom. 12:17–13:7)?" unpublished paper presented at the SBL conference, November 1994, 16.

countability to the central Christian norm of love in this way is surely undesirable. On the other hand, even if we accept that secular institutional life stands under the imperative of love, we still need to recognize that the way in which love can be expressed in, say, the criminal justice system will be different from (and lesser to) what is possible in interpersonal I-Thou relationships or in relations within the Christian community of faith.

(3) *Mode of Public Discourse:* A third key question relates to the mode of ethical discourse Christians should use in the public arena. In what terms do Christians commend ethical considerations, especially those based on eschatological redemption, to policymakers who neither understand nor accept the Christian gospel? This has always been a problem for Christians wishing to contribute to political or moral discussion in the wider community, but it has become particularly acute in recent decades as even the memory — never mind the intelligibility — of Christian language and concepts fades from the collective consciousness.[77]

In the past, Christian ethicists have advocated the use of "middle axioms" in which a social critique derived from theological belief is clothed in terms and principles that secular authorities can understand, as a kind of ethical Esperanto. This approach was first proposed in the 1930s and has been particularly popular with Anglican social ethicists. On the positive side, it facilitates intelligibility and enables Christians to make full use of their equal citizenship in society. On the negative side, it raises questions about the validity, relevance, and integrity of the Christian message. Jonathan Boston challenges the assumption that the distinctive features of Christian language and faith should be filtered out in order to arrive at axioms that invite general consent regardless of people's worldview. "Surely, if Christians are to be faithful to the gospel, if they are to take their prophetic responsibility seriously, they have no choice but to emphasise the gospel's central features, its distinctive dogmatics as well as its distinctive ethics, no matter how disagreeable, or even offensive, some may find the message."[78]

---

77. In light of this, M. McKenzie expresses pessimism about the capacity of Christians to articulate biblical norms in the marketplace unless they recapture the ethical square through evangelism. See "Christian Norms in the Ethical Square: An Impossible Dream?" *JETS* 38, no. 3 (1995): 413-27.

78. Boston, "Christianity in the Public Square: The Churches and Social Justice," in *Voices for Justice: Church, Law, and State in New Zealand,* ed. J. Boston and A. Cameron (Palmerston North, N.Z.: Dunmore Press, 1994), 29.

Another problem with the middle-axioms approach is that it assumes Christian values and moral principles can be separated from the larger narrative framework of the Christian story without loss to either and without substantially altering their meaning. The principles are considered timeless, the story expendable. But Christian values make most sense when seen in light of the canonical biblical story, and it is that story which gives even commonsense values a distinctive flavor. Arguably it is the biblical narrative of God's creative love and redemptive justice made known in the life of Israel and in the person of Christ and the experience of his followers, rather than a set of timeless moral axioms, that represents the real Christian contribution to collective ethical discourse. For this story offers more than a code of morality. It reveals the *character* of God demonstrated in word, deed, and relationships; it mediates *participation* in the life of God; and it has the power to shape *moral character* in conformity to God, both individually and communally.[79]

Yet there is still the problem that both knowledge of the biblical story and the intelligibility and credibility of Christian theological beliefs are at an all-time low ebb in contemporary Western society. If Christians are to speak meaningfully in current moral and political debates, including those relating to criminal justice, they must find ways of doing so that will command common understanding, if not assent, across the spectrum of pluralist society,[80] yet without shrinking from justifying and explaining their perspectives in light of the faith-story to which they subscribe. The dilemma Christians face, then, is not only deciding how Christian values derived from the eschatological experience of God's redemptive love and saving justice recorded in Scripture can be and should be applied in a mixed and fallen society, but also deciding how they are to be expressed in terms that are intelligible in the marketplace, yet faithful to and explicitly anchored in the distinctive claims of the Christian story. That story does not furnish a ready-made theory of criminal justice, but it does a great deal to en-

---

79. See the excellent discussion by B. C. Birch, "Moral Agency, Community, and the Character of God in the Hebrew Bible," *Semeia* 66 (1995): 23-41.

80. For a sophisticated attempt to do this by means of the concept of relationism, see C. Townsend et al., *Political Christians in a Plural Society: A New Strategy for a Biblical Contribution* (Cambridge: Jubilee Policy Group, 1994).

large our understanding of justice and to foster a commitment to its pursuit.

The discussion so far on the task and complexities of Christian social ethics has been necessarily selective and incomplete. A comprehensive analysis would need to consider many other factors, especially those of a hermeneutical and political nature. But what has been said is enough to warn against two opposite errors in using the New Testament as a guide to thinking about such issues as crime and punishment. One error is to attempt to apply the discipleship ethics of the New Testament directly and legalistically to the machinery of the state, which is bound to end in compromise or failure. The other is to confine the ethical demands of the New Testament entirely to the Christian community and regard them as substantially irrelevant to wider social issues. Neither approach does justice to the normative authority of New Testament scripture. While New Testament ethical teaching is directly relevant to the community of faith, it is at least indirectly relevant to the larger community, since both communities are involved in the realization of God's will on earth as it is in heaven (Matt. 5:13-16; 6:10; 28:19-20).

The Goal and Limitations of This Study

In light of these methodological reflections, it is time to clarify the goal and concede the limitations of the present investigation. Plainly there is much more to Christian ethics than shuffling selected biblical texts into some convenient arrangement, then seeking to apply them directly to modern problems. Not only do a wide range of theological, philosophical, moral, and pragmatic considerations need to be taken into account, but the historical and cultural conditionedness of the biblical texts themselves must be reckoned with. As Richard Hays outlines in his magisterial study *The Moral Vision of the New Testament*, there are four main tasks entailed in moving from the biblical text to normative ethical judgments: the descriptive task of exegeting the relevant texts, the synthetic task of placing texts in their canonical context, the hermeneutical task of relating the ancient text to the contemporary situation, and the pragmatic task of embodying the text's imperatives in the concrete life of the community of faith. In view of the enormity of such an undertaking, what follows is by no means a fully fledged study in Christian ethics on the topic of crime and punishment. My aim is more modest than that in two respects.

On the one hand, although in places (especially in Chapter 3) I explore wider legal and moral questions so as to provide a "realistic" context for my exegesis, I make no pretense to being a criminal justice specialist or a social ethicist, or to have mastered the relevant literature in these fields, which is mountainous. My training is in New Testament studies, and my main intention is to survey a broad range of New Testament texts pertinent to the subject of crime and punishment in order to ascertain the extent to which they reflect what might be called a vision of restorative justice. On the other hand, although this is mainly a biblical study, I do not undertake a thoroughgoing historical-critical investigation for its own sake. My primary concern is to marshal and discuss canonical texts in a manner that will be useful to the larger task of Christian ethical reflection. This enterprise is logically distinct from historical-critical analysis, for it is the final form of the text that possesses canonical authority, not some hypothetical reconstruction of the community behind the text or of the historical Jesus behind the gospel traditions.[81] My handling of the biblical data is intended to facilitate this aim. I do not analyze every text with the exegetical, critical, and hermeneutical rigor one might expect of a technical exercise in historical-critical scholarship. I make no attempt to assess the authenticity of the sayings ascribed to Jesus but am content to assume that a reliable recollection of Jesus' own perspectives on such issues as forgiveness and nonretaliation has been a major factor — surely the dominant factor — in shaping the available sayings tradition. Nor do I claim to have identified every text of potential relevance to my subject. Indeed, it has been difficult to avoid a kind of exegetical domino effect where discussion of one text leads inexorably to analysis of dozens of related or parallel texts. The discussion of love of the enemy in Chapter 2, for example, or of excommunication in Chapter 4, could easily have spilled over into a wider consideration of the pronounced dualism of the Johannine writings, which some interpreters see as a failure of the Christian ethic of

---

81. On this point, see Hays, *The Moral Vision of the New Testament,* 14, 158-68; Matera, *New Testament Ethics,* 1-10; L. E. Keck, "Rethinking 'New Testament Ethics,'" *JBL* 115, no. 1 (1996): 3-16; and J. D. G. Dunn, *The Living Word* (London: SCM, 1987), 141-74.

enemy-love.[82] Investigation of the meaning of the "sword" in Romans 13:4 (Chapter 5) could well have led into consideration of the political ramifications of the passage as a whole, as well as of other New Testament texts on the state. But to keep the study within manageable proportions, I have avoided chasing the dominoes. I have also restricted my discussion of divine justice in Paul's theology mainly to the letter to the Romans, while my characterization of Jesus as the justice of God concentrates only on the themes of forgiveness and nonretaliation (Chapter 2).

The exploration that follows is therefore limited in scope. My premise is that the first Christians experienced in Christ and lived out in their faith communities an understanding of justice as a power that heals, restores, and reconciles rather than hurts, punishes, and kills, and that this reality ought to shape and direct a Christian contribution to the criminal justice debate today. I trust the representative soundings of early Christian thought that follow are sufficient to establish this thesis and will help to furnish a biblical foundation for Christians engaged in the critique and reform of our present system of criminal justice.

82. See, for example, P. Perkins, "Apocalyptic Sectarianism and Love Commands: The Johannine Epistles and Revelation," in *The Love of Enemy and Nonretaliation in the New Testament*, ed. W. M. Swartley (Louisville, Ky.: Westminster John Knox, 1992), 287-96.

CHAPTER 2

THE ARENA OF SAVING JUSTICE

The Justice of God in Paul and Jesus

We have seen how first impressions can be misleading. An initial impression that the New Testament writers have little to say about crime and punishment needed revision in light of the wealth of detail the New Testament contains on each of the major components of the criminal justice system: laws, crimes, criminal offending, courts, police, prisons, and punishments. While much of this detail is incidental in nature, it still affords unexpected insight into the underbelly of first-century criminal justice systems and gives us reason to question any strong "law and order" agenda allegedly based on the Bible. There is another reason too why perceptions about the New Testament's lack of attention to penal justice issues need questioning — because of how much the New Testament has to say about justice in the broader sense. It is this general conception of justice, and especially God's justice, that provides an indispensable framework for elaborating a Christian perspective on crime and punishment.

Modern readers seldom realize how often justice language features in the New Testament. This is mainly because English translations render the key terms — those employing the *dik-* stem — with a double set of equivalents deriving from two different linguistic stocks (Anglo-Saxon and Latin). Sometimes the terms are translated with "right-" terms ("right," "righteous," "righteousness"), at other times with "just-" terms ("just," "justify," "justification"). Because of this linguistic peculiarity, English-speaking readers sense little obvious connection between the "right" language of the New Testament and the concept of justice. Even the words "justification" and "justify" are rarely associated with the notion of justice, despite the obvious lexical resemblance, because these terms have acquired an exclusively theological meaning in Christian discourse. As we will see later, a parallel problem is found in the Hebrew Bible, where the corresponding Hebrew terms, those derived from the *sdq* root, are also often translated with "right" terminology.

The problem is compounded by the fact that in contemporary English usage, "righteousness" and "justice" have quite distinct connotations. "Righteousness" carries the sense of personal ethical purity and religious piety (indeed, the term "righteousness" is now virtually obsolete in secular discourse), while "justice" relates to public judicial fairness and equality of rights. One belongs to the private, moral, religious realm, the other to the public, political, legal realm. But this is not necessarily so in the Bible. In biblical usage the same terms may carry ethical and juridical applications and may relate to both private and public spheres. What this means is that in the New Testament "righteousness," "justice," and "justification" belong to the same complex of ideas. They derive from a single linguistic stem and fall within the same semantic field. Accordingly, when the New Testament writers, especially Paul and Matthew, make such extensive use of "right" language, they are trading in justice-related ideas.

This is not to say that we can invariably use "justice" as a translation substitute for "righteousness" and related "right" terms. In Western usage, the term "justice" is closely tied to the public arena of lawmaking and enforcing, whereas in biblical usage "justice" goes beyond the legal sphere to evoke the idea of comprehensive well-being, wholeness, and peace.[1] Always to replace the term "righteousness" with "justice" would somewhat obscure the nonforensic applications and holistic character of the biblical terminology and tend to encourage the use of Western concepts of legal justice to interpret the biblical notion of justice. In fact, the "right" word group is so loaded with potential meaning in biblical usage that no single translation equivalent can bear the semantic weight the terms may carry in diverse contexts. This is es-

---

1. See H. G. Reventlow, "Righteousness as Order of the World: Some Remarks Towards a Programme," in *Justice and Righteousness: Biblical Themes and Their Influence,* ed. H. G. Reventlow and Y. Hoffman (Sheffield: Sheffield Academic Press, 1992), 164-65, 171.

pecially true of Paul's usage. Still, the point to be stressed here is that righteousness terminology in the New Testament, like its Old Testament counterparts, has a wide semantic range embracing forensic, sociopolitical, ethical, and religious applications. At the most general level it signals "doing, being, declaring, or bringing about what is right," with the specific connotation being dictated by context. Biblical righteousness is a more comprehensive reality than Western justice, but it is still indissolubly connected with what we mean by justice, and "justice" is often preferable to "righteousness" as a translation equivalent, though neither term is entirely adequate.[2]

In this chapter I will offer some reflections on the role and meaning of justice in Paul's theology (especially in Romans) and in the ministry of Jesus. This is a huge area to address, and all I can hope to do here is take some initial bearings on the terrain. But the issue is plainly relevant to our inquiry, since the criminal justice system claims to dispense justice and operates according to a pre-understanding of what justice means, an understanding that may be compared with what the New Testament understands by justice. For Christian ethics, such a comparison also implies a critique, for as Duncan Forrester notes, "The relative justice which is all that is possible in this sinful broken world, the justice which comes from the balancing of claims and interests and acts to restrain sin, must constantly be measured against the divine justice and love we know in Jesus Christ, and in our experience of justification."[3] What then does Paul mean when he describes the gospel in Romans as the revelation of the justice of God (Rom. 1:16-17)? What does Jesus mean when he instructs us to seek first God's royal justice (Matt. 6:33)?

---

2. D. G. MacGuire says that "when we speak of the Bible's justice . . . we fall victim to the translator. . . . Our pale and wan 'justice' is not worthy of biblical words like *sedeqah*. The traitor plays even more mischievously when *sedeqah* is translated 'righteousness,' with all the unfortunate relatives that word has gathered" (*The Moral Core of Judaism and Christianity: Reclaiming the Revolution* [Minneapolis: Fortress, 1993], 130). In "Is 'Righteous' Right?" (*SJT* 41 [1988]: 1-10), G. A. F. Knight maintains that the English word "righteousness" is a "wholly inept" translation of the corresponding biblical (in particular Hebrew) terms, especially when applied to God, because "it conjures up a vision of an unattractive, self-righteous individual who knows how to blow his own horn" (9).

3. Forrester, "Political Justice and Christian Theology," *StChEth* 3, no. 1 (1990): 13.

Paul's Gospel of Divine Justice

A strong case can be made for regarding "righteousness" *(dikaiosunē)* in general, and "the righteousness of God" *(dikaiosunē theou)* in particular, as the central theme of Paul's letter to the Romans. One clear indication of this is the sheer preponderance of "right" terminology in the epistle. There are sixty-three instances of the seven main *dik-* words associated with the concept.

GREEK WORD	TRANSLATION	FREQUENCY IN ROMANS
dikaiosunē	righteousness, justice	33
dikaioō	to justify, rectify	15
dikaiōma	regulation, requirement	5
dikaiōs	justly, uprightly	—
dikaiōsis	acquittal, setting free	2
dikaiokrisia	righteous judgment	1
dikaios	upright, just, righteous	7

The key phrase "the righteousness of God" occurs eight times in Romans (1:17; 3:5, 21, 22, 25, 26; 10:3), as against twice in the other Pauline letters (2 Cor. 5:21; Phil. 3:9) and three times in the rest of the New Testament (Matt. 6:33; James 1:20; 2 Pet. 1:1). The most revealing occurrence of the phrase is in 1:16-17, where Paul states programmatically the theme to be expounded throughout the epistle:

> For I am not ashamed of the gospel; it is the power of God for salvation to everyone who has faith, to the Jew first and also to the Greek. For in it the righteousness of God is revealed through faith for faith; as it is written, "The one who is righteous will live by faith."

Arguably this passage identifies "the gospel" rather than righteousness as the main theme of the epistle. But even if that is so, the content of this gospel is given as "the revelation of the righteousness of God," and it is the righteousness motif that unifies the epistle as a whole.[4] Chapters 1 through 4 explicate the meaning of this righteousness for both Jew and Gentile, using Abraham as a scriptural example; chapters 5 through 8 discuss the human and cosmic implications of righteous-

---

4. P. Stuhlmacher, "The Theme of Romans," *ABR* 36 (1988): 31-44.

ness by faith; chapters 9 through 11 explore the implications of God's righteousness for Israel; and chapters 12 through 15 deal with righteousness in the daily life of the Christian community. The centrality of divine righteousness in Romans is also apparent in the selection of Old Testament texts Paul uses to buttress his argument. There are more than fifty formal quotations from the Old Testament in Romans as well as countless allusions to scriptural themes and concepts. In his stimulating study of intertextual echoes in Romans, Richard Hays demonstrates that Paul's formal quotations of Scripture all spiral around a common focus — the fulfillment of God's saving righteousness in relation to Israel.[5]

Clearly, then, divine righteousness is a dominant concern of the book of Romans. At the same time, the exposition of the theme in Romans is foundational to Paul's entire theology of righteousness, for here more comprehensively than anywhere else Paul expresses the essence of the gospel in terms of God's justifying righteousness. While most commentators agree on the importance of the righteousness theme in Romans, there has been vigorous debate on the precise meaning of the phrase "the righteousness of God,"[6] on its most appropriate translation into English,[7] and on its relationship to the more general notion of righteousness. For some interpreters, "righteousness" and "the righteousness of God" are more or less synonymous terms for the new status God bestows on believers; the general category is "righteousness," while the genitive construction "of God" designates the source or object of that righteousness.[8] For others, a clear distinction exists between these two terms.[9] They note that whereas Paul speaks of the righteousness of God as being "revealed," "shown," and "disclosed" (Rom.

5. R. B. Hays, *Echoes of Scripture in the Letters of Paul* (New Haven: Yale University Press, 1989), 34-83. Cf. *Paul and the Scriptures of Israel,* ed. C. A. Evans and J. A. Sanders (Sheffield: JSOT, 1993), 13-96.

6. For a very helpful summary of options, see N. T. Wright, *What Saint Paul Really Said* (Oxford: Lion, 1997), 100-103; and Wright, "On Becoming the Righteousness of God: 2 Corinthians 5:21," in *Pauline Theology,* vol. 2: *1 and 2 Corinthians,* ed. D. M. Hay (Minneapolis: Fortress, 1993), 200-203.

7. For options, see J. A. Fitzmyer, *Romans* (New York: Doubleday, 1993), 258.

8. See, for example, G. Bray, "Justification: The Reformers and Recent New Testament Scholarship," *Churchman* 109, no. 2 (1995): 102-26.

9. See S. K. Williams, "The Righteousness of God in *Romans,*" *JBL* 99 (1980): 241-98.

1:17; 3:5, 21, 25; 10:3), he talks of righteousness as being "received," "reckoned," "given," or "attained" (Rom. 4:5; 5:17, 21; 8:10; 9:30; 10:4, 10; 14:17). The genitive phrase "of God" is therefore best taken as a reference to God's own righteous character or activity, and the simple noun "righteousness" (as well as the passive of the verb "to justify") as depicting the gift of righteousness imparted to believers. Whether this imparted righteousness is essentially a legal status or includes moral qualities or moral power as well has also long been debated.[10]

It would take us much too far from our focus to enter this debate in any substantial way. For our purposes it is sufficient to register four points of importance: Paul's deliberate use of justice language in explaining God's work of salvation in Christ; his conception of divine justice as a saving, restorative justice more than a retributive or vindictive justice; his utilization of this idea in his theology of justification by faith; and his understanding of the cross of Christ as a means of emancipation, not an occasion of substitutionary punishment. In light of these four observations, Romans may be fairly described as "a treatise on the justice of God."[11]

Justice at the Heart of the Gospel

In their useful discussion of Paul's understanding of the death of Jesus, John Carroll and Joel Green comment that interpreters have not always appreciated the dazzling array of colors in the mural of Paul's theology of the cross. Paul has dozens of ways of explicating the meaning of the cross. He never seems to tire of adding new images to his interpretive vocabulary; he plunders his theological thesaurus for terms to lay bare the benefits of Christ's death. This multiplicity cautions against positing for Paul a single (or central) conception of atonement.[12] This is an

---

10. For a useful summary, see P. J. Achtemeier, *Romans* (Atlanta: John Knox, 1985), 61-66.

11. C. Gunton, *The Actuality of Atonement* (Grand Rapids: William B. Eerdmans, 1989), 102.

12. Carroll and Green, *The Death of Jesus in Early Christianity* (Peabody, Mass.: Hendrickson, 1995), 114, 125, 127. See also C. B. Cousar, "Paul and the Death of Jesus," *Interpretation* 52, no. 1 (1998): 42. C. J. Den Heyer goes much too far, however, in arguing that the diversity of metaphors in the New Testament is such that it rules out any realis-

important insight. The various "theories" of atonement that have emerged in the history of Christian thought have often failed to reckon sufficiently with both the metaphorical nature of New Testament language and the diversity of metaphors employed.[13] At the same time, it should be noted that not all of the several dozen metaphors in Paul's letters are utilized to the same degree; some are developed more extensively than others. The "right" or juridical metaphor is a case in point. Statistically it looms much larger in Paul's reflections on the cross than do other metaphors. Certainly it is not Paul's only way of explaining the cross, nor is it necessarily his primary way of doing so, though this is debatable. (It could be argued that inasmuch as they convey the idea of the restoration of broken relationships, all of Paul's atonement metaphors describe in some way the nature of justice.)[14] But it is hugely significant, especially for this study, that in order to explain what God has accomplished in Christ, Paul deliberately employs the categories and terminology of justice and justice-making.

In so doing Paul shows that the gospel is all about justice. Fundamentally, it is a manifestation of *God's justice* (1:17; 3:21-22, 25) — that is, a demonstration of God's rectifying power to accomplish justice on earth. At the same time, it is a manifestation of *justice for the oppressed*. Through the cross of Christ, God has worked justice for those oppressed by the tyranny of law, sin, and death, those unable to free themselves from such cruel oppressors. Paul states both sides of this justice equation in Romans 3:26: the gospel demonstrates that "[God] himself is righteous [just] *and* that he justifies [or secures justice for] the one who has faith in Jesus" (italics mine).

---

tic doctrine of atonement at all. See *Jesus and the Doctrine of Atonement* (London: SCM, 1998), passim.

13. On the metaphorical nature of soteriological images in the New Testament, see S. B. Marrow, "Principles for Interpreting the New Testament Soteriological Terms," *NTS* 36, no. 2 (1990): esp. 278-80.

14. So J. R. Donahue, "Biblical Perspectives on Justice," in *The Faith that Does Justice: Examining the Christian Sources for Social Change*, ed. J. C. Haughey (New York: Paulist, 1977), 103. On the debate over the center of Paul's theology, see J. Plevnik, "The Center of Paul's Theology," *CBQ* 51 (1989): 461-78; D. N. Howell Jr., "The Center of Pauline Theology," *BS* 151 (1994): 50-70; and J. P. Sampley, "From Text to Thought World: The Route to Paul's Ways," and P. J. Achtemeier, "Finding the Way to Paul's Theology: A Response to J. Christiaan Beker and J. Paul Sampley," in *Pauline Theology*, ed. J. M. Bassler (Minneapolis: Fortress, 1991), I:3-14, 25-36.

This justice connection is routinely referred to in theological scholarship as the "forensic" character of justification.[15] This means that justification is primarily a legal concept having to do with the legal status of a person before God. Paul pictures God as a royal judge before whom sinners are arraigned. Though they are deserving of judgment, God graciously pronounces a verdict of acquittal, a free pardon that excludes all possibility of condemnation and settles forever the question of acceptance by God. Paul's intention in using forensic imagery, it is said, is to safeguard the notion that salvation is wholly a work of God, that the believer can never stand before God on the basis of personal merit and spiritual attainments but only because of the vicarious work of Christ.

While there is obvious truth in this, to speak of justification as "forensic" and to explain it principally in terms of law may unwittingly serve to conceal what is fundamentally at issue — namely, God's work of justice-making. There is more to justice than the vindication of law, even God's law, and there is more to our justification than a mere verdict of acquittal. Scholars usually recognize that Paul's description of salvation goes well beyond a cold, hard, legal abstraction and so caution against taking the forensic metaphor too far. Some suggest that justification describes the form salvation takes, an acquittal of all charges against us, but not the content of salvation, which is a free outpouring of grace that shatters the forensic image and exceeds the legal sphere.[16] Others seek to subordinate the forensic imagery to other allegedly more fundamental metaphors in Paul's theology. E. P. Sanders, for instance, notes that while Paul speaks of justification as a juridical acquittal, his notion of participation in Christ is more crucial, for "it is not clear how a forensic declaration frees one from hostile powers, puts one under new lordship and gives one a totally new life."[17]

But perhaps the problem interpreters have in relating Paul's justification language to his depiction of the comprehensive content of sal-

15. See, for example, R. Y. K. Fung, "The Forensic Character of Justification," *Themelios* 16, no. 1 (1977): 16-20.

16. See, for example, J. Jeremias, *The Central Message of the New Testament* (London: SCM, 1965), 51-66; G. Schrenk, "δίκη κτλ.," *TDNT* II:204-5. Cf. T. W. Manson, *On Paul and John: Some Selected Theological Themes* (London: SCM, 1963), 56.

17. E. P. Sanders, *Paul and Palestinian Judaism* (London: SCM, 1977), 440n.47.

vation derives from the way the forensic character of justification is conceptualized in terms of law codes and law courts rather than in terms of justice and justice-making. For when the forensic dimension is reduced to rendering a not-guilty verdict in the court of heaven, it fails patently to comprehend the scope of Paul's theology of salvation. If, however, it is understood as a process of *doing justice,* and restorative justice at that, then it becomes clear, as we will see shortly, why Paul could summarize his entire exposition in Romans as the manifestation of God's saving justice (1:17). But why has the justice nature of justification traditionally been equated with the rendering of a legal verdict, which has sometimes virtually been regarded as a legal fiction?[18] And why, as Robert Morgan observes, has "the explosion of judicial metaphors in western theology and devotion . . . fueled readings of Romans which Paul would scarcely have acknowledged"?[19] Largely because Paul's interpreters have unwittingly brought to the text an essentially Western concept of retributive justice based on metaphysical law rather than a Hebraic concept of covenant justice based on relationship.[20]

In formulating the doctrine of salvation, traditional theology has made heavy use of Western or Latin concepts of justice. (Even in Paul's day, especially in Rome, *dikaiosunē* was a term for legal justice.) Many of the early Latin Fathers were lawyers and so were predisposed to conceive of divine-human relationships in terms of legal obligations, as operative in the Greco-Roman tradition.[21] This conception of justice was based on the notion of an abstract moral order in which imbalances must be righted and each person receive precisely what each is due.[22] In practice such justice entails securing a fair balance or harmonization of the rights and duties of different parties. This has two major expressions: distributive or social justice, which concerns the fair distribution of goods and services in society, and penal or retributive justice, which concerns the punishing of offenses against the moral and legal order.

---

18. Cf. W. Sanday and A. C. Headlam, *A Critical and Exegetical Commentary on the Epistle to the Romans,* 5th ed. (Edinburgh: T. & T. Clark, 1902), 36.

19. Morgan, *Romans* (Sheffield: Sheffield Academic Press, 1995), 114.

20. See A. E. McGrath, "'The Righteousness of God' from Augustine to Luther," *StTh* 36 (1982): 63-78.

21. Gunton, *The Actuality of Atonement,* 86-87.

22. Gunton, *The Actuality of Atonement,* 96-100.

In the retributive sphere, justice and mercy stand in tension. Justice entails giving persons their just deserts; mercy involves setting aside the demands of justice and treating persons contrary to what they justly deserve.

Against this background, divine justice has typically been equated in the theological tradition with God's right to punish people for their transgression of God's law, in conformity to the ideal ethical norm of strict retributive justice. God is duty bound, by God's own righteous character, to punish wrongdoers and thus uphold the moral order God has created. God cannot overlook breaches of universal law, for then the universe would become a disordered and irrational place. While God is loving and merciful, God cannot simply forgive sin, for God's justice also demands satisfaction. The genius of the cross is that it allows God to satisfy the demands of retributive justice by inflicting the penalty of sin on Christ, while at the same time satisfying his mercy by conferring forgiveness on sinners.

This identification of divine righteousness with God's vindictive or punitive justice has had a complex and often distorting effect on Christian thinking about justice. One result has been an almost total divorce between the doctrine of justification and issues of *social* justice. Justification has been confined to the religious sphere of thought, while social justice has been assigned to the ethical or sociopolitical sphere. As a result, few people today sense any positive relationship between the doctrine of justification by faith and issues of social justice, and Paul's discussion of justifying righteousness is largely ignored in attempts to formulate a theology of social involvement. Worse than that, since securing social justice requires doing "good works," an emphasis on social responsibility is often seen as a direct threat to the Pauline doctrine of justification by grace and not by works. A different thing has happened with respect to the doctrine of justification and *criminal* justice. Here a two-way traffic of ideas has occurred. Moving in one direction, the logic of criminal law and punishment has had a formative influence on how God's justice has been conceptualized. From the other direction, punitive understandings of divine justice in general, and the atonement in particular, have had a powerful and often deleterious influence on Western penal thought and practice. As Timothy Gorringe documents, the belief that God punished Christ retributively for the sins of the world in defense of his own holiness has frequently been used in Western history to justify excessively harsh treatment of criminals.[23]

Such effects flow, in large part, from the inadequate concept of justice that has been used to interpret the implicit justice-dimension of justification. Rather than assuming a holistic, biblical conception of "shalom-justice"[24] that is capable of embracing the whole work of salvation, interpreters have presupposed a narrow, law-based conception of retributive justice that effectively confines the justice dimension to the law-court facet of the metaphor and ascribes all else to grace. But the scenario looks dramatically different when a model of restorative or relational justice is employed, a model that is arguably more appropriate to the Hebrew realities Paul presupposes.

Divine Justice as Restorative Justice

It is crucial to recognize that Paul's theology of justifying righteousness in Romans is constructed on Jewish rather than Greco-Roman presuppositions.[25] Paul himself insists that apart from law, "the righteousness of God has been disclosed, and is attested by the law and the prophets" (3:21), and that his own conception of righteousness by faith upholds biblical teaching (3:31; 8:4), something he seeks to prove by citing Scripture extensively to bolster and explain his position. Some appreciation of this Hebraic/Jewish/biblical background is therefore essential for grasping Paul's understanding of divine justice.

Justice is a multifaceted concept in the Old Testament, and it is not possible to capture its richness in a simple definition. Of the wide range of terms used to convey the idea of justice,[26] the two most commonly

23. Gorringe, *God's Just Vengeance: Crime, Violence, and the Rhetoric of Salvation* (Cambridge: Cambridge University Press, 1996). See also T. Grimsrud and H. Zehr, "Rethinking God, Justice, and Treatment of Offenders," *Journal of Offender Rehabilitation* 31, no. 3 (forthcoming).

24. P. B. Yoder, *Shalom: The Bible's Word for Salvation, Justice, and Peace* (Newton, Kans.: Faith and Life Press, 1987), 24-38.

25. J. D. G. Dunn, *The Theology of Paul the Apostle* (Edinburgh: T. & T. Clark, 1998), 342.

26. See C. J. H. Wright, *An Eye for an Eye: The Place of Old Testament Ethics Today* (Downers Grove, Ill.: InterVarsity Press, 1983), 133-47.

translated this way are *mishpat* and *sedeq* or *sedeqah*.[27] Each term, together with its related verbs and modifiers, has a broad semantic range, and each is rendered in English translations in a variety of ways in different contexts.[28] There is also considerable overlap in meaning between *mishpat* and *sedeq[ah]*; G. A. F. Knight describes them as "Siamese twins."[29] They are frequently used together in parallel statements (e.g., Amos 5:24; Isa. 16:5; 32:1), while the hendiadys "righteousness and justice" is possibly a stock phrase for what today we call "social justice."[30] Individually, *mishpat* is more typically tied to legal settings and decisions. As well as designating the whole process of litigation, it can be used to represent any component of that process and its outcome, such as arraignment, indictment, trial, verdict, sentence, and penalty. It can also be used for legal ordinances or customs and for the legal rights of the plaintiff.[31] From this usage it might be said that *mishpat* denotes applied justice, that which is done in concrete situations to achieve or administer justice, especially in forensic settings. *Sedeq[ah]*, on the other hand, refers to justice in a more general or normative or objective sense. As the common translation "right-eousness" implies, it refers to the "right order of things," to the correct ordering of the world according to the divine intention, and to actual conduct, both human and divine, that corresponds to the way things ought to be.

Now whether we approach the biblical theme of justice through one or the other of these terms, we encounter a complex, multidimensional phenomenon. Rolf P. Knierim examines the *mishpat* word group, together with some other key terms, and identifies at least sixteen different facets or conceptual presuppositions to the Old Testament con-

27. Old Testament scholars differ on whether the masculine and feminine forms of this noun are synonymous or have different applications or nuances. Here I regard them as more or less equivalent in meaning. So too J. J. Scullion, "Righteousness (OT)," *ABD* V:725-26.

28. A whole variety of renderings are used for terms from the *sdq* root, such as "uprightness," "vindication," "requirement," "judgment," "acquittal," "victory," "salvation," "prosperity," "triumph," "innocence," "truth," "mercy," "correctness," and so on. The *shpt* root also yields a variety of meanings, such as "justice," "judgment," "rights," "vindication," "deliverance," "custom," and "norm."

29. Knight, "Is 'Righteous' Right?" 8.

30. For this proposal, see M. Weinfeld, *Social Justice in Ancient Israel and in the Ancient Near East* (Minneapolis: Fortress, 1995).

31. T. L. J. Mafico, "Just, Justice," *ABD* III:1127-29.

ception of justice. "The evidence shows that the concern for justice was one, if not the central, factor by which ancient Israel's multifaceted societal life was united throughout its historical changes."[32] A similar conclusion emerges from consideration of the verbs, nouns, and adjectives deriving from the *sdq* root, which occur some 476 times in the Old Testament, 90 percent of which are translated by *dik-* terms in the Septuagint. According to Gerhard von Rad, "There is absolutely no concept in the Old Testament with so central a significance for all the relationships of human life as that of *sdqh*. It is the standard not only for man's relationship to God, but also for his relationship to his fellows, reaching right down to . . . the animals and to his natural environment . . . for it embraces the whole of Israelite life."[33] It is a "protean and many-sided term,"[34] says John Donahue, with personal, judicial, cultic, and moral associations.

While allowing for the all-embracing nature of the concept, it is still possible to make some generalizations about Hebrew conceptions of righteousness that will help to illuminate Paul's teaching on God's righteousness or justice. The first is that the Hebrew idea of righteousness is *comprehensively relational*. It is not a private attribute that an individual can have on her or his own, independent of anyone else. It is something that one has specifically in one's relationships as a social being. Righteousness is, at heart, the fulfillment of the demands of a relationship, whether this relationship is with other human beings or with God. For this reason, righteousness language frequently appears in covenant-making contexts, for "covenant" was Israel's term for a committed relationship. Righteousness in this setting is the wholehearted loyalty of both parties to the demands of the covenant relationship.[35]

This applies pre-eminently to Israel's covenant with Yahweh. On the one side, *Israel's righteousness* consists in exhibiting the ethical and religious conduct specified in the terms of the covenant, in the "judgments" or "laws" *(mishpatim)* codified in the Torah. Law, covenant, and righteousness are thus interpenetrating concepts. To be righteous is to be faithful to the law of the covenant-keeping God and thus to treat fel-

---

32. Knierim, *The Task of Old Testament Theology: Substance, Method, and Cases* (Grand Rapids: William B. Eerdmans, 1995), 86-122 (quote from 88).

33. von Rad, *Old Testament Theology*, 2 vols. (London: SCM, 1962), 2:370, 373.

34. Donahue, "Biblical Perspectives on Justice," 68.

35. E. R. Achtemeier, "Righteousness in the Old Testament," *IDB* IV:80.

low members of the covenant community with justice. To be unrighteous is to act in ways that break covenant. The central concern of biblical law was the creation of *shalom,* a state of soundness or "all-rightness" within the community. The law provided a pattern for living in covenant, for living in *shalom.* Specific laws were considered to be just, not because they corresponded to some abstract ethical norm or reflected the will of the king or protected the welfare of the state, but because they sustained *shalom* within the community. This, in view of Israel's origins as liberated slaves, necessarily required provision for the impoverished and oppressed, which is why so much biblical legislation is devoted to "social justice" concerns, such as care for widows, orphans, aliens, and the poor, the remission of debts, the manumission of slaves, and the protection of land rights. In this connection, covenant justice could be understood as positive succor for, and intervention on behalf of, the poor and the oppressed. As Isaiah puts it, "Cease to do evil, learn to do good; seek justice, rescue the oppressed, defend the orphan, plead for the widow" (1:16-17; cf. Mic. 6:8; Ps. 146:7-10; 119:153-59).[36]

A similar understanding underlay the Israelite law-court procedure. In the Western judicial system, a person is brought before the court when the police have reason to suspect his or her guilt. The judge is expected to be objective and impartial and to apply the law dispassionately. By contrast, in the legal processes described in the Old Testament, the accuser is not a neutral policeman but the personal enemy of the accused, who might be acting with malicious intent. The judge is expected not simply to apply the law but to vindicate the righteous. If he gives a verdict in favor of the defendant, he would be considered to have rescued the innocent person from oppression, so that even forensic justice could be understood as a positive act of remedy, an intervention on behalf of the defenseless.[37]

36. See further S. C. Mott, "The Partiality of Biblical Justice," *Transformation* 10, no. 1 (1993): 23-29; MacGuire, *The Moral Core of Judaism and Christianity,* 127-64; and K. Leech, *True God: An Exploration in Spiritual Theology* (London: Sheldon Press, 1985), 379-420.

37. On law enforcement in ancient Israel, see G. J. Wenham, "Law and the Legal System in the Old Testament," in *Law, Morality, and the Bible: A Symposium,* ed. B. N. Kaye and G. J. Wenham (Leicester: Inter-Varsity Press, 1978), 44-50. Cf. N. Watson, "Justification — A New Look," *ABR* 18 (1970): 41-43.

Two other points are worth making about this forensic context, both of which are pertinent to Paul's use of forensic imagery. One is that the category of "righteousness" applies differently to the judge and to the litigant. The judge is righteous insofar as he handles the case without favor or prejudice (Exod. 23:2-3; Lev. 19:15; Deut. 1:16-17). The litigant is deemed righteous if the case is decided in his or her favor. If the defendant is declared righteous, it means he or she is found to be "in the right," to be innocent of the accusation. It does not imply that he or she is morally virtuous in every other respect of their lives, nor does it mean that the judge has somehow imparted, bequeathed, or imputed *his* moral righteousness to the vindicated party. As N. T. Wright observes, "Righteousness is not an object, a substance or a gas which can be passed across the courtroom."[38] So, applied to the judge, righteousness is a reference to his *action;* applied to the litigant, it is a reference to his or her *right standing* in the covenant. The other point to note is that the goal of the whole forensic process is the restoration of fellowship within the community. If the defendant is found to be blameworthy, penalties might be imposed on the guilty party. But these punitive measures are intended not merely to uphold the rule of law or to maintain some cosmic balance, but rather to put right what has gone wrong, and so restore the integrity of the community's life and its relationship with God. Covenant justice is satisfied by the restoration of *shalom,* not by the pain of punishment, even if the infliction of pain might be entailed in the process (e.g., Deut. 25:1-5). Isaiah makes clear the connection between justice and peace, even if his focus is not strictly forensic: "Then justice *[misphat]* will dwell in the wilderness, and righteousness *[sedeqah]* abide in the fruitful field. The effect of righteousness will be peace *[shalom],* and the result of righteousness, quietness and trust forever" (Isa. 32:16-17; cf. Ps. 85:10).

On the other side of the covenant partnership, *God's righteousness* consists in Yahweh's steadfast loyalty toward the covenant people and his saving intervention on their behalf.[39] God is "righteous" inasmuch as God fulfills the obligations he took upon himself to be Israel's God.

38. Wright, *What Saint Paul Really Said,* 98.

39. Although God is often called "righteous" or "upright" in the Old Testament (e.g., Ps. 35:28; 36:7; 51:6; 103:17; 112:9; 116:5; Prov. 16:10; Isa. 46:13; 59:16), Paul's precise phrase "the righteousness of God" does not occur in the Hebrew scriptures as such. (The closest parallels are found in Deut. 33:21 and Judg. 5:11.) An exact equivalent is found in the Dead Sea Scrolls, however (1QM 4:6; 1QS 11:12).

These included rescuing Israel in times of need and of war,[40] forgiving her sins, and defending the rights of the poor and weak within Israel's own borders through the promulgation and enforcement of law, the inspiration of prophetic word, and the appointment and instruction of kings.[41] For Israel, then, the justice of God was not an abstract theological or philosophical axiom; it was something about God's being learned from the concrete experience of God's actions of claiming, blessing, and rescuing Israel. Righteousness language in the Hebrew Bible is thus *action* language as well as relational language. The king is righteous when he acts to bring about justice and equity in the covenant community, by remitting debts, releasing lands, protecting the weak, and so on.[42] The Divine King is righteous because he intervenes to save those who cannot save themselves, thus proving his faithfulness to covenant commitments. This is why God's righteousness is characteristically associated in the Hebrew scriptures with God's love and grace, with God's generosity, forgiveness, and liberation.[43] God's justice and God's mercy stand, significantly, in parallel, not in opposition.[44]

40. For example, Exod. 9:27; Judg. 5:11; 1 Sam. 12:7; Mic. 6:5; Isa. 59:15-18; 63:1; Dan. 9:16; cf. Pss. 48:5, 8, 11-12; 97:8. There are also many other texts where Yahweh's warfare against foreign aggressors is seen as a manifestation of God's justice (e.g., Exod. 7:1-5; 17:8-15; Num. 33:3; Deut. 32:34-43; Judg. 6-8; 1 Sam. 20:16; 2 Sam. 5:17-25; 8; 22:47-49/Ps. 18:46-48; 2 Kings 18-20; Isa. 36-39; Pss. 2; 46:6, 9; 48:4-8; 59; Isa. 10:5-19; 29:6; 34:8; 47; 63:1-6; Jer. 30:18-21; 46-51; Ezek. 25-32; Nahum).

41. For example, Ps. 99:4; 78:5; 103:6-8 (cf. Exod. 33:13); Ps. 50:2 (cf. Deut. 33:2); Ps. 119:142, 144; Isa. 51:7. See further Weinfeld, *Social Justice in Ancient Israel and in the Ancient Near East*, ch. 9.

42. 2 Sam. 8:15; 1 Kings 10:9; Ps. 72; Jer. 22:3, 15; 23:5; 33:15; Ezek. 45:9; Isa. 42. So too of the eschatological king: Isa. 9:1-7 (cf. 2 Sam. 8:15); Isa. 11:1-12; 16:5; Jer. 23:5 (cf. 33:15); Ps. 45; Hos. 2:1-25; Amos 9:11-15; Ezek. 34:11-31.

43. See, e.g., Judg. 5:11; 1 Sam. 12:7; Pss. 9:7-9; 10:16-18; 19; 24; 31:1; 35:10; 48:10; 66:1-6; 71:15-17; Mic. 6:4-5; Isa. 46:13; 51:5-12; 56:1; 61:10.

44. Like justice, mercy is a covenant term. To show mercy is to act compassionately toward those in need within the covenant community, so as to bring about justice or communal well-being. In the Bible, the term mercy pre-eminently designates God's steadfast loyalty to the covenant people, which God expresses by intervening repeatedly to help them. In one sense, such mercy is undeserved, for the covenant people are constantly faithless. In another sense, it can be expected, for God is faithful to commitments. (In the Septuagint, *eleos* mainly translates the Hebrew term *hesed*, the term that denotes God's steadfast loyalty to the covenant.) Obviously, then, mercy and justice are inseparable, and in several texts they occur as almost synonymous pairs (with *sedeqah*,

"He will rise up to show mercy to you," declares Isaiah. "For the LORD is a God of justice" (Isa. 30:18; cf. Ps. 85).

At the same time, there is also a forensic and punitive dimension to God's righteousness. This features when God calls his people to account when they have forgotten or broken the covenant. The prophets sometimes picture a courtroom setting in which a lawsuit between Israel and Yahweh is being heard. Yahweh or the prophet summons Israel before the bar of God, recites acts of past beneficence, levels accusations, and then calls on the witnesses to the covenant in both heaven and earth. Repentance is required if Israel is to be acquitted or justified in God's tribunal.[45] Sometimes Israel comes before God to argue her cause against the wicked who are oppressing her, pleading with God to be faithful to his covenant promises.[46] In such settings, God's righteousness may be linked with the idea of punishment, whether of recalcitrant Israel as a whole or of the wicked within Israel or of Israel's pagan enemies. But even here God's justice is shown in the liberation of the afflicted or the purification and refinement of the wayward more than in the destruction of the oppressor, which is but a means to that end. After distinguishing two basic notions of divine judgment in the Old Testament — judgment as an act of punishment or destruction and judgment as a forensic or judicial inquiry — Marius Reiser comments,

> In both cases, what is at stake is that God creates justice where human beings have been unable or unwilling to bring it about. The true pur-

---

Jer. 9:24; Ps. 36:10; 40:11; 85:10; 143:11; with *mishpat*, Hos. 12:6; Mic. 6:8; Jer. 9:24; Zech. 7:9). In mercy, God works justice for the covenant people. God's people are to imitate God's actions, showing compassion to those in need and thus acting to restore well-being, to bring about justice. As M. Lind points out, "Justice in the Bible is not the opposite to mercy, but is parallel to it. Both justice and mercy arise out of the covenant relationship of God and people. The first centres on keeping covenant relations; the second, on re-establishing covenant when it is broken. Both are informed by a humble walk with God whose righteous acts save the people." See "Transformation of Justice: From Moses to Jesus," *NPCJ* 5 (1986): 1. So too A. J. Heschel, *The Prophets* (New York: Jewish Publication Society of America, 1962), 201; and K. Turner, "Justification and Justice in a Theology of Grace," *Theology Today* 55 (1999): 510-23.

45. See, e.g., 1 Sam. 12:7; Isa. 1:2-9; 3:13; Hos. 4:1-20; 12:3; Mic. 6:1-8; Jer. 2:4ff.; 12:1ff.

46. See, e.g., Isa. 51:9-10; 62:1-2; Neh. 9:6-37; Pss. 7:6-11; 17:2; 26:1-3; 28:3-4; 31:1; 143.

pose of the judgment is thus not the elimination of sinners or the punishment of those condemned, but the salvation of the righteous, the poor, and the weak that is thereby made possible. That is why devout believers hope for God's judgment and pray, as in the psalms, that God will intervene as judge.[47]

Accordingly, as Donahue observes, "Though Yahweh punishes sinners, there is no text in the Old Testament where his justice is *equated* with vengeance on the sinner. Yahweh's justice is saving justice where punishment of the sinner is an integral part of restoration."[48] God's justice is a restorative or reconstructive justice before it is a punitive or destructive justice.

Under the circumstances of the Exile, assertions about God's saving justice became problematical. How could God be considered righteous if Israel had been abandoned to her enemies? In exilic and post-exilic writings, especially in Deutero-Isaiah, God's righteousness becomes the ground and the content of an eschatological hope for the ultimate revelation of divine power to vindicate Israel's trust and lead all nations to acknowledge God's cosmic lordship.[49] Here God's righteousness is virtually synonymous with "salvation,"[50] God's intervention to restore and sustain his people within the covenant. In the Second Temple period,

47. Reiser, *Jesus and Judgment: The Eschatological Proclamation in Its Jewish Context* (Minneapolis: Fortress, 1997), 6.

48. Donahue, "Biblical Perspectives on Justice," 72 (my emphasis). So too von Rad, *Old Testament Theology,* 377; K. Koch, "Is There a Doctrine of Retribution in the Old Testament?" in *Theodicy in the Old Testament,* ed. J. L. Crenshaw (Philadelphia/London: Fortress/SPCK, 1983), 77. The key word here is "equated"; in some texts God's righteousness does entail retributive judgment on evil, though this is usually a means to an end, not the end in itself (e.g., Exod. 9:27; Pss. 7:12-17; 9:5-8; 75:3; Isa. 5:6-7, 15-16; 10:2, 18, 22; 28:14, 17-18, 22; Lam. 1:18; Mic. 7:9-10; Neh. 9:33; 2 Chron. 12:6; Ezra 9:15; Dan. 9:13-19; Zeph. 3:5-6). On this, see S. H. Travis, *Christ and the Judgment of God: Divine Retribution in the New Testament* (London: Marshall & Pickering, 1986), 6-13, 54-55; J. Piper, "The Demonstration of the Righteousness of God in Romans 3:25, 26," *JSNT* 7 (1980): 2-32; and H. G. L. Peels, *The Vengeance of God: The Meaning of the Root* NQM *and the Function of the* NQM-*Texts in the Context of Divine Revelation in the Old Testament* (Leiden/New York/Köln: E. J. Brill, 1995), 287-92.

49. See, e.g., Pss. 31:1; 35:23-24; 51:14; 65:5; 71:2, 15; 98:2; 143:11; Isa. 41:2; 42:6; 45:8, 21; 46:13; 51:5-6, 8; 62:1-2; 63:1, 7; Ezek. 9:6-13; Neh. 9:6-37.

50. On righteousness terminology in Second Isaiah, see J. W. Olley, "Righteousness — Some Issues in Old Testament Translation into English," *TBT* 38 (1987): 309-13; and Scullion, "Righteousness (OT)," 728-30.

these texts became the matrix for the view that justice is no longer something that God will establish in the sphere of history but will be reserved for the end-time and will be characteristic of the new age. Some writers see their own age as entirely devoid of righteousness. Others affirm the existence of a righteous minority who will welcome the coming Messiah. All agree, however, that at the end of time God will visit judgment upon evildoers and bring deliverance to the righteous, and that the eschatological age will know universal and everlasting righteousness.[51]

In Hebrew usage, then, righteousness language is not primarily "status" or "being" or "ideal" or "principle" language but *power* language or *action* language, for, as Stephen C. Mott comments, "justice in the Bible is an intervening power."[52] The most common image for justice in the West is a set of scales, symbolizing the balancing of rights and obligations or deeds and deserts. The prophetic symbol of justice is a mighty, surging river (Amos 5:24). Biblical justice is thus not a static state but, says Abraham J. Heschel, "a power that will strike and change, heal and restore, like a mighty stream bringing life to the parched land. . . . Justice is more than an idea or a norm: justice is charged with the omnipotence of God. What ought to be, shall be!"[53] Applied to God, divine righteousness denotes God's concrete deeds of deliverance for his people in keeping with God's covenant commitments to them, thus upholding the honor and integrity of God's own name. The justice of God is not primarily or normatively a retributive justice or a distributive justice but a restorative or reconstructive justice, a saving action by God that recreates *shalom* and makes things right.[54]

Justification by Faith as Restorative Justice

It is this biblical background Paul has in mind when at the beginning of Romans he announces the eschatological manifestation of God's

51. See A. Cronbach, "Righteousness in Jewish Literature, 200 B.C.–A.D. 100," *IDB* IV:89-90; and J. Reumann, "Righteousness (Early Judaism, Greco-Roman World, New Testament)," *ABD* 5:736-37.

52. Mott, "The Partiality of Biblical Justice," 25.

53. Heschel, *The Prophets*, 213.

54. P. M. Ramsey, "The Biblical Norm of Righteousness," *Interpretation* 24, no. 4 (1970): 420-21.

righteousness, which is "the *power* of God for salvation" (Rom. 1:16-17). His doctrine of justifying righteousness represents a distinctive development within Jewish tradition rather than a complete innovation. In particular, Paul deliberately picks up from the Psalms and Deutero-Isaiah (which together supply the bulk of his theological vocabulary in Romans) motifs that portray God's righteousness as God's unswerving covenant-faithfulness manifested in the act of eschatological deliverance to restore justice to the world. For Paul, the Passion event, Christ's death and resurrection, is that act of eschatological deliverance, that decisive demonstration of God's unbreakable fidelity to covenant commitments, and hence the supreme vindication of God's justice (3:21-26).

In the opening chapters of Romans, Paul first establishes the need for such deliverance. In 1:18-32 he graphically describes humanity's plight under the wrath of God, using the excesses of Gentile behavior, as well as muted allusions to Israel's own history of idolatry, to illustrate the extremity of the situation.[55] Then, beginning in chapter 2, Paul systematically dismantles any Jewish claim to exemption from condemnation by virtue of Israel's unique relationship to God. Despite Israel's role as God's covenant partner and despite her possession of God's law, the Jewish people are as guilty as the Gentiles of wickedness and disloyalty to God. Sin, Paul argues, is no respecter of ethnic boundaries. Israel's "covenantal nomism"[56] has afforded her no real protection from the contamination of evil. The conclusion Paul arrives at is all-inclusive: "All, both Jews and Greeks, are under the power of sin" (3:9).

Both these assertions — the radical dominion of sin over humanity

---

55. Romans 1:18-32 may be regarded as a multilayered exposition of the human plight. At one level, it serves as a classical Jewish denunciation of contemporary pagan idolatry and moral depravity. At another level, Paul's description of human rebellion calls to mind the history of Israel's own slide into idolatry (cf. v. 23 with Ps. 106:20; Jer. 2:11; Deut. 4:16-18), which even more graphically shows how entrenched the problem of human sin is and shows why the gospel is for "the Jew first" (1:17). But at the deepest level, Paul's account echoes the story of Adam's fall, from which originates the idolatrous dynamic of human history. Cf. M. D. Hooker, "Adam in Romans," *NTS* 6 (1959/60): 297-306.

56. This term was coined by E. P. Sanders to depict the self-understanding of first-century Judaism and has since won widespread acceptance. For Sanders's definition, see *Paul and Palestinian Judaism*, 75, 236.

and the radical failure of the law to remedy this situation — set Paul apart from his Jewish contemporaries. According to Jewish thought, the law was given precisely to deliver people from the tyranny of the sinful impulse within human nature.[57] But for Paul, sin is more than a latent disposition. It is a dominating cosmic principle, a kind of systemically embedded apostasy that holds universal sway, even over God's chosen people.[58] Because of Adam's primeval act of idolatry (1:18-32), sin has invaded God's good creation and become an enslaving power (3:9; 5:12-21; 6:1-23). So tyrannical is its power that even God's law is impotent to do anything about it; on the contrary, the law itself has fallen victim to sin and become a weapon in its hands (7:7-25). Consequently, all who are in Adam, Jew as well as Gentile, are subject to both the power and the consequences of Adam's original rebellion,[59] a fact patently demonstrated by the universality of death (5:12-21). In Paul's analysis, sin and death form an inseparable alliance: "sin exercises its dominion in death" (5:21; cf. 7:9, 13; 1 Cor. 15:56).[60] They are the supreme powers of the present age, which in turn determine the function of the law and the flesh.[61] Without the saving intervention of God, then, Israel's lot is hopeless.

Now since God is just, God is obligated to treat Jewish and Gentile sin alike. If God were to wink at Jewish sin while condemning Gentile sin, it would pervert justice, for equity or impartiality is an essential feature of

57. J. A. Ziesler, *Paul's Letter to the Romans* (London/Philadephia: SCM/Trinity, 1989), 85.

58. On sin as apostasy, see D. B. Garlington, "The Obedience of Faith in the Letter to the Romans, Part 3: The Obedience of Christ and the Obedience of the Christian," *WTJ* 55, no. 1 (1993): 100-112. On the lordship of sin, see Sanders, *Paul and Palestinian Judaism,* 502-8. (For a different emphasis, see R. H. Gundry, "Grace, Works, and Staying Saved in Paul," *Biblica* 66 [1985]: 28-34.) For a helpful discussion of how the Bible sometimes speaks of sin as the preserve of the wicked and sometimes as the common state of all humanity, see J. Goldingay, "Your Iniquities Have Made a Separation between You and Your God," in *Atonement Today,* ed. J. Goldingay (London: SPCK, 1995), 45-50.

59. S. E. Porter, "The Pauline Concept of Original Sin, in Light of Rabbinic Background," *TynBul* 41, no. 1 (1990): 3-30. Cf. G. J. Wenham, "Original Sin in Genesis 1-11," *Churchman* 104, no. 4 (1990): 309-28.

60. J. C. Beker, "The Relationship between Sin and Death in Romans," in *The Conversation Continues,* ed. R. T. Fortna and B. R. Gaventa (Nashville: Abingdon, 1990), 55-61.

61. On Paul's understanding of the powers that oppress humanity, see J. D. G. Dunn, *Christian Liberty: A New Testament Perspective* (Carlisle: Paternoster, 1993), 53-77. See also Ziesler, *Paul's Letter to the Romans,* 39-52.

justice (Exod. 23:2-3; Lev. 19:15; Deut. 1:16-17). Paul therefore asserts that God will judge all people according to their deeds, not according to their ethnic or covenantal status. "For God shows no partiality" (2:11). And since sin is as rampant within Israel as without, notwithstanding her possession of God's law, "every mouth may be silenced, and the whole world may be held accountable to God" (3:19). But this creates a major problem for Paul. If God's justice is comprised merely of impartiality, if it is solely a matter of treating all people alike, what becomes of God's commitment to Israel? God has promised to be faithful to Israel, to save her in time of need, to be her God and they his people, forever.[62] If, at the end of the day, God ultimately treats all people alike, has God lied? Can God be trusted? Does God keep faith? Is God true to sworn commitments? Paul poses this troubling question explicitly in Romans 3:3-6: "Will [Israel's] faithlessness nullify the faithfulness of God [to Israel]? By no means! Although everyone is a liar, let God be proved true." "Our injustice," Paul continues, our failure to keep covenant, merely serves "to confirm the justice of God" — that is, God's unbreakable bond with Israel.

Paul's point here is that Israel's sin breaches her covenant with God. Because God is just, God must regard Jewish sin with the same seriousness as Gentile sin. Accordingly, Israel falls under divine wrath. Yet, equally because God is just, God must remain true to the covenant with Israel. God cannot simply abandon Israel to judgment, for that would be unjust, a failure on God's part to honor his word. The solution to this apparent impasse lies in a further demonstration of justice — God's eschatological intervention to deliver Israel from her plight of radical enslavement to sin and death and to restore her to full covenantal status. But to save Israel, God must rectify the human condition itself, for it is Israel's membership in Adam that lies at the root of the problem (5:12-17). And if God is to redeem the human condition, it must be done "apart from law" (3:21), both because the law has proved incapable of dealing with sin (3:20) and because it is a uniquely Jewish possession (2:17-24). Therefore, if God is to "justify the ungodly" (4:5), it must be achieved and appropriated simply on the basis

---

62. The covenant formula "I will be your God, and you shall be my people" occurs frequently in the biblical tradition: see Lev. 26:12; Ruth 1:16; Jer. 7:23; 11:4; 24:7; 30:22; 31:1, 33; 32:38; Ezek. 11:20; 14:11; 36:28; 37:23, 27; Zech. 2:11; 8:8; 2 Cor. 6:16; Heb. 8:10.

of the universal human capacity of faith. Where the law is confined to Israel and fails to deal with sin, faith is open to the world and participates in the conquest of sin (3:27-30; 5:1).

God's definitive eschatological justice-initiative takes place in the death and resurrection of Christ. God sent his Son into the world to do "what the law, weakened by the flesh, could not do" (8:3), rescue humanity from its terrible predicament. Christ was "born under the law" (Gal. 4:4) and perfectly fulfilled the fundamental intention of the law, a life of conformity to God's will and fidelity to God's covenant, a life of love and justice under the rule of God (Rom. 10:4; 13:8-10; cf. 14:17). Such a life challenged the existing unjust order and threatened those in positions of power, Jewish and Roman, so they deemed Christ to be a dangerous criminal and crucified him (1 Cor. 2:8).[63] Christ freely accepted this experience of criminalization and rejection. In so doing he journeyed into "the far country of our estrangement and despair,"[64] and tasted the bitterness of death (Rom. 5:8, 10; Phil. 2:7-8). Yet his death was also willed by God, because through it God would use human sin and rebellion to achieve salvation. In his death, Christ plumbed the depths of human wickedness without reserve; he exposed and absorbed human religious and political violence without retaliation, and in so doing broke the inner "payback" logic of evil (something beyond the reach of any display of coercive power, even God's power). At the same time, in some unfathomable way, Christ became identified with all that is hostile to God and accepted the divine verdict against human evil and injustice, as "for our sake, [God] made him to be sin who knew no sin, so that in him we might become the righteousness of God" (2 Cor. 5:21; cf. Rom. 8:3). A remarkable interchange of destinies took place. Christ absorbed human sin and its accompanying penalty, so that we might be absorbed by the saving justice of God that he embodied.[65] In Christ sin ran its inevitable course of self-

63. Cf. N. Elliott, *Liberating Paul: The Justice of God and the Politics of the Apostle* (Maryknoll, N.Y.: Orbis, 1994), 93-139.

64. P. S. Fiddes, *Past Event and Present Salvation: The Christian Idea of Atonement* (London/Louisville, Ky.: Darton, Longman & Todd/Westminster John Knox, 1989), 109.

65. The syntax and exegesis of this verse are disputed. For one attempt to maintain the technical meaning of divine righteousness as God's covenant fidelity, as opposed to a righteous status conferred on believers, see Wright, "On Becoming the Righteousness of God," 200-208. For the idea of interchange, see M. D. Hooker, *From Adam to Christ: Essays on Paul* (Cambridge: Cambridge University Press, 1990), 13-69.

destruction — and Christ died. But God raised him from the dead and in so doing triumphed over the power of both sin and death. "The death he died, he died to sin, once for all" (6:10), with the result that "death no longer has dominion over him" (6:9). And those who by baptism are united with Christ in his death share also in his liberation, "so that as Christ was raised from the dead by the glory of the father, we too might walk in newness of life" (6:4).

Thus, the justice of God is fully disclosed in the gospel because, in the first place, it shows that God has treated the sin of the covenant people with deadly seriousness. God has not perverted justice by showing favoritism to his own; instead, God has consigned Israel to the same plight of subjection to wrath and judgment as the rest of humanity. But, in the second place, this has not entailed God reneging on his covenant promises to Israel, to be her God forever and to deliver her from oppression. God keeps faith with Israel. For in putting forth Christ as "a sacrifice of atonement [*hilastērion*] by his blood" (3:25),[66] a means of eradicating sin definitively, God has acted to restore Israel to full covenant relationship on the basis of the faithful action of Jesus. Where Israel proved faithless (3:3), Christ remained faithful (3:22).[67] This act of eschatological deliverance is the third and decisive way in which God's justice is demonstrated. And because the benefit of the atoning work of Christ — restored covenantal relationship — is made freely available to all who respond in faith ("justice by faith"), Gentiles as well as Jews, the impartiality of God's justice is still further confirmed.

God's justice is vindicated, then, not by some cold, legal transaction in which people are examined according to the standards of codified law and discharged because someone else has paid the penalty. The atonement is an all-encompassing act of justice-making that overthrows oppressing powers (cf. Rom. 8:38-39; 1 Cor. 15:24-26), forgives

---

66. The grammar, meaning, and translation of this term have been enormously controverted, as all the standard commentaries discuss. Whether translated "expiation," "propitiation," "place of atonement," or "sacrifice of atonement," the essential thought is one of dealing definitively with sin.

67. There is ongoing debate over whether Paul speaks directly of "the faith or faithfulness of Christ." On this, see in the bibliography the writings of D. A. Campbell, B. Dodd, J. D. G. Dunn, R. A. Harrisville, D. M. Hay, R. B. Hays, M. D. Hooker, A. Hultgren, L. T. Johnson, L. E. Keck, B. Longenecker, R. N. Longenecker, and S. K. Williams.

all those guilty of collaboration with the enemy (5:6-10),[68] and restores to full covenant-relationship all who believe, Gentiles as well as Jews. As Robert Brinsmead explains,

> To justify a person means "to secure justice for him," "to champion someone's cause." This is what God has done for all who believe in Jesus, whether Jew or Gentile. All have been hopelessly oppressed by the legacy of sin (Rom 1–3), all have fallen short of God's glorious ideal (Rom 3:23), and all are helpless — candidates for God's justice, which is biased in favour of the weak (Rom 5:6). In Jesus Christ, God has acted in a manifestation of justice far above what any man could ask or think. He has acted to restore the rights of those who are clearly in the wrong and to champion even the cause of his enemies (Rom 5:10). He declares that all who believe in Jesus, whether Jew or Gentile, are declared to be in the right and are entitled to all the rights which belong to members of his family.[69]

Accordingly, as Perry Yoder suggests, "we should understand justification not as a punishing justice but as shalom justice — justification is liberation from sin in order that things may be right."[70] Justification by faith is a manifestation of restorative justice.

Redemptive Solidarity, Not Penal Substitution

I have proposed that Paul locates the justice-making activity of God at the heart of the gospel, and that for Paul, in keeping with the biblical tradition he draws upon, such activity centers on God's intervention, in the person and work of Christ, to deliver his people from their subjection to the power of sin and death and to restore them, together with all humanity, to the full blessings of their covenant relationship with God. The righteousness disclosed in the gospel is God's liberative, forgiving, transformative justice at work in Christ.

68. A. D. Clarke, "The Good and the Just in Romans 5:7," *TynBul* 41, no. 1 (1990): 128-42.

69. Brinsmead, "Justification by Faith Re-Examined," *CV*, Special issue, 1 (1983): 16.

70. Yoder, *Shalom*, 65.

Yet it is often urged that God's mercy toward humanity was possible only because retributive justice was first satisfied through the substitutionary punishment of Christ. The doctrine of penal substitution stems from the Reformers, especially Calvin, who recast Anselm's "satisfaction theory" into more strictly legal and penal categories. God passed the penalty of condemnation on humanity that the law demanded, but carried it out on a substitute. A legal transfer took place. Our guilt and its punishment were imposed on Christ, and his righteousness was imputed to us. (This, of course, is not the only way the atonement has been understood in the Western tradition, and the retributive model itself has had a variety of historical forms.[71] But notions of legal satisfaction and substitutionary punishment have exercised a dominant influence in Western theology, so much so that other theories of atonement, such as the moral influence theory, have been developed in conscious dissent from the dominant penal tradition. Furthermore, as noted earlier, the dominance of retributive theologies of atonement has had a demonstrable impact on criminal justice practices in Western society. "Wherever Calvinism spread," Timothy Gorringe observes, "punitive sentencing followed."[72])

Several scholars have argued that substitutionary punishment is basic to how Paul understands the atonement.[73] Furthermore, in popular Christian thought some version of penal substitution remains the dominant way of explaining — and proclaiming — the work of the cross. Tom Smail deems penal substitution to be "one of the main bastions of evangelical orthodoxy, second only in importance to the supreme authority of Scripture."[74] But powerful and persuasive objections have been raised to the logic, morality, and theological coherence of this model, especially in its popular forms but also in its more sophisticated renderings.[75]

71. See Fiddes, *Past Event and Present Salvation*, 96-104.

72. Gorringe, *God's Just Vengeance*, 83-219 (quote from 140).

73. J. I. Packer, *What Did the Cross Achieve? The Logic of Penal Substitution* (Leicester: TSF Monograph, 1974); L. Morris, *The Cross in the New Testament* (Exeter: Paternoster, 1966), 382-88.

74. Smail, "Can One Man Die for the People?" in *Atonement Today*, ed. J. Goldingay (London: SPCK, 1995), 75.

75. See, e.g., T. Talbot, "Punishment, Forgiveness, and Divine Justice," *RelSt* 29 (1993): 151-68; Fiddes, *Past Event and Present Salvation*, 83-111; Gorringe, *God's Just Ven-*

Rather than reviewing these in detail, I will limit myself to two observations.

The first is that Paul himself does not understand the atonement as a matter of penal substitution as *conventionally understood*. He does not view Christ's sacrificial death as an act of vicarious punishment that appeases God's punitive wrath. The elements of sacrifice, substitution, wrath, and penalty are all part of Paul's reflections on the cross. But he does not put them together into a thoroughgoing theory of penal substitution.

It is true, to begin with, that Paul sees a *substitutionary dimension* to Christ's death. But it is substitutionary not in the sense of one person *replacing* another, like substitutes on a football team, but in the sense of one person *representing* all others, who are thereby made present in the person and experience of their representative. Christ died not so much instead of sinners as on behalf of sinners, as their corporate representative.[76] Paul frequently speaks of Christ dying "for us" or "for our sins."[77] It it is true that there is a vicarious or "instead of" dimension to representation, since it is the one instead of the many who is the focus of attention, and the many derive vicarious benefit from the action of the one. But Paul's understanding seems to be that when Christ died, in some mysterious way fallen humanity died with him and through him.[78] "For the love of Christ urges us on," Paul writes, "because we are convinced that one has died for all; therefore all have died" (2 Cor. 5:14). And, further, "I have been crucified with Christ . . . the Son of God, who loved me and gave himself for me" (Gal. 2:19-21; cf. Rom. 6:6). If anything, the substitutionary aspect of Christ's death applies not to his role as an innocent third party substituting for humankind in the face of God's punishment but to the

---

geance, 99-103, 136-41, 229-47; Smail, "Can One Man Die for the People?" 84-86; R. D. Brinsmead, "The Scandal of God's Justice," Part 3, *CV* 8 (1983): 3-11; and C. A. Baxter, "The Cursed Beloved: A Reconsideration of Penal Substitution," in *Atonement Today,* ed. J. Goldingay (London: SPCK, 1995), 68-70.

76. See M. D. Hooker, *Not Ashamed of the Gospel: New Testament Interpretations of the Death of Christ* (Carlisle: Paternoster, 1994), 20-46.

77. See 1 Cor. 15:3; 1 Thess. 5:10; Rom. 5:6, 8; 2 Cor. 1:5; 5:14; Gal. 3:13. Cf. Eph. 5:2; Titus 2:14.

78. See J. D. Harvey, "The 'With Christ' Motif in Paul's Thought," *JETS* 35, no. 3 (1992): 329-40.

activity of God (in Christ) substituting himself for humankind in the face of sin. God was the subject; God provided the atoning sacrifice (Rom. 3:23); God sent the Son into the world as a sin offering (Rom. 8:3); God was in Christ reconciling the world to himself (2 Cor. 5:19). And it makes no sense at all to speak of God inflicting punitive retribution on himself, much less "damning himself,"[79] in order to satisfy divine justice![80]

It is true nevertheless that Paul speaks of sin carrying a *penalty,* the penalty of death (Rom. 6:23; cf. 1:32; 1 Cor. 15:56), and of Christ undergoing that penalty for us (Rom. 4:25; 1 Cor. 15:3). But this is not a matter of a penalty being added on to an offense as an arbitrary, external retributive punishment. It is the penalty of inherent consequences, something intrinsic to the nature of the offense itself. Perhaps a better term than penalty is "cost" or "price" or "consequence" (Romans 6:23 uses the term "wages," and 1 Corinthians 15:56 uses "sting.") The penalty is fundamentally one of alienation from God, experienced both as *shame,* stemming from the uncleanness or defilement of sin and the pervasive brokenness in which all share, and as *guilt,* stemming from our blameworthiness or responsibility for perpetuating the reign of sin through sinful actions that hurt others. Christ suffers the penalty of sin not because God transfers our punishment onto him as substitute victim but because Christ fully and freely identifies himself with the plight and destiny of sinful humanity under the reign of death and pays the price for doing so. The thought is not one of legal imputation of guilt to Christ but of Christ's costly solidarity with humanity in its shameful and culpable situation. Christ takes our guilt in the sense that, as our "representative substitute," he accepts the deadly consequences of our guilt; as Norman Krauss explains, "he accepts solidarity with us in our responsibility for sin in the sense that he assumed the responsibility to correct the intrinsic consequences, namely, alienation

---

79. D. J. Williams writes, "God has deemed Christ to be bearing our sin and, as a consequence, damned him for doing so, in a sense therefore damning himself." See *Paul's Metaphors: Their Context and Character* (Peabody, Mass.: Hendrickson, 1999), 146.

80. On a different note, R. G. Hamerton-Kelly proposes that Paul uses the idea of God offering himself as a propitiation as a reductio ad absurdum of the idea of vengeance and to parody the whole logic of sacrifice as an appeasement to God. See "Sacred Violence and the Curse of the Law (Galatians 3:13): The Sacrifice of Christ as Sacrificial Travesty," *NTS* 36, no. 1 (1990): 115-16. Cf. Gorringe, *God's Just Vengeance,* 81-82.

and death."[81] It should go without saying that Paul does not see the agonies and tortures of crucifixion as some kind of divine punishment. Not only would this have disturbing implications of a sadistic God, but it would require us to conceive of Christ as still being under continuous punishment, for Paul seems to regard Christ's sufferings as, in some sense, ongoing (2 Cor. 1:5; 2:15; 4:10; Col. 1:24).

It is also true that Paul depicts Christ's death in *sacrificial* terms.[82] But it is simplistic and misleading to equate sacrifice with punishment. In ancient Israel, sacrifices were made for a variety of purposes — to seal covenants, to offer thanksgiving, to remember past deeds of salvation, to commune with God, to respond to God's goodness, to express shame and regret, and to deal with sin.[83] Paul interprets Christ's death as a covenant sacrifice (1 Cor. 11:25), a Passover sacrifice (1 Cor. 5:7-8), a sacrifice of firstfruits (1 Cor. 15:20, 23), a sacrifice of self-oblation (Rom. 8:32; Gal. 2:20), and a sin offering (Rom. 3:25; 4:25; 8:3; 1 Cor. 15:3, 20, 23; 2 Cor. 5:21; Gal. 1:4). None of these entail retributive punishment. Even in the depiction of Christ's death as a sin offering, the fundamental thought is not one of punishment but one of expiation. The atonement rituals of the Old Testament depended not on the idea that God punished the animal instead of punishing sinners, thus appeasing his anger, but on the understanding that God somehow transferred the contamination and consequences of sin to the sacrificial vic-

---

81. Krauss, *Jesus Christ Our Lord: Christology from a Disciple's Perspective* (Scottdale, Pa.: Herald Press, 1987), 226. The Western theological tradition has related the cross almost exclusively to the problem of guilt. But, as Krauss helpfully demonstrates, the biblical writers portray the human plight as both shame and guilt. Significantly, the experience of shame cannot be removed by substitutionary punishment but only by a forgiveness that covers the past and restores relationship (211).

82. That Paul sees Christ's death in sacrificial terms is asserted by J. D. G. Dunn in "Paul's Understanding of the Death of Jesus," in *Reconciliation and Hope,* ed. R. Banks (Grand Rapids: William B. Eerdmans, 1974), 125-41; and in *Romans,* 2 vols. (Dallas: Word, 1988), 1:181. This assertion is strongly contested, however, by B. H. MacLean, "The Absence of an Atoning Sacrifice in Paul's Soteriology," *NTS* 38, no. 4 (1992): 531-53.

83. See J. Goldingay, "Old Testament Sacrifice and the Death of Christ," in *Atonement Today,* ed. J. Goldingay (London: SPCK, 1995), 3-20; I. Bradley, *The Power of Sacrifice* (London: Darton, Longman & Todd, 1995), 86-102; Gorringe, *God's Just Vengeance,* 33-57; and J. V. Dahms, "Dying with Christ," *JETS* 36, no. 1 (1993): 15-23. Cf. B. D. Chilton, "The Hungry Knife: Towards a Sense of Sacrifice," in *The Bible in Human Society: Essays in Honour of John Rogerson,* ed. M. D. R. Carroll, D. J. A. Clines, and P. R. Davies (Sheffield: Sheffield Academic Press, 1995), 122-38.

tim in order to remove them from the community.[84] As John Goldingay explains, "Sacrifice does not involve penal substitution in the sense that one entity bears another's punishment. By laying hands on the offering, the offerers identify with it and pass on to it not their guilt but their stain. The offering is then not vicariously punished but vicariously cleansed."[85] Such expiation simultaneously propitiated God's wrath, not because God had exacted punishment but because the breach of covenant relationship occasioned by sin had been restored. What was efficacious in this was less the death of the sacrificial victim per se than the dedication of heart and will shown by the people's participation in the event.[86] In the same way, Christ's death serves to remove the contamination of sin and thus clear the way for restoration and renewal, not to pacify God's anger through bloody punishment.

It is true, finally, that Paul speaks of God's *wrath* (e.g., Rom. 1:18; 2:5, 8; 3:5) and sees Christ's death as delivering us from this wrath (Rom. 5:9; 8:1; 1 Thess. 1:10; 5:9). But, like sacrifice, wrath cannot simply be taken as a theological synonym for retributive punishment. I will consider the meaning of divine wrath more fully in Chapter 4, but two brief points may be made here. One is that when wrath is understood as God's personal consent to the intrinsic outworking of people's estrangement from God, as Paul understands it in Romans 1, Christ's death may be seen as an expression of divine wrath against sin without any suggestion that God punishes Christ on our behalf. In freely identifying with the human condition of enslavement to evil, Christ inevitably falls under divine wrath, which is intractably opposed to sin. The other point is that for Paul the work of wrath in the death of Christ is God's action of "condemning sin in the flesh" (Rom. 8:3), not of destroying the flesh of sinners! It is a work of curative justice, not punitive retribution.[87] It is po-

---

84. According to Bradley, "The general consensus among scholars . . . is that the sin offerings made by the Israelites were conceived of in expiatory terms with the sacrificial victims being regarded as representatives of, rather than substitutes for, the lives of the offerers" (*The Power of Sacrifice*, 94). Goldingay points out that the idea of God's anger hardly appears at all in the book of Leviticus. Sacrifice is seen as God's provision for dealing with the pollution and repulsiveness of sin, not for appeasing his anger ("Your Iniquities Have Made a Separation between You and Your God," 51).

85. J. Goldingay, "Old Testament Sacrifice," 10.

86. 1 Sam. 15:22; Amos 5:22-25; Mic. 6:7-8; Hos. 6:6; Pss. 40:6-8; 50:13-14; 51:16-17.

87. Cf. Dunn, "Paul's Understanding of the Death of Jesus," 139.

tentially misleading to speak of God's wrath being "appeased" by Christ's death, since it could evoke the thought of a pent-up emotion being spent in a bout of vigorous punishment. It is better to think of God's wrath being fully "revealed" (Rom. 1:18) in his death, and paradoxically in the nonretributive way in which Christ triumphed over evil. As a result of that triumph, the destructive consequences of God's wrath may now be turned away from humankind because the root of human sin has been dealt with in the dying and rising of Christ.[88] Thus, as Stephen Travis rightly concludes,

> Paul's understanding of the death of Christ does not include the idea that he bore the retributive punishment for our sins which otherwise would have been inflicted on us. To understand the atonement in those terms is to misunderstand what Paul means by "the wrath of God." It is to press too far the implications of his legal metaphor. It is to risk driving a wedge between the action of God and that of Jesus.[89]

This leads to my second observation. Penal substitution gives primacy in the work of Christ to the retributive features of divine justice, whereas, as we have seen, Paul employs a conception of covenant justice where the keynote is covenant faithfulness, liberation, and restoration. Penal atonement asserts that God forgives us because an equivalent penalty has been paid through Christ's death, in accordance with the law of *talion*, where offending requires a proportionate punishment, "eye for eye, tooth for tooth." But this necessarily exalts punitive justice over love as the driving force of atonement. As Krauss notes, "The *lex talionis* is a way to restrain the action of anger and not the way of prescribing the reaction of love. . . . It reveals something of the nature of God, but it in no way defines the ultimate necessity of his nature."[90] The logic of the cross actually confounds the principle of retributive justice, for salvation is achieved not by the offender compensating for

88. On this idea, see C. Schroeder, "'Standing in the Breach': Turning Away the Wrath of God," *Interpretation* 52, no. 1 (1998): 16-23.

89. Travis, "Christ as Bearer of Divine Judgment in Paul's Thought about the Atonement," in *Jesus of Nazareth: Lord and Christ*, ed. J. B. Green and M. Turner (Grand Rapids/Carlisle: William B. Eerdmans/Paternoster, 1994), 345; cf. 341. So too Carroll and Green, *The Death of Jesus in Early Christianity*, 123, 263, 277-78; Fiddes, *Past Event and Present Salvation*, 98; and Morgan, *Romans*, 28, 91-92.

90. Krauss, *Jesus Christ Our Lord*, 225.

his crimes by suffering, but by the victim, the one offended against, suffering vicariously on behalf of the offended — a radical inversion of the *lex talionis*.[91] In effect, as Paul Fiddes notes, "the New Testament picture of atonement uses legal language only to blow the legal system wide open."[92]

By building on retributive categories, the penal theory inherits all the defects of retributive conceptions of justice (which I will detail in the next chapter). Among these is the tendency to conceive of justice in abstract, legal terms more than in personal, relational terms. The penal model portrays the atonement as a forensic transaction between God the Father and God the Son, acting virtually as independent subjects,[93] rather than as a healing of relationships between estranged humanity and God, in which God takes the initiative and personally bears the cost of doing so. Such is the emphasis on law in the penal model that even God's own freedom is constrained by it. God *cannot* forgive until the punishment demanded by the law is exacted. The law becomes the supreme principle, and punishment becomes a necessity imposed on God by a superior rule. In reply to this point, it might be argued that God exercises freedom in allowing a substitute to take the retribution owing to others. But why then is God not free to dispense with retribution altogether? Why not forego punishment? If the answer given is that God cannot act against God's own holy character, which cannot tolerate sin, the question then becomes why, and whether, punitive retribution truly safeguards God's holiness.

This leads to another key defect in retributive theories of justice — their propensity to invest punishment with too much efficacy. Punishment is a finite mechanism; there is a limit to what it can achieve. The penal theory of atonement ascribes too much potency to punishment, and too little to sin. It conceives of sin as a debt incurred against God,

---

91. For this helpful insight, see Conrad Brunk's response in W. Northey, "Justice Is Peacemaking: A Biblical Theology of Peacemaking in Response to Criminal Conflict," *NPCJ* 12 (1992): 50; cf. 59.

92. Fiddes, *Past Event and Present Salvation*, 86.

93. It is true that in many accounts of penal substitution an effort is made to avoid the idea of Father and Son acting as independent parties with Christ serving as the object of God's punishment and God as the object of Christ's propitiation. The question is whether it is theologically credible to say that God acts both *in* Christ (cf. 2 Cor. 5:19) and *against* Christ at one and the same time.

which the punishment imposed on Christ serves to discharge. But Paul takes sin more seriously than that. Sin is more than a moral debt on the pages of the divine ledger. It is an alien power that distorts personality, corrupts relationships, and enslaves the human will. Sin is not merely an affront to God's dignity requiring reparation, or a breaking of God's rules requiring correction; it is a state of volitional-moral enslavement and relational distortion that requires deliverance and reconciliation. It is not clear how punishment can effect the kind of comprehensive deliverance from the power of sin and renewal of relationship with God which Paul ascribes to the atoning work of Christ. Nor is it clear why, if God cannot tolerate sin as much as penal advocates insist, God should be concerned primarily to exact punishment rather than root out the causes and effects of sin in the lives of those it infests. Why shouldn't a healing remedy, instead of payment of damages, satisfy God's justice? And if it is the lethal punishment of Christ that vindicates justice, where does resurrection fit in? Why is it even necessary? How can Paul speak of Christ "being raised for our justification" (Rom. 4:24)?

A good deal more could be said about the inadequacies of penal substitution, including, for example, its vulnerabilities to feminist critique.[94] It might be possible to reformulate the theory to take into account the sort of criticisms listed above. But to the extent that any such reformulation continues to depend on essentially retributive conceptions of justice, it will fail to comprehend Paul's approach. For Paul, and for the biblical tradition in which he stands, the justice of God is a dynamic, active power that breaks into situations of oppression and evil in order to bring liberation and restore freedom. Its basic concern is not to treat each person as each deserves but to do all that is necessary to make things right, even though it is totally undeserved and immensely costly. It is a restorative justice more than a retributive or distributive justice. It is God acting to end oppression and secure harmony and well-being, especially by meeting the needs of the disadvantaged and downtrodden.

The death of Christ is a work of justice-making, then, not because

94. Cf. E. Moltmann-Wendel, "Is There a Feminist Theology of the Cross?" in *The Scandal of a Crucified World: Perspectives on the Cross and Suffering,* ed. J. Tesfai (Maryknoll, N.Y.: Orbis, 1994), 87-98; and N. J. Duff, "Atonement and the Christian Life: Reformed Doctrine from a Feminist Perspective," *Interpretation* 53, no. 1 (1999): 21-33.

it entails secondary retribution on human sin, but because it demonstrates God's unfailing faithfulness to his people and because it liberates, cleanses, heals, and restores. Rather than pressing a legal right to punish and condemn, God, like the righteous judge of Old Testament times, has taken the side of the accused party and acted in Christ to deliver all humanity from the legacy of Adam's rebellion. "God's justice is his love in action," suggests N. T. Wright, "to right the wrongs of his suffering world by taking their weight upon himself. God's love is the driving force of his justice, so that it can never become a blind or arbitrary thing, a cold system which somehow God operates, or which operates God."[95] Human shame and guilt are dealt with not by vicarious punishment but by gratuitous forgiveness. As Krauss explains,

> God is justified in forgiving us on the basis of his own holy love and not on the basis of an equivalent penal statisfaction which has been paid to him through the death of Jesus. The cross itself as an act of solidarity with us is the divine ethical justification for forgiveness, and the resurrection of Jesus demonstrates the effectiveness of God's love in Christ to forgive and cleanse us from sin.[96]

As well as forgiving and cleansing sinners, God has intervened to remedy the environment of sin and evil that causes offending in the first place, defeating the malignant powers that enslaved the human race. Thus, God's justice is vindicated not through prosecution and punishment but through forgiveness, restitution, and liberation — restorative justice par excellence. And the outcome of God's justice-making in Christ is the restoration of *shalom* (Rom. 5:1), both peace with God and, in what is Paul's primary agenda in Romans, peace between Jew and Gentile (Rom. 14–15; cf. Eph. 2:11-22), peace within the human community (cf. Gal. 3:28-29). Justification is, as Markus Barth puts it, "a social event."[97]

Finally, as Paul makes clear in Romans 6 and elsewhere, it is this

95. Wright, *What Saint Paul Really Said,* 110-11.

96. Krauss, *Jesus Christ Our Lord,* 225.

97. Barth, "Jews and Gentiles: The Social Character of Justification in Paul," *JES* 5 (1968): 241-67. See also K. Stendahl, *Paul among Jews and Gentiles* (Philadelphia: Fortress, 1976), K. Stendahl, *Final Account: Paul's Letter to the Romans* (Minneapolis: Fortress, 1995); and H. Boers, *The Justification of the Gentiles: Paul's Letters to the Galatians and Romans* (Peabody, Mass.: Hendrickson, 1994).

character of divine justice that provides the model and the empowerment for Christian ethical conduct.[98] Having been set free from slavery to sin, Christians have become slaves to God's liberating righteousness and are to offer themselves to God as "instruments of righteousness" (6:13), vehicles of restorative justice in God's afflicted world. Applied to the realm of criminal justice, this means taking evil seriously, holding wrongdoers to account and summoning their repentance, as God does with Israel (Rom. 1–2). It also means refusing to deny our relationship with wrongdoers, refusing to abandon them or exclude them entirely from the human community, just as God remains steadfastly loyal to his sinful people (Rom. 3). It means, further, seeing criminals not solely as perpetrators of evil, though indeed they are that, but also as victims of the crushing power of sin, from which they are in need of liberation and renewal. And it means not regarding their punisment per se as the satisfaction of justice. Punishment may be necessary, as we will see in the next chapter, but it is not the pain of punishment itself that achieves justice, as though justice resides in creating an equity of suffering, the pain of the offenders' punishments compensating for the pain inflicted on victims. True justice resides in the restoring of relationships and the recreation of *shalom* (Rom. 5). It is only when the cycle of evil is broken and, as far is possible, the consequences of criminal action remedied, consequences which blight the lives of both crime victims and their abusers — only then is true justice, the justice modeled by God, attained in measure.

Jesus as the Justice of God

Divine justice for Paul is a saving, reconciling justice, and the death and resurrection of Christ represent the concrete realization and visible demonstration of this justice. Whereas Paul sees the cross and resurrection as the focal point of God's justice, the Gospel writers consider Jesus' entire life and ministry also to be a demonstration of divine justice.[99] In the Gospel narratives, Jesus personally embodies the saving

98. See B. J. Byrne, "Living Out the Righteousness of God: The Contribution of Rom. 6:1–8:13 to an Understanding of Paul's Ethical Presuppositions," *CBQ* 43, no. 4 (1981): 557-81. See also Yoder, *Shalom*, 63-70.

99. Cf. J. C. Haughey, "Jesus as the Justice of God," in *The Faith That Does Justice*, 264-

justice of God. He is, in Matthew's view, God's chosen servant who proclaims "justice to the Gentiles" and will bring "justice to victory" (Matt. 12:18-23; cf. Isa. 42:1-4; Matt. 23:23).[100] To what extent this is demonstrably consistent with the self-understanding of the historical Jesus might be debated, but there is little reason to doubt that it is.[101]

According to the Synoptic tradition, the central burden of Jesus' ministry was the announcement and establishment on earth of the eschatological kingdom of God (Mark 1:14-15).[102] On this, New Testament scholarship has been agreed for a very long time. Notwithstanding its manifold expressions and sometimes conflicting details, the Jewish hope at the time of Jesus for the coming of salvation was essentially the hope for a definitive revelation of divine power to vindicate Israel's trust in God, to punish the wicked and liberate the oppressed, and to make Israel "the epicentre of international peace and justice and order."[103] In proclaiming the advent of God's kingdom, Jesus was suggesting that the fulfillment of this hope for national and cosmic salvation was at hand.

It is not possible to arrive at a single, precise definition of what Jesus meant by the phrase "kingdom of God." It functions as a kind of umbrella term that embraces all the diverse ways that God's eschatological sovereignty impinges on human life. Nonetheless, it is possible, as I have proposed elsewhere,[104] to identify three major facets of Jesus' kingdom proclamation that, taken together, provide a kind of summary conception of what he meant by the term. First, the advent of God's kingdom meant the presence of God's end-time power to put things right on the earth, in accordance with God's ultimate intentions for creation. This is seen pre-eminently in Jesus' miracles and exorcisms. Second, the coming of the kingdom meant the closeness of

90. On the extent of Paul's knowledge of and interest in the historical Jesus, see C. D. Marshall, "Paul and Jesus: Continuity or Discontinuity?" *Stimulus* 5, no.4 (1997): 32-42.

100. That *krisis* here designates "justice" (so NRSV) rather than eschatological judgment is persuasively argued by R. Beaton, "Messiah and Justice: A Key to Matthew's Use of Isaiah 42:1-4?," *JSNT* 75 (1999): 5-23.

101. See W. R. Herzog II, *Jesus, Justice, and the Reign of God: A Ministry of Liberation* (Louisville, Ky.: Westminster John Knox, 2000).

102. On this passage, see C. D. Marshall, *Faith as a Theme in Mark's Narrative* (Cambridge: Cambridge University Press, 1989), 34-56.

103. Haughey, "Jesus as the Justice of God," 267.

104. C. D. Marshall, *Kingdom Come: The Kingdom of God in the Teaching of Jesus* (Auckland, N. Z.: Impetus, 1993).

God's personal presence to bring men and women into a new relationship of intimacy with God. This is demonstrated, for example, in Jesus' table fellowship with outcasts, in his forgiveness of sins, and in his emphasis on God as *Abba* ("father"). Third, the dawning of the kingdom meant the creation of a messianic community that was to live in a manner consistent with the demands of the new age in the midst of the old, challenging the unjust status quo by its very existence as a dissident community of equals. This is the chief concern in Jesus' ethical teaching. Taken as a whole, Jesus' message of the inbreaking of God's kingdom may be understood, according to Richard Hays, as a declaration of "the radical restoration of God's justice, setting things right but bringing judgment and destruction to those who resist God's will."[105]

Jesus summoned his hearers to "strive first for the kingdom of God and his righteousness" (Matt. 6:33; cf. Deut. 16:20),[106] and in his words and deeds he demonstrated precisely what this entails. To seek first God's kingdom means making the agenda of God's reign the supreme concern of one's existence, to dedicate oneself to serving God's redemptive rule in present history. This is done by following the example of Jesus in serving the needs of the poor (Luke 6:20), liberating the oppressed (Luke 4:18-19), and caring for the victims of injustice and violence (Luke 10:25-37). Seeking first the kingdom also means pursuing the ultimate goal of the kingdom, which is the realization on earth of the justice of God, the bringing of human life into harmony with God's will (Matt. 6:10). There is nothing passive about seeking God's kingdom; the present imperative verb *zēteite* ("seek unceasingly") implies a continuous, strenuous, enduring commitment to the values, priorities, and ethical standards of God's new order, now made manifest in Jesus.[107]

Jesus calls his followers, then, to strive for the triumph of God's

---

105. Hays, *The Moral Vision of the New Testament: A Contemporary Introduction to New Testament Ethics* (Edinburgh: T. & T. Clark, 1996), 163.

106. On this text, see G. R. Beasley-Murray, "Matthew 6:33: The Kingdom of God and the Ethics of Jesus," in *Neues Testament und Ethik*, ed. H. Merklein (Freiburg/Basel/Wein: Herder, 1989), 84-98.

107. On the kingdom as both a "divine performance" and a "human performance," see B. D. Chilton and J. I. H. McDonald, *Jesus and the Ethics of the Kingdom* (London: SPCK, 1987), 115-29. So also B. Wiebe, "Messianic Ethics," *Interpretation* 45, no. 1 (1991): 33-35.

royal justice on earth, a healing justice that puts right what is wrong. It is also a suffering justice, one that is prepared to endure wrong without retaliation and to practice costly forgiveness for the sake of reconciliation. According to the Gospel's witness, Jesus demonstrated in his own life the saving power of forgiving, nonretaliatory love. He refused to condemn the woman taken in adultery (John 7:53–8:11), he forgave the sins of other supplicants (Mark 2:5, 10; Luke 7:47), and he repudiated the use of violence against his opponents (Matt. 26:52; Luke 22:51; John 18:10-11). Ultimately he forgave even his own executioners (Luke 23:34).[108] He prayed not for the justice of swift retribution on his abusers but for their pardon, for the higher justice of God. As 1 Peter observes, "When he was abused, he did not return abuse; when he suffered, he did not threaten; but he entrusted himself to the one who judges justly" (1 Pet. 2:23; cf. Heb. 12:3). In all this, Jesus provided the paradigm for those who would follow him (Mark 8:34-38; cf. Heb. 12:2).

To deal adequately with the paradigmatic significance of Jesus' life and teaching would require an entire book in its own right, and a very long one at that. In what remains of this chapter, I will confine my comments to the two features of Jesus' teaching that have the most immediate pertinence to criminal justice concerns: his teaching on forgiveness and on nonretaliation. Other aspects of Jesus' teaching with criminal justice implications, such as his perspective on punishment, will be picked up in later chapters.

Forgiveness of Offenders

As well as offering forgiveness himself to individuals, Jesus repeatedly stressed the need for his hearers to forgive those who hurt them. His teaching on forgiveness is far-reaching both in scope and significance.

In *scope*, Jesus required an unlimited readiness to forgive. On one occasion, Peter asks, "Lord, if another member of the church sins against me, how often should I forgive? As many as seven times?" Jesus says to him, "Not seven times, but, I tell you, seventy-seven times" (Matt. 18:21-

---

108. The textual status of this verse is uncertain. Internal considerations favor its inclusion, but its omission in several early and diverse witnesses is striking. The dominical origin of the saying is beyond serious doubt.

22; cf. Luke 17:3-4). Rabbis of the period taught that people should be prepared to forgive others for repeated offenses up to three times; it was unreasonable to expect forgiveness on the fourth occasion.[109] Peter, perhaps suspecting that Jesus will expect more than other teachers of the law, attempts to second-guess him by proposing a new "perfect" limit of sevenfold forgiveness, more than double the existing standard. But even this remarkable level of generosity is light years removed from Jesus' intention: "Not seven times, but, I tell you, seventy-seven times" (Matt. 18:22). Jesus is not simply adjusting the arithmetic. He is ruling out all calculation when it comes to forgiveness. Jesus' followers are to forgive, and to go on forgiving, without counting the cost. In Genesis 4:24, Lamech demanded unlimited, "seventy-sevenfold" revenge. The gracious justice of God's kingdom demands unlimited, "seventy-sevenfold" forgiveness. An obligation is laid on the messianic community, therefore, to be a visible fellowship of forgiveness as a picture to the wider world of what God's rule is all about (cf. Matt. 18:21-23, 35).

In Luke's version of the saying (17:3-4), the offender's repentance is mentioned as the basis of forgiveness. But even here, emphasis lies on the uncalculating nature of forgiveness. "If the same person sins against you seven times a day, and turns back to you seven times and says, 'I repent,' you must forgive." For a broken relationship to be restored, forgiveness by the victim alone is not enough; there must also be repentance by the offender, since relational repair is, of necessity, a two-sided process. But even if repentance is not forthcoming, even if the relationship cannot be restored, the disciple is still obligated to nurture forgiveness; after all, Jesus forgave his murderers in the absence of their repentance (Luke 23:34). The need to be forgiving is as much for the sake of the injured party as it is for the offender, for forgiveness is a process whereby those who have been wounded let go of the power of the offense and the offender over them, and move toward freedom and wholeness. I will develop this concept further in the concluding chapter of the book.

Further-reaching still is the *significance* with which Jesus invests forgiveness. He makes the readiness to forgive others a condition for appropriating the forgiveness of God. In the Lord's Prayer, he instructs his disciples to petition God to treat them in precisely the same manner

109. See F. W. Beare, *The Gospel According to Matthew* (Oxford: Blackwell, 1981), 381.

as they treat others. "Forgive us our debts, as we also have forgiven our debtors" (Matt. 6:12/Luke 11:4). This petition stands out, strikingly, as the sole reference to human activity in the entire Prayer. This suggests that the obligation to forgive, as well as the humility to receive forgiveness, is not simply one among many desirable qualities for disciples of Jesus. It is the sine qua non of eschatological existence in the messianic community, for without the disciplined practice of forgiveness, no eschatological community is possible.[110] This may be why, in Matthew's account, immediately after teaching the Prayer, Jesus returns to this petition to clarify and reinforce it. "For if you forgive others their trespasses, your heavenly Father will also forgive you; but if you do not forgive others, neither will your Father forgive your trespasses" (6:14-15; cf. 5:7, 23-24). The same point is made in an independent saying in Mark that emphasizes the comprehensive nature of the obligation to forgive: "Whenever you stand praying, forgive, if you have *anything* against *anyone;* so that your Father in heaven may also forgive you your trespasses" (Mark 11:25, italics mine). The essential thought common to all these sayings is put most crisply by Luke: "Forgive, and you will be forgiven" (Luke 6:37).

These sayings cannot mean, of course, that divine forgiveness conforms to the pattern of human forgiveness, or that God's pardon is somehow earned or merited by the granting of human pardon. Quite the contrary. While there is a definite emphasis in these sayings on the conditional nature of divine forgiveness, elsewhere in the Jesus tradition there is a clear indication that it is the prior gift of God's forgiveness that impels commitment to human forgiveness. This emerges directly in the story of the sinful woman who anoints Jesus' feet at the home of Simon the Pharisee. Jesus says to Simon, "'Therefore, I tell you, her sins, which were many, have been forgiven; hence she has shown great love. But the one to whom little is forgiven, loves little.' Then he said to her, 'Your sins are forgiven'" (Luke 7:47-48).[111] The

110. So G. Soares-Prabhu, "'As We Forgive': Interhuman Forgiveness in the Teaching of Jesus," in *Forgiveness,* ed. C. Floristán and C. Duquoc, Concilium 177 (Edinburgh: T. & T. Clark, 1986), 59.

111. It is possible to read vv. 47-48 in two different ways. According to one interpretation, Jesus confers forgiveness on the woman as a reply to her act of love, which he takes as a sign of her repentance. According to the other, Jesus regards the woman's act of love as evidence that she had previously experienced God's forgiveness, declaring

point made here, and echoed in several other New Testament texts (Matt. 18:32-33; Eph. 4:32; Col. 3:13; 1 John 4:7, 21), is that the vertical reality of God's love and forgiveness motivates and empowers the recipients' practice of horizontal forgiveness. Human forgiveness is *motivated* by believers' profound sense of gratitude to God for the gracious forgiveness of their sins and by their knowledge of the obligation placed on them to imitate or conform themselves to the character of God, whose nature it is to be merciful (Matt. 5:48; cf. 7).[112] The experience of God's forgiveness also *empowers* the offering of human forgiveness. The innate human capacity to forgive (without which society could not function) is intensified and augmented by the experience of God's forgiving mercy. Participation in the reality of God's forgiveness enables believers to mediate to others the kindness and generosity of God they have freely received.[113]

So in Jesus' teaching, as elsewhere in the New Testament, forgiveness is both a gift and a task, and it is a gift *before* it is a task. Yet there is also a reverse loop from task to gift, for Jesus repeatedly warns that the failure to forgive others nullifies the benefits of God's forgiveness. "If you do not forgive others, neither will your Father forgive your trespasses" (Matt. 6:15). This circular relationship between gift and task is explicable only if we understand God's forgiveness as an ongoing relational dynamic rather than a punctiliar legal transaction. Through acceptance of the person and mission of Jesus, believers enter into a "covenant [that is, an ongoing relationship] . . . for the forgiveness of sins" (Matt. 26:28). Within this covenant, God's forgiveness is the steadfast orientation that God exhibits toward his covenant partners — or, to change the metaphor, it is an everflowing stream of pardoning mercy

---

"Your sins are forgiven" to add certitude to the woman's own perception of this fact. The latter reading is preferable. See J. J. Kilgallen, "Forgiveness of Sins (Luke 7:36-50)," *NovT* 40, no. 2 (1998): 105-16; and Kilgallen, "Luke 7:41-42 and Forgiveness of Sins," *ExpT* 111, no. 2 (1999): 46-47.

112. In *Embodying Forgiveness: A Theological Analysis*, L. G. Jones helpfully grounds the Christian discipline of forgiveness, not in human therapeutic needs but in friendship with the Triune God who ever lives in, and creates out of, the communion of self-giving love (Grand Rapids: William B. Eerdmans, 1995). "We need the schooling provided by the Triune God," he says, "so that we can learn to envision and to embody costly forgiveness" (7).

113. J. Sobrino, "Latin America: Place of Sin and Place of Forgiveness," in *Forgiveness*, 45.

that God directs toward them. Because of the inherent character of forgiving mercy, it is simply not feasible for its recipients to keep it self-
ishly for themselves. They are compelled, by the very nature of the reality itself, to channel it on to others. When they stubbornly refuse to do
so, they block the flow, so to speak, and consequently cease to be bene-
ficiaries themselves. They close themselves off to the continuing experience and benefits of God's mercy. God goes on being forgiving, just as
the sun goes on shining. (It cannot do otherwise.) But it is still possible
to remove oneself from the liberating power of this mercy, just as it is
possible to hide oneself from the sun and lose its benefits. Practically
speaking, Jesus is suggesting that when we fail to entertain the possibility of extending forgiveness to others, we show that we have lost sight
of our own staggering need for forgiveness, we have underestimated the
enormity of God's grace toward us, and we have failed to appreciate the
moral obligations that come with the experience of grace (cf. Luke
7:47). If we are unwilling to pass on to others the forgiving grace we
have received from God, we have not really "received" that grace at all. It
has become a nullity.

This is the point of the parable of the unforgiving servant (Matt.
18:23-35). When the indebted servant asks the king for time to repay
his staggering debt of ten thousand talents (the equivalent of billions —
even zillions — of dollars today),[114] the king sets aside his legal rights to
restitution and freely forgives the entire debt, at great financial cost to
himself. Then the forgiven servant meets a fellow servant who owes
him a minor debt of a hundred denarii. But instead of passing on the
gracious justice he has received, he enforces strict legal justice and has
his debtor thrown into prison. In so doing, he shows that he has not in-
ternalized the principle of mercy employed by the king. By refusing to
treat others in the same way he has been treated, he effectively nullifies
the forgiveness he has been offered and ends up suffering a worse fate
than he inflicted on his debtor (v. 34). The story ends with a stern warning: "So my heavenly Father will also do to every one of you, if you do
not forgive your brother or sister from your heart" (18:35). Some readers sense an inner contradiction at this point. Jesus urges unlimited forgiveness (18:22), but the king in the parable does not grant forgiveness

---

114. R. H. Gundry, *Matthew: A Commentary on His Literary and Theological Art* (Grand
Rapids: William B. Eerdmans, 1982), 373.

even a second time, never mind seventy-seven times. But it is probably unwise to press the logic of the parable too far. The reaction of the king is intended to underline the eschatological seriousness of the demand placed upon the messianic community to practice forgiveness, as well as to clarify that forgiveness is not a matter of cheap grace or eternal leniency.

For the follower of Jesus, then, forgiveness is not an optional response to wrongdoing; it is an obligation. If God's presence with Israel was demonstrated by the temple, then God's presence with the new community is demonstrated by the community's faith-filled prayer and readiness to forgive (Mark 11:20-25).[115] The messianic community is the place where God's eschatological mercy becomes a social reality. This is not to say that forgiveness is a simple, univocal concept. Nor is it to say that forgiveness is easy or comes quickly. To arrive at the place of forgiveness is often a long and painful process, and the ability finally to let go of the hurt is ultimately the work of God. As I said earlier, I will return to this matter in the final chapter. The point to make here is that the willingness to enter into that process is essential if believers are to be true to the gracious love of God upon whom they depend for life itself. Athol Gill underscores the point with this apt metaphor: "Our forgiveness of others is the outstretched hand by which we are able to grasp the forgiveness of God."[116]

The Stance of Nonretaliation

Obviously, then, Jesus sees no place for vindictiveness or retaliation as a response to crime. Jesus rebuked James and John for wanting to call down fire on a Samaritan village (Luke 9:51-56). When Peter resorted to "justifiable violence" in Gethsemane, Jesus reprimanded him by exposing the vicious logic of violence: "All who take the sword will perish by the sword" (Matt. 26:52). More appropriate to divine justice is the gracious logic of the Beatitudes. "Blessed are the merciful, for they will receive mercy. . . . Blessed are the peacemakers, for they will be called chil-

---

115. On this saying, see Marshall, *Faith as a Theme in Mark's Narrative*, 170-74.

116. Gill, *Life on the Road: The Gospel Basis for a Messianic Lifestyle* (Homebush West, N.S.W.: Anzea, 1989), 232-33.

dren of God" (Matt. 5:7, 9). To be a child of God is to be like God; to be a peacemaker is to be a child of God and therefore to be like God, for God makes peace with his enemies while they are "still sinners" (Rom. 5:1, 6-8; 6:20; cf. Luke 1:79; 19:39; Acts 10:36; Eph. 2:14-18). Revenge is totally excluded; as C. S. Macalpine explains, "It cannot justify itself to those who have seen God in the face of Jesus Christ."[117]

This raises the question of the meaning and status of the *lex talionis*, or "law of retaliation," specified in Scripture and discussed by Jesus. The "eye for an eye" principle is undoubtedly the best-known and perhaps most misunderstood biblical text on crime and punishment. It is often cited as justification for retributive justice. But, as Howard Zehr observes, "There is more to 'an eye for an eye' than meets the eye."[118] Closer examination indicates that the *lex talionis* is neither as central to biblical justice nor as vengeful in meaning as many people think. To appreciate this, we need to consider first its function within Jewish law and practice, then look at Jesus' commentary on it.

The Lex Talionis *in Biblical and Jewish Tradition*

The *lex talionis* is found three times in the Mosaic law, although the talionic "like for like" principle underlies several other references to divine judgment.[119] It is important to note the full context of the references.

When a slave owner strikes a male or female slave with a rod and the slave dies immediately, the owner shall be punished. But if the slave survives a day or two, there is no punishment; for the slave is the owner's property. When people who are fighting injure a pregnant woman so that there is a miscarriage, and yet no further harm follows, the one responsible shall be fined what the woman's husband demands, paying as much as the judges determine. If any harm follows, then you shall give life for life, eye for eye, tooth for tooth, hand for hand, foot for foot, burn for burn, wound for wound, stripe for stripe. (Exod. 21:20-25)

---

117. C. S. Macalpine, "Vengeance," *HDCG*, 2:792.

118. Zehr, *Changing Lenses: A New Focus for Crime and Justice* (Scottdale, Pa.: Herald Press, 1990), 126.

119. See, for example, Exod. 4:23; 1 Sam. 2:30; 2 Chron. 12:5; 24:20; Ps. 18:26; Prov. 3:34; Isa. 3:11; 59:18; Jer. 14:13-16; 17:10; 34:17; 50:15; Ezek. 7:8, 27; Mic. 2:1-5; Joel 3:4-8; Obad. 1:15; Mal. 3:7; 1 Cor. 3:16-17; Gal. 6:7-8; 2 Thess. 1:6-7.

Anyone who maims another shall suffer the same injury in return: fracture for fracture, eye for eye, tooth for tooth; the injury inflicted is the injury to be suffered. One who kills an animal shall make restitution for it; but one who kills a human being shall be put to death. You shall have one law for the alien and for the citizen: for I am the LORD your God. (Lev. 24:19-22)

If the witness is a false witness, having testified falsely against another, then you shall do to the false witness just as the false witness had meant to do to the other. So you shall purge the evil from your midst. The rest shall hear and be afraid, and a crime such as this shall never again be committed among you. Show no pity: life for life, eye for eye, tooth for tooth, hand for hand, foot for foot. (Deut. 19:18-21)

Compare: Whoever sheds the blood of a human, by a human shall that person's blood be shed; for in his own image God made humankind. (Gen. 9:6)

The law of retaliation seems to have been part of most ancient Semitic law codes, since it was current in almost identical words in Babylon and Canaan.[120] But there are distinctive aspects to the biblical use of the principle. The Hebrew *lex talionis* was, at least in some respects, more humane than the *lex talionis* in other ancient Near Eastern law codes.[121] The law governed willful injuries to the person, not to property or possessions. Unlike Mesopotamian codes, where the law was ap-

---

120. According to D. J. Weaver, "Widespread literary evidence — from the Code of Hammurabi and the Middle Assyrian Laws to Greek, Roman, and Jewish formulations, both scriptural and rabbinic — points to the virtual universality of such a 'law of retaliation' in the ancient world." See "Transforming Nonresistance: From *Lex Talionis* to 'Do Not Resist the Evil One,'" in *The Love of Enemy and Nonretaliation in the New Testament*, ed. W. M. Swartley (Louisville, Ky.: Westminster John Knox, 1992), 37.

121. For parallels, see *Ancient Near Eastern Texts Relating to the Old Testament*, ed. J. B. Pritchard (Princeton: Princeton University Press, 1955), 175. See also J. Westbrook, "Crimes and Punishments," *ABD*, 5:552, 554-55; and Wenham, "Law and the Legal System in the Old Testament," 38-39, 41. This is not to say that penalties were always milder in Israel than they were elsewhere. For example, in Babylon the punishment for a son assaulting his father was amputation of his hand; in Israel it was death (Exod. 20:12; 21:15, 17). Again, it was common in other legal systems to allow compensation in the case of homicide; Hebrew law expressly excludes this arrangement (Num. 35:31-34).

plied differently according to one's place in the class system, the biblical law applied equally to persons of all classes: there was one standard for all, rich and poor, native and stranger.[122] The biblical law also restricted the talion to the offender alone. Vicarious or collective punishment was not permitted (Deut. 24:16; 2 Kings 14:6; Ezek. 18:1-32), when dealing with interpersonal offending.[123]

It is crucial to understand that, contrary to popular perception, the *lex talionis* was never intended to sanction revenge. Revenge is expressly forbidden in biblical law (Lev. 19:18; Deut. 32:35; cf. Prov. 20:22; 24:29). Instead, the *lex* served the twofold purpose of limiting the destructive effects of retribution on the one hand, especially in blood feuds between clans and families, and providing an equitable basis for making restitution or reparation in personal injury cases on the other. Far from encouraging revenge, the *lex* limited retaliation to the appropriate measure of the offense, so that excessive reprisal was ruled out. The "eye for an eye" was a law of proportion: *only* an eye for an eye *and no more*. But its role in restitution was perhaps even more important. Although the formulation of the principle implies physical mutilation was to be exacted for corresponding harm caused, there are many reasons to doubt that the Hebrew *lex* was ever understood or applied literally as a judicial penalty, except in the case of certain capital offenses. Several things point in this direction:

(1) To begin with, there are too many cases where the infliction of an exactly equivalent penalty upon the wrongdoer could not have been achieved by the literal application of the *lex*. For example, if a person blind in one eye had his other eye destroyed, requiring a single eye from the offender would not be a precise equivalent, since only one party would end up totally blind. Again, in injuries that only partially incapacitated the organ of another, it would be extremely difficult to inflict a literal, in-kind injury. Taken as a hard-and-fast rule, then, the *lex talionis* provides only a rough-and-ready method of dispensing justice, and could, if applied legalistically, result in grave injustice. This must have been apparent to Hebrew jurists from the earliest of times, as it certainly was to the later rabbis. (See below.)

122. On the social radicalism of biblical law in this respect, see M. C. Lind, "Law in the Old Testament," in *The Bible and Law*, ed. W. M. Swartley (Elkhart, Ind.: Institute of Mennonite Studies, 1982), 9-41.

123. Contrast the situation of offenses against cultic or taboo law — see Josh. 7:24-28; Judg. 21:10-11; 1 Sam. 22:19; 2 Sam. 21; 2 Kings 9:26; cf. Exod. 20:5.

(2) It is significant that nothing is said about how the law was to be implemented, although judges are mentioned in Exodus 21:22. Unlike Assyrian law, which provided for expert officials to be attached to the court to supervise the mutilation of offenders, biblical law does not provide for a court executioner or mutilator, which makes it doubtful that the literal infliction of talion was ever seriously contemplated as a judicial penalty. Mutilation is recorded in the Old Testament, but the examples of its practice are without the direct sanction of covenant law (Judg. 1:6-7; 2 Sam. 4:12; Dan. 2:5; 2 Macc. 7:1-40; but cf. Deut. 25:12).[124] It is also important to allow for the hypothetical or rhetorical nature of the language used in specifying penalties in biblical law. James Barr points out that ancient Near Eastern and biblical law codes have a certain theoretical quality to them, with horrendous punishments being prescribed that were not necessarily carried out literally in the manner suggested.[125]

(3) The very fact that in certain cases, such as murder or idolatry, the law expressly forbade the commuting of the penalty ("Show them no pity," Deut. 13:8; 19:13, 21; 25:12; Num. 35:31-34) implies that in other cases, including accidental homicide, the injury could be compensated for by ransom or monetary payment (Exod. 21:30; Num. 35:31, 32). In other words, the *lex talionis* presupposes that in crimes involving no blood guilt, compensatory payments were widely practiced, and it seeks to set limits on these payments as well as to forbid application of the practice to homicide (although even this was not enforced in a rigid matter – e.g., Gen. 4:11-15; 2 Sam. 12:13; 14:11). This explains Martin Buber's translation of the formula as "an eye for the value of an eye, a tooth for the value of a tooth,"[126] and Pinchas Lapide's version, "eye-compensation for eye, tooth-compensation for tooth."[127]

(4) That "an eye for an eye" was not understood woodenly is indi-

124. M. Greenberg, "Crimes and Punishments," *IDB*, 1:742. It is unlikely that the law in Deuteronomy 25:12 permitting mutilation was ever enforced. Cf. J. A. Hoyles, *Punishment in the Bible* (London: Epworth, 1986), 23-24.

125. Barr, "Ancient Biblical Laws and Modern Human Rights," in *Justice and the Holy: Essays in Honour of Walter Harrelson*, ed. D. A. Knight and P. J. Peters (Atlanta: Scholars Press, 1989), 28-29.

126. Cited in H. Bianchi, "The Biblical Vision of Justice," *NPCJ* 2 (1984): 3.

127. Lapide, *The Sermon on the Mount: Utopia or Program for Action?* (Maryknoll, N.Y.: Orbis, 1986), 128-30.

cated by the context in which the earliest citation of the principle occurs (Exod. 21:18-25). The talion is linked directly with what would be an exceedingly rare case: a miscarriage caused by brawling men hurting a pregnant woman (v. 22). But the penalty laid down is a monetary fine levied by the woman's husband; there is no suggestion that the wife of the guilty party should have her next pregnancy forcibly terminated, as "like for like" might justify. The fact that the editor of Exodus quotes the whole formula, as was current in oral tradition, even though none of the items listed (eye, tooth, hand, foot, burn, stripe, or even life) are applicable to the situation envisaged, suggests that it is employed not as a technical legal ruling but because of its rhetorical impact on the hearer in underlining the seriousness of the matter. Other cases mentioned in the immediate context also treat the law of talion creatively. The penalty for temporarily incapacitating someone in a fight is compensation and coverage of his medical costs, not blow for blow, stripe for stripe (vv. 18-19). The penalty for knocking out the eye or tooth of a slave is manumission of the slave, not presentation with the master's eye or tooth in return (vv. 26-27). All these examples suggest that talion is understood in the sense of moral vindication, not of literal physical retribution.[128]

(5) The context in which the *lex talionis* is cited in Deuteronomy 19:15-21 and Leviticus 24:17-21 also points in this direction. In Deuteronomy 19, the *lex* is used to explain why the penalty for perjury should be the same as the penalty the accused would have suffered if convicted. Why? Because lying about someone else's involvement in a crime is *morally*, not literally, equivalent to committing the crime oneself. In Leviticus 24, the discussion of talion (vv. 17-21) is located between two indications that the sin of blasphemy warrants the death penalty (vv. 16, 23). The writer's intention in appealing to the *lex talionis* is to show that blasphemy is morally equivalent to murder and therefore deserves the same punishment. (A strict application of "like for like" would imply that blasphemy should incur a punishment of shame and dishonor, since God's life has not been diminished by the blasphemer's words.) In both passages, then, the law of talion is applied not as a law of equivalent retribution but as a way of underlining the seriousness of certain offenses and of expressing the principle of moral equivalency.

128. E. J. Fisher, "Explorations and Responses: *LEX TALIONIS* in the Bible and Rabbinic Tradition," *JES* 19, no. 3 (1982): 585.

(6) Closer to the New Testament period, Jewish opinion on the role of talion was somewhat mixed. Some writers, like Philo of Alexandria, perhaps under pagan influence, thought that justice demanded literal talion.[129] Josephus, writing for a Roman audience, reflected the Roman practice of giving victims the choice between receiving monetary compensation from the offender or demanding his literal mutilation.[130] Some Sadducees and at least one Talmudic authority (R. Eliezer) also seem to have favored actual retaliation, perhaps as a consequence of hermeneutical literalism. But prevailing Jewish legal opinion recognized the problems associated with a rigid and exact application of the law of retaliation, and prescribed strict tests of intentionality and specified monetary substitutes for "eye," "tooth" and so on.[131] The Mishnah specifies four kinds of monetary loss incurred by injury which the offender is responsible to recompense.[132] Interestingly, in the later Babylonian Talmud (5th-6th century C.E.), arguments are mounted against the justice of literal talion. One person's eye will inevitably be larger, smaller, sharper, or weaker than another's. What if a blind person takes another's eye, or a cripple injures another's leg? Moreover, removal of any organ or limb involves loss of blood and hence risks the life of the offender, with the result that "it could sometimes happen that eye and life would be taken for eye." A convoluted argument is constructed to the effect that "an eye for an eye" really means monetary compensation, just as it does in the case of striking an animal (Lev. 24:18, 21). It is also argued that the imposition of the death penalty for killing a person in Leviticus 24:17 really means pecuniary compensation.[133] Jacob Milgrom observes of this discussion that "the rabbis' logic is better than their exegesis." Their "exegetical convolutions" express their unease at enforcing "retributive equality" as the basis of justice, despite the apparently plain meaning of the scriptural text.[134]

It appears, therefore, that from the outset the *lex talionis* was designed to express, with maximum memorability, the principle of eq-

129. Philo, *Special Laws*, III:181-82.
130. Josephus, *Antiquities*, IV:280.
131. For references, see *Str-B*, 1:337-41.
132. *m. B. Qam.* 8:1.
133. *b. B. Qam.* 83b-84a.
134. See Milgrom, "Lex Talionis and the Rabbis," *BR* 12, no. 2 (1996): 16, 48.

uity.[135] It was understood to require not physical punishments that replicated the crime in exact detail but penalties that "marked" the seriousness of the offence and that bore both moral equivalency and material proportionality to it. It is likely that from the earliest times, these penalties mainly took the form of monetary compensation. The actual formula, with its implications of bodily amputation, was retained for its rhetorical power to instill in people an appreciation of the evil being proscribed. But in practice it was a canon of proportionate restitution, not imitative retribution. The one exception was in cases of premeditated murder, where "life for life" retained its literal meaning. David Daube suggests that the fact that Jesus omits "life for life" when quoting the biblical maxim indicates that, both in the law and in the minds of ordinary people, the two parts of the *lex* had drifted apart and become separate. "An eye for an eye" was assigned to private law and understood in terms of financial compensation. "Life for life" retained its literal meaning and was taken to mandate capital punishment, at least in principle.[136]

Jesus and the Lex Talionis

We have seen that, as an articulation of the principle of proportionate penalties and equitable restitution, the *lex talionis* played an important and legitimate role in the administration of biblical and Jewish justice. Why then is Jesus' teaching set in stark antithesis to it in Matthew 5:38-42?[137]

> You have heard that it was said, "An eye for an eye and a tooth for a tooth." But I say to you, Do not resist an evildoer. But if anyone strikes you on the right cheek, turn the other also; and if anyone wants to sue you and take your coat, give your cloak as well; and if anyone forces

135. D. A. Kidner, "Retribution and Punishment in the Old Testament in Light of the New Testament," *SBET* 1 (1983): 5.

136. Daube, *The New Testament and Rabbinic Judaism* (London: The Atholone Press, 1956), 257-58.

137. The antithetical format of Matthew 5 is usually ascribed to Matthean redaction. For our purposes what is significant is that the extant, canonical version of the Jesus tradition perceives and depicts an antithetical contrast between Jesus' teaching on nonresistance and the biblical *lex talionis*.

you to go one mile, go also the second mile. Give to everyone who begs from you, and do not refuse anyone who wants to borrow from you. (Matt. 5:38-42; cf. Luke 6:27-45)

It is unlikely that Jesus (or Matthew) would have been troubled by the restitutive implications of the *lex talionis* (cf. Matt. 7:12; Luke 6:31, 38). Nor is it sufficient to think that Jesus was simply repudiating a prevailing literalism in the interpretation and application of the *lex* in contemporary Jewish legal practice (though it is possible that such a literalism existed in some circles, as it does today). It is more probable that Jesus was inviting his hearers to learn to respond to wrongdoing in ways that transcended the principle of equivalence expressed in the *lex,* however acceptable it may be by human standards of fairness, and to emulate the gratuitous goodness of divine justice. Even when it is not taken literally, the *lex* may still be used to justify legal, even violent, retaliation, albeit circumscribed or limited by the principle of proportion. But for Jesus equivalent recompense is not the heart of justice or the supreme principle of morality. There is something more fundamental to achieving true justice than justifiable revenge. The impulse to strike back may seem basic to human nature, and violence may appear inescapable and pervasive. But, as Gregory Jones observes, humankind's origin in the creative love of God and its destiny of participation in the kingdom of God mean that peace, not vengeance or violence, is the ontological ground of human existence, a view Jesus doubtlessly shared (Matt 5:9, 43-48).[138] Accordingly, those captured now by the impinging Kingdom of God must do more than merely limit the extent of retaliation or channel violence; they must practice a peacemaking justice that points beyond the talion to the *telos* of the kingdom.

Interpreters are sharply divided over whether Jesus here abrogates the biblical commandment or merely opposes the intrusion of a judicial principle into the realm of interpersonal I-Thou relationships, relegating it to its proper forensic setting. The latter proposal is problematic, for as a judicial principle the *lex* applied precisely to the realm of interpersonal injury, and it is its operation in this domain that Jesus challenges. If the choice, then, is between abrogation or relegation, the evidence favors abrogation. Dorothy Jean Weaver speaks of Jesus "disal-

---

138. Cf. Jones, *Embodying Forgiveness,* 101-34.

lowing" and "invalidating" the ancient principle of punishment in kind.[139] Richard Hays says that in this antithesis "Jesus actually overrules the Torah,"[140] while Gordon Zerbe considers it to be "the only antithesis which rejects the law," since in it "Jesus seems to overthrow the provision of the law for legal vindication."[141] Yet abrogation is probably not the best word to describe what transpires here. Jesus is not abolishing the Old Testament commandment (cf. Matt. 5:17-18) so much as setting it aside as a guiding norm or rule of thumb for the conduct of his followers. He renders it redundant rather than repudiates it in principle (though a principle not practiced soon loses its persuasive power). When Jesus' saying is understood this way, Hays' comment is appropriate: "The law's concern for maintaining stability and justice is supplanted by Jesus' concern to encourage non-violent, long-suffering generosity on the part of those who are wronged. This extraordinary change of emphasis constitutes a paradigm shift that effectually undermines the Torah's teaching about just punishment for offenders."[142]

Both the established function of the *lex talionis* as a judicial principle and the concrete illustrations or "focal instances"[143] that immediately follow its citation in Matthew 5:38 indicate that the focus of Jesus' commentary is principally on the practice of taking legal action against opponents (cf. Deut. 19:15-21). In this context, the injunction "Do not resist an evildoer" (v. 39a) is not advocating a general stance of passivity toward all evil but is, in the first instance, forbidding the employment of coercive judicial power against an opponent; as Robert Guelich proposes, "The antithesis specifically commands one to forego the legal right to seek judicial redress against an offending party."[144] This does not mean that all the sayings grouped around the fifth antithesis (Matt. 5:38-42) relate solely to formal judicial situations. They deal

---

139. Weaver, "Transforming Nonresistance," 54; cf. R. A. Guelich, *The Sermon on the Mount* (Waco, Tex.: Word, 1982), 224.

140. Hays, *The Moral Vision of the New Testament*, 325.

141. Zerbe, *Non-Retaliation in Early Jewish and New Testament Texts: Ethical Themes in Social Contexts* (Sheffield: Sheffield Academic Press, 1993), 205 (and n. 119).

142. Hays, *The Moral Vision of the New Testament*, 325.

143. R. C. Tannehill, "The 'Focal Instance' as a Form of New Testament Speech: A Study in Matthew 5:39b-42," *JR* 50 (1970), 372-85.

144. Guelich, *The Sermon on the Mount*, 25; cf. 219-20. Contrast this with Zerbe, *Non-Retaliation in Early Jewish and New Testament Texts*, 205.

more generally with conflict situations where the wronged party could appeal to his or her "rights" under the law to antagonize his or her opponents. The four sayings, like those that follow with the sixth antithesis (Matt. 5:43-48), really exemplify nonviolent love toward one's enemies in situations where the law might sanction a more hostile response.

One such situation is on an occasion of physical attack: "if anyone strikes you on the right cheek, turn the other also" (v. 39b; cf. Luke 6:29). Many exegetes think that reference to the "right cheek" signals a backhanded slap rather than a closed-fist punch (which a right-handed person would normally land on the left jaw of the victim), so that the offense envisaged is one of calculated insult rather than common assault. Daube explains that in both rabbinic argument and Roman law, smiting another's cheek was regarded as an unqualified insult, paradigmatic of all legal insult. For the rabbis, insult was such a terrible sin because it was aimed at the victim's dignity as one made in God's image. Jesus' lengthy discussion of the legal — and eternal — implications of deliberately insulting one's fellows (5:21-26) suggests that he shared this view.[145] Other exegetes, however, think a full-blown physical assault is envisaged.[146] Whichever the case, striking someone in this way was subject to prosecution under the biblical and oral law of damages.[147] Jesus exhorts his hearers not to avail themselves of this provision, but rather to absorb such an attack and not to seek legal vindication.

A second occasion for such a response is when one is being "taken to the cleaner's" by a creditor: "and if anyone wants to sue you and take your coat [*chitōn*, or undergarment], give your cloak [*himation*, or outer garment] as well" (v. 40). According to biblical law, a borrower's cloak was his one legally inalienable asset; it could not be held as a pledge by a creditor for more than one day (Exod. 22:25-26; Deut. 24:10-13; cf. Amos 2:8). Jesus exhorts his hearers not to rely on this legal protection, but rather to take the initiative in turning over their cloaks freely to the lender, possibly as a means of facilitating reconciliation (cf. 5:25-26) or perhaps as a symbolic protest at the injustice being perpetrated. (Luke's

---

145. Daube, *Rabbinic Judaism*, 257, 259-65. See also Zerbe, *Non-Retaliation in Early Jewish and New Testament Texts*, 180-84.

146. Hays, *The Moral Vision of the New Testament*, 325-26.

147. Exod. 21:12–22:17. Cf. *m. B. Qam.* 8.6; Matt. 5:21-26.

version of the saying [6:29] reverses the sequence of surrendering garments and seems to envisage a situation of forcible theft rather than legal prosecution.)

A third occasion for laying aside one's rights occurs when a member of the occupying army exercises his privilege, under Roman custom, of requiring a member of the subject population to render forced labor (*angareuein;* cf. Mark 15:21): "and if anyone forces you to go one mile, go also the second mile" (v. 41). If "one mile" designates the limit of one's legal obligation to conform with this practice, Jesus is again urging rejection of legal protection or customary rights in favor of offering generous service to one's enemy. The fourth example captures this same spirit with respect to giving to those in need, which is the very opposite of retaliation: "Give to everyone who begs from you, and do not refuse anyone who wants to borrow from you" (v. 42). This recapitulates the law in Deuteronomy 15:7-11 on giving and lending to the poor, and perhaps also alludes to laws on lending to the poor without interest (Exod. 22:25-27; Lev. 25:35-38; Deut. 23:19-20). It is these laws that counsel open-handed generosity toward the disadvantaged, and not the law of limited retaliation, that best evoke the nature of divine justice.

Each of these examples underlines the same essential point: when injured by others, Jesus' followers are not to retaliate or sue for reparation or resist all but minimal cooperation; instead, they are to practice reconciling, self-giving love that meets their opponents more than halfway. If enforced legalistically and applied across the board, such teaching would lead to the collapse of the legal system. To avoid this implication, interpreters have spared no effort to bring the sayings on nonretaliation within the bounds of common sense and social realism. But Jesus' intention was not to replace one legal prescription with another, and he does not frame his call to nonretaliatory forgiving love in legal idiom.[148] Instead, he advocates a different starting point in human relationships, one made possible by his conquest of evil. Rather than perceiving human relationships as controlled by legal rights and tit-for-tat equivalence, which in turn presupposes that sinful self-centeredness is the ruling principle, Jesus calls for relationships in

148. See A. E. Harvey, *Strenuous Commands: The Ethic of Jesus* (London: SCM, 1990), 76-91.

which sin and self are no longer the controlling factors. As Guelich explains, "Justice for justice's sake is no longer viewed as the basis of one's behaviour but the restored relationships between individuals in which the other's interests are foremost."[149]

Jesus and Love of Enemies

The same concern for the welfare of others underlies Jesus' call to love of enemies, which constitutes the obverse of the *lex talionis* (vv. 43-48). There has long been debate over the original social setting of the saying, on who is meant by "enemies," and on what practical implications flow from a commitment to love them.[150] Richard Horsely, for example, insists that the saying applies not to national enemies like the Romans but only to persecutors within the village community and that it does not proclaim "some noble principle of non-violence."[151] In a similar vein, Aaron Milavec argues that the commands to turn the other cheek and to love the enemy are instructions to new recruits to the Jesus movement on how to deal with fierce opposition from members of their own families and synagogues.[152] Walter Wink and Richard Hays, on the other hand, insist that the Roman occupiers cannot be excluded from the referent of the sayings.[153] Gerd Theissen shows how the sayings could have different applications at different times. Jesus formulated them at a time dominated by opposition to Roman rule; his wandering disciples applied them to situations of persecution and rejection by their compatriots; Matthew orients them to the aftermath of the Jewish revolt; Luke applies them to local situations of conflict over money (cf. Luke 6:30, 34, 35, 38). Therefore, the setting of the sayings

149. Guelich, *The Sermon on the Mount*, 252; cf. 224.

150. See W. Klassen, "'Love Your Enemies': Some Reflections on the Current Status of Research," in *The Love of Enemy and Nonretaliation in the New Testament*, 1-31.

151. Horsely, "Ethics and Exegesis: 'Love Your Enemies' and the Doctrine of Nonviolence," in *The Love of Enemy and Nonretaliation in the New Testament*, 72-101, 126-32 (quote from 93). So also Zerbe, *Non-Retaliation in Early Jewish and New Testament Texts*, 193-94; and Herzog, *Jesus, Justice, and the Reign of God*, 213-16.

152. Milavec, "The Social Setting of 'Turning the Other Cheek' and 'Loving One's Enemies' in Light of the *Didache*," *BTB* 25, no. 3 (1995): 131-43.

153. Wink, "Neither Passivity nor Violence: Jesus' Third Way (Matt 5:38-42 par)," *The Love of Enemy and Nonretaliation in the New Testament*, 102-25, 133-36; Hays, *The Moral Vision of the New Testament*, 319-29.

cannot be restricted to a single context. For Theissen, "Economic, political and religious enemies are all meant."[154] On a similar note, Dorothy Jean Weaver shows how Matthew's redactional placement of the love-of-enemy saying serves to include within its scope all those — both fellow Jew and foreign Gentile — who revile, persecute, abuse, and tell lies about the disciples (5:1, 44), as well as the adversary, the council, the judge, and the court assistant (5:22, 25), collectively designated "the evil one."[155]

Of more relevance to us than the scope of the sayings is the underlying rationale for this novel way of treating adversaries. Jesus was not unique in counseling nonretaliation as such. Zerbe demonstrates how "the non-retaliatory ethics in the New Testament stand solidly in the tradition of the non-retaliatory ethics in early Judaism."[156] It is still the case, however, that Jesus' formulation of the demand is "uniquely clear and emphatic,"[157] in that he explicitly calls for "love" and "blessing" of opponents.[158] But why does Jesus call for such aggressive goodwill toward one's abusers? Several motives are discernible in Matthew's text. One is a desire for reciprocity, expressed most crisply in the Golden Rule: "In everything do to others as you would have them do to you; for this is the law and the prophets" (7:12; cf. Luke 6:30). This may entail

154. Theissen, "Nonviolence and Love of Our Enemies (Matthew 5:38-48; Luke 6:27-38)," in Theissen, *Social Reality and the Early Christians: Theology, Ethics, and the World of the New Testament* (Edinburgh: T. & T. Clark, 1992), 115-56 (quote from 154). For a traditio-historical analysis, see also Zerbe, *Non-Retaliation in Early Jewish and New Testament Texts,* 176-210.

155. Weaver, "Transforming Nonresistance," 49.

156. Zerbe, *Non-Retaliation in Early Jewish and New Testament Texts,* 294.

157. Theissen, "Nonviolence and Love of Our Enemies," 197.

158. Zerbe concedes the distinctiveness of Jesus' language of loving enemies (e.g., 239; cf. 171-72) but insists that similar sentiments are found in Judaism (*Non-Retaliation in Early Jewish and New Testament Texts,* 194). Other scholars believe the uniqueness of Jesus' call to enemy-loving at this point is more substantial. According to J. Charlesworth, "This aspect of Jesus' thought is the most distinctive or unique aspect of his ethical teachings. As far as we know, no other Jew, or Jewish group, drew that extreme inference from the relevant ethical passages in the Old Testament" (*Jesus within Judaism* [New York: Doubleday, 1988], 38). So also Harvey, *Strenuous Commands,* 99. Lapide accepts that "the body of Jewish teaching knows no explicit demand of love of one's enemy. To be precise, 'love your enemy' is an innovation introduced by Jesus" (*The Sermon on the Mount,* 91). For similar Jewish views, see D. A. Hagner, *The Jewish Reclamation of Jesus* (Grand Rapids: Zondervan, 1984), 144-50.

some enlightened self-interest, such as when Jesus encourages debtors to reach out-of-court settlements in order to avoid legal punishment (5:25-26; cf. Luke 12:57-59), or when he promises eschatological reward to those who bless their persecutors (5:46; cf. Luke 6:36-38). Another motive for loving enemies is to differentiate the righteousness of the new eschatological community from the Torah righteousness of the mainstream Jewish community, which could be construed, wrongly, as sanctioning hatred of enemies (5:38, 43),[159] as well as from the normal patterns of reciprocal love and friendship found among Gentiles and tax collectors (5:46-47). But the profoundest motivation is Jesus' desire for his hearers to emulate God's justice:

> But I say to you, Love your enemies and pray for those who persecute you, so that you may be children of your Father in heaven; for he makes his sun rise on the evil and on the good, and sends rain on the righteous and on the unrighteous. . . . Be perfect, therefore, as your heavenly Father is perfect. (Matt. 5:44-45, 48).

The imitation of God here is a matter not merely of copying this or that aspect of divine behavior but of measuring one's whole way of life against the character or "perfection" of God (cf. Lev. 19:1-2; Deut. 18:13). By placing the demand for perfection at the conclusion and climax of the six antitheses in chapter 5, Matthew indicates that it explicates each one of the preceding antitheses. Furthermore, the clear upward progression within the antitheses — from surmounting inward aggression (5:21-26) to the practice of enemy love (5:43-48) — identifies love of enemies as the heart of the imitation of God and God's royal justice.

---

159. It is possible that this saying alludes to Psalm 139:21-22, but more probably it echoes a popular maxim of folk wisdom or a conventional interpretation that limited the Torah's call to neighbor love (Lev. 19:18) to members of one's own community. Such an attitude is found at Qumran. "Love all that he has elected. . . . Hate . . . all that he has cast aside" (1QS 1:9-11); "Love all the sons of light . . . and hate all the sons of darkness" (1QS 10:17-20). In *The Sermon on the Mount* (85-95), Lapide denies that Matthew 5:43 stems from Jesus, for the "strange imperative, 'hate your enemy,' turns the ethos of the entire Bible into a lie" (85). It is Matthew who is the "the author of this slander" (86). But Jewish resistance toward integration with Gentiles was perceived by some outsiders as hatred. Tacitus, for example, comments that they show "their stubborn loyalty and ready benevolence towards brother Jews, but the rest of the world they confront with the hatred reserved for enemies" (*Histories* 5.4, 5).

Now since it is of the nature of God's justice, as we have seen, to raise up the downtrodden and empower the weak, the renunciation of violence and the eschewing of retaliation cannot be — and must never become — a posture of supine passivity in the face of evil. On the contrary, nonviolent love is a participation in divine sovereignty, a manifestation of power that even the politically powerless and outwardly inferior can display toward their oppressors. Both Pinchas Lapide and Walter Wink suggest that, far from counseling passivity in the face of evil, Jesus is actually advocating nonviolent forms of resistance that employ shock tactics to expose the injustice of oppression.[160] For Wink, Jesus teaches a "third way" between violence and passivity that seeks to transform the relationship of oppression that dehumanizes both the aggressor and the victim, and in so doing sets forth "a way of fighting evil with all one's power without being transformed into the very evil we fight. It is a way of not becoming what we hate."[161] This is the secret and the genius of true justice.

Let it be said again that in none of these sayings does Jesus set out to amend or rewrite Pentateuchal law, nor had he the institutional authority to do so. His teaching was primarily for his own disciples and was not meant to be enforced legislatively in a mixed society. Nonetheless, the way in which Jesus places relationships and the restoration of relationships above the dictates of strict legal justice, and his recognition that evil can never be overcome by more evil but can be defeated only by reversing the violent payback mechanism of evil, do have considerable relevance for the public legal system. At the very least they are a reminder that genuine justice, the justice that makes things better, is never satisfied merely by following the rules, however equitable they are, or by asserting one's legal rights, however fair that may be. It is satisfied only when relationships are restored and the destructive power of evil is defeated, and this requires a freely chosen relinquishment of the logic of — and legal right to — an eye for an eye and a tooth for a tooth.

---

160. Lapide, *The Sermon on the Mount;* Wink, "Neither Passivity nor Violence," 104-12; Wink, *Violence and Non-Violence in South Africa: Jesus' Third Way* (Philadelphia/Santa Cruz: New Society Publishers, 1987), passim.

161. Wink, "Neither Passivity nor Violence," 117; cf. Weaver, "Transforming Nonresistance," 55-58.

Summary

In this chapter I have argued that underlying Paul's interpretation of the Christ-event and the Gospel writers' presentation of the life and teaching of Jesus is an understanding of God's justice as a redemptive power that breaks into situations of oppression or need in order to put right what is wrong and restore relationships to their proper condition. Paul speaks of God's act of eschatological deliverance in the death and resurrection of Christ as a comprehensive work of justice-making that liberates oppressed humanity from the power of sin and death and from the guilt of actual transgression, and brings peace with God and reconciliation between former enemies. Jesus speaks of the inbreaking of divine justice as the coming of God's kingdom, which starts to put right what is wrong on earth, establishes a relationship of new intimacy between God and humanity, and calls into being a new community to live a transformed way of life in the midst of the old order. Distinctive of this life is the call to radical forgiveness of offenders and nonretaliation toward opponents, virtues taught and exemplified by Jesus himself and repeatedly affirmed throughout the New Testament.[162] These virtues are not arbitrary requirements; they flow from the inherent character of divine justice itself. For throughout the biblical witness, as Paul Ramsey explains,

> [God's saving justice] is the source and at the same time the measure of human righteousness. Expressly excluded from the heart and soul of biblical ethics is the notion that we should deal with people only according to their merits, earned or unearned; or that we are simply to treat all men as their manhood intrinsically deserves. Not corrective justice or distributive justice or any other humanitarian standard is the measure, but a *contributory* justice, a helpful, redeeming, caring justice, since the day God began to form the consciences of men and to shape their lives to the measure of God's own righteousness that stooped to conquer wrong.[163]

162. On the similarities between Paul and Jesus on nonretaliation, see D. Wenham, *Paul: Follower of Jesus or Founder of Christianity?* (Grand Rapids: William B. Eerdmans, 1995), 250-71. On nonretaliation in Paul and 1 Peter, see Zerbe, *Non-Retaliation in Early Jewish and New Testament Texts,* 211-90. See also K. L. Yinger, "Romans 12:14-21 and Nonretaliation in Second Temple Judaism: Addressing Persecution within the Community," *CBQ* 60 (1998): 74-96.

163. Ramsey, "The Biblical Norm of Righteousness," 420-21.

A conception of justice that centers on forgiveness and restoration cannot be faulted for minimizing sin. It takes the reality of evil just as seriously as does the form of justice that centers on retribution or vengeance. Indeed, it takes it more seriously, since it recognizes the full extent of the damage sin does to interpersonal relationships, which is in no way repaired by simple retribution. Divine justice may entail punitive sanctions against wrongdoers, as we will see in the next chapter, but it does not rest content with punishment, for it is fully satisfied and fully vindicated only when healing and repair occur.

But is forgiveness always possible? Does not Jesus also speak of the "unforgivable sin" (Mark 3:28-30), while other New Testament writers refer to "mortal sins" or "sins which lead to death" (1 John 5:16-18) and sins for which no repentance is possible (Heb. 6:4-6; 10:26-31)? Do not these texts imply that there are certain offenses which are inherently beyond forgiveness and redemption? Since the time of the early church fathers, there has been a tendency to distinguish between forgivable (or venial) and unforgivable (or mortal) sins and to specify especially grave "crimes," such as murder, apostasy, idolatry, and adultery, as belonging to the latter category. The New Testament itself, however, does not identify a certain class of offenses as beyond forgiveness. The essential character of the unforgivable sin, and of sins that are death-inducing or beyond repentance (even though each category should be kept distinct),[164] lies not in the outward form of the act itself but in the subjective mentality of the offender. The warnings against such offenses suggest that it is possible for recalcitrant offenders to place themselves in a position of such inner resistance to grace that repentance becomes subjectively impossible and God's forgiveness remains unappropriated. "The unforgivable sin," says L. Gregory Jones, "is the refusal to accept the forgiveness God always offers. It is unforgivable because there is no way for us to accept forgiveness if we refuse to acknowledge our own need of forgiveness."[165] It is not that there are certain kinds of *offenses* that do not deserve forgiveness. (Forgiveness is never deserved!) Rather, there are certain kinds of *offenders* who run the risk of so stubbornly repudiating forgiving grace that they make restoration of relationship

164. See T. Ward, "Sin 'Not unto Death' and Sin 'unto Death' in 1 John 5:16," *Churchman* 109, no. 3 (1995): 226-37.

165. Jones, *Embodying Forgiveness,* 297.

with God effectively impossible, since relational renewal always requires both parties to be willing. They condemn themselves to unforgiveness; they remain wedded to sin, which brings alienation and death.

It is worth emphasizing that the question of unforgivable sin relates principally to the individual's relationship with God. There is no justification for designating certain interpersonal crimes, such as adultery or murder, as inherently beyond human forgiveness (cf. Luke 23:34; Acts 7:60). If the texts on unforgivable and mortal sins have any relevance to interpersonal relationships, it is as sober warnings to offenders of the need to take responsibility for their offenses and not to harden themselves against repentance and change. For the rest, Jesus' instruction stands: "Forgive, and you will be forgiven" (Luke 6:37; cf. Matt. 6:14-15; Mark 11:25). Forgiveness is not an optional response to wrongdoing; it is an obligation placed upon all who celebrate the saving justice of God made manifest in the life, death, and resurrection of Jesus Christ.

CHAPTER 3

PUNISHMENT THAT FITS

The Purpose and Ethics of Punishment

S o far we have seen that divine justice, as understood by Paul and embodied by Jesus in the Gospel narratives, is primarily a redemptive rather than a punitive justice. It is God acting in mercy to deliver those powerless to save themselves, thus demonstrating faithfulness to covenant commitments and upholding the honor and integrity of God's name. But what about punishment? If Christian faith compels us toward a notion of justice as something that redeems, reconciles, and restores, what role does punishment have in the operation of such justice? Punishment may be defined as the deliberate infliction of an unpleasant or painful experience on a person, such as the deprivation of something greatly valued, like freedom or money or even life itself, as the response to a perceived offense and corresponding in some way to the action that evoked it.[1] "Legal punishment," Karen Kissane suggests, "is the imposition of calmness and intellect on what, often, is an experience of pain or injury almost primal in intensity."[2] In light of what we have said so far about divine justice, the question arises as to whether the infliction of injury upon wrongdoers is to be understood as an alien or an inalienable dimension of the administration of justice, whether divine or human.

1. For expanded definitions of punishment, see W. Moberly, *The Ethics of Punishment* (London: Faber & Faber, 1968), 35-36; B. A. Hudson, *Understanding Justice: An Introduction to Ideas, Perspectives, and Controversies in Modern Penal Theory* (Buckingham: Open University Press, 1996), 1-3; and N. Christie, "Crime, Pain, and Death," *NPCJ* 1 (1984): 1-4.
2. Kissane, "Punish and Be Damned," *Time Magazine,* 28 June 1993, 28.

In the next chapter I will explore New Testament teaching on the place of punishment in human affairs and in the divine-human relationship. In this chapter I provide a realistic context for that investigation by reviewing the perennial debate in criminology over the grounds on which it is justifiable to punish wrongdoers and the appropriate ends to which punishment should be directed. Walter Moberly frames the issue this way: "Should a criminal be regarded by society chiefly as a nuisance to be abated, an enemy to be crushed, a debtor to be made to pay, a patient to be treated, or a refractory child to be disciplined? Or should he be regarded as none of these things, but simply as an example through which it can be demonstrated to other men that anti-social conduct does not pay?"[3]

The Debate over Criminal Punishment

There has been a long-standing debate among legal and social philosophers over both the *purpose* of punishment — Why do we punish? What are our goals in administering punishment? — and its *moral justification:* What entitles us to punish? How much should we punish? If it is wrong to inflict pain, and two wrongs do not make a right, what justifies adding the pain of punishment to the pain already caused by the offense? In this debate, which can be traced back to Greek antiquity, two main approaches have been taken to establish the legitimacy of punishment. On the one side, there are those who justify punishment by appealing to its inherent justness. Crime upsets the moral or social order, and punishment is required to restore the balance. Where an offense has been committed, the offender *deserves* punishment. No further justification is needed; it is all but obligatory to deliver such punishment. On the other side, there are those who appeal to utilitarian considerations to defend punishment. Punishing wrongdoers is justifiable because, in terms of curbing antisocial behavior, it yields better results than not punishing them. Because it causes suffering, punishment is not a good thing in itself. But if the suffering it prevents is even greater, or if it serves to bring about a greater good, then the desirable consequences that punishment produces outweigh the harm it causes the offenders.

3. Moberly, *The Ethics of Punishment,* 30.

The first approach legitimates punishment by reference to the past, to the crime already committed; the second approach legitimates punishment by reference to the future, to the prevention or reduction of crimes that have not yet been committed.

Several different ways of explaining punishment have emerged from this discussion. From the utilitarian side have come explanations that stress the value of punishment in rehabilitating offenders and others that give primacy to deterrence. From the just-deserts side have issued several variations on retributivism as a penal philosophy. Each of these major rationales for punishment has held sway at certain periods in Western legal thinking, with legal codes and penal administration being altered to reflect the prevailing fashion in penal thought, and each continues to have an influence on current penological practice. Each rationale has both strengths and weaknesses, and each, as we will see, can claim some biblical warrant, which is not surprising, given the bewildering diversity of biblical teaching on the theme of punishment.

The Rehabilitation Theory

One way of justifying punishment is to appeal to its capacity for generating change in the recipient. Punishment is acceptable as a way of reforming the offender, as the means of achieving his or her return to the law-abiding community and its values. It has a corrective goal; it might even be regarded as a form of "treatment" for antisocial tendencies, a system of social hygiene that seeks to "cure" the propensity to offend.

That an important — though subordinate — aim of punishment is the reform of the offender was a relatively novel idea when it was mooted by the eighteenth-century philosopher Jeremy Bentham (1748-1832).[4] The existing system of punishment was largely arbitrary and often brutal. There was little proportionate gradation of penalties. The sanctions imposed upon offenders depended largely on the whim of

4. For utilitarians like Bentham, reformation is only a secondary goal of punishment. The primary purpose is deterrence. The magistrate must consider the well-being of the many before that of the one. The effect of the punishment upon the offender is much less significant than its effect upon the community at large. The reformative theory has an older lineage than this, however; Plato saw reform as a goal of punishment (*Laws*, 862, 934; *Republic*, 380B, 591B).

the magistrate or prince, and there was a much stronger emphasis on hurting the body — by torture, mutilation, the stocks, or the gallows — than on reforming the mind or changing the character of the offender. But as the idea of rehabilitation took hold, it contributed considerably to mitigating the severity of criminal law. In the space of forty years, the number of capital offenses in England fell from several hundred to just four. The spectacle of public executions, preceded or accompanied by torture and followed by the dismemberment or incineration of the body, had largely disappeared by the beginning of the nineteenth century. The function of imprisonment also changed from being primarily a means of holding people awaiting trial or of inducing compliance with payment orders to being a mode of punishment in its own right, as a more humane alternative to death or exile. "The age of sobriety in punishment had begun," Foucault observes, even if the intention was "not to punish less but to punish better" — better because now the mind or soul of the criminal was being targeted, not just the body, and it was being done so away from the public gaze, behind prison walls.[5] Prisons were built throughout Western Europe and America with the intention not only of incarcerating but also of reforming prisoners through a combination of work, discipline, and penance (the latter encouraged by individual cells where offenders had space for solitary reflection). At first, reform strategies were unsophisticated and undifferentiated; all prisoners were subject to the same regime. But as the human sciences developed, offenders were divided into categories and rehabilitation programs adjusted to meet their specific needs. In twentieth-century penal theory and practice, there was unprecedented growth of concern for the reformation of criminals and their reintegration into society.

The obvious strength of the rehabilitative approach is the way it recognizes that an offender does not stop being a member of the community while under correction. The offender's interests are part of society's interests, and it is in everyone's interest that the lawbreaker is rid of the behavior that injures the community to which he or she belongs.

---

5. Foucault, *Discipline and Punish: The Birth of the Prison* (New York: Vintage Books, 1979), quotes from 14, 82. See also Hudson, *Understanding Justice*, 26-31; and D. Cayley, *The Expanding Prison: The Crisis in Crime and Punishment and the Search for Alternatives* (Toronto: Anansi Press, 1998), 89-164.

Rehabilitation also gives expression to important virtues, such as charity, care, hope, and compassion. Giving scope to such values is crucially important, not least for officials working within the penal system, since it would be psychologically and morally unhealthy for judges and prison officers to see themselves simply as agents of society's vengeance.[6] From a Christian perspective, rehabilitation is consistent with the strong biblical emphasis on repentance and redemption. "Whether in the judgment of Israel in the Old Testament or the discipline of church members in the New," observes Robertson McQuilkin, "God's primary purpose in punishment has always been the restoration of the sinner. 'Have I any pleasure in the death of the wicked, says the Lord GOD, and not rather that they should turn from their ways and live?' (Ezek 18:23)."[7] While it is true that in the Old Testament disciplinary punishment aimed at repentance and reform plays a larger part in national punishments than in penalties laid down for serious individual offenses,[8] the individual dimension is not entirely lacking, and it is certainly prominent in the New Testament.[9] Foundational to both testaments, Rolf Knierim points out, is the firm belief that "the divine justice of forgiveness in principle outweighs the divine justice of momentary or periodic judgment."[10] There is, then, sound biblical precedent for seeing rehabilitation as a purpose of punishment.

However, criticism has been leveled at the rehabilitative theory of punishment on both philosophical and pragmatic grounds.[11] Philo-

6. C. Wood, *The End of Punishment: Christian Perspectives on the Crisis in Criminal Justice* (Edinburgh: Saint Andrew Press, 1991), 57-63, 96.

7. R. McQuilkin, *An Introduction to Biblical Ethics* (Wheaton: Tyndale, 1989), 357. So too S. H. Travis, *Christ and the Judgment of God: Divine Retribution in the New Testament* (London: Marshall & Pickering, 1986), 4.

8. For example, Deut. 4:24-31; Lev. 26:14-33; 1 Kings 8:33-34; Amos 4:6-11; cf. Isa. 9:13; 42:25; Jer. 2:19, 30; 5:3; 30:4; 31:18; Dan. 9:13; Zech. 1:1-6; Ps. 78:34. See D. A. Kidner, "Retribution and Punishment in the Old Testament in Light of the New Testament," *SBET* 1 (1983): 3-5.

9. Cf. 2 Thess. 3:13-15; 1 Cor. 5:5; 2 Cor. 2:6-8; 1 Tim. 1:19-20; Heb. 12:7-11.

10. Knierim, *The Task of Old Testament Theology: Substance, Method, and Cases* (Grand Rapids: William B. Eerdmans, 1995), 102.

11. A classic critique is that of C. S. Lewis, "The Humanitarian Theory of Punishment," reprinted, among other places, in *Essays on the Death Penalty*, ed. T. R. Ingram (Houston, Tex.: St. Thomas Press, 1963), 1-12. Less impressive, in the same volume, is E. L. H. Taylor, "Medicine or Morals as the Basis of Justice and Law," 81-102.

sophically, critics have warned of the dangers of confusing punishment with treatment. While treatment may usefully accompany punishment, to equate the two presumes that crime is a kind of disease or abnormality to be cured rather than the expression of particular choices for which the offender stands accountable. This in turn rests on a deterministic view of human nature that diminishes the moral autonomy of the offender and locates the cause of crime in some inherited psychological predisposition or in social factors such as poverty, unemployment, or family upbringing. Such denial of personal liability can lead to two opposite kinds of injustice — laxity and tyranny. In the former case, criminal behavior is too easily excused and the criminal exempted from taking responsibility for his or her actions. The offender is treated as an infant to be socialized, or even as an animal to be trained, rather than as a rational, self-directed, morally culpable individual. In the latter case, there is the potential for "treatment" to be extended for an inordinately long time until social conformity is secured. How do we know when the treatment has been successful? Who decides? What is there to prevent inhumane techniques from being used to achieve success? If the object of punishment is not to penalize the offender for a past crime but to render him or her unlikely to re-offend in the future, the duration and form of the punishment are logically linked not to the seriousness of the offense but to subjective assessments about the offender's progress toward harmlessness. This opens the door to attempts to coerce personality change, such as through aversion therapy, chemical manipulation, or shock treatment. The well-documented use of psychiatric medicine to enforce ideological conformity in the former Soviet Union is an example of the dangers of confusing punishment and treatment.

Another reason for distinguishing punishment from therapy is that each operates on different terms. One is exclusively aimed at reform and is structured to achieve this end, while the other sees reform as a possible by-product of pursuing a different — perhaps contradictory — goal of "getting even" with a wrongdoer. According to some critics, punishment, as the deliberate, forcible imposition of suffering or injury on a person, is itself an evil that can do nothing to transform the mental or spiritual disposition of the recipient. As George Bernard Shaw put it, "If you are to punish a man retributively, you must injure him. If you are to reform him, you must improve him.

And men are not improved by injuries."[12] The pain or prospect of punishment may succeed in deterring antisocial behavior and encouraging conformity to the rules of the penal environment. But behavior based on fear or habituation is not the same as a genuine transformation of moral and spiritual disposition. Permanent organic change requires the criminal's personal cooperation and commitment, and these are not readily elicited by deliberately hurting the person. Those who work to reform offenders must work *with* them, not merely *upon* them. This is not necessarily to say that punishment *prevents* reform. Far from it. If the punishment is appropriate, if it is accepted by the offender as thoroughly deserved, and if it has been imposed by an authority that the offender respects, it may well serve to awaken in the offender the moral shame and regret which are essential preconditions for genuine interior change. But it is not the pain of punishment per se that amends character; punishment is simply one of several mechanisms for helping to release springs of reformation within the criminal's own personality. I will return to this point later.

There is also a major pragmatic objection to the reformative theory: it appears not to work! Despite the introduction of rehabilitation programs, recidivism rates remain high. New Zealand is typical: around 30 percent of current female prisoners and 60 percent of current male prisoners have already served previous prison sentences.[13] It is sometimes said that the only thing known to rehabilitate criminals is old age. But this objection may not be as persuasive as it first appears. Many rehabilitation programs were doomed from the outset because they were incorporated into regular prison life and thus were required to function in extremely punitive, inhumane environments where official attitudes were often hostile to the concept of rehabilitation. Furthermore, many of the programs were inadequately constructed, and few resources were put into the reintegration of prisoners released into the community or into longer-term support strategies. This is not to say that every rehabilitation program has been an unqualified failure. Some targeted schemes, such as those that deal with sex offenders, can claim considerable success in reforming offenders.

---

12. Shaw, *The Crime of Imprisonment* (New York: Citadel Press, 1961), 26.

13. Cited in *Restorative Justice: Contemporary Themes and Practice,* ed. H. Bowen and J. Consedine (Lyttelton, N.Z.: Ploughshares Publications, 1999), 84.

Be that as it may, what Kissane has called Western society's "creeping sense of helplessness about its ability to rehabilitate those who commit crime"[14] is undoubtedly a major reason for the declining influence of the reformative theory of punishment. Even the most ardent defenders of the current prison system, such as leaders of the massive commercial enterprises that benefit from it (the so-called prison-industrial complex), rarely claim anymore that it rehabilitates its inmates. Although some thinkers have sought to reformulate the reformative theory, arguing for rehabilitation efforts within the context of fixed sentences and proportionate penalties in order to protect offenders from indefinite, excessive, or draconian treatment, most criminologists insist that rehabilitationism has had its day.[15] By the 1980s, many Western jurisdictions had effectively given up correctionalist goals in favor of deterrent-retributivist strategies.

The Deterrence Theory

According to the deterrence theory, which can claim a lineage as far back as Plato,[16] punishment is designed to discourage future wrongdoing, whether by the offender ("specific deterrence" through "incapacitation") or by others tempted to follow his or her example ("general deterrence"). The miscreant becomes an object lesson to society of the serious consequences of wrongdoing. Punishment is justified as the most appropriate way of instilling in the offender, and reinforcing in the wider community, respect for the legal code that has been violated. In contrast to the reformative theory, the deterrence theory is more honest about what punishment is actually doing: it is delivering pain, not administering therapy.

There can be little doubt that the likelihood of arrest and punishment does have some deterrence value: acting so as to avoid unnecessary pain is a common human trait. Deterrence works best with certain

14. Kissane, "Punish and Be Damned," 29.

15. See Hudson, *Understanding Justice*, 63-67, 140.

16. According to Plato, punishment "is to be inflicted not because of the crime [what's done can't be undone], but for the sake of the future: we hope that the offender himself and those who observe his punishment will either be brought to loathe injustice unreservedly or at any rate recover appreciably from this disastrous disease" (*Laws*, 934).

premeditated crimes, particularly those aimed at material gain, and with certain sections of the population, especially those who would generally be law-abiding citizens. Insofar as deterrent penalties may reduce the danger of copycat offending, exemplary punishment serves to protect innocent victims from further crime. Scripture is filled with admonitions for the protection of the innocent, and the Bible seems to recognize a deterrent dimension to punishment. Rebellion in ancient Israel was punished with the death penalty so that "all the people will hear and be afraid, and will not act presumptuously again" (Deut. 17:12-13; cf. 13:11; 21:21; Rom. 13:3-5). A similar rationale underlies instructions relating to church discipline in 1 Timothy. "As for those who persist in sin, rebuke them in the presence of all, so that the rest also may stand in fear" (5:20; cf. Acts 5:11).

It needs to be recognized, however, that punishment by itself is usually not an adequate deterrent, especially for serious crime or crimes of desperation. Punishment will do little to deter offending in social contexts of economic despair, political hopelessness, or systemic violence. As most criminologists and sociologists recognize, crime rates are more influenced by social and economic policies and by the prevailing political climate than by penal policies.[17] Moreover, deterrence research indicates that formal sanctions imposed by remote legal authorities, whatever their severity, have far less impact on deterring criminal behavior than do informal sanctions imposed by family, friends, and associates or internal sanctions imposed by one's own moral convictions. In other words, most people are dissuaded from offending not by the fear of legal punishment but by the fear of being shamed, whether that shame stems from personal conscience or from the disapproval of one's intimate circle.[18]

Deterrence reasoning also assumes a high level of rational control and freedom of choice on the part of offenders or potential offenders. It presumes that criminal activity is the outcome of carefully made calculations of self-interest. Sometimes this is the case. Yet many serious offenses, such as murder and assault, are crimes of impulse committed in the heat of the moment, with no thought to personal consequences

17. Hudson, *Understanding Justice,* 67; cf. also 17-26.
18. On this, see J. Braithwaite, *Crime, Shame, and Reintegration* (Cambridge: Cambridge University Press, 1989), 69-83.

or likely penalties. Those who commit them often live chaotic lives, unable to measure present decisions and actions in light of their longer-term consequences. Even in premeditated crimes, as long as the felons think there is a reasonable chance of evading arrest, the allotted punishment will have little deterrent value. It is the certainty of apprehension more than the dread of punishment that has a deterrent effect. Walter Moberly made the point succinctly: "The busiest hangman can do little for the protection of society in comparison with an efficient police force."[19]

The deterrence approach also encounters a range of empirical quandaries. How do we know just how severe penalties have to be in order to make people decide against crime? Individuals are different; what might deter one person will not necessarily deter another. The inconsistency of sentencing suggests that judges are not agreed on what will constitute effective deterrence. Furthermore, how can we be sure that potential lawbreakers will learn about the penalties devised to deter them? The theory requires that intending offenders will know about the sentences which the courts hand down for particular crimes and have these uppermost in their minds at the moment they are tempted to offend. But not all criminals read newspapers or court reports, much less criminal legislation. Again, how can we verify the effects of deterrence? It is very difficult to determine *real* crime rates, since statistical fluctuations may reflect reporting or detection rates rather than offending rates. If the actual offending rate is hard to know, how much harder is it to know whether the rate has been affected by particular penalties or their absence? Even if real reductions in particular crimes could be pinpointed after the use of deterrent penalties, such reduction may be due to growing public disapproval of particular behaviors, like drunken driving, rather than the specific fear of punishment.

But there are two more substantial criticisms of the deterrent theory of punishment. The first is that it depersonalizes the offender. It is interested in the criminal (or the victim) not as a person but only as a means to an end. That end is compliance with the law in society at large, and the mechanism for securing it is fear, not inward disposition. This means that the individual rights of the offender might be sacrificed for

19. Moberly, *The Ethics of Punishment*, 55, 276.

the sake of the higher good of crime prevention. There is nothing in the deterrence theory that supplies normative criteria for limiting the extent of the punishment. No necessary connection need exist between the offense and the punishment. The nature, scope, and severity of the penalty are determined more by the message the courts want to send to the community, than by the gravity of the offense or the culpability of the offender. And if the prescribed medicine fails to effect a communal cure, the strength of the dose must be increased, resulting in penalties becoming out of all proportion to personal culpability, as well as in the mechanisms of crime control becoming ever more entrenched in the fabric of social life. Barbaric punishments may be defended, and historically have been defended, on the grounds that they maximize deterrence. It might be argued that while the penalty is disproportionate to the actual harm done by the particular offender, it is proportionate to the total harm that would follow if potential offenders were not deterred. But this is the logic that totalitarian regimes use to justify the most horrific abuses of human rights, a link Jürgen Moltmann recognizes when he asserts that "anyone who wants to take a stand against torture and have it abolished will also have to abandon an expiatory criminal law, and the notion of punishment as a deterrent."[20]

The utilitarian principle that the pain inflicted in punishment should not exceed the pain avoided through crime provides little safeguard against potential abuse, since there is no rational way to quantify either the pain avoided or the pain inflicted. This point is even more pertinent when it is realized that the pain of punishment falls not just on the offender but also on the offender's immediate family and friends, as well as on the people who staff penal institutions. The wider community also suffers. Social civility and public safety are diminished, not enhanced, when societies become increasingly acclimatized to regimes of harsh punishment, such as imprisonment. Far from deterring crime, prison fosters the corrupt and violent behavior it purports to control, then returns it to the streets when prisoners are released. A vicious cycle is set up in which where crime demands punishment, punishment entrenches crime, and continuing crime demands yet more and more punishment.

The other main criticism of the deterrent theory is that it circum-

20. Moltmann, *Jesus Christ for Today's World* (London: SCM, 1994), 62.

vents the moral element of punishment. The reason for punishing is largely functional. It is not the moral or legal guilt of the offender that is primary but whether a particular behavior is thought to represent a danger to society. Logically speaking, the recipients of punishment need not even be guilty of an offense for the penalty to be justified. As long as crime is deterred, the purpose of the punishment has been satisfactorily achieved. It may be true that the deterrent impact will be enhanced when the party is clearly guilty, but it is not in principle dependent on it. Furthermore, when primary emphasis is placed on society's reaction to crime rather than on the responsibility or needs of the offender, the importance of offenders knowing they can atone for their wrongdoing and be discharged of the burden of guilt is minimized. Yet to bypass issues of guilt, desert, and atonement in justifying punishment is to rob moral life of all meaning. Instinctively we know that to punish in the absence of guilt would be a moral travesty. The strongest condemnation that can ever be passed on any punishment is that it is unjust — that is, it is undeserved by virtue of innocence. In evaluating the rightness or wrongness of a punishment, therefore, the first question to be asked is not whether it will convey a salutary warning to society but whether it is deserved by the recipient. Accordingly, Moberly points out, "the doctrine that crime is punished, not because it is wicked, but simply because it is a public nuisance or a public danger, is only a half-truth."[21]

Even where personal guilt is demonstrably present, deterrence reasoning can still lead to scapegoating, in that an individual offender is made to suffer not only the consequences of her or his own misdeeds, past and potential, but also the full weight of communal anxiety about crime.[22] Scapegoating is both morally wrong and potentially self-defeating, for if the offender, or the criminal fraternity he or she represents, does not accept the legitimacy of the punishment, it is not going to be effective in deterring future offending. A punishment that is perceived to be unfair, unwarranted, or excessive may in fact encourage rather than discourage crime by embittering and further alienating offenders (and their acquaintances) from society and increasing their

21. Moberly, *The Ethics of Punishment*, 75.
22. See V. Redekop's insightful analysis, "Scapegoats, the Bible, and Criminal Justice: Interacting with René Girard," *NPCJ* 13 (1993): 33.

propensity toward criminal activity. They may choose to pursue the very lifestyle that the penalty was intended to dissuade them from. Utilitarians argue that it is precisely these considerations which provide a check against excessive or unfair punishment in the deterrence approach. This may be true, but if so, justice is demoted from normative principle to pragmatic calculation, and the ethical problem of hurting an offender in the name of crimes not yet committed remains unsolved. Thus, while a concern to deter or prevent criminal offending is a valid social goal, it does not give the community unlimited rights over the offender. As Elizabeth Moberly insists, "Ethical seriousness and redemptive possibilities must be continually interlinked in the concerns of penology."[23]

The Retributivist Theory

Strictly speaking, the term "retribution" (from the Latin *retribuere*) simply means "repayment" — that is, giving back to someone what he or she merits or deserves, either in terms of punishments or rewards. The term is normally used, however, in the negative sense of punitive recompense for wicked deeds rather than positive reward for good deeds. There are several different versions of retributionism as a penal philosophy, and as a consequence considerable conceptual confusion in the literature, but for our purposes four key elements in retributivism, especially modern retributivism, may be identified.[24]

The first is the notion of *guilt*. Criminals are regarded as morally responsible agents who, by voluntarily breaking the law, incur personal legal guilt that must be dealt with. From this flows the concept of *desert*, the second key element. Punishment is meted out solely because it is deserved and because it would be unjust not to punish. No other justification is necessary. Wrongdoers deserve to suffer for what they have done, whether or not the punitive suffering produces any desir-

23. Moberly, "Penology," *NDCE*, 464.
24. H. Zehr identifies five key elements of retributivism: Crime is understood essentially as lawbreaking (1). When a law is broken, justice involves establishing guilt (2), so that just deserts can be meted out (3) by inflicting pain (4) through a conflict in which rules and intentions are placed above outcomes (5). See *Changing Lenses: A New Focus for Crime and Justice* (Scottdale, Pa.: Herald Press, 1990), 63-82.

able consequences. Proponents of retributivism frequently use metaphors for punishment such as "restoring the moral balance," "neutralizing the poison," "repaying the debt to society," "wiping the slate clean," or "nullifying the crime." Punishment of wrongdoers achieves something that is morally — even cosmically — important. The third key concept is *equivalence* or, as it is more commonly expressed today, *proportionality*. In order to be just, the punishment inflicted must be commensurate with the offense committed. The penalty exacted should be proportionate to the harm done. The fourth concept is *reprobation* or *denunciation*. Punishment is the fundamental means by which society communicates its abhorrence for certain deeds and sets the boundaries of acceptable behavior. It is a way of disowning the offense, of openly exhibiting the guilt incurred, and of demonstrating to the wider community the "just deserts" that ensue. Murderers are punished, for example, not simply to reform them or to deter others, but so that they may serve as a powerful witness to the constraints imposed by the moral and legal order.

Underlying classical retributivism was the notion of a rational metaphysical order where imbalances must be righted and each person receive precisely what each is due. Aristotle argued that the essential feature of justice is equality or equivalence: corrective justice requires an exact correspondence between an offense and its punishment, while distributive justice aims at giving each member of the community a share of honors and goods proportionate to their merit (however merit is determined). This understanding of justice has had a vast influence on the Western legal tradition and on Christian theology, particularly through Augustine and Aquinas. Thus it became widely accepted that the essence of justice, both human and divine, entails the distribution of rewards and punishments in direct proportion to people's deserts.

Up until the advent of constitutional governments in Western Europe, retribution was the dominant rationale for punishment. Retributivism fell into increasing disfavor during the nineteenth century, partly in reaction to the savage levels of retribution exacted by judges in the eighteenth century. During the twentieth century, the reformative ideal became more prominent, with most criminologists regarding retribution as simple vengeance and arguing for greater discretion to be given to judges to impose sentences that would encourage rehabilitation. Yet, as Howard Zehr insists in his book *Changing Lenses,* the fundamental "paradigm" of the Western justice system has remained retributivist. Moreover, both at a theoretical level and in popular sentiment, retributivist theories of punishment have regained ascendancy over the past thirty years. Disquiet among liberals over the excesses of rehabilitative sentencing, especially in America, together with the anger of conservatives at what were perceived to be soft and ineffective penalties and wildly inconsistent sentencing for the same crimes, gave rise to a "back-to-justice" movement. During the 1970s, old retributivist ideas were revived and new formulations put forward, and by the 1980s the new retributionist version of "just deserts" had become the most influential penal theory. This continued into the 1990s, sustained in part by the dominance of New Right political thinking. The neo-conservative dogma of nonintervention by governments in the marketplace and a significantly reduced role for the state in the provision of social welfare services creates the dilemma of how governments can project themselves to their electorates as strong and responsible. Crime control is one major area of social life where state intervention is still acceptable and where governments can gain political advantage by playing the "law and order" card. While the redistributive functions of the state have been curtailed, the repressive functions of the state have been extended.[25]

Now there are significant strengths in the retributivist theory. In contrast to the deterrence theory, it focuses on the criminal as an individual, not on the betterment of wider society. It rightly recognizes that wrongdoing entails personal choice and moral responsibility. Punishment is justified only if it is just, it is just only if it is deserved, and it is deserved only if the crime is the result of free will. As Walter Moberly observes, "In deciding *how* to punish, deterrence and reformation may be our guiding principles; but the question *whether* we have a right to punish at all is, first and foremost, a question of justice."[26] It follows from this that punishment should be limited to the guilty party alone. Notions of collective or vicarious punishment are excluded. All citizens can therefore be assured that whether or not they are punished depends entirely on their own actions and choices. This means that the protection

25. For this insight, see Hudson, *Understanding Justice*, 110-11; and Cayley, *The Expanding Prison*, 74-81.

26. Moberly, *The Ethics of Punishment*, 95.

of the innocent is anchored more normatively in retributivism than in utilitarian theories. The guilty are also afforded greater protection in retributivism. The retributive concepts of just deserts and proportionate punishment, if applied carefully, can help to eliminate vindictiveness, cruelty, and bias based on race, class, or gender in punishment.

A further strength of retributivism, at least according to its proponents, is the way that it takes seriously the entitlement of the criminal to be treated as a rational human being with an inherent right to receive just repayment, positive and negative, for his or her actions.[27] To punish someone in order to intimidate, as in deterrence theory, is to treat the person as less than human; to punish in order to correct, as in rehabilitation theory, is to treat the person as a juvenile; but to punish because it is due, and simply because it is due, is to treat the recipient as a reasonable and responsible agent. Punishment could almost be seen as a privilege or an honor. At a social level, it is an implicit tribute to the criminal's fellow citizenship in a society where, by social agreement, rules are expected to be enforced. It offers the offender a chance to discharge the debt incurred through crime and to rejoin society's moral consensus by choosing to live within the terms of the social contract. At a metaphysical level, as Daryl Charles explains, "to be punished — however severely — because we in fact deserved it is to be treated as a dignified human moral agent, created in the image of God."[28]

Notwithstanding these strengths, retributivism has been subjected to serious criticism on philosophical, moral, biblical, and theological grounds. It is important to review these considerations in some detail in view of the current dominance of retributivism in Western penal thinking, in view of its ready acceptance by many Christians as the theory that best squares with Christian belief, and because restorative jus-

---

27. H. W. House writes, "Rehabilitation of criminals, the deterrence of crime, and the protection of society from crime are valid and proper concerns of a legal system. However, they cannot be its ultimate goal, for they ignore the criminal's individuality, his rights to personally receive the payment of his acts, and his freedom to be treated as a person in terms of punishment" ("Crime and Punishment," in *The Death Penalty Debate*, ed. H. W. House and J. H. Yoder [Dallas: Word, 1991], 26-27). Hudson deems this emphasis to be "a principle of utmost importance in all modern versions of retributivism" (*Understanding Justice*, 51). See also Cayley, *The Expanding Prison*, 94-96.

28. Charles, "Crime, The Christian, and Capital Justice," *JETS* 38, no. 3 (1995): 438n.31.

tice is often presented by its advocates as a radical alternative to prevailing conceptions of retributive justice.

(1) *Philosophical Considerations:* David Dolinko insists that retributivism is unable to offer a coherent, rationally defensible justification of punishment. It is not enough to say that crime should be punished because of its inherent wrongness or that lawbreakers deserve punishment simply because of their moral wrongdoing, for not all moral transgression is deemed by society to be criminal, and the state does not invariably mete out punishment (or reward) whenever it is deserved. To say that punishment is merited is not to establish that it is required or needed or that there is an inescapable moral obligation to deliver it. It is only particular misdemeanors that are deemed worthy of punishment, and the decision as to which acts should be penalized usually entails culturally specific utilitarian considerations.[29] Furthermore, it is worth noting that only a tiny percentage of those who actually commit wrong acts are ever caught and sentenced, which raises questions about the equity of punishing only those offenders who are fortuitously apprehended, while most go scot free. It is also not clear why it should be the function of the political authorities to ensure that wrongdoers are given their deserts. Certainly the state has the task of protecting its citizens, and punishing crime is one instrument for doing so. But insofar as retributivism refuses to justify punishment philosophically on the basis of its positive effects, it cannot appeal to the protective functions of the state to vindicate its interest in ensuring that criminals suffer.

Retributivism's core principle of proportionate punishment runs into at least three interrelated problems. It depends, in the first place, on the ability to rank crimes in terms of their seriousness. But judgments about seriousness vary over time (as changing attitudes toward child abuse, sexual harassment, and drunken driving indicate), and there are so many variables involved that it is impossible to come up with a satisfactory scale of gravity. It may be possible to secure general agreement about the most and least serious offenses, but problems arise in ranking offenses between these poles. Is shoplifting more or less serious than minor tax evasion? Is cruelty to an animal more or less serious than burglary or arson? Some just-desert theorists have attempted to devise ways of measuring the seriousness of crimes in terms

---

29. Dolinko, "Some Thoughts about Retributivism," *Ethics* 101 (1991): 537-59.

of their impact on the living standards of the victim. But the emotional or psychological impact of a crime often bears little relation to the material or physical loss suffered.

A second difficulty relates to determining what constitutes a commensurate punishment for a specific crime. Hypothetically, it is feasible to graduate penalties from least severe to most severe. But how are the levels of punitive severity to be objectively correlated with degrees of seriousness in offending? What are the anchoring points on the scale? On what grounds can it be decided whether fifteen or twenty or fifty years in jail, or some different penalty, is proportionate to the loss of a victim's life? And how would such a scale work in practice, since the same penalty will have a different severity for different parties? A $10,000 fine may be deemed a proportionate penalty for a particular crime, but it will have a more severe impact on a poor person than on a wealthy one. It is impossible to measure pain in standard doses. What hurts one person moderately may hurt another very severely.

The third problem concerns the measuring of guilt. In practice the severity of penalties is determined not only by the nature of the crime but also by the degree of moral culpability of the criminal. Not just the criminal act but the intentions behind the act *(mens rea)* and the circumstances in which the act occurred are considered relevant to deciding on the appropriate punishment. Rightly so. Yet no human court can ascertain true moral character. Moral guilt is not coterminous with legal guilt. Moral culpability cannot be quantified objectively. It varies from person to person and depends on innumerable intricate circumstances. Nor, from a moral (or theological) point of view, are guilt and innocence mutually exclusive categories. As Miroslav Volf observes, "From a distance, the world may appear neatly divided into guilty perpetrators and innocent victims. The closer we get, however, the more the line between the guilty and the innocent blurs and we see an intractable maze of small and large hatreds, dishonesties, manipulations, and brutalities, each reinforcing the other."[30]

What these observations amount to is a recognition that while moral blameworthiness may be an *essential* element in the justification

---

30. Volf, *Exclusion and Embrace: A Theological Exploration of Identity, Otherness, and Reconciliation* (Nashville: Abingdon Press, 1996), 81. So too L. G. Jones, *Embodying Forgiveness: A Theological Analysis* (Grand Rapids: William B. Eerdmans, 1995), 116-17.

of punishment, it is rarely a *sufficient* reason. Retributivism is better able to tell us when *not* to punish (i.e., when the person is innocent of legal wrongdoing) than when *to* punish, since it is neither expedient nor necessary to punish every moral infringement. Consequently, just as utilitarian theories of punishment must take the moral dimension of punishment into account to be adequate, so retributivist theories must take utilitarian considerations into reckoning to operate effectively. As a social institution, punishment occupies the borderland between morality and social expediency. It cannot be understood without reference to morality, as retributivism insists, but it cannot be governed solely by moral considerations, as utilitarians are quick to point out.

Another philosophical difficulty with retributivism concerns its frequent confusion of personal and impersonal categories. In practice, punishment is focused personally on the individual criminal, yet its purpose is seen as vindicating the impersonal moral order that the crime has outraged. In this way retribution distinguishes itself from revenge. Whereas revenge is an expression of personal indignation against a personal enemy, retribution is impersonal in the sense that it is the evil more than the evildoer that is the target, with the punishment serving as what Walter Moberly calls "an act of homage to righteousness."[31] But such an understanding of retribution is seriously flawed. Punishment is unavoidably a transaction between persons. There are always at least two persons involved, and any moral valuation of punishment must have regard to the personal condition of those involved. Furthermore, in practice it is not every offense against righteousness that attracts punishment. It is usually only those that are experienced in some way as personal injury and that evoke strong moral indignation in the community, and moral indignation is the reaction of persons to persons. Retribution cannot, therefore, be so neatly distinguished from revenge, and often the attitude shown toward the culprit is one of unmitigated hostility. He or she is regarded as the embodiment of evil and treated with considerable brutality.

One helpful feature of the retributive theory is the way it seeks to endow punishment with not just a negative value but a positive one as well: that of clarifying and publicly proclaiming fundamentally shared values. But while punitive retribution may in practice serve as an ex-

31. Moberly, *The Ethics of Punishment*, 101.

pression of social censure and revulsion, this is not the same as saying that punishment is intrinsically necessary to the expression of opprobrium. Its role of denunciation does not in itself justify punishment. It might be argued, for example, that the function of censure is adequately fulfilled by the pronouncement of guilt and rebuke more than by the carrying out of the sentence; indeed, the courts sometimes decide on a suspended sentence and deem the conviction of guilt to be a sufficient public sanction. The same could be said for efforts to shame offenders publicly or to rehabilitate them or to have them repair the damage caused. As C. F. D. Moule observes, "If a community tries to reclaim or reform the offender and to prevent a repetition of the offence, surely that is a clear enough expression of its disapproval."[32] Retributive punishment is not therefore essential to the goal of reprobation; at times it may be quite superfluous.

(2) *Moral Considerations:* Retributive practice is also dogged with moral problems. Retributivism tends to sanction society's most punitive reflexes and to bolster demands for greater pain in punishment. It appeals to the darker, more fearful side of human nature. For all their theoretical weaknesses, historically it has been utilitarian rather than retributive theories of punishment that have contributed most to moderating the severity of criminal law. The massive institutions of punishment that characterize the present criminal justice system are sustained largely to service the popular demand for retribution, with a corresponding lack of imagination being shown in the development of mechanisms of restitution and reform. This is one factor in explaining why there is no direct correlation between crime rates and rates of imprisonment. Although reported crime rates in the United States and Canada have fallen over recent years, levels of imprisonment in those countries have continued to rise at an alarming rate.[33] Burgeoning social problems such as drug abuse are partly to blame, but current sentencing practices in America such as "three strikes and you're out," aimed at reducing judicial discretion and increasing retributive severity, have also contributed to this sad state of affairs. In this connection, the argument that punishing offenders demonstrates respect for them

---

32. Moule, "Punishment and Retribution: An Attempt to Delimit Their Scope in New Testament Thought," *NPCJ* 10 (1990): 19.

33. See Cayley, *The Expanding Prison,* 1-11, 43-62.

as free moral agents is potentially dangerous. If punishment is equated with personal respect rather than seen as something that stands in tension with respect, an important check against excessive punishment is lost. It is also not clear, despite its theoretical claim, that retribution actually functions as an annulment of the crime or a repayment of the individual's moral debt to society. If it did so, ex-prisoners would not suffer from the continuing stigma, suspicion and mistrust they almost invariably do. Far from wiping the slate clean, a period of imprisonment almost serves, in the eyes of society, to establish criminality as "an indelible ontological attribute."[34]

Again, the concepts of just deserts and of the punishment fitting the crime are open to question on moral grounds. As general principles they have some value in guiding the administration of justice, even though, as we have seen, it is impossible to measure objectively what a person's just deserts really are. (This is why Walter Moberly describes the concept of just desert as "a myth, but a wholesome myth.")[35] More significantly, while it makes moral sense to repay good deeds with further good, it is surely unjustifiable to requite evil deeds with further evil. Malice is unquestionably a vice, and to insist that evildoers be repaid in kind is surely to make a virtue out of a vice. It also runs directly counter to perhaps the most distinctive emphasis in the moral teachings of the New Testament: the obligation to show goodwill toward all people, including one's enemies (Matt. 5:38-48; Rom. 12:14-21).

Retributivism also tends toward an exaggerated individualism. Punishment may theoretically be explained in terms of restoring the social or even cosmic balance upset by the crime, but in practice, attention focuses on the criminal as an isolated unit in society. Retributivism treats crime primarily as an offense against the law by an autonomous individual rather than as an injury to the community by a member of the community who has been fundamentally shaped, for good or for ill, by that community. The retributivist emphasis on personal responsibility and choice is valuable and important; individuals do *choose* to commit crimes. But choices are constrained by environmental circumstances, and it is naïve, if not dishonest, to speak of crime solely in terms of personal free will. People who would remain

34. I owe this phrase to Cayley, *The Expanding Prison*, 41.
35. Moberly, *The Ethics of Punishment*, 156.

law-abiding in certain social climates will turn to crime under other social conditions. Poverty, unemployment, racial inequality, social prejudice, and drug and alcohol abuse all have a role in fostering crime. A
significant proportion of criminal offenders have been offended
against as children before they became offenders. It is crucial, therefore,
to inquire into the societal causes of crime — and collective responsibility for it — rather than being content to divide individuals into categories of guilty and innocent, and calculating commensurate punishments for the guilty. Society's own complicity in the creation of
criminals is quickly lost sight of in outpourings of moral indignation
at individual offenders. As Karen Kissane comments,

> The legal principle that each person is responsible for his or her ac-
> tions has collided with growing knowledge about how little control
> some people have over their lives; about the links between physical and
> emotional poverty and abuse and crime. How just is it for society to
> cast from its midst the misshapen creatures of its own making, like a
> biblical figure casting out demons? Is not crime part of the body
> proper, a systemic illness? Legal academics make the analogy that the
> Black Death was not defeated by medical cures but by preventive mea-
> sures, such as better hygiene.[36]

It is also important to recognize that the law which criminals break is
not a neutral transcription of absolute morality. It is an irrefutable fact,
Barbara Hudson insists, that the law is predominantly reflective of the
standpoint of the powerful, property-owning, white male, and that the
justice system bears down more heavily on the poor and disadvantaged
than on the rich and the powerful.[37] One recent study in New Zealand
shows how the government puts far more money and resources into
cracking down on welfare-benefit fraud than on white-collar crime,
even though the cost of white-collar crime and corporate fraud is up to
ten times higher than the cost of all other crime combined.[38] There is
also a significant link between business cycles and punishment. Times
of economic depression are also times of punishment, with the ratio-

36. Kissane, "Punish and Be Damned," 28-29.
37. Hudson, *Understanding Justice,* 149-50.
38. The study is by M. Thornton of Victoria University of Wellington, reported in
the campus newspaper *Salient* 61, no. 12 (1998).

nale shifting from reform to retribution. This may be seen in the way that the rehabilitative ethos of the expansionary 1960s gave way to the retributive ethos of the recessionary 1970s and 1980s. Hudson offers this commentary:

> Whether or not times of depression really do lead to increased crime is debatable, but what is not debatable is that in times of recession the vocabulary of justice becomes harsher. Blame is attached to individuals, and social responsibility for crime is denied; lack of investment in areas of high unemployment is blamed on crime rates rather than on the flight of capital; the unemployed are said to be happy to depend on welfare payments, to have a different (pro-crime) set of values from those of the rest of society. Theories of justice in such times inevitably emphasize punishment rather than help or treatment, and the economic downturn has indeed seen the demise of rehabilitative orthodoxy and the rise of deterrence, retribution and incapacitative strategies.[39]

Retributivism thus faces the problem of explaining how there can be just deserts for individuals in the context of an unjust society, and a society where the justice system most benefits those with vested interests in maintaining the status quo. In light of the social realities surrounding crime, the retributivist claim to be delivering "justice" through the imposition of proportionate penalties needs considerable tempering. In fact, as Howard Zehr observes, by separating criminal justice from wider questions of social justice, retributivism attempts "to create justice by leaving out many of the relevant variables."[40] In David Cayley's words, "Justice must be enacted, not simply invoked."[41]

This almost exclusive focus on the individual offender also highlights another weakness in retributivism (a weakness shared by deterrence and reform theories as well) — neglect of the victim. Retributive justice is held to be satisfied by the vindication of the law and punishment of the lawbreaker. There is no need to refer to the real victim at all, particularly when the system redefines the victim as the impersonal state, not the human being actually hurt by the crime. But crime nearly

39. Hudson, *Understanding Justice*, 109-10.
40. Zehr, *Changing Lenses*, 72-73.
41. Cayley, *The Expanding Prison*, 11.

always involves the rupturing of relationships.[42] Not only is the proper relationship between victim and offender distorted by the crime, but the emotional, material, and physical hurt experienced by the victim radiates out through his or her relational world. When conceived as the fracturing of relationship between victim and offender, and between their respective relational networks, punitive retribution is clearly an inadequate response, since it does little or nothing to bring about recovery. A more promising strategy is to begin where the problem began, in the fractured relationships.

(3) *Biblical Considerations:* It is debatable whether retribution, strictly understood, is as foundational to biblical conceptions of law and justice as is sometimes claimed. Discussion at this point often becomes very confused because interpreters use the word "retribution" in different ways. Some use the term broadly to embrace all indications in the Bible that human deeds carry certain inescapable moral consequences, some of which are experienced as the intrinsic outcome of the deeds themselves, and some of which are personally imposed from outside, by God or by human agents, as extrinsic punishments. Both are regarded as retributive since they express the same underlying law of recompense, for which God is ultimately personally responsible: "Whoever digs a pit will fall into it" (Eccles. 10:8; Prov. 1:32; 26:27; Ps. 7:15); "Do not be deceived; God is not mocked, for you reap whatever you sow" (Gal. 6:7).[43] According to Jerome Quinn, "A basic conviction that grounds the whole scriptural teaching is that the one God ultimately punishes those who do evil and rewards those who do good. The God who gives human beings commands to act upon reserves ultimately to himself retribution for the actions that he has ordered."[44] Others, however, use the term more precisely to designate only externally imposed penalties (or benefits), which are imposed by a higher authority after judicial assessment according to a pre-existing norm, and regarded as sufficient and proportionate rec-

---

42. On the primacy of relationships, see M. Schluter and D. Lee, *The R Factor* (London: Hodder & Stoughton, 1993), especially 258-63. See also the essays in *Relational Justice: Repairing the Breach,* ed. J. Burnside and N. Baker (Winchester, U.K.: Waterside Press, 1994).

43. Kidner, "Retribution and Punishment in the Old Testament in Light of the New Testament," 3-9; cf. G. A. Herion, "Retribution," *ISBE,* 4:154-59.

44. J. D. Quinn, "Scriptures on Merit," in *Justification by Faith,* ed. H. G. Anderson, T. A. Murphy, and J. A. Burgess (Minneapolis: Augsburg, 1985), 83.

ompense for particular actions. Only when these penalties are imposed from outside and as an end in themselves should they be regarded as strictly retributive.[45] When this narrower conception of retributive punishment is employed, retribution is arguably a much more limited theme in Scripture than is often assumed.

Certainly it is not difficult to find evidence of retributivist elements and language in the Bible, especially in connection with God's activity, although the actual term "retribution" appears in English translations infrequently.[46] The four central concepts of guilt, desert, equivalence, and censure or reprobation are widely attested in Scripture. The notion of guilt and atonement underlies certain parts of the Old Testament sacrificial system, and is foundational to many of the procedures of Pentateuchal law. The concept of desert is expressed, for instance, in the frequent assertion of the impartiality and justness of divine judgment, since it is meted out according to deeds,[47] and is attested in the principle that "it is only the person who sins that shall die" (Ezek. 18:4), not his or her wider family group.[48] The idea of equivalent recompense is captured in the *lex talionis*[49] and other talionic expressions of divine judgment.[50] And the notion of censure or reprobation is perhaps echoed in the oft-repeated refrain in Deuteronomy, "So you shall purge the evil from your

45. See especially Travis, *Christ and the Judgment of God,* passim; K. Koch, "Is There a Doctrine of Retribution in the Old Testament?" in *Theodicy in the Old Testament,* ed. J. L. Crenshaw (Philadelphia/London: Fortress/SPCK, 1983), 58-59; and Moule, "Punishment and Retribution," passim. Cf. E. R. Moberly, *Suffering, Innocent and Guilty* (London: SPCK, 1978), 83.

46. In the RSV, the term occurs only in Romans 11:9 and Hebrews 2:2. The NRSV employs the word nine times, but all uses are in Jeremiah (5:9, 29; 11:20; 15:15; 20:12; 46:10), with the exception of Isaiah 66:6 and Romans 11:9. The NJB consistently uses the term "retribution" for *orgē,* or "wrath," in Paul and Revelation, while the NEB also uses the term "retribution" in Revelation 11:18; 19:15.

47. For example, Pss. 9:8, 11; 37:9, 33; 58:12; 62:12; Job 34:11; Prov. 10:16; 24:12; Eccles. 12:14; Isa. 3:10-11; 59:18; Jer. 17:10; 25:14; 32:19; Lam. 3:64; Hos. 4:9; Matt. 12:37; 16:27; 23:35; Rom. 2:1-16; 14:7-12; 1 Cor. 3:1-17; 4:1-5; 5:1-5; 6:9-11; 9:24-27; 11:27-34; 2 Cor. 5:9-10; Gal. 5:19-21; 6:7-10; Col. 3:25; Eph. 6:8; 1 Tim. 5:24-25; 2 Tim. 4:14; Heb. 2:2; 1 Pet. 2:14; Rev. 22:12.

48. Cf. Exod. 20:5 (note the qualification "of those who reject me"); Deut. 24:16; 2 Kings 14:6; Ezek. 18:1-32.

49. Exod. 21:24; Lev. 24:19-22; Deut. 19:21. Cf. Matt. 5:38-48; Luke 6:27-45.

50. See, e.g., Jer. 14:13-16; Mic. 2:1-5; Exod. 4:23; Ps. 18:26; Prov. 3:34; Isa. 59:18; Jer. 34:17; Joel 3:4-8.

midst,"[51] and in instances where punishment is inflicted for revelatory purposes, so that others, such as the Egyptians, might know God's character and power.[52] Retribution is most clearly in view when God's wrath is said to destroy the objects of judgment, thus ruling out any hope of their reformation or restoration,[53] and in texts where the object of God's judgment is neither the offender nor the victim but the nature of the injury.[54] Retribution is also evident where God is said to inflict punishment by the agency of natural phenomena — such as plagues (Exod. 7–11), disease (Num. 11:33; 2 Sam. 24:15), drought (Jer. 14:1-7), famine (Ezek. 5:12, 16), earthquake (Isa. 29:6; Amos 8:8), and lightning (Num. 11:1) — since such punishments are imposed from outside rather than being the inevitable result of wrong moral choices.[55]

Clearly, then, there is a theme of retribution in the Bible.[56] And it serves an important theological function. According to W. S. Towner, "The theme stands as a constant reminder of the seriousness with which the biblical writers understood God's hatred of evil and injustice and his will to overcome them," as well underscoring the relationship between deeds and their moral consequences.[57] But this is *not* to say that the Bible advocates *a full-fledged, coherent theory of retributive justice*, and certainly not in the classical Western sense. Biblical law and justice operate according to certain values, convictions, and assumptions that are largely foreign to the model of retributive justice in the Western tradition.

Klaus Koch argues, for example, that assertions in the Old Testament about Yahweh's punitive intervention in human affairs need to be understood in light of the basic worldview conviction that deeds carry their own inherent outcome. There are forces at work within the actions themselves that carry the doer along in their wake, bringing either blessing or bane depending on whether the deeds are good or bad. It is not that Yahweh assesses deeds according to some higher moral or

---

51. Deut. 13:5; 17:7, 12; 19:19; 21:21; 22:21, 22, 24; 24:7; Judg. 20:13.

52. Exod. 7:17; 10:2. Cf. Ps. 9:16; Ezek. 6:11-13; 7:4, 9, 27; 38:22-23.

53. For example, Deut. 7:4; 9:8, 19, 25; Num. 16:21; Ezek. 22:31; 43:8.

54. Deut. 32:43; 2 Kings 9:7; Ps. 79:10. Cf. Rev. 6:10; 19:2; Matt. 23:35.

55. See Travis, *Christ and the Judgment of God*, 6-13.

56. See the major study by H. G. L. Peels, *The Vengeance of God: The Meaning of the Root NQM and the Function of the NQM-Texts in the Context of Divine Revelation in the Old Testament* (Leiden/New York/Köln: E. J. Brill, 1995), esp. 269-97.

57. Towner, "Retribution," *IDB Suppl*, 743-44.

legal norm and allocates rewards or punishments accordingly. Rather, actions and their consequences are intrinsically linked, so that there is a Sin-Disaster connection on the one hand and a Righteousness-Blessing connection on the other. "Misfortune pursues sinners, but prosperity rewards the righteous" (Prov. 13:21). This helps explain why a whole series of Hebrew roots are used to describe both an action and its consequences. The word *hatta't*, for example, means both "sin" and "disaster," and is perhaps the closest Hebrew word for "punishment." It is also the basis on which the problem of theodicy arises. That the wicked prosper while the good suffer is a paradox precisely because of the "Deed-Consequence" construct.

This is not understood, Koch is careful to explain, as some kind of impersonal cause-and-effect mechanism that operates independently of God. Yahweh is pictured as intimately involved in the process. God is active in the interplay between human actions and their consequences. God sets the Deed-Consequence construct in motion and consents to its operation. God sometimes hurries it along and brings it to completion, and ensures that the consequences of actions are directed back on the person who performed them. This is intended not only to bring retributive punishment on the wicked but also to contain the consequences of the evil so that the entire land is not ruined. Even where God's wrath brings disaster for Israel in the short term, it is still "motivated by the long-range purpose of restoring Israel to the status of being blessed." Furthermore, in acting this way, God is not keeping some metaphysical order of justice finely tuned; he is preserving the covenant. Every action, whether good or wicked, spreads out to affect or infect others within the covenant community, and therefore Israel's relationship with Yahweh. God proves true to his covenant commitments by purging evil from the land, and thus protecting his people, through establishing, sustaining, and symbolically dramatizing (in judicial procedures and penalties) the Deed-Consequence construct.[58]

Koch's approach has been subjected to considerable criticism, and it does not entirely dispose of the theme of retribution in the Old Testa-

---

58. Koch, "Is There a Doctrine of Retribution in the Old Testament?" 57-87 (quote from 68). See also G. von Rad, *Old Testament Theology*, 2 vols. (Edinburgh: Oliver & Boyd, 1962), 1:266, 384-86, 436, 439.

ment.[59] But his study is an important warning against overemphasizing the extent and unity of the theme, conceptualizing it wholly in forensic terms, and treating it in isolation from the wider conceptual framework in which deeds carry inherent consequences and where God's vengeance is activated primarily by internal or external threats to the covenant.[60]

In this covenantal setting, criminal offending was viewed by Israel as a breaching of covenant relationships. The basic concern in administering justice was twofold: to constrain or overcome the intrinsic consequences of the evil act (whether through punishment, by which the evil effects of the deed are turned back on the evildoer, or through pardon, where the effects are dealt with by repentance, forgiveness, and atonement), and to restore the relational integrity of the community. "In contradistinction to Roman and western justice," Erich Renner observes, "the fundamental purpose of a trial in the Old Testament was to settle disputes so that the community might thrive and prosper. Indeed, all punishments were designed to help communal living."[61] In this setting, justice is not "due process" or "giving each his due." It is principally about the restoration of relationships. While certain religious offenses and crimes against human life required strict retributive punishment, including "cutting off" and death,[62] even here the goal was the restoration of the community to its covenant commitment to be a holy people.[63] Moreover, the actual execution of those guilty of mur-

---

59. For critiques of Koch, see Y. Hoffman, "The Creativity of Theodicy," in *Justice and Righteousness: Biblical Themes and Their Influence*, ed. H. G. Reventlow and Y. Hoffman (Sheffield: Sheffield Academic Press, 1992), 117-130; and Peels, *The Vengeance of God*, esp. 302-05.

60. On the primarily (but not exclusively) covenantal character of divine vengeance, see Peels, *The Vengeance of God*, 284-87.

61. Renner & V. C. Pfitzner, "Justice and Human Rights: Some Biblical Perspectives," *LTJ* 24, no. 1 (1990): 5. See also D. B. Forrester, "Political Justice and Christian Theology," *StChEth* 3, no. 1 (1990): 13.

62. Old Testament law refers to God "cutting off" an offender (e.g., Exod. 12:15; Lev. 7:20-21, 25; 17:4, 9, 14; 18:29; 19:8; 20:3, 5-6, 17-18; Num. 15:30-31). Opinion differs on whether this is an alternative way of referring to capital punishment (cf. Lev. 20:6 and 20:27), a reference to excommunication from the covenant community, or a threat of direct punishment by God, usually in the form of premature death.

63. This is particularly true of the so-called priestly strand of Pentateuchal law, where a major concern was to uphold the ritual status of the community. The death penalty is prescribed for several offenses. But, notes J. A. Hoyles, "it is not automatic ret-

der or certain religious and sexual crimes was not simple tit-for-tat judicial retribution. It was a kind of communal cleansing or ceremonial expiation of especially serious sins which, if left unchecked, threatened the actual survival of the community as a covenant people. According to Douglas Knight, "Their readiness to eliminate certain criminals and enemies arose out of a desire to eradicate what was held to be severe threats to the very existence of all other Israelites. . . . The imperative to live was not to be subverted by any others, whether from within or without, who might take the life of Israelites."[64] It is significant that often these penalties are justified in the Old Testament in terms of a "purging" or "cleansing" of evil.[65] Such expiatory penalties cannot be simply equated with the retributive punishment, for in some cases collective guilt attaches to the offenses, something ruled out under retributivist thinking (cf. Deut. 5:9 and 24:16).

In noncapital offenses, the emphasis in biblical jurisprudence falls on restitution rather than retribution (Lev. 17–27; Num. 5–8). As John Hayes explains, "The basic principle operative in Israelite laws dealing with injured parties was restitution. That is, the concern of Israelite law was for restoration of the victim to the status prior to the wrong rather than *punishment* of the offender."[66] Restitution restored *shalom,* which flourishes only when true justice has been done, where harm has been repaired. Specific acts of restitution are prescribed in Mosaic law, based broadly on equivalence of value (Exod. 21:26-36). A punitive element might be seen in the way some offenses demanded double restitution or more, according to the seriousness of the offense and the attitude of the offender (Exod. 22:4, 7). If penitent, the thief restored what was stolen plus a fifth more (Lev. 6:5). If the thief was caught with the goods

---

ribution or ineluctable vengeance. It has a disciplinary intent. Its aim is to preserve the religious worship which expressed a relationship with God, symbolized their existence as a chosen race and provided hope of deliverance from sin. In other words, the aim of punishment was reconciliation with God." See *Punishment in the Bible* (London: Epworth, 1986), 35.

64. Knight, "The Ethics of Human Life in the Hebrew Bible," in *Justice and the Holy: Essays in Honour of Walter Harrelson,* ed. D. A. Knight and P. J. Peters (Atlanta: Scholars Press, 1989), 86.

65. Deut. 13:5; 17:7, 12; 19:19; 21:21; 22:21, 22, 24; 24:7; Judg. 20:13.

66. Hayes, "Atonement in the Book of Leviticus," *Interpretation* 52, no. 1 (1998): 11 (author's emphasis).

on him, he restored double. If he had already disposed of the goods and tried to conceal the offense, he had to restore fourfold or fivefold. But fourfold, fivefold, even sevenfold reparation of a theft (Exod. 22:1, 4, 9; Prov. 6:30-31) was intended not merely to penalize the offender but also to bring both restitution and compensation to the victim, as well as to "mark" the gravity of the situation. If the thief could not pay, he might be taken as a slave by the injured party until he had worked off the debt (Exod. 22:3). Enslavement could last for a maximum of six years (Exod. 21:1-6; Deut. 15:12-17) or until the Year of Jubilee (Lev. 25:39-55). Slavery was not as ghastly in the ancient Orient as in modern times; in fact, it could be argued that Hebrew slavery was a more humane institution than its modern equivalent of imprisonment.[67]

The theme of retribution is also tempered or moderated by the existence of controls and counter-themes. The controls include legal provisions that placed restraints on vengeance, such as the *lex talionis,* the creation of cities and other places of refuge (Num. 35; Deut. 4, 19; Josh. 20; 1 Kings 1:50-53; 2:28-29),[68] and stated limitations on punishment to prevent excessive degrading of the offender (e.g., Deut. 25:1-3).[69] The counter-themes include the recognition of nonretributive expressions of divine judgment,[70] the oft-repeated assertion that "God's redemptive purpose is greater than the literal requirements of his justice,"[71] the way in which vengeance is reserved for God alone (Deut. 32:35; Lev. 19:18; Rom. 12:19), and those texts that celebrate forgiveness and mercy instead of retribution (e.g., Exod. 34:6-7; Ezek. 33:11; Mic. 7:18; Ps. 103:3, 10). It is also important to recognize the use of rhetorical flourish in some of the descriptions of divine retribution. In the opening chapters of Amos, God repeatedly declares, "I will not revoke the punishment,"

67. G. J. Wenham, "Law and the Legal System in the Old Testament," in *Law, Morality, and the Bible: A Symposium,* ed. B. N. Kaye and G. J. Wenham (Leicester: Inter-Varsity Press, 1978), 44; C. J. H. Wright, *An Eye for an Eye: The Place of Old Testament Ethics Today* (Downers Grove, Ill.: InterVarsity Press, 1983), 165-66.

68. On places of refuge, see M. Weinfeld, *Social Justice in Ancient Israel and in the Ancient Near East* (Minneapolis: Fortress Press, 1995), 120-32.

69. Cf. Wright's discussion of Israel's "scale of values" in *An Eye for an Eye,* 163-65.

70. These include the recognition of disciplinary, purificatory and revelatory judgment, the notion of intrinsic rewards and punishment, and judgment that takes the form of God's withdrawal of his presence and protection. See Travis, *Judgment of God,* 6-13.

71. Towner, "Retribution," 744.

but later God promises to be gracious if the offenders become penitent (5:15). "I will by no means leave you unpunished," God declares in Jeremiah 30:11, but in almost the next breath says, "I will have compassion" (30:18). The ultimate counter-theme is the Christian gospel, where the whole notion of just deserts and repayment in kind is turned on its head.[72] In the judgment of Timothy Gorringe, "The New Testament, far from underscoring retributivism, actually deconstructs it."[73]

It is one thing, then, to identify certain retributivist dynamics in biblical law and narrative; it is quite another to read out of the text a wholly retributivist theory of punishment that can be transferred directly into the secular criminal justice system today. The retributivist features that exist need to be understood and evaluated in light of several key factors, such as the Hebrew understanding of the intrinsic connection between deeds and their consequences, the use of rhetorical language, the cultic and covenantal character of Israelite society, the restorative goal of covenantal justice, and the role of nonretributivist features in the operation of divine justice.

(4) *Theological Considerations:* There are, finally, theological reasons to question the assumption that God's order operates according to the principle of retributive justice. Two may be mentioned here.

First, inasmuch as judicial retribution entails recompense for overt acts only, retribution operates on less than a fully personal level, since it deals with external actions rather than personal character. In the human sphere, this is necessarily so, for while we may agree that intention is crucial to the moral valuation of deeds, and while human courts may strive to take intention into account (e.g., in distinguishing between murder and manslaughter), it is exceptionally difficult to discover what a person's true motives are. Intentionality is not a matter of direct observation but a matter of precarious inference. Furthermore, attempts to discern motives for a particular action cannot be isolated from the person's entire moral history and character. A single action, even if ill-intentioned, may not be the best gauge of a person's true character and disposition. Genuine justice requires that all relevant factors be taken into account, but human beings can never know all these factors and

---

72. See, e.g., Matt. 5: 38-42; 20:1-16; Luke 15:11-32; John 8:7-11; Rom. 4:5; 5:6.

73. Gorringe, *God's Just Vengeance: Crime, Violence, and the Rhetoric of Salvation* (Cambridge: Cambridge University Press, 1996), 58.

are simply not equipped to make final judgments on people. In practice we can achieve only a rough justice, which may be preferable to no justice at all but is still less than ideal. By contrast, God deals with people not merely on the basis of external deeds but on the basis of their intentions, motivations, and enduring moral character, which God alone can know perfectly (1 Sam. 16:7; Matt. 5:8). For this reason, C. F. D. Moule insists that "the fittingness of retribution and the idea that punishment is proper, simply *qua* punishment, do need to be challenged in the name of personal values, and especially, in the name of the Christian gospel."[74] Retribution, Moule insists, has no place in Christian vocabulary.

Second, in his penetrating critique of penal theologies of the atonement, Thomas Talbot argues that the retributivist theory of justice is fundamentally flawed because punishment as punishment can never fully satisfy the demands of justice. Justice is fully satisfied only when the harm caused by wrongdoing is undone, when the damage is repaired, when the bad consequences of wrong actions are canceled out. Punishment does none of these things. Inasmuch as sin is anything that separates us from God and from each other, "perfect justice requires *reconciliation* and *restoration*. It requires, first, that sinners repent of their sin and turn away from everything that would separate them from others; it requires, second, that God forgive repentant sinners and that they forgive each other; and it requires, third, that God overcome, perhaps with their own co-operation, any harm that sinners do either to others or to themselves."[75] Paul Fiddes makes the same point: "What justice demands is not payment but repentance; it is finally 'satisfied' not by any penalty in itself but by the change of heart to which the penalty is intended to lead."[76] In short, God's justice can be ultimately vindicated not by retribution but only by reconciling forgiveness, for only thus are things made right.

Taken together, these philosophical, moral, biblical, and theological considerations warn us against seeing the satisfaction of retributive

74. Moule, "Punishment and Retribution," 5; so too Travis, *Christ and the Judgment of God*, 5.

75. Talbot, "Punishment, Forgiveness, and Divine Justice," *Rel St* 29 (1993): 151-68 (quote from 163).

76. Fiddes, *Past Event and Present Salvation: The Christian Idea of Atonement* (London/Louisville, Ky.: Darton, Longman & Todd/Westminster John Knox, 1989), 104.

justice as a fully adequate justification for the imposition of criminal punishment, and caution us against basing such a view on a superficial appeal to biblical texts that speak of God's punitive activity. Retributivism contains valid insights, and there are retributivist features in the biblical tradition. But on its own, retributivism is inadequate to deal with the complexities of the social institution of punishment and the depth and breadth of the biblical witness.

Other Approaches

The ideas of reform, deterrence (including prevention), and retribution (including reprobation) have been the dominant categories used in the long-running debate over the purpose of and moral justification for punishment. Each of these categories is valid and morally defensible in itself, but no single category is sufficient to account for all the dimensions of punishment. Not surprisingly, then, there have been several attempts to combine the strengths and insights of each of these categories. Many penal specialists today would insist that, far from being mutually exclusive, utilitarian and retributivist explanations are interdependent and mutually corrective. Certainly in practice, Western penal codes and courts have sought to achieve a variety of goals in imposing punishment, even if periodically certain goals have been prioritized at the expense of others.

Attempts have also been made to conceptualize the problem of crime and punishment in fresh terms. The use of human rights theory is a case in point. Here crime is understood as an interference with the rights and freedoms of others. But punishment is also an interference with the rights and freedoms of others — namely, offenders — and therefore requires special justification. The general justification for punishment is the protection of human rights through crime reduction and the promotion of the positive freedom of victims and potential victims. But there are limits to punishment guaranteed by the offender's continuing possession of human rights, limits that cannot be set aside for utilitarian or talionic purposes. Capital punishment is ruled out as a violation of the offender's right to life. "Cruel, inhuman and degrading punishments," such as torture, physical abuse, and forced public humiliation, are also excluded, since in the Universal Declaration of Human Rights they are considered abuses of inalienable human rights. Perpetual punishment without prospect of rehabilitation is also disallowed as a permanent denial of the offender's right to participate in social, cultural, and communal life. Rights also imply corresponding duties, especially from a biblical perspective.[77] If the state claims the right to punish the offender by depriving him or her of rights and freedoms, it has a corresponding duty to ensure that it inflicts no more harm on the offender than was intended by the sentence. The intention of imprisonment is the deprivation of liberty; that is the punishment. But other suffering inevitably ensues, such as the loss of family ties, the limited ability to make decisions for oneself, impaired prospects for future employment, and the dehumanizing impact of the prison community. The state has a duty to offset these handicaps by rehabilitative efforts, which will also enhance the offender's positive freedom by increasing his or her capacity to refrain from crime and to live as a responsible citizen.[78]

Human rights theory thus offers a helpful new framework for explaining and justifying criminal punishment, especially in view of the vitality, if not the imperialism, of human rights thinking in all other areas of contemporary social life.[79] But whether it achieves fundamental shifts at the institutional level of the criminal justice system remains to be seen.

The current justice system is a hybrid of many different — and, to some degree, conflicting — theories of punishment. No one penal theory has been able adequately to justify the institution of punishment in its present form. The result is a profound crisis in the penal system itself and widespread confusion among the general public over what purpose punishment is intended to serve. One public opinion poll in New Zealand showed that 36 percent of the population saw the aim of imprisonment as re-education of the offender, 29 percent as protection of other citizens, 24 percent as punishment, and 3 percent as providing a lesson to others. Twenty-three percent of the population favored physically disabling offenders, and 39 percent were in favor of the reintro-

77. On this, see C. D. Marshall, "'Made a Little Lower Than the Angels': Human Rights in the Biblical Tradition," in *Human Rights and the Common Good: Christian Perspectives,* ed. B. Atkin and K. Evans (Wellington, N.Z.: Victoria University Press, 1999), 14-76.

78. For a fuller summary with references, see Hudson, *Understanding Justice,* 67-74.

79. See Marshall, "'Made a Little Lower Than the Angels,'" 14-15, 60-62, 65-66.

duction of corporal punishment.[80] Obviously the community is not of a common mind on why criminals are punished. This places impossible demands on those running the system. Prison administrators are required to deter, hurt, and rehabilitate all at the same time, then denied the resources to do so and widely criticized for failing to meet such an incoherent and contradictory remit.

Howard Zehr argues that the Western penal system, although a mixture of several theoretical perspectives, remains largely committed to retribution.[81] A fundamentally retributive model has been subjected to a number of utilitarian adjustments (such as the concept of rehabilitation and alternatives to incarceration) to make it work better or appear more humane. But none of these adjustments have remedied the basic dysfunctionality of the retributive model. What is needed, he argues, is a new paradigm, a model of restorative justice, committed not merely to administering punishment but to making right what has gone wrong through crime, and employing appropriate institutional mechanisms for doing so. Advocates of restorative justice are often reluctant to speak of punishment at all, or to justify it on moral or philosophical grounds for fear of reinforcing the very notion of retributivism they are seeking to supplant.[82] Does this mean there is no place for punishment in a restorative model? Is the notion of punishment *replaced* by the concept of restoration? Or is there such a thing as *restorative* punishment?

Restorative Punishment?

One of the strengths of restorative justice, as of utilitarian theories of punishment, is the way it challenges us to subject to critical scrutiny the complex of impulses that lead us to punish other human beings. In light of such scrutiny, many of these impulses appear to be dishonorable and indefensible, especially when tested against the demands of Christian faith. Punishment for the sake of punishment is difficult to justify morally or theologically. Yet, as retributivism re-

---

80. As reported in the *New Zealand Listener,* 14 May 1994, 15.
81. Zehr, *Changing Lenses,* 83-94.
82. See Zehr, *Changing Lenses,* 209-10.

minds us, the link between justice and punishment is too important to be ignored or downplayed, and, as we will see in the next chapter, the theme of punishment is too well-entrenched in Scripture to be disregarded or minimized. The real question to be asked is whether punishment can play a positive role in the attainment of restorative justice. I believe it can, as long as, on the one hand, we broaden the concept of punishment to include the suffering involved in working for restoration and, on the other hand, understand the role of external punitive sanctions in essentially symbolic terms.

Punishment as the Pain of Taking Responsibility

It is now widely conceded that a significant weakness in the conventional criminal justice system is that it takes too little account of the needs of victims in dispensing justice. Technically the victim of crime is the impersonal state, and the responsibility of the courts is to enforce state law. In criminal legislation, the category of punishment is usually distinguished from that of restitution. Where an offender is ordered to pay reparation to the actual victim, it is typically in addition to some other punishment that is imposed for the act of lawbreaking itself and that is intended to satisfy the principle of justice and to uphold the public interest. But if justice is truly satisfied only when the harm done to the real victim is remedied, as restorative justice insists, then there is no reason why a serious and concrete contribution to doing so should not be regarded as a form of punishment. Certainly the suffering involved in confronting the personal consequences of one's actions, accepting responsibility for seeking reconciliation with those harmed, and working to restore (so far as is realistic) the damage caused will be sufficiently intense to qualify as punishment. Of course, in cases where an offender refuses to enter the process of reparation or remains a serious danger to the safety of others, different penalties may be justified. But the goal of the exercise should never be simply to make an offender suffer an appropriate measure of pain in order to "pay" for the pain he or she has caused the victim, as in retributivism. This simply increases the amount of misery in the world. Rather, the goal should be to facilitate a situation where the suffering that must inevitably be experienced in the wake of the crime serves to restore and repair.

Such an approach recognizes that in the aftermath of a crime, there is need for repair. The need is at least threefold. It is partly a matter of restitution and/or compensation by the offender to the victim, which brings with it a sense of vindication as well as a contribution to restoring what has been forcibly taken away by the crime.[83] It is partly a matter of resolution, if not reconciliation, between victim and offender, as well as between the offender and the wider community — that is, the resolving of what has distorted the appropriate relationship between them as fellow citizens and as human beings. And it is partly a matter of promoting restoration or healing within the offender's own character by clarifying that moral wrong has been done and that a change in the offender's behavior and disposition is necessary. This is the case because wrongdoing brings its own baneful consequences on the character of the offender, consequences that can be arrested only when the person accepts the pain of responsibility for his or her actions and strives to make amends to those injured. Such striving enables the offender to begin to expiate his or her own feelings of guilt and shame as well as offering the victim(s) the chance for closure.

The extent to which genuine restoration can be achieved in the wake of crime will vary from case to case. It will never be easy or painless, for there is nothing an offender dreads more than confronting his victim (and, often, vice versa). But if each of the three areas of injury listed above is addressed by the wrongdoer, he or she will experience intense suffering, which may fairly be called punishment. But it will be suffering in the service of restoration and reformation, not simply suffering as a consequence of society or the victim getting even with the culprit. It will be a form of punishment that stands in creative opposition to the wrong done, that seeks to arrest its influence and undermine its sway, not the kind of punishment that stands in continuity with wrongdoing and extends it further through payment in kind.

But what about crimes where grave physical or psychological injuries have been incurred, where full repair and restoration are impossible? Is retributive punishment the only remaining option? Not necessarily. Certainly the situation that prevailed before the crime can never be reproduced as though nothing had happened. Something *has* hap-

83. On the needs and experience of victims, see A. Hayden and P. Henderson, "Victims: The Invisible People," in *Restorative Justice*, 78-82.

pened, and it has made a permanent difference. The question is, What kind of difference? Need the victim's sense of violation continue forever? Must the offender be abandoned to the evil he or she has unleashed? The past cannot be undone literally, but all those affected by a crime may decide to react in retrospect to what has happened in such a way that its original negative significance is, eventually, reversed, so that the past ceases to control the present and becomes an occasion for growth and healing. Such a response can never be coerced and is not without emotional cost, especially for victims, and it may not be attainable for some individuals. But where it is possible, it requires offenders to take responsibility for the things they have done; they must submit to the inherent punishment of acknowledging their own guilt and accepting responsibility to deal with the full consequences of their wrongful actions.

A significant factor in the pain of taking responsibility is accepting the shame that public exposure of one's wrongdoing brings. In his seminal work on the topic, John Braithwaite contends that the experience of shaming, if mediated in the context of a supportive community committed to the ultimate well-being of offenders, can serve to restore and re-integrate wrongdoers into the community. Whereas *disintegrative* shaming stigmatizes and ostracizes wrongdoers and often drives them into deviant subcultures, *reintegrative* shaming maintains the bonds of respect or love and leads beyond reproval to repentance, forgiveness, and restoration. The most potent vehicle of re-integrative shaming is disapproval by one's immediate family and friends. But formal punishments too, if they are visible and nurture relational involvement in the community, such as restitution and community service, can also serve this end. In both cases the true punishment is not the penalty itself but the shame it symbolizes and the accountability it brings. "Punishment is often shameful and shaming usually punishes," Braithwaite says. "But whereas punishment gets its symbolic content only from its denunciatory association with shaming, shaming is pure symbolic content."[84] Positive shaming is not terminal, however; in the right environment it issues in restoration.

Punishment, by definition, entails the deliberate imposition of pain on an offender as a response to an offense. But arguably the most

---

84. Braithwaite, *Crime, Shame and Reintegration*, 73.

exquisite pain and the most profound shame associated with criminal offending comes not from incurring secondary penalties but from facing up to one's responsibility for violating another human being and striving to remedy its consequences. (I recently heard a former prisoner say that whereas the walls of his prison were ten feet thick, the wall of fear and shame he had to cross to face his rape victim, and her extended family and local community, was one hundered feet thick.) Such pain and shame are an inherent punishment, one imposed by the offense itself and by the offender's deliberate acceptance of responsibility for it. It is a restorative punishment, a punishment that promises healing. Can the same be said for the imposition of external, secondary sanctions?

Punishment as Symbol and Invitation

At this point, some of the insights of the "symbolic" theory of punishment propounded by Sir Walter Moberly and refined by his niece Elizabeth Moberly may have something to offer the model of restorative justice.[85] The symbolic theory seeks to overcome the dichotomy between the retributivist and utilitarian theories of punishment, which for the last two centuries have generally been defined in contrast to one another. The starting point of the symbolic theory is the recognition that there are two basic, perhaps universal human drives or instincts which underlie the practice of punishment — the drive for *just deserts*, the feeling that punishment "serves one right" for doing wrong, and the drive for *annulment*, the deep craving to undo or annul the wrong that has been committed. The singular attraction of retributivism is the way it speaks directly to these two drives. But its great weakness is that it sees punishment as both the consummation of wrongdoing and the undoing of wrongdoing at one and the same time. In actual fact, it is neither. The true consequences of wrongdoing, and the undoing or annulment of those consequences, belong to the moral and spiritual realm. Criminal punishment, however, belongs to the material and social realm; it is external and physical, something that is "added" to the crime. Punish-

---

85. W. Moberly, *The Ethics of Punishment*, 210-25; E. Moberly, *Suffering, Innocent and Guilty*, esp. 61-101, and "Penology," 463.

ment is not the automatic result of wrongdoing, nor does it possess the power, in and of itself, to undo or cancel the effects of wrongdoing. Yet it derives its moral quality from its relation to both these ideas.

The conception of two different orders, the moral and the material, is crucial to grasping the purpose and potential of punishment in the symbolic theory. Crime is an evil of the first order; it is a moral offense that carries its own inevitable repercussions. For the offender, the result of crime is a process of moral and spiritual deterioration in his or her own person. An inner moral degradation occurs. It may be gradual and imperceptible, but it is nonetheless real and, if left unchecked, will result in total ruination. It is this moral debasement, not external punishment, that is the true retribution for crime. Strictly speaking, it is not possible to confer just deserts upon a wrongdoer, for the real desert for crime is interior and automatic. As Walter Moberly explains, "The most certain and the most terrible retribution of our wrongdoing will then be nothing that is done *to* us, but simply what we ourselves have *become*."[86] The New Testament is full of this idea.[87] It is what Paul means when he says "the wages of sin is death" (Rom. 6:23). Death is not "added" to sin as a secondary penalty; it is the inherent outworking of sin. For society too, the true damage of crime is its impact on the moral fabric of the community, while for the victim the most injurious aspect of an offense is usually emotional and spiritual rather than physical and material.

Given the moral nature of criminal offending, society is duty-bound to react against evil, to repudiate it in principle by social censure and condemnation and to seek its annulment or negation lest it spread like a disease. The act of wrongdoing has set in motion an insidious process of moral decay. It is desirable and in the long run essential for both individual and social well-being that this process be arrested and, if possible, reversed. For society this is an act of self-preservation as well as a moral obligation. As a member of society, the offender *deserves* to be treated in a way that will help to check the process of deterioration and promote restoration to goodness. The victim also *deserves* to be treated

86. W. Moberly, *The Ethics of Punishment,* 179. See also E. Moberly, *Suffering, Innocent and Guilty,* 78, 84.

87. See, e.g., John 3:19; 8:34; Gal. 6:7; 1 John 3:14; 5:12; James 1:15. See further Chapter 4 below.

in a manner that will address the internal damage suffered through crime. It is in this connection that punishment has an important role to play. As already noted, punishment is not the true retribution for wrongdoing, nor is it the true undoing of wrongdoing. The real battle between good and evil takes place in a region deeper than any punishment can reach directly. But punishment can reflect this battle and may, indirectly, influence its course. It can do so by *symbolizing* or signifying the two deeper realities of retribution and annulment, thereby inviting or encouraging them to take place.

(1) On the one hand, punishment *symbolizes the corrupting impact of the misdeed on the wrongdoer's own person*. The punishment *refers* to this retribution but is not identical with it, as Walter Moberly points out: "The physical pain or material loss inflicted is designed to be a garish but arresting picture of the spiritual injury which he has inflicted both on himself and on his fellows. The ritual indignity which society puts upon him is only a parable of the spiritual indignity which he has put upon himself."[88] Just as in the biological realm physical pain serves as a danger signal that serious injury may occur, so in the social realm punitive pain is intended to awaken criminals to the danger they are in of doing permanent moral damage to themselves, as well as to the damage they have already done to others. The key point to note is that punishment is intended to foreshadow and forestall — not to inflict — the true consummation or retribution of wrongdoing. "Moral ruin is foreshadowed precisely in order that it may *not* be achieved," Walter Moberly writes. "In this sense punishment is *a kind of inverted sacrament*. Its object is, not to effect or to ratify that which it images, but to bring it to naught."[89] Punishment is intended to promote the moral restoration of the offender, but it can only do so by first identifying and seeking to arrest the moral harm unleashed by the criminal act.

> In punishment, the individual wrongdoer is himself an object of attention. His own pain and humiliation are partly designed to bring home to him symbolically the real nature of his deed, both its moral damage to himself and its calamitous repercussions on others. . . . His punishment is intended to induce him to rue his deed and to be ashamed of

88. Moberly, *The Ethics of Punishment*, 207.

89. W. Moberly, *The Ethics of Punishment*, 208. See also E. Moberly, *Suffering, Innocent and Guilty*, 78.

himself. If it is to fulfil this purpose, penal pain must ultimately be transmuted into penitential pain.[90]

It is penitential pain — that is, repentance and amendment of character, or conversion — that halts the moral debilitation that accompanies wrongdoing. This leads to the second symbolic dimension of punishment.

(2) As well as signifying the retributive consequences of wrongdoing (i.e., moral deterioration), thus satisfying the underlying drive to see wrongdoers get their deserts, albeit indirectly or symbolically, punishment *signifies the reversal or cancellation of wrongdoing*, thus satisfying the underlying drive to see crime annulled or put right. Once again, annulment is a fundamentally moral — that is to say, voluntary — matter. It requires repentance and reparation. No punishment can of itself annul. It is no more than a token payment for the injury suffered, a vivid gesture that symbolizes the need for the crime to be canceled, an invitation for the criminal to face the reality of the hurt he or she has caused and seek to make amends. Whereas retributivism equates the punishment with cancellation, and utilitarianism refuses to accept that cancellation is necessary, the symbolic theory sees punishment as a symbol of or invitation to annulment. The goal of annulment is not some abstract cancellation of wrong by virtue of having suffered sufficient pain under punishment. True annulment is the reformation of the offender and, I would add, the healing of the victim and restoration of the damaged relationships to wholeness.

All this, I suggest, has much to offer the theory and practice of restorative justice. Among the criticisms leveled at restorative justice is that it underestimates the social and moral function that the ceremonies of criminal law and infliction of penalties play in relieving the feelings of victims and the community. It is also ill-equipped to deal adequately with those who refuse to admit guilt or who represent an ongoing threat to the safety of the community. Whatever the merit of these or other criticisms,[91] they underline the need for restorative justice to articulate a theory of punishment that matches its agenda. Such

90. Moberly, *The Ethics of Punishment*, 221.

91. Cayley offers a sympathetic review of some of the problems and pitfalls associated with restorative and other alternative modes of handling criminal offending in *The Expanding Prison*, 358-65.

a theory would understand punishment not as identical to retribution and annulment, as retributivism views it, nor as incidental to reformation, as utilitarianism may regard it, but as an instrument for accessing the moral realm. It does so by mirroring, albeit imperfectly, the moral consequences of criminal offending and thereby inviting transformation and restoration. From this it follows that the form of punishment should be what is most conducive to achieving these goals. In fact, if the symbolic theory is to attain in practice what it espouses in principle, it is essential that the nature of the punishments imposed correspond with the goal sought. Since punishment is but a symbol of and an invitation to penitence and restoration, it will not achieve automatically the realities it seeks to portray, since any real change in the moral sphere demands the exercise of the offender's free choice. But the potency of the appeal issued by the punishment depends almost entirely on the shape of the punishment itself.

That punishment is a source of pain is not a persuasive objection to the practice of punishment as such, since pain is an essential component in all personal and spiritual growth. Suffering is not intrinsically evil. But to cause pain for its own sake, to strive only to inflict injury and hurt as just deserts for doing wrong, is both irrational and immoral. It is one thing to punish *although* it hurts; it is quite another to do so *because* it hurts.[92] While it makes sense to repay good deeds with further good, it makes little sense, morally or pragmatically, to repay evil deeds with further evil. Far better, and far more consistent with the Christian gospel, is to requite evil with a counteraction that seeks to redeem and restore (Rom. 12:21; 1 Thess. 5:15; 1 Pet. 3:9). Such counteraction may need to be imposed by society and may be painful, and hence may legitimately be regarded as punishment. But the intention of the punishment is to reclaim the offender, restore relationships, and bring healing to the victim.

This requires developing modes of punishment that focus on restoration rather than simply on more effective ways to deliver pain. In devising such punishments, certain considerations should be uppermost. Does the punishment express, clarify, and publicly declare that the offender's behavior was wrong? Does it include the opportunity for the offender to clarify and acknowledge his or her moral responsibility for

---

92. Cf. Moberly, *The Ethics of Punishment,* 68.

the crime and its impact? Does it involve reparation to the victim and the opportunity, should the victim concur, for reconciliation and forgiveness? Does it entail the wrongdoer rendering service to the victim or to others in the community? Does it contribute in some way to remedying the social context that helped spawn the crime and the criminal? Does it provide for the eventual re-integration of the offender in the community, and include ways of symbolizing his or her re-acceptance into the community that are as powerful and effective as the current rituals that symbolize the condemnation and exclusion of offenders? Does it, in short, minimize the dangers always inherent in the deliberate infliction of pain and maximize the potential for restoration and new life?

Summary

The question we have begun to pursue in this chapter is whether punishment has a legitimate role to play in a concept of justice as something that redeems, restores, and reconciles. In the following chapter I will turn more directly to New Testament teaching on this theme; for the present I have confined myself largely to the criminological debate over the purpose of punishment and its moral justification. In this debate, two main approaches have been taken to establish the legitimacy of punishment: the retributivist position, which sees punishment as a particular application of the principle of justice, and the utilitarian position, which insists that punishment needs to be judged not by justice but by utility. The former views punishment in terms of moral obligation; the latter asks not whether it is right to punish but whether it is necessary.

These two lines of thought have spawned several different ways of explaining and defending the social institution of punishment. Some defend punishment as a form of rehabilitation; others emphasize its role as a deterrent; others insist on its inherent justice when applied to those who deserve it and its value in publicly affirming key social values. Each of these approaches contains truth, each can lay claim to some biblical support, and each has a contribution to make to any new theory of punishment that seeks to go beyond the limitations of the established views. The sharp antithesis between retributive and utilitarian theories is not only unfortunate but quite false.[93] To administer punishment in the absence of guilt would be a monstrous injustice; this is the irreducible truth of retributivism. To punish solely because of guilt would be impossible, for we are all sinners, and decisions must be made about which wrongs to punish and how much to punish them, decisions that require utilitarian considerations to be taken into account. That punishment must serve some end beyond itself is the crucial insight of utilitarianism.

Restorative justice places emphasis on the moral and spiritual obligations that come with crime to respond in a way that endeavors to make things right. As such, it combines retributivist and utilitarian concerns, although restorative justice can be ascribed to neither school of thought, since it is concerned primarily with reconceptualizing justice, not justifying punishment. Yet punishment cannot be easily sidelined in any theory of justice. The practice of punishment is itself bound up with two deeply rooted human drives triggered in the aftermath of crime: the drive to see the offender held accountable for his or her actions and receive in some sense the just deserts of wrongdoing, and the drive to undo or annul the crime, to see restoration and healing occur. To deepen our appreciation of how restorative justice can respond to these two drives, we explored the symbolic theory of punishment, which, like restorative justice, transcends the dichotomy between utilitarianism and retributivism. Contemporary retributivists, drawing on sociological studies of crime and punishment,[94] commonly stress the expressive role of criminal punishment — that is, its indispensable function in demonstrating a society's moral boundaries, the limits of its tolerance. But the "audience" of punishment is not only the wider community; it is also — and perhaps principally — the individual offender. Punishment may be

---

93. E. Moberly observes that utilitarian theories of punishment logically include retributivist considerations. For example, by what right may a person be subject to reformative treatment unless it is deserved? How will punishment deter from crime unless it is imposed for crime? She insists that the dichotomy between retributivist and utilitarian approaches is a false one, and that "the current agenda for secular and Christian criminologists must be the reintegration of retributive and reformative ideals, to prevent further oscillation from one extreme to the other" ("Penology," 464). For a fuller defense of this position, see E. Moberly, *Suffering, Innocent and Guilty*, 82-101.

94. For a discussion of such sociological analysis, see Hudson, *Understanding Justice*, 79-138.

seen as a symbolic enactment of the inner consequences of wrongdoing and hence a call to penitence by the offender, and a symbolic demonstration of the need for annulment or cancellation of the wrong, and hence an invitation to reparation. Seen in such terms, punishment is not merely the negative infliction of pain but an attempt to check the evil consequences that flow from wrongdoing. Punishment is, in other words, a legitimate — perhaps necessary — instrument of restoration, though it is by no means an infallible instrument.

As such, all depends on what form punishment takes. If blameworthiness automatically implies that there is a situation to be remedied, any accompanying punishment should be, as far as possible, of a remedial kind. Restorative punishment is partly a matter of restitution or compensation for the victim, which brings with it a sense of vindication; it is partly a matter of resolution between victim and offender, as well as reconciliation between the offender and the community she or he has spurned; and it is partly a matter of promoting restoration or healing within the offender's own character and conduct. Measured against these criteria, many of the punishments employed in the current penal system, such as long periods of incarceration, are far from restorative; they are inherently destructive. Some criminal justice specialists now speak of the "tragic quality" of punishment: it is simultaneously necessary yet destined to a degree of futility.[95] But both the tragedy and the futility of punishment would be eased by the forging of stronger links, both conceptual and practical, between punishment and restoration.

According to David Cayley, Western criminal justice systems now stand at a crossroads. "They have inherited a procedural account of justice that proliferates rights but has nothing to say about what justice actually is; a retributivist theory of punishment that satisfies the public cry for the restoration of the moral order, but degenerates into pure revenge in the absence of a convincing mode of punishment; and a prison system, based on a mishmash of incoherent and unbelievable principles, that in reality does little more than warehouse the problem."[96] This crisis situation needs both alternative ways of dealing with criminal offending and fresh understandings of what justice and punishment are all about.

95. See Hudson, *Understanding Justice*, 88-89.
96. Cayley, *The Expanding Prison*, 347.

For too long, Christian thinking about justice and punishment has been dominated by notions of retribution. L. Gregory Jones accepts that considerations of retribution, deterrence, and rehabilitation may all have a contribution to make to a Christian view of punishment. "More strongly, however, Christian understandings and practices ought to challenge the adequacy of even thinking in terms of such theories; the aim ought to be the reform of actual practices of punishment within the context of a Christian vision of forgiveness and reconciliation."[97] The concept of restorative punishment is a move in that direction. It coheres well with Christian themes of repentance, reconciliation, and redemption, each of which entails not a denial or forgetting of the past but its creative re-appropriation. While it is possible, as we have seen, to identify reformative, reprobative, deterrent, and retributive dimensions to punishment in Scripture, the fundamental and distinctive concern of biblical jurisprudence is best expressed in terms of restoration or reconstruction. With that in mind, we turn now to consider New Testament teaching on divine and human punishment.

97. Jones, *Embodying Forgiveness,* 275.

CHAPTER 4

VENGEANCE IS MINE

Divine and Human Punishment in the New Testament

I have argued that divine justice, as portrayed by Paul and embodied by Jesus, is principally a redemptive or restorative justice rather than a vindictive or retributive justice. If this is true, we are confronted with the task of explaining the recurring emphasis in the New Testament, and in Scripture generally, on punishment. What is the relationship between justice that seeks to liberate and transform and penalties inflicted by God or human beings because of wrongdoing? In the previous chapter I approached this question mainly from the perspective of penological theory. The conclusion I reached was that there can be such a thing as restorative punishment, that punitive measures can be imposed in the ultimate service of reclaiming the wrongdoer and repairing the damage done. It is now time to consider whether the New Testament data on divine and human punishment points in the same direction.

The first thing to observe in turning specifically to New Testament teaching is that use of the terminology of punishment is strikingly confined. The ordinary Greek noun for "punishment" *(poinē)* does not even occur, while other common verbs and nouns for punishment appear only a handful of times,[1] sometimes figuratively and often as a result of dependence on Old Testament or Jewish tradition. Given the prominence of punitive terminology in the Septuagint and contemporary Jewish literature, this is an observation of some significance. In

---

1. These include *timoria/timōreō, kolasis/kolazō, ekdikos/ekdikeō, paideia/paideuō,* and *basanos/basanizō.*

145

light of it, Stephen Travis asserts that in the New Testament, "retributive concepts are almost displaced because of the nature of the Christian gospel."[2] The gospel announces a new relationship to God based on grace, forgiveness, and love, and this emphasis virtually eclipses the concept of retributive punishment.

We must beware, however, of the "word-concept fallacy." The idea of punishment may be present and intended even where the technical vocabulary is lacking. Notwithstanding the infrequency of punitive terminology, there is still a considerable amount of material in the New Testament on the matter of punishment that requires our attention. In assessing this material, it is helpful to distinguish, on the one hand, between divine punishment (penalties inflicted by God for wrongdoing) and human punishment (penalties inflicted by human agents), and, on the other hand, between punishments administered within the community of faith (the church) and those that operate in wider society (the state). These distinctions are not absolute, however. God's punishment may be seen to operate through human intermediaries (Rom. 13:4; cf. Acts 5:1-11; 1 Cor. 11:30), while human punishment may entail the ceremonial handing over of offenders to God, or to Satan, for discipline (1 Cor. 5:5; 1 Tim. 1:20). Nonetheless, for the sake of clarity I will work with these categories.

Punishment by Human Agency

There is a large body of material in the New Testament that depicts punishments administered by human agents, sometimes expressly on behalf of God, sometimes not. In some texts these penalties are administered within the community of faith; in other texts they occur in a wider social setting.

Punishment in Society

Many of the references to human punishment in the New Testament are purely descriptive. They describe physical chastisements, such as

2. Travis, *Christ and the Judgment of God: Divine Retribution in the New Testament* (London: Marshall & Pickering, 1986), 168.

whippings or beatings, inflicted on slaves by their masters[3] or on members of the Jesus movement by the judicial authorities.[4] These narrative texts simply attest to the disciplinary practices of the day; they imply neither approval nor disapproval of specific punitive actions. In Romans 13:4 and 1 Peter 2:14, however, the role of governing authorities in punishing crime is referred to with obvious approval.[5] In both cases, when the state punishes wrongdoing, it is understood to be an instrument of divine wrath and vengeance on evildoers (*ekdikos eis orgē,* Rom. 13:4; *eis ekdikēsin,* 1 Pet. 2:14), something which, by engendering fear, is expected to have a deterrent effect on others (Rom. 13:2-4). Whether possession of the sword in Romans 13:4 implies divine sanction for capital punishment is something I will consider in the next chapter. But there can be no doubt that it refers at the very least to punitive or disciplinary action by those in political authority to control and requite criminal activity.

It is important to note that the terms used in these texts for the state's punishment of crime — "wrath" *(orgē)* and "vengeance" or, better, "requital" *(ekdikos, ekdikēsis)* — are elsewhere reserved for God alone. "Beloved, never avenge yourselves, but leave room for the wrath of God; for it is written, 'Vengeance is mine, I will repay, says the Lord.'"[6] This means that the state is said to do what God alone has the right to do, and which Christians are expressly forbidden to do — namely, avenge wrongdoing. In some sense, then, the state acts as God's instrument or "servant" *(diakonos,* Rom. 13:4) for visiting wrath on wrongdoers in present history. It would be going too far, however, to conclude that these texts give an unqualified mandate to the state to act in the place of God by punishing sinful conduct. (After all, both texts are referring to pagan Roman authorities who wrongly punished Christians for their faith, which would hardly be understood as an experience of God's wrath.) The writers presumably have in mind God's providential judgment on evil being exercised, in part, through the me-

3. See, e.g., Matt. 18:34; 24:45-49/Luke 12:42-49; 1 Pet. 2:18-25.

4. See, e.g., Mark 13:9; Matt. 24:9; Acts 4:21; 22:5; 26:11; Luke 23:16, 22; 2 Cor. 6:9; 11:23-24.

5. More neutral references to state actions can be found in John 19:11; Acts 24:25; 25:11; 1 Tim. 2:1-4; Titus 3:1-2.

6. Rom. 12:19; cf. Luke 18:7; 21:22; 1 Thess. 4:6; 2 Thess. 1:8-9; Heb. 10:30; Rev. 6:10; 19:2; cf. Acts 7:24.

dium of human magistrates acting to punish transgression. It is not so much that God instructs or empowers human courts to administer vengeance autonomously on God's behalf. Rather, the state's punishment of evil deeds may, in certain circumstances, be seen as a vehicle of God's wrath against sin. What these circumstances are is hinted at in the description of the state's task as that of restraining those who do evil (*tō to kakon prassonti*, v. 4), which evildoing believers are expressly forbidden to engage in (*ean de to kakon poiēs, phobou*, v. 4), and of promoting what is good (*to agathon*, v. 4), which coincides with the calling of believers to "do what is good" (*to agathon poiei*, v. 3). In other words, to the extent that the state acts in a manner consistent with the moral standards and responsibilities incumbent on believers, it acts as a servant of God, albeit unawares. With respect to evil, it functions as a medium of divine wrath, which Paul understands as God's way of providentially controlling human sin by permitting its deadly consequences to fall back on its perpetrators.

This understanding of divine wrath is consistent with Paul's classical discussion of the topic in Romans 1:18-32. I will examine this passage in more detail in the next section on divine punishment. To anticipate that discussion here, we may simply observe that in this passage Paul sees divine wrath working itself out in the fallen world not by God's periodic intervention to wreak retribution on individual sinners, but by the measured withdrawal of God's protective influence and control so that sinners "receive back" (v. 27) in their own experience the degenerative consequences of their rejection of God. This is not some impersonal, immanent cause-and-effect mechanism, for God is personally involved in the process. But neither is it individually planned personal reprisal, for three times Paul defines wrath as God's "giving up" of people to reap the harvest of their own choices (vv. 24, 26, 28). As C. F. D. Moule observes in a different context, "If God willed the dire consequences that ensue on sin, it does not necessarily follow that he has willed them retributively, punitively. It may be that he has willed them as the only way of doing justice to the freedom and responsibility of the human personality, as he has created it."[7] Divine wrath, then, is a kind of "intrinsic punishment" whereby human destiny unfolds under the

7. Moule, "Punishment and Retribution: An Attempt to Delimit Their Scope in New Testament Thought," *NPCJ* 10 (1990): 6.

ultimate control of a loving God who acts personally but nonretributively to resist evil. The same sort of scenario is envisaged in Romans 13:1-7. Here God's wrath is activated against sin on the human scene through an established authority in society punishing criminal actions. It is important to stress the providential character of the state's role as wrath-bearer. For if the state per se is seen as God's vice-regent with an obligation to exact revenge on criminals, there is a real danger of absolutizing, even divinizing, the coercive power of the state, which the first Christians certainly did not do (cf. Phil. 2:11; 3:20; Rev. 13:1-18). If, on the other hand, the state's God-intended role in promoting good and restraining evil is seen as one of the ways God exercises providentially the divine prerogative of wrath upon wrongdoers, there is room for a more nuanced, critical understanding of the state.

Punishment in the Church

The language of punishment is also occasionally found in connection with church discipline, most notably in the Corinthian correspondence. It goes without saying that such discipline was not administered on the basis of canon law or any codified system of church membership. Nor did it entail the imposition of any disadvantages on offenders or any form of physical chastisement, such as employed in synagogue discipline. The penalties ranged from personal admonition,[8] to overt rebuke,[9] to temporary expulsion from the community.[10] In applying these sanctions to its members, the church had no established disciplinary law it could appeal to. It relied instead on the direction and leading of the Spirit-in-community to determine appropriate sanctions in specific instances. This is not to say that there was no "law" involved at all. Ernst Käsemann insists that the early communities were conscious of standing under a divine law, the eschatological law of God, mediated in the power of the Spirit through the authoritative pronouncements of charismatic figures such as prophets and apostles.

---

8. Rom. 15:14; Col. 3:16; 1 Thess. 5:14; 2 Thess. 3:14, 15; Titus 3:10, 11.

9. Matt. 18:15; 2 Cor. 2:6; Eph. 5:11; 1 Tim. 5:20; 2 Tim. 4:2; Titus 1:9, 13; 2:15. Cf. John 16:8; Rev. 3:19.

10. Matt. 18:17; 1 Cor. 5:11, 13; 2 Thess. 3:14; 2 Tim. 3:1-5; Titus 3:10. Cf. Rom. 16:17.

Käsemann identifies on form-critical grounds several examples of these pronouncements, or "sentences of holy law," in which "a real edict of the Holy Spirit is being promulgated" in response to wrongdoing and in the interests of preserving what we call "order" and what Paul calls "peace" (1 Cor. 14:33). In other words, in the exercise of church discipline, Spirit and "law" were not separated; the Spirit granted insight into the exigencies of a particular situation and inspired those endowed with the task of discipline, in the context of communal discernment, to declare authoritatively how the "law of Christ" applied (Gal. 6:2; 1 Cor. 9:21).[11]

1 Corinthians 6:1-11

Before examining specific texts relating to punishment in the community of faith, it is worth emphasizing that Paul, like Jesus, encourages Christian communities to resolve disputes internally and not to drag one another into pagan courts.[12] In 1 Corinthians 6:1-11, Paul expresses indignation at the use of litigation by Corinthian believers to settle even the trivial disputes of daily life (vv. 2, 4). Paul's outrage would have stemmed from a number of factors. As a Jew, he no doubt shared the view of the rabbis that God was defamed if Jewish disputes were brought before Gentile judges, which necessitated the establishment of arbitration courts in Diaspora communities to settle matters internally. At the same time, Paul considered it ludicrous for Christians, who were destined to judge the world and angels, to submit minor disputes to worldly courts (1 Cor. 6:2, 5). But what weighed most heavily with Paul was his belief that the gospel itself was shamed by the inability of Christians to reconcile their differences in a manner consistent with Christian love. This is why he describes the Corinthians' penchant for litigation as "already a defeat for you" (v. 7).

11. Käsemann, "Sentences of Holy Law in the New Testament," in Käsemann, *New Testament Questions of Today* (London: SCM, 1969), 66-81. The legal nature of these utterances is disputed by E. Schüssler Fiorenza, "Judging and Judgment in the New Testament Communities," in *Judgment in the Church*, ed. W. Bassett and P. Huizing (New York: Seabury Press, 1977), 3.

12. See 1 Cor. 6:1-11; cf. 2 Cor. 13:1-2; Matt. 18:15-17. On Paul's knowledge of the Jesus tradition at this point, see D. Wenham, *Paul: Follower of Jesus or Founder of Christianity?* (Grand Rapids: William B. Eerdmans, 1995), 210-13.

Seen in the context of the wider problem of social division in the Corinthian community and in light of the realities of civil litigation in first-century Roman Corinth,[13] the use of worldly courts by Christians to adjudicate disputes represented a defeat for the gospel in two ways. First, the courts would probably favor those of higher social status in the dispute. It was generally forbidden in the Roman legal system for people to sue their social superiors, so we should probably envisage a situation in which a powerful plaintiff brings a suit against someone of lower or equal rank.[14] In the former case, the plaintiff's greater wealth and status would sway the decision; in the latter case, the court might vindicate the party that offered the highest bribe or exerted the greatest extrajudicial leverage. This would result not just in a subversion of justice but in a practical defrauding of fellow Christians (vv. 7-8), since financial penalties would be imposed on the losing parties, the severity varying according to the social rank of the accused. Second, insofar as litigation in antiquity was intensely acrimonious and involved the need to blacken the character of one's opponent, going to court would aggravate still further the enmity and broken relationships within the congregation itself.

In both respects, recourse to pagan courts manifested "the community's assimilation to values of the outside world."[15] Because Christian believers belong to an alternative community, Paul expects them to have significantly different values and practices, not least with respect to the use of public litigation to exact justice, impose retribution, and defend personal honor. He therefore advocates private arbitration, an extrajudicial procedure available under Graeco-Roman law[16] and supported by Scripture (Deut. 16:18-20), wherein a community member is selected to mediate between the disputing parties. If verse 4 is part of Paul's instructions about the appointment of congre-

13. See B. Winter, "Civil Litigation in Secular Corinth and the Church: The Forensic Background to 1 Corinthians 6:1-8," *NTS* 37, no. 4 (1991): 557-72.

14. See D. G. Horrell, *The Social Ethos of the Corinthian Correspondence: Interests and Ideology from 1 Corinthians to 1 Clement* (Edinburgh: T. & T. Clark, 1996), 109-112, 137-42.

15. A. C. Mitchell, "Rich and Poor in the Courts of Corinth: Litigiousness and Status in 1 Corinthians 6:1-11," *NTS* 39, no. 4 (1993): 562. See also J. M. G. Barclay, "Thessalonica and Corinth: Social Contrasts in Pauline Christianity," *JSNT* 47 (1992): 49-74.

16. On methods of dispute settlement in antiquity, see J. D. M. Derrett, "Judgment and 1 Corinthians 6," *NTS* 37, no. 1 (1991): 22-36.

gational arbiters, which is possible though not certain,[17] he advises that they be drawn from the lowest social ranks in the church, those most despised by the litigious elite. This would serve to discourage status-seeking believers from using litigation to gain social clout and would allow for dispute settlement in a manner consistent with the Christian conception of justice. It would also be good practice for saints whose destiny it is to judge the world (vv. 2-3; cf. Matt. 19:28/Luke 22:28-30).[18]

While the entire discussion relates to civil and not to criminal matters (there was little chance of the church evading the criminal law of the Roman state), the underlying principles — namely, the concern for equal and just relationships between disputants, the priority given to securing right relationships over financial or social advantage, and the role of wider relational networks in resolving disputes — all have implications for criminal concerns as well.

1 Corinthians 5:1-8 and 1 Timothy 1:19-20

In 1 Corinthians 5:1-8, Paul calls for the punishment of a member of the church, probably a man of high social status, who was living in a sexual relationship with his (deceased?) father's wife. Paul is alarmed not simply by an individual instance of immoral — even illegal[19] — conduct but by the congregation's willing acceptance of the practice. The congregation had failed to discipline the man, not only because of his

17. Cf. B. Kinman, "'Appoint the Despised as Judges!' (1 Corinthians 6:4)," *TynBul* 48, no. 2 (1997): 345-54.

18. On the eschatological statement in verses 2-3, see M. Delcor, "The Courts of the Church of Corinth and the Courts of Qumran," in *Paul and the Dead Sea Scrolls,* ed. J. Murphy-O'Connor and J. H. Charlesworth (New York: Crossroad, 1990), 80-84.

19. If the woman was the man's stepmother, marriage to her would have been considered incestuous, and as such was expressly forbidden under both Jewish law (Lev. 18:8; 20:11; Deut. 22:30; 27:20) and Roman law. (For references to Roman law, see H. Conzelmann, *A Commentary on the First Epistle to the Corinthians* [Philadelphia: Fortress, 1975], 96n.29.) If the woman was the former concubine of the deceased father, not his legal wife, as C. S. De Vos argues, then the son's relationship with her was not technically illegal and perhaps not uncommon. But Paul still considered it to be immoral, since he would have counted the woman's relationship to the father as ethically equivalent to marriage (cf. 1 Cor. 6:16). See further C. S. De Vos, "Stepmothers, Concubines, and the Case of PORNEIA in 1 Corinthians 5," *NTS* 44, no. 1 (1998): 104-14.

social position but also because they applauded his action as a demonstration of Christian liberty. This is suggested by the references to the Corinthians' arrogance and boasting in verses 2 and 6; by the way in which Paul addresses the entire community, not the specific offender; and by the libertarian slogans that enjoyed currency in the Corinthian church (1 Cor. 6:12; 8:1; 10:23).[20]

The punishment Paul calls for — "you are to hand this man over to Satan for the destruction of the flesh, so that his spirit may be saved in the day of the Lord" (v. 5) — is very mysterious. (The woman is not handed over, presumably because she is not a member of the church.) There is little consensus on its precise meaning. Some sort of ritual expulsion or excommunication from the community, and hence exposure to Satan's power,[21] is clearly involved. Such an action is motivated by a concern to protect the community, God's temple (3:16), from contamination by the man's immoral behavior by means of "cleaning out the old yeast so that you may be a new batch" (v. 7).[22] But the meaning of the "destruction of the flesh" and "salvation of the spirit" continues to be debated.[23] One widespread view is that Paul envisages the church pronouncing a curse on the offender that will result in physical debilitation and eventual death, and Ivan Havener even speaks of "the capital punishment required by Paul."[24] The offender's death is expected somehow to facilitate his ultimate salvation, perhaps by means of a deathbed repentance. If this interpretation is sound, it is significant that physical penalties such as flogging or stoning are not employed, as they sometimes were in the synagogue.[25] The ultimate penalty of death

20. So A. Y. Collins, "The Function of 'Excommunication' in Paul," *HTR* 73, no. 1-2 (1980): 253; and G. Harris, "The Beginnings of Church Discipline: 1 Corinthians 5," *NTS* 37, no. 4 (1991): 1-21. M. D. Goulder thinks the episode was an isolated exception to a prevailing sexual asceticism in the church. See "Libertines? (1 Cor. 5-6)," *NovT* 41, no. 4 (1999): 334-48.

21. Cf. 2 Cor. 4:4; Eph. 2:2, 6; 6:12; Col. 1:13; Acts 26:18; 1 John 5:19; Rev. 2:13.

22. See B. S. Rosner, "Temple and Holiness in 1 Corinthians 5," *TynBul* 42, no. 1 (1991): 137-45.

23. See B. Campbell, "Flesh and Spirit in 1 Cor. 5:5: An Exercise in Rhetorical Criticism," *JETS* 36, no. 3 (1993): 331-42; and G. D. Fee, *God's Empowering Presence* (Peabody, Mass.: Hendrickson, 1994), 324-27.

24. Havener, "A Curse for Salvation — 1 Corinthians 5:1-5," in *Sin, Salvation, and the Spirit*, ed. D. Durken (Collegeville: Liturgical Press, 1979), 341.

25. On the judicial and other functions of Diaspora synagogues, see M. D. Nanos,

is exacted not by literal execution but by exclusion from the community, which is thereby to be "cut off from Christ" (Gal. 5:4) and exposed to Satan, who has the power of death (cf. Heb. 2:14).

This interpretation is by no means certain, however. The detailed analysis of the passage by J. T. South subjects it to devastating critique.[26] South insists that Paul was concerned for the welfare of the offender as well as the purity of the community and that the goal of his excommunication was to bring him to repentance and restoration to the congregation. "There is little warrant for the idea that Paul would have been content to 'sacrifice' one member of the community for the benefit of the whole without making every effort to redeem the one along with the many."[27] South concludes that "Paul did not, as often maintained, admonish the Corinthians to curse and destroy a deviant member. Rather he admonished them to expel such a person from their midst in the hope of regaining him and of protecting the community from his deviant behaviour."[28] That is to say, the punishment imposed was intended to be both reformative of the offender and restorative for the community.[29] Paul's assumption of corporate responsibility by the Corinthian church for the situation is also noteworthy. While the individual offender is disciplined, he is not made a scapegoat; instead, the whole community is called to account for the "crime" and summoned to change.[30]

This interpretation coheres well with 1 Timothy 1:19-20, the only genuine verbal parallel in the New Testament to 1 Corinthians 5:5. Here Hymenaeus and Alexander, two false teachers (cf. 2 Tim. 2:17; 4:14-15), are "turned over to Satan, so that *[hina]* they may learn not to blaspheme." Unless the purpose clause expresses a purely vindictive

---

The Mystery of Romans: The Jewish Context of Paul's Letter (Minneapolis: Fortress Press, 1996), 41-50.

26. South, "A Critique of the 'Curse/Death' Interpretation of 1 Corinthians 5:1-8," *NTS* 39, no. 4 (1993): 539-61.

27. South, "A Critique of the 'Curse/Death' Interpretation of 1 Corinthians 5:1-8," 559.

28. South, "A Critique of the 'Curse/Death' Interpretation of 1 Corinthians 5:1-8," 561.

29. Contra Harris, "The Beginnings of Church Discipline," 18.

30. Cf. B. S. Rosner, "'Οὐχὶ μᾶλλον ἐπενθήσατε': Corporate Responsibility in 1 Corinthians 5," *NTS* 38, no. 3 (1992): 470-73.

motive, the intention of the penalty is to encourage repentance and restoration (cf. 2 Tim. 2:25). In this text, as in 1 Corinthians 5, the author conceives of the world in terms of two opposed realms, which, to use the language of Colossians, may be called "the domain of darkness" and "the kingdom of [God's] beloved son" (Col. 1:13; cf. 1 John 5:19). To belong to the community of faith, and thus be incorporated into Christ's kingdom, is to enjoy protection from the ravages of Satan. To be expelled from the community is to forfeit that protection and be "turned over" *(paradidōmi)* to the realm controlled by Satan. This "turning over" is a matter of the withdrawal of God's protective hand (here the fellowship of believers) so that unrepentant malefactors experience the full consequences of the choice they have already made to "abandon themselves" to sin (cf. *heautous paredokan,* Eph. 4:19). The clear expectation is that the result of this delivering over will be suffering, stemming both from the shame of being openly repudiated by God's people (and in some sense also by God — cf. Matt. 18:18; John 20:23), and from the hostility elicited from Satan. But the purpose of inflicting such punishment is not merely vindictive. The aim is two-fold: to protect the community from contamination with evil, and to encourage repentance and restoration of the obstinate sinner. While the suffering is caused directly by Satan, it is indirectly used by God for positive educative purposes, an idea that recurs frequently in the New Testament, as we will see later (e.g., 2 Cor. 12:7-10).[31]

2 Corinthians 2:5-11; 7:5-13

Punitive action against errant Christians is also mentioned in 2 Corinthians. In 2 Corinthians 2:5-11 and 7:5-13, Paul refers to a punishment imposed by the Corinthian congregation on someone who had personally offended him. In 2 Corinthians 7:11, the punishment is referred to by the term *ekdikēsis* ("punishment," NRSV), which could carry the sense of vengeance. But in light of Romans 12:19, the term here cannot denote spiteful revenge or even simple retribution. It is a forensic metaphor for some form of congregational discipline or rebuke aimed at

---

31. On Paul's view of Satan, see S. R. Garrett, "The God of This World and the Affliction of Paul," in *Greeks, Romans, and Christians,* ed. D. L. Balch, E. Ferguson, and W. A. Meeks (Minneapolis: Fortress Press, 1990), 104-09.

producing repentance and reformation.[32] Indeed, Paul terms the punishment a "rebuke" *(epitimia)* in 2 Corinthians 2:6 and speaks of his desire to see the man forgiven, consoled, and restored to full fellowship (cf. 7:9-10).

The identity of the offender is unclear. The traditional view is that he is the incestuous man disciplined in 1 Corinthians 5:1-8, who had come to his senses and was now seeking re-admission to the church. But most contemporary exegetes reject this identification, since the offense in 1 Corinthians 5 is against the community and the law, whereas the offense in 2 Corinthians 2 and 7 is against Paul personally. The latter offense is now commonly attributed to some unknown party who had directly challenged Paul's apostolic authority or insulted his personal representative. Margaret Thrall even speculates that the culprit had robbed Paul of some of the money he was collecting for the saints in Jerusalem (cf. 1 Cor. 16:2).[33] Colin Kruse, however, has sought to rehabilitate the case for seeing the offender as the same in both epistles. Kruse proposes that when the church received Paul's instructions to discipline the incestuous member, it failed to carry out the punishment immediately. The man remained unrepentant and subsequently mounted a strong personal attack on Paul, questioning Paul's authority to discipline him. When, after further urging from Paul, the church did instigate discipline, the man repented and was forgiven by Paul.[34]

If Kruse is correct, the case for seeing the punishment called for in 1 Corinthians 5:5 as restorative in intention is strengthened further. The identity of the offender in 2 Corinthians 2:5 and 7:11 must remain uncertain, however. What *is* certain is the remarkable concern that Paul shows for his welfare. Paul acknowledges that the offense has been a great source of pain to him and others (2:5) and has needed correction or rebuke (2:6). But the penalty has now served its purpose of stimulating what Paul later calls a "godly grief that produces repentance" (7:10), so that to prolong the man's punishment may cause him to be "overwhelmed by excessive sorrow" (2:7). Paul, who is the victim of the of-

32. So R. P. Martin, *2 Corinthians* (Waco: Word, 1986), 235-36.

33. Thrall, "The Offender and the Offence: A Problem of Detection in 2 Corinthians," in *Scripture: Meaning and Method,* ed. B. P. Thompson (Hull, U.K.: Hull University Press, 1987), 65-78.

34. Kruse, "The Offender and the Offence in 2 Corinthians 2:5 and 7:12," *EvQ* 88, no. 2 (1988): 129-39.

fense, speaks of having already forgiven the offender (2:10) and summons a similar response from the rest of the church. This will serve to thwart Satan's destructive designs (2:11), to confirm the zeal of the church for Christian truth (cf. 7:12-13), and to restore the well-being or peace of the community. Strikingly, Paul speaks of forgiveness being necessary not only for the sake of the offender but also for the sake of the community (2:10). If the church fails to move beyond its punitive stance and bring closure to the offense and reconciliation to relationships, Satan will get the upper hand. It is clear, then, that Paul saw church discipline not as a matter of personal retribution but as a matter of corporate restoration. "It must be practised in love," Kevin Quast explains, "with the best interests of both the offender and the church in mind. Without a willingness to forgive, discipline will destroy the church."[35]

2 Corinthians 10:6

In 2 Corinthians 10:6, Paul speaks of standing "ready to punish every disobedience, when your obedience is complete." Paul is using a combination of military and forensic imagery[36] to refer to his intention to discipline intruders in the Corinthian congregation who have been undermining Paul's authority and hindering the church in its obedience to the gospel. Again the term *ekdikēsai* ("punish," NRSV) denotes not personal revenge or mere retribution but an authoritative refutation of theological error (cf. v. 5) and formal repudiation of those who promote it (cf. 2 Tim. 2:25; 3:16; 4:2; Titus 1:13; 2:15).

Social Ostracism: Matthew 18:15-20; Romans 16:17; 1 Corinthians 5:11, 13; 2 Thessalonians 3:6, 14-15; 2 Timothy 3:1-5; Titus 3:10; cf. Galatians 6:1

There are several instances in the New Testament where some form of social ostracism or excommunication from the community is recommended as a penalty for wrongdoing (although it would be anachronis-

---

35. Quast, *Reading the Corinthian Correspondence: An Introduction* (Mahwah, N.J.: Paulist Press, 1994), 115; cf. 135-36.
36. See V. P. Furnish, *II Corinthians* (New York: Doubleday, 1984), 458-59, 463-64.

tic to envisage the elaborate excommunication procedures of later times). The most notable examples are the "handings over to Satan" referred to in 1 Corinthians 5:5 and 1 Timothy 1:19-20, which we have just discussed. The withholding of fellowship is prescribed for cases of immorality, drunkenness, greed, idolatry, dishonesty, indolence, fractiousness, and false teaching.[37] But it is not the case that certain sins in themselves are thought to merit excommunication; it is persistent impenitence on the part of offenders that attracts the penalty. For this reason excommunication can be seen as a kind of self-judgment, or more accurately as an external, symbolic enactment by the church of what the offender has already done at a moral and spiritual level — separate himself or herself from the sanctity of the community. It might also function as a forewarning of future divine judgment on those that have done so (cf. 1 Cor. 11:31). But the immediate goal of the procedure, as we will see, is redemptive.

Of particular interest is Matthew 18:15-20, where Jesus instructs his followers to treat a persistent and unrepentant offender in the community like a Gentile or a tax collector. Since Gentiles are, by definition, outside the Jewish community, and tax collectors were considered apostate, most commentators understand the Matthean penalty as a form of excommunication. Given the significant in-group/out-group distinction in Mediterranean society, for an insider now to be treated as an outsider would be a cause of deep shame or dishonor (cf. *hina entrapē*, 2 Thess. 3:14). In a perceptive discussion, Marlin Jeschke insists that such excommunication or social avoidance is intended to have a redemptive intent. It is not a loveless condemnation, nor does it represent a departure from grace or a denial of the inclusivism of the gospel. "On the contrary, its function is to prevent persons from anaesthetising themselves against grace. Excommunication is the form under which the church continues to make grace available to the impenitent."[38] The goal is to preserve the integrity of the church and to clarify a person's true standing with respect to Christian discipleship, so that the one under correction may avail himself or herself of the grace of re-

37. Rom. 16:17; 1 Cor. 5:11, 13; 2 Thess. 3:6, 14-15; 1 Tim. 1:19-20; 6:3-5; 2 Tim. 3:1-5; Titus 3:10; 2 John 7-11.

38. Jeschke, *Discipling the Brother: Congregational Discipline According to the Gospel* (Scottdale, Pa.: Herald Press, 1972), 105.

pentance and restoration. Arguably this is what is implied in an offender assuming the status of a Gentile or a tax collector (Matt. 18:17). It need not mean, as is often assumed by exegetes, that the person is to be treated as a pariah, for while Gentiles do serve sometimes in Matthew as negative paradigms,[39] Matthew's Jesus also has considerable contact with Gentiles and outcasts and earns notoriety as "a friend of tax collectors and sinners" (Matt. 11:19).[40] Furthermore, according to Bruce Malina and Richard Rohrbaugh, "reconciliation is a primary social feature of Matthew's presentation of the teaching of Jesus."[41] The point of 18:17 may therefore be that in reverting to the condition of an outsider ("Gentile or tax collector"), the offender once again becomes a candidate for the gospel, a recipient of the call to discipleship, a lost sheep awaiting restoration (cf. 18:10-14).[42]

It is not coincidental that the saying about excommunication is followed by a statement on the gathered community's divinely delegated authority to bind and loose (18:18-20) and by a saying and parable dealing with forgiveness (18:21-35). David McClister has proposed that the passage on binding and loosing lies at the center of a chiastic arrangement of material that spans Jesus' first (17:22-23) and second (20:17-19) passion predictions. Chiastic arrangements usually serve to draw the reader's or hearer's attention to the material at the center of the structure as being the key, climax, or main point of the discussion. They also place related materials in parallel with each other on either side of the center, thus encouraging readers to compare or contrast the paired units.[43] If McClister's analysis of the literary structure of chapters 17 through 20 is plausible, it sharpens our appreciation of the intention of the disciplinary instructions in 18:15-20. The center of the chiasm is the saying on

---

39. Matt. 5:47; 6:7, 32; 7:6 (?); 20:19, 25; 24:9.

40. See also Matt. 2:1-12; 3:23-25; 4:24; 8:5-13; 10:9-13; 11:19; 15:21-28; 24:14; 28:19-20.

41. Malina and Rohrbaugh, *Social Science Commentary on the Synoptic Gospels* (Minneapolis: Fortress Press, 1992), 119.

42. So Jeschke, *Disciplining the Brother,* 134-35; and R. B. Hays, *The Moral Vision of the New Testament: A Contemporary Introduction to New Testament Ethics* (Edinburgh: T. & T. Clark, 1996), 102. Cf. W. M. Swartley, *Israel's Scripture Traditions and the Synoptic Gospels: Story Shaping Story* (Peabody, Mass.: Hendrickson, 1994), 93.

43. McClister, "'Where Two or Three Are Gathered Together': Literary Structure as a Key to Meaning in Matt. 17:22-20:19," *JETS* 39, no. 4 (1996): 549-58.

"binding and loosing" (18:18-20). There has been a long debate over the specific referents of binding and loosing. According to Robert Gundry, the immediate context favors a primary reference to the "disciplinary retention of sins by means of ostracism, and to forgiveness of sins by means of restoration to fellowship."[44] Yet when seen as the heart of the entire subsection of Matthew's narrative, the saying can be applied to every aspect of discipleship discussed in the larger context. All actions of disciples should be characterized by an agreement between heaven and earth — that is, by an effort to act on earth in a way that corresponds to God's will in heaven (cf. 6:10). This applies especially to dealing with broken relationships. The discussion on discipline (18:15-17) is to be seen not in isolation, as some clinical strategy for disciplining recalcitrant offenders, but, in its literary context, as one further example of how disciples are to emulate God's concern for others. The emphasis is not on reproach or punishment but on the primacy of forgiveness and reconciliation for those whose relationships have been damaged by sin. No effort must be spared to regain the lost brother or sister. So important is the repairing of a sin-damaged relationship that a disciple's effort to regain his or her estranged brother or sister should enlist ever-widening sources of help. The preceding parable of the lost sheep (18:10-14) and the ensuing parable of the unforgiving servant which stands in parallel relationship with the disciplinary text (18:23-35) underline that such commitment corresponds to and should be motivated by God's own concern to seek out and be reconciled with the lost.

The restorative purpose of social ostracism is implied in the contexts of several other excommunication texts as well. For instance, the instruction in 2 Thessalonians 3:15 to count the disciplined person as a brother or sister rather than an enemy presupposes that the "shaming" of verse 14 has produced repentance and restoration. The call to avoid wrongdoers in 2 Timothy 3:1-5 is preceded by an instruction to correct opponents with gentleness in the hope that God may grant them repentance (2:24-26). Similarly, the command to "drive out the wicked person from among you" in 1 Corinthians 5:13 is followed by a reminder that the Corinthians were themselves once guilty of identical sins yet have been washed, sanctified, and justified in Christ (6:9-11), a

---

44. Gundry, *Matthew: A Commentary on His Literary and Theological Art* (Grand Rapids: William B. Eerdmans, 1982), 369.

recollection that would provide a check against treating an expelled offender as a lost cause.

The above survey of texts shows that notwithstanding the many places in the New Testament where believers are warned against judgmentalism,[45] adjudication and punishment have a definite role in church discipline. Indeed, in situations of serious abuse, such as in the Corinthian church, their use is positively commended. But even there, Stephen Travis points out, "the suffering imposed . . . is remedial rather than retributive in purpose."[46] The goal of every type of church discipline, whether it is admonition, public rebuke, or social ostracism, is not merely the maintenance of group boundaries, though this is essential for the survival and flourishing of any community committed to a distinctive way of life; the ultimate goal is always the repentance and restoration of the offender to fellowship. This is made unmistakably clear in Paul's instructions to the Galatians:

> My friends, if anyone is detected in a transgression *[paraptōmati]*, you who have received the Spirit *[humeis hoi pneumatikoi]* should restore *[katartizete]* such a one in a spirit of gentleness. Take care that you yourselves are not tempted. (6:1)

Whether the transgression *(paraptōma)* mentioned here is understood as an unwitting or isolated moral lapse,[47] or as a deliberate flouting of accepted standards that has come to light despite the offender's best efforts at concealment,[48] the fundamental instruction is clear: the offender must be rehabilitated, not abandoned. The present tense of the verb *(katartizete)* indicates that this task of rehabilitation, of restoring everything to its proper condition, may be a lengthy one. But to undertake it is identified as a mark of spiritual maturity *(hymeis hoi pneumatikoi)* and evidence of a sober awareness of one's own vulnerability to similar failure. It is surely significant, as James Dunn observes,

45. For example, Matthew 7:1-2/Luke 6:37; Romans 14:4, 10, 12 — compare 2:1; 1 Corinthians 4:5. These texts presumably rule out censoriousness and hypocritical judgmentalism rather than all communal discernment and discipline.

46. Travis, *Christ and the Judgment of God,* 89.

47. F. F. Bruce, *The Epistle to the Galatians: A Commentary on the Greek Text* (Exeter: Paternoster, 1982), 260.

48. J. D. G. Dunn, *The Epistle to the Galatians* (Peabody, Mass.: Hendrickson, 1993), 319.

that Paul's immediate response to transgression is not punitive retribution but a concern "to restore the erring fellow member to his former
condition and mend the injured relationships."[49]

Punishment by Divine Agency

There is a pervasive emphasis on divine judgment in the New Testament. This judgment may be temporal or historical in character, which
is a fundamental emphasis in Old Testament tradition, but more often
it is eschatological in nature. Eschatological judgment is also discussed
in the Old Testament, but the idea is developed more extensively in the
New Testament, as in Second Temple Judaism generally. In Matthew's
Gospel alone, a full 25 percent of the Gospel's 148 pericopae relate human behavior to its eschatological consequences.[50] There is, however,
still a body of material on present or temporal judgment, which I will
consider first.

Historical Judgment

The New Testament writers usually depict temporal judgment as reformative or educative in purpose. The writer to the Hebrews, for example,
speaks of God using trials to discipline *(paideuein)* his children and doing so "for our good, in order that we may share his holiness" (Heb.
12:5-11; cf. Titus 2:11-12; Rev. 3:19). Similarly, Paul considers the sickness and death experienced by Corinthian believers as a result of abuses
of the Lord's Supper as potentially reformative in impact:

> For all who eat and drink without discerning the body, eat and drink
> judgment against themselves. For this reason many of you are weak
> and ill, and some have died. But if we judged ourselves, we would not
> be judged. But when we are judged by the Lord, we are disciplined so
> that we may not be condemned along with the world. (1 Cor. 11:29-32)

49. Dunn, *The Epistle to the Galatians*, 320-21.
50. For references, see K. Weber, "The Image of the Sheep and the Goats in Matthew 25:1-46," *CBQ* 59, no. 4 (1997): 674n.52.

Most commentators take Paul to be saying here that God is punishing those in the church guilty of sacramental abuse by visiting illness and death on them, a judgment mediated to them by the eucharistic elements themselves. But it is more likely, in my view, that Paul is thinking of God "using" tragic events to further his disciplinary purposes with the community. The sickness and death in question were not being inflicted retributively by God but were the predictable outcome of the selfish and discriminatory behavior of the pneumatic Corinthians (vv. 20-22, 33-34). While the elite feasted in style, the needs of the poor and the weak in the church were being neglected to the point that they suffered physical debilitation and premature death. That this should be happening was an implicit judgment on their spiritual pretensions. In other words, Paul sees God using the cause-effect mechanism of sinful behavior as a way of reproving the community and summoning it to change, just as God sometimes even uses satanic activity for such ends (1 Cor. 5:5; 2 Cor. 12:7-10; 1 Tim. 1:20).

In a similar vein, Jesus seems to have accepted the possibility that some physical afflictions may be the result of personal sin, as a kind of temporal judgment, and summons to repentance (Mark 2:10). He insisted, however, that this must not be assumed in any specific case (Luke 13:1-5; John 9:2-3), any more than earthly comfort should be taken as an infallible sign of divine approval (Mark 12:38-44; 10:30; Matt. 6:2; Luke 12:13-21; 16:14). James too sees an educative role in sickness inasmuch as it prompts self-examination and confession of sin (5:13-18). The same could be said of Luke's accounts of penalties imposed on unbelievers in the book of Acts, such as the temporary blindness inflicted on Saul (9:8-12) and Elymas (13:8-11). In his confrontation with Simon Magus, Peter's response is first to condemn him to perdition ("May your silver perish with you!"), then to summon him to repentance so that, "if possible, the intent of your heart may be forgiven you" (8:20-22). The beating given to the sons of Sceva by the demon-possessed man, though not expressly identified as a divine punishment, serves similarly to provoke awe, repentance, and renunciation of magic among the residents of Ephesus (19:13-19).

On other occasions, however, temporal judgment seems more destructive than restorative in intent, at least for its immediate recipients. The most dramatic example of this is the story of Ananias and Sapphira in Acts 5:1-11. Luke indicates that the apostles deemed their offense to be especially serious ("Why has Satan filled your heart to lie to the Holy Spirit?" v. 3; "How is it that you have agreed together to put the Spirit of the Lord to the test?" v. 9), and their punishment is uniquely severe. Their expulsion or excommunication from the community (they are "carried out," vv. 6, 10) costs them their lives. Both the interpretation of their offense as lying to the Holy Spirit and the ensuing punishment of death suggest that Luke regards the crime as one of blasphemy.[51] Contrary to Ernst Haenchen's exaggerated claim that Peter "kills" and "wants to kill" Sapphira,[52] the punishment is considered to have been imposed ultimately by God, even if Peter foresaw it. (The immediate cause of death was probably the culprits' profound shock at the realization that they had breached a religious taboo.) The definitive nature of the penalty and its swift imposition mean that no restoration was possible for the offenders. No opportunity was given for repentance or restitution. But the extreme severity of the punishment serves the positive purpose of dramatizing the identity and preserving the holiness of the community. Twice Luke refers to the "great fear" that seized both the "whole church" and "all who heard of these things" (vv. 5, 11). It is a reverential fear, a sense of awe at how God has identified his own holy name with the new messianic movement so that offenses against community norms acquire transcendent significance. It is also a cautionary fear, a sobering realization of the dreadful consequences of transgressing the sanctity of the community that would deter others from similar deception (cf. v. 13). The chastened community then experiences dramatic fresh growth (5:12-16).

The striking down of Herod Agrippa in Acts 12:18-23 is another instance of a divinely imposed death sentence for the sin of blasphemy (vv. 22-23). Luke uses the same verb for death *(ekpsuchein)* in this story as in the story of Ananias and Sapphira (5:5, 10; 12:23), indicating that in both events it is God who executes judgment. In Herod's case, death is not instantaneous but is the outcome of a terminal illness caused by his failure to "give the glory to God" (12:23).[53] We might speculate that God intended the sickness to provoke Herod's repentance, which

51. So too H. Havelaar, "Hellenistic Parallels to Acts 5:1-11 and the Problem of Conflicting Interpretations," *JSNT* 67 (1997), esp. 79-82.

52. Haenchen, *The Acts of the Apostles: A Commentary* (Philadelphia: Westminster, 1971), 239.

53. Cf. Josephus's account in *Antiquities,* XIX:343-53.

would bring healing, and hence was reformative in intention. But Luke does not say this, and even if it were the case, death still occurs (v. 23). The oppressor dies, the oppressed thrive, "and the word of God continued to advance and gain adherents" (v. 24).

There are other places too where the harshness of historical judgment is emphasized. Jesus refers to past acts of divine judgment on Noah's contemporaries and on Sodom and Gomorrah to warn his hearers of the consequences of disobedience (Matt. 11:20-24/Luke 10:13-15; 17:26-32), and he depicts the approaching historical destruction of Jerusalem as "the days of vengeance" and "wrath" (Luke 21:22, 23). There are several other sayings in which Jesus warns of divine judgment within history on Jerusalem or on the whole community of Israel, many of which allude to Hosea 9 and 10.[54] Yet just as Hosea's threats are followed by the counternote of mercy ("My heart recoils within me; my compassion grows warm and tender. I will not execute my fierce anger; I will not again destroy Ephraim; for I am God and no mortal, the Holy One in your midst, and I will not come in wrath"; 11:8-9), so Jesus' warnings of judgment are not necessarily the last word on the matter but are meant to provoke Israel to repentance. Even the Old Testament paradigms used for destructive judgment — Noah's flood, the annihilation of Sodom and Gomorrah, the sacking of Jerusalem — are not always viewed in the New Testament as definitive or irrevocable. Jesus speaks of a future reckoning with Sodom and Gomorrah (Matt. 10:15; 11:24; cf. Ezek. 16:53, 55, 61); 1 Peter talks mysteriously of a proclamation of the gospel to the generation of Noah (3:18-20; 4:6); Paul seems to anticipate the salvation of "all Israel" (Rom. 11:26); and the Apocalypse uses the image of a new and glorified Jerusalem as the symbol for eschatological redemption (Rev. 21:2, 9-21). Temporal judgment is intended to issue in restoration.

Cursing and Consigning to Destruction

A concern for change and renewal can even be detected behind the curses and declarations of divine condemnation on human opponents that figure several times in the New Testament and that, on the surface, appear

---

54. Mark 13:2/Hos. 10:2; Mark 11:11-14, 20-22/Hos. 9:1-17; Luke 13:6-9/Hos. 9:10, 13, 16; Luke 19:41-44/Hos. 9:7; 10:2, 4; Luke 21:22/Hos. 9:7; Luke 23:28-31/Hos. 10:8. See also Luke 13:34-35; 19:41-44; Matt. 23:37-39.

to be the antithesis of nonretaliatory love or restorative justice. The phenomenon of pronouncing curses on real, imagined, or potential wrongdoers is found in many — perhaps all — human cultures, and is attested frequently in the Hebrew Bible. Curses serve a variety of ends, from enabling the ruling classes to secure social conformity from their people to arming the weak and powerless in society with a weapon they can use against their oppressors.[55] Curses also function to reinforce the moral and social boundaries of a community. *Moral boundaries* are strengthened by the way in which curses identify certain kinds of behavior as especially offensive or dangerous. To curse certain deeds is to create an extremely powerful taboo, powerful both because it plays on a latent fear of retaliation and because the enforcer of the curse is considered beyond merely human control. *Social boundaries* are clarified by the exclusionary power of curses. Those cursed are punished not merely by the calamities wished upon them but by their symbolic ostracism from the community. The excommunication of those who threaten the well-being of the community or its individual members serves to enhance social solidarity. Curses might also serve as a substitute for political or judicial action. Where an individual or group has no available means for seeking institutional redress for wrongs suffered, curses can serve as an extrajudicial means of pursuing the guilty party until justice is finally done.

Against this backdrop, when Paul pronounces curses *(anathema)* on his adversaries in Galatia (1:8-9) and Corinth (1 Cor. 16:22), or issues sentences of eschatological condemnation on those who damage his apostolic workmanship (1 Cor. 3:17; 2 Cor. 11:15), he is not simply revealing how little he has learned about loving his enemies, as J. Massyngbaerde Ford surmises.[56] Certainly Paul's readers would have sensed the full negative force of the term *anathema*. It is used in the Septuagint to translate *herem*, or "ban," a term that denotes "something delivered up to divine wrath, dedicated to destruction and brought under a curse."[57] But the translation "eternally condemned"

55. See J. S. Anderson, "The Social Function of Curses in the Hebrew Bible," *ZAW* 110, no. 2 (1998): 223-37. Cf. also A. Luc, "Interpreting the Curses in the Psalms," *JETS* 42, no. 3 (1999): 396-410.

56. Ford, "Cursing and Blessing as Vehicles of Violence and Peace in Scripture," in *Peace in a Nuclear Age: The Bishops' Pastoral Letter in Perspective*, ed. C. J. Reid Jr. (Washington: Catholic University of America Press, 1986), 24.

57. J. Behm, *TDNT*, 1:354. The term *anathema* occurs only a handful of times in the

(NIV) or "condemned to hell" (GNB) is much too strong. The fact that Paul includes his own missionary team and even angels under an *anathema* should any distort the gospel (Gal. 1:8) suggests his primary thought is that certain *actions* deserve destruction.[58] With respect to the people guilty of such actions, perhaps more fundamental in Paul's mind than destruction is the idea of *separation,* since in biblical practice things under a ban were separated from all human contact. In pronouncing a curse, then, Paul is drawing lines of separation between his own churches and his opponents. This serves, on one side, to distance his enemies from the faithful so they can do no harm to them, and on the other side, to remove his communities from a source of danger and contamination.

In handing his adversaries over to divine judgment in this way, Paul affirms both his confidence in ultimate justice and his belief that such justice is already operative in present events. His very words of condemnation represent an initial realization of God's final judgment. But the verdict of condemnation paradoxically makes room for restoring grace. Käsemann suggests that such declarations, as "sentences of holy law," fulfill the double function of threat and proclamation. They announce the "already present power" of the eschatological Judge recompensing evil as he will do on the last day. They are therefore more than mere warnings, since the process of judgment has already commenced. Yet, as an anticipation of the last day, such judgment stands always in the service of grace, granting wrongdoers space for repentance and therefore exemption from final destruction. Thus, even declarations of judgment or curses are not to be separated from God's saving action. Even God's wrath "manifests the will of him who has not given us up."[59] God's judgment is a judgment of grace — a judgment in that it confronts and condemns, rather than ignores or excuses, the destructive-

---

New Testament, and only twice in connection with church discipline (Mark 14:71; Acts 23:14; Rom. 9:3; 1 Cor. 12:3; 16:22; Gal. 1:8-9). The word is used in the Septuagint to translate *herem*, or "ban," something dedicated to God for destruction. But in view of the association of *herem* with excommunication rather than execution in postexilic Judaism, there is no need to see Paul's references to anathema as implying anything more punitive than exclusion from the community of Christ and its consequences.

58. Dunn, *The Epistle to the Galatians,* 46-47.

59. Käsemann, "Sentences of Holy Law in the New Testament," 66-81 (quote from 80). For a qualification on the legal nature of such statements, see above p. 150n.11.

ness of present human conduct, and a work of grace in that it aims at repentance, transformation, and restored communion.[60]

This provides a clue to the perplexing tension that exists in the New Testament between the call to nonretaliatory enemy-love on the one hand, which we explored in a previous chapter, and the frequent consignment of opponents to the destruction of divine judgment on the other hand.[61] Both ideas are juxtaposed sharply in Romans 12:19-20: "Beloved, never avenge yourselves, but leave room for the wrath of God; for it is written, 'Vengeance is mine, I will repay, says the Lord.'"[62] This injunction is followed by a mysterious reference to "heaping burning coals upon your enemy's head" (v. 20), which may be an allusion to eschatological punishment.[63] In explaining the relationship between these two lines of thought, some interpreters subordinate the former to the latter. They argue that retaliation is not renounced in principle in favor of reconciliation; it is simply remitted to a higher court. Revenge is still contemplated but given over to God to execute. There is a sense in which this is true, since it is the certainty of God's ultimate triumph over evil that Paul gives as the reason for nonretaliation in the present. Miroslav Volf even argues that it is *only* through such conscious displacement or transference of violence to God, rather than its complete relinquishment, that Christian nonviolence and forgiveness are possible in a violent world.[64]

But Paul's thought goes deeper than simply deferring retaliation to God, for he enjoins believers not simply to endure present opposition

60. Cf. L. G. Jones, *Embodying Forgiveness: A Theological Analysis* (Grand Rapids: William B. Eerdmans, 1995), 135-62.

61. See, e.g., Matt. 10:14-15/Luke 10:10-12; Matt. 11:21-23/Luke 10:13-15; Matt. 12:38-42/Luke 11:29-32; Matt. 23:29-30, 34-36/Luke 11:47-48, 49-51; Matt. 23:37-39/Luke 13:34-35; Matt. 24:45-51/Luke 12:42-46; Rom. 2:5; 3:8; 12:19; 2 Cor. 11:15; Gal. 5:10; Phil. 1:28; 3:19; 1 Thess. 1:10; 2:16; 5:9; 2 Thess. 1:6-9; Col. 3:6; Eph. 5:6; 1 Pet. 3:12.

62. For a survey of exegetical opinion on this passage, see G. M. Zerbe, "Paul's Ethic of Nonretaliation," in *The Love of Enemy and Nonretaliation in the New Testament*, ed. W. M. Swartley (Louisville, Ky.: Westminster John Knox, 1992), 177-222.

63. For different views on this, see W. Klassen, "Coals of Fire: Sign of Repentance or Revenge?" *NTS* 9, no. 4 (1962/1963): 337-50; G. M. Zerbe, *Non-Retaliation in Early Jewish and New Testament Texts: Ethical Themes in Social Contexts* (Sheffield: Sheffield Academic Press, 1993), 249-64; and Zerbe, "Paul's Ethic of Nonretaliation," 194-202.

64. Volf, *Exclusion and Embrace: A Theological Exploration of Identity, Otherness, and Reconciliation* (Nashville: Abingdon Press, 1996), 301-4.

while savoring the prospects of ultimate revenge, but to love, feed, bless, pray for, and actively do good to their enemies (Rom. 12:14-21). Unless the implication is that believers are to be more generous to their opponents now than God will be to them in the future, some material connection must be thought to exist between the obligation to love one's enemies and the inherent nature of God's recompensing justice, on which the obligation is grounded. Even God's vengeance, in other words, must be suffused with enemy-love.[65] This is illustrated by the way in which God's temporal judgments are intended to awaken sinners to their dangerous predicament and thus escape final loss, and by the way in which God continually delays ultimate judgment to give people time for repentance (Rom. 3:25; cf. Acts 17:30-31). And even God's final judgment, when it comes, notwithstanding its destructive impact on the impenitent, must also in some way manifest the enemy-love of God (which we will consider further in the following sections). Only God loves enough to avenge with true justice. Believers are thus called to love and pray for their abusers and to call down God's gracious power upon them, not simply as an interim measure before the Great Reversal, but as a reflection of God's own steadfast orientation of unmerited love toward his enemies, made known even in God's punitive judgments, both now and in the future.

The Present Wrath of God: Romans 1:18-32;
cf. 1 Thessalonians 2:14-16

So far we have seen how the New Testament writers discern the judging actions of God at work in cases of human misfortune and calamity, whether associated with sickness, war, disability, or premature death. In doing so they stand in a long biblical tradition that associates the negative side of human experience with the outworking of divine wrath on human wickedness and injustice. Interestingly, the first reference to God's wrath in the Bible appears as Yahweh's response not to generic human sinfulness but to whatever impedes God's efforts to deliver his

---

65. On the relationship between God's vengeance and God's love in the Old Testament, see H. G. L. Peels, *The Vengeance of God: The Meaning of the Root* NQM *and the Function of the* NQM-*Texts in the Context of Divine Revelation in the Old Testament* (Leiden/New York/Köln: E. J. Brill, 1995), 292-95.

people from injustice and oppression (Exod. 4:13-14; 15:7). After the establishment of the covenant with Israel, the major cause of divine wrath is Israel's failure to abide by the terms of the covenant, including her obligation to provide social justice.[66] Yahweh's wrath is also directed at foreign nations who oppress his people[67] and who idolize their own autonomy from God, though in reality they are but instruments in God's hands,[68] often used to chastise his own people.[69] God's wrath, then, is double-sided. It is positive insofar as it is directed at evil and oppression that hinders God's purposes of deliverance for the covenant people; it is negative in that God's people, both corporately and individually, suffer under punishment for their own sinfulness and injustice, a punishment that at times seems excessively cruel and unjust and raises questions about the character and faithfulness of God.

For Paul it is the Christ event that vindicates God's faithfulness to his people while at the same time displaying God's wrath. Most references to wrath in the New Testament are found in the Pauline epistles and the Apocalypse of John. There are scattered references in the Gospels and the general epistles,[70] but it is Paul who offers the most extensive reflection on the nature and meaning of God's wrath, and nowhere more so than in the letter to the Romans.[71] I have already discussed Romans 13:1-7, where the state's action in requiting evil is viewed as an expression of divine wrath, and I will return to aspects of that passage again in the next chapter. Here I will consider Paul's classic discussion of the outworking of divine judgment in present human experience in Romans 1:18-32, a passage that Anthony Hanson deems "a handbook to the working of wrath."[72]

In the opening section of Romans, sin, wrath, and judgment occupy central stage (1:18–3:20). Paul offers a step-by-step indictment of humanity for its rebellion against God. The indictment begins in 1:18 with the announcement of the revelation of the wrath of God from

---

66. Ps. 50:16-22; Isa. 1:23-24; 42:24-25; Amos 8:4-10; Mic. 6:9-16.

67. Jer. 10:25; Ezek. 25; Jer. 50–51; Nahum; Obadiah.

68. Cf. Isa. 10:5-19; Jer. 25:7-14; 50:25; Ezek. 36:1-7; Mal. 1:2-5.

69. Judg. 2:11-15; 2 Kings 13:3; 2 Chron. 36:15-17; Zech. 7:11-14; Lam. 2.

70. Mark 14:36; Luke 14:21; 21:23; Matt. 18:34; 22:7; John 3:36; Heb. 3:11; 4:3; James 1:19-20.

71. Rom. 1:18; 2:5, 8; 3:5; 4:15; 5:9; 9:22; 12:19; 13:4; 1 Thess. 1:10; 2:16; 5:9; cf. Col. 3:6; Eph. 5:6.

72. Hanson, The Wrath of the Lamb (London: SPCK, 1957), 83.

heaven against all human wickedness, and it climaxes in 3:9-20 with the declaration that all peoples, both Jew and Gentile, are "under the power of sin" (3:9). Three crucial questions emerge about Paul's understanding of divine wrath in this discussion: what is meant by wrath, why is it being revealed, and how is it experienced?

The concept of God's wrath is so firmly anchored in the biblical tradition that there can be little doubt that Paul's readers would have understood what he meant by the term. It designates God's fervent reaction against human wickedness, God's refusal to tolerate, compromise with, or indulge evil. God's wrath, says C. E. B. Cranfield, is God's personal "indignation against injustice, cruelty and corruption, which is an essential element of goodness and love in a world in which moral evil is present."[73] There has been extensive debate, however, over whether Paul understood God's wrath specifically as *affective* (something God feels) or *effective* (something God does). According to C. H. Dodd, by employing the term "wrath" Paul is not meaning to ascribe to God the irrational and capricious passion of anger but is thinking of the "inevitable process of cause and effect in a moral universe."[74] But most recent commentators think it is unlikely that Paul saw God's wrath purely in terms of a detached, impersonal causal connection of deed and effect. The thrice-repeated "God gave them up" (1:24, 26, 28) implies God's personal involvement in the process. Even so, Paul is not thinking of God's emotions so much as God's actions. Wrath is not a chronic case of ill temper on God's part but a measured commitment to act against evil and injustice in order to contain it and destroy it. Wrath is not, therefore, an ontological attribute of God's nature or a function of God's personality. It is an expression of God's will that is contingent upon the existence of evil. If there were no sin in the world, there would be no occasion for wrath.

This answers the second question about why God's wrath is revealed. The object of God's wrath is "all human ungodliness [*asebeia*]

73. Cranfield, *A Critical and Exegetical Commentary on the Epistle to the Romans,* 2 vols. (Edinburgh: T. & T. Clark, 1975, 1977), 1:109.

74. Dodd, *The Epistle of Paul to the Romans* (London: Hodder & Stoughton, 1932), 20-24; also Hanson, *The Wrath of the Lamb,* 68-111 (esp. 69, 110), 179; W. Barclay, *The Letter to the Romans* (Edinburgh: St. Andrews, 1957), 17-20. See also the helpful discussion by G. H. C. MacGregor, *The New Testament Basis of Pacifism* (London: Fellowship of Reconciliation, 1953), 51-64.

and wickedness [*adikia*]." Either these two terms reinforce each other by synonymous parallelism, or else the former accents an attack upon God's majesty and the latter on the justice of God's governance of the world. Those responsible for such offenses are identified as persons who hinder or suppress the truth of God in unrighteousness *(adikia)*. The "truth" that is repressed is not merely the fact of God's existence but the nature of God's moral character and will for human life. ("Truth of God" would, to Jewish ears, convey the idea of God's reliability and trustworthiness, God's own moral character.)[75] Rebellious creatures deny or pervert the truth about the kind of God that God is: the faithful Creator, Lord, Judge, and Redeemer of humanity. In the unit that follows (1:19-23), Paul defines more precisely what is entailed in the "suppression of the truth in unrighteousness." At root it is the willful rejection of the knowledge of the Creator-God made available through general revelation, and the elevation of some creature into the place of God, which is the sin of idolatry.

Where, then, is this wrath revealed, and how is it experienced? This is open to debate,[76] but Paul seems to detect the present revelation of God's wrath in two main arenas. One is in the gospel itself, or more specifically in the gospel events to which the *kerygma* points. This is implied by the carefully constructed parallelism between 1:17 and 1:18. Just as God's righteousness is now "being revealed" *(apokaluptetai)* in the gospel (v. 17), so too is God's wrath against unrighteousness now "being revealed" *(apokaluptetai)* from heaven (v. 18). The implication seems to be that the death of Christ is concurrently a revelation of God's saving justice toward his people and a demonstration of heavenly wrath against the sin and injustice that all people are guilty of. Against this interpretation it is sometimes objected that nowhere else does Paul explicitly include the negative concepts of judgment and wrath in the message of the gospel, which would hardly qualify as "good news." But this is not so. In Romans 2:16 Paul expressly includes final judgment, previously depicted as the "day of wrath" (v. 5), in "my gospel." Yet it is worth repeating here the point made in my earlier discussion of Paul's theology of divine justice — that for Paul to see the death of Christ as a

75. Dunn, *Romans,* 2 vols. (Dallas: Word, 1988), 1:56.

76. See G. Bornkamm, "The Revelation of God's Wrath (Romans 1-3)," in Bornkamm, *Early Christian Experience* (London: SCM, 1969), 47-70.

demonstration of divine wrath is *not* to say that he regarded it as an act of retributive punishment. The cross supremely reveals God's wrath not because sinners are vicariously punished in the experience of Christ but because the cross definitively subverts and destroys the principle of sin itself. Facing the horror of crucifixion, Jesus totally refused to compromise with evil or to meet evil with evil in order to defend himself. He triumphed over evil without employing the mechanisms of evil to do so, thereby breaking the grip of evil over the human heart, thus satisfying the ultimate purpose of God's wrath.[77]

While in verse 18 God's present wrath is manifest in the story of the dereliction of Christ, in the discussion that ensues it is manifest, secondly, in human dereliction in general (1:24-32), which Christ's own death epitomizes (cf. Gal. 3:13; 2 Cor. 5:21). Paul argues that by rejecting dependence on God and surrendering to the lie of idolatry (vv. 19-23), humankind has fallen victim to degenerative processes which, in reality, are visible expressions of God's "giving up" of people (vv. 24, 26, 28) to "receive in their own persons" (v. 27) the consequences of their choice. God's wrath, in other words, works itself out through everyday sociological, psychological, and physiological expressions of human decadence and depravity. In Dodd's view, Paul is portraying "the disastrous progress of evil in society . . . as a natural process of cause and effect, and not as the direct act of God."[78] However, the emphatic statement "God gave them up" *(paredōken autous ho theos)* does seem to imply some overt, deliberate action on God's part. But God's act is not so much a matter of direct, individually tailored punitive intervention as it is a matter of measured withdrawal of his protective influence and control, a refusal to intervene to stem the deleterious effects of human rebellion.[79] "He withdraws the gracious power of his absolute lordship

---

77. Cf. C. N. Krauss, *God Our Saviour: Theology in a Christological Mode* (Scottdale, Pa.: Herald Press, 1991), 210-11.

78. Dodd, *The Epistle of Paul to the Romans,* 55.

79. Not infrequently in the Old Testament, divine judgment is said to involve God hiding his face from Israel (e.g., Deut. 31:17-18; 32:20; Mic. 3:4; Isa. 54:8; 57:17; 59:2; 64:7; Jer. 3:5; Ezek. 39:23-24; cf. Gen. 4:14; 1 Sam. 28:15; 2 Sam. 7:15; Job 13:24; Pss. 31:1; 27:9; 88:14; 89:46; 102:2; 104:29; Isa. 64:7), or withdrawing his protective presence from them (Hos. 1:9; cf. 2:4; 4:6, 17; 5:6; Isa. 1:15; Zech. 7:13-14; Num. 32:15; 2 Chron. 12:5; 15:2; 24:20), something especially felt in the catastrophe of the Exile (Jer. 7:29; 16:10-13; Lam. 5:20-22; cf. Jer. 12:7-13; Pss. 78:58-66; 106:40-48).

and allows other lordships to prevail," says Paul Achtemeier.[80] But God does this with redemptive more than punitive intent, hoping that human beings will recoil from the disastrous outworkings of their rebellion and, as Paul puts it in Romans 2:7, "by patiently doing good seek for glory and honor and immortality" (cf. 1:23) and thus escape the eschatological consummation of God's wrath (2:5, 8; 5:9).

Accordingly, when Paul speaks of shame, perversity, and ethical corruption as the historical experience of God's wrath, he is not thinking merely of divine punishment but also of God's redemptive commitment to contain and destroy sin. Israel understood the Torah as part of God's containment mechanism. But for Paul, such is the cosmic sweep of sin that not even obedience to the Torah is enough to escape captivity to evil. "The law," Paul declares, "brings wrath" (Rom. 4:15; cf. 3:20). By contrast, the revelation of saving justice in the gospel brings definitive deliverance from wrath (Rom. 5:9; 8:1; 1 Thess. 1:10; 5:9). It effects an escape for believers from having their fate determined by humanity's captivity to that sinful reality which is irretrievably destined for destruction. Consequently, Paul never speaks of God's wrath being directed at Christians, and he views their present sufferings not as an experience of wrath but as a participation with Christ in redemptive suffering.[81]

There is another reference to God's present wrath in 1 Thessalonians 2:14-16. Here Paul speaks of God's wrath having at last overtaken the Jews because "they have constantly been filling up the measure of their sins," particularly by their murderous opposition to Jesus and his followers (v. 16). The meaning of this passage, which is felt by some scholars to be so virulently anti-Semitic as to be inauthentic,[82] is highly ambiguous. It is not clear whether Paul is speaking about all Israel or just some Jews. Nor is it clear whether he is referring to the imminence or irrevocability of eschatological judgment, or to recent or

80. Achtemeier, *Romans* (Atlanta: John Knox, 1985), 40.

81. Rom. 5:3-5; 8:18-25, 31-39; 2 Cor. 1:5; 4:10; 12:9-10; Phil. 3:10; Col. 1:24. See C. D. Marshall, "'For Me to Live Is Christ': Pauline Spirituality as a Basis for Ministry," in *The Call to Serve: Biblical and Theological Perspectives on Ministry*, ed. D. A. Campbell (Sheffield: Sheffield Academic Press, 1996), 111-13.

82. So, for example, N. Elliott, *Liberating Paul: The Justice of God and the Politics of the Apostle* (Maryknoll, N.Y.: Orbis, 1994), 25, 27. Cf. R. A. Wortham, "The Problem of Anti-Judaism in 1 Thess. 2:14-16 and Related Pauline Texts," *BTB* 25, no. 1 (1995): 37-44.

approaching historical events as expressions of divine punishment. If by "wrath" Paul has in mind recent Roman actions against the Jews in Jerusalem and/or in Rome (cf. Rom. 13:4-5; Luke 21:23), as David Wenham suggests,[83] then it is likely that he would have seen it, like other historical judgments in Israel's history, as punishment intended to elicit obedience and renewal. If, on the other hand, by "wrath" he means that condition of spiritual blindness toward the gospel that keeps Israel on the path to ultimate destruction, then it is important to note that elsewhere Paul diagnoses this condition as temporary and educative. It serves as temporal discipline that will lead eventually to repentance (cf. Rom 9:22-23 and 11:11-12, 26-27).

In light of human sinfulness, then, Paul understands historical adversity in terms of divine wrath working itself out against sin and evil. Such wrath is not, strictly speaking, retributive in character in the sense of the external infliction of equivalent penalties for the deeds done. Rather, it is an intrinsic punishment in which people experience the ruinous consequences of their own choices. And the purpose of such wrath is not purely punitive but, ultimately, redemptive or restorative. The point is not to torment human beings but to enable them to see their moral frailty and their consequent need for God's healing assistance. Furthermore, the task of believers is not to offer themselves to God as instruments of divine wrath in present history (Rom. 12:19), but to declare the present and future activity of God's wrath as a work of both judgment and grace. This task is fulfilled by the authoritative proclamation and embodiment of God's word, not by concrete actions of vengeance and punishment. It is God's prerogative to exercise wrath, and God does so in service of his saving justice. For, as James reminds his readers in a proverbial turn of phrase, "human anger [*orgē andros*, "your anger," in NSRV] does not produce God's righteousness [*dikaiosunē theou*]" (1:20).

Final Judgment

Most references to divine judgment in the New Testament are eschatological in reference. The wrath of God upon sin, partially reflected in historical experiences, is definitively located at the close of history, "the

83. Wenham, *Paul,* 319-26.

day of wrath, when God's righteous judgment will be revealed" (Rom. 2:5). This conviction permeates New Testament literature from beginning to end. Indeed, the canonical narrative closes with this announcement: "See, I am coming soon; my reward is with me, to repay according to everyone's work" (Rev. 22:12, 18-21; cf. 11:18).

There is no uniform conception of final judgment and its consequences to which all New Testament authors subscribe.[84] They speak selectively and allusively about realities which, by definition, lie beyond human experience and knowledge, each author giving emphasis to different aspects of the traditions he draws upon and employing a diversity of terms, images, and genres in doing so. Nevertheless, a sufficient number of common or similar convictions emerge in their writings to give us reasonable insight into how, in broad terms, they understood eschatological judgment. At the end of the age, all people, both the living and the dead, both "the righteous and the unrighteous,"[85] will appear before the judgment seat of God or Christ,[86] where each will receive "recompense for what has been done in the body, whether good or evil."[87] A separation will occur. The righteous will depart into eternal life.[88] For them there will be "rewards" or "prizes" or "treasure in heaven."[89] The wicked, however, "will go away into eternal punishment *[kolasin aiōnion]*."[90] In the Gospels, Jesus speaks frequently of "Gehenna,"[91] or the place of outer darkness and unquenchable fire where there

---

84. According to M. Reiser, "The coexistence of what, from a logical point of view, are mutually exclusive eschatological conceptions, a situation apparently regarded as unproblematic — this is characteristic of Jewish and to a great extent of Christian intellectual history." See *Jesus and Judgment: The Eschatological Proclamation in Its Jewish Context* (Minneapolis: Fortress Press, 1997), 162.

85. Acts 24:15; cf. Luke 13:28-29; John 5:28-29; Heb. 9:27.

86. Rom. 14:10; 2 Cor. 5:10.

87. 2 Cor. 5:10; cf. Matt. 25:31-46; Rom. 2:6-11; Rev. 20:11-15; 21:5-8.

88. Matt. 7:14; 19:29; 24:46; Luke 10:25; John 3:15-16; 5:29; Acts 11:18; 13:46-47; Rom. 2:7; 2 Cor. 5:4; 1 Pet. 3:7; cf. Heb. 5:9; 9:12.

89. Mark 9:41; 10:21, 28-30; Matt. 5:12, 46; 6:1-6, 16-21; 10:41; 19:28-29; 20:1-16; 24:46-47; 25:21, 23; Luke 6:23, 38; 12:33-34; 14:12, 14, 15; 18:28-30; cf. 1 Cor. 3:5-15; 4:4-5; 2 Cor. 5:10; Phil. 3:12-16; Col. 3:24-25; Eph. 6:8-9.

90. Matt. 25:46; cf. Mark 3:28-29; Mark 9:42; 12:9; 14:21; Matt. 5:26; 10:15, 28, 33; 11:20-24; 12:31-32, 36-37; 13:30, 41-42; 18:35; 25:41, 46; Luke 12:47; 13:9, 22-30; 16:23-31; 18:7-8; 19:27; 23:41; John 3:36; 5:28-29; cf. Matt. 3:7/Luke 3:7 (John the Baptist).

91. Cf. C. Milikowsky, "Which Gehenna? Retribution and Eschatology in the Synoptic Gospels and in Early Jewish Texts," *NTS* 34, no. 2 (1988): 238-49.

will be "weeping" (signifying misery or fear) and "gnashing of teeth" (denoting anger or frustration) by those excluded from salvation.[92] He also indicates that judgment will fall not just on individuals but on cities and nations as well.[93] Many other New Testament texts speak of the eternal loss the wicked will face, which is described variously as an experience of "wrath,"[94] "vengeance,"[95] "repayment,"[96] "tribulation and distress,"[97] "fire,"[98] and, most often, of "destruction," "death," or "disintegration."[99] Particularly graphic is 2 Peter 2:9, which speaks of the unrighteous being "kept under punishment *[kolazomenous tērein]* until the day of judgment."[100]

Now, inasmuch as retributive justice consists in proportionate recompense according to deserts, the New Testament descriptions of final judgment as a matter of God assessing and recompensing human works,[101] sometimes with the suggestion that there will be varying de-

92. Mark 9:42-48; Matt. 5:22, 29-30; 8:11-12; 10:28; 13:41, 42, 50; 18:8-9; 22:13; 23:15, 33; 24:51; 25:30; Luke 12:4-5; 13:28-29; cf. James 3:6.

93. Matt. 10:15; Matt. 11:21-24/Luke 10:13-15; Matt. 21:43-44; 23:35-38.

94. Matt. 3:7; Luke 21:33; John 3:36; 1 Thess. 1:9-10; 5:9; 2:14-16; Rom. 2:1-11; 3:5; 4:15; 5:9; 9:22-23; 12:19-21; Eph. 2:3; 5:6; Col. 3:6; Rev. 6:16-17; 11:18; 14:10, 19; 15:1, 7; 16:1; 16:19; 19:15.

95. 2 Thess. 1:6-10; Heb. 10:28-30; Jude 7; cf. Rom. 12:19; 1 Thess. 4:6; Luke 18:7-8.

96. Rom. 12:19; 2 Thess. 1:6; 2:9-12; Rom. 6:23; cf. 1 Cor. 3:17; Gal. 6:7-8; Rom. 1:27, 32.

97. Rom. 2:9; 2 Thess. 1:6.

98. Matt. 5:22; 13:42, 50; 24:41; Mark 9:47-48; Luke 17:29-30; 2 Thess. 1:8; Heb. 10:27; 2 Pet. 3:7; Rev. 11:5; 18:8; 19:20; 20:9-10, 14-15; 21:8.

99. Destruction, death *(olethros)*: 1 Thess. 5:3; 2 Thess. 1:9 (1 Tim. 6:9); death *(thanatos)*: Rom. 1:32; 6:21-23; 7:5; 8:6; 1 Cor. 15:21-22; 15:56; 2 Cor. 2:16; 7:10; James 1:15; 1 John 5:16; Rev. 2:11; 20:6; 20:14; 21:8; annihilation, ruin, destruction *(apoleia)*: Matt. 7:13; John 17:12; Acts 8:20; Rom. 9:22-24; Phil. 1:28; 3:19; 2 Thess. 2:3; 1 Tim. 6:9; Heb. 10:39; 2 Pet. 2:1; 3:7, 16; decay, disintegration *(phthora)*: Gal. 6:8; 2 Pet. 1:4; 2:12; end *(telos)*: Rom. 6:21-22; 2 Cor. 11:15; Phil. 3:19; 1 Pet. 4:17.

100. The text could be construed to mean either that the unrighteous will be punished before the day of judgment, in some intermediate state (so NRSV), or that the unrighteous will be punished on the day of judgment. See R. J. Bauckham, *Jude, 2 Peter* (Waco: Word, 1983), 253-55.

101. This theme pervades both Old and New Testaments. See, e.g., Pss. 9:8-21; 37:9, 33; 58:12; 62:10, 13; Job 34:11; Prov. 10:16; 24:12; Eccles. 12:14; Isa. 3:10-11; 59:18; Jer. 17:10; 25:14; 32:19; Lam. 3:64; Hos. 4:9; Rom. 2:1-16; 14:7-12; 1 Cor. 3:10-17; 4:1-5; 5:1-5; 6:9-11; 9:24-27; 11:27-34; 2 Cor. 5:9-10; Gal. 5:19-21; 6:7-10; Col. 3:25; Eph. 6:8; 1 Tim. 5:24-25; 2 Tim. 4:14.

grees of reward or punishment depending on merit,[102] could easily be understood to teach that divine justice is essentially and ultimately retributive justice. More worrisome is that the doctrine of final damnation could be taken to mean that the God we are to imitate is finally vindictive, not forgiving; that salvation is, ultimately, the achievement of coercive power, not of self-surrendering love; that punitive pain is an everlasting reality, not a remedial or restorative mechanism. Any such implications, if applied to criminal practice today, would have disastrous results. Nor is this merely a hypothetical concern. Throughout Christian history, the fear of being consigned to hell by a truly merciless God has fueled and justified all manner of horrific violence. It is a short step from denying the future existence of one's opponents after death to denying their right to exist before death. Moreover, for centuries the use of torture to convert heretics and infidels was considered justifiable, even merciful, since it would serve to deliver them from eternal torture in hell. Thus, as Hans Küng explains,

> All who were worthy of damnation, destined for hell, were opposed with the sword, with torture and continually with fire, so that by the death of the body here below the soul might perhaps be saved for the hereafter. Forced conversions, burning of heretics, Jewish pogroms, crusades, witch hunts in the name of a religion of love, cost millions of lives (in Seville alone in the course of forty years four thousand persons were burned by the Inquisition).[103]

The most prolonged and sadistic forms of public execution were employed both to serve as a foretaste of God's judgment to come and to afford victims the chance to influence their eternal destiny by their manner of endurance. Judicial judgment and eternal judgment were mutually related, as Michel Foucault explains:

> The eternal game has already begun: the torture of the execution anticipates the punishments of the beyond; it shows what they are; it is the theatre of hell; the cries of the condemned man, his struggles, his

102. See, e.g., Mark 10:29-30; Luke 12:47-48; Matt. 10:15; 11:22, 24; 12:40; 1 Cor. 15:41; Eph. 6:8.

103. Küng, *Eternal Life? Life after Death as a Medical, Philosophical, and Theological Problem* (Garden City, N.Y.: Doubleday, 1984), 136. See also J. Moltmann, *Jesus Christ for Today's World* (London: SCM, 1994), 59-60.

blasphemies, already signify his irremediable destiny. But the pains here below may also be counted as penitence and so alleviate the punishments of the beyond: God will not fail to take such a martyrdom into account, providing it is borne with resignation. The cruelty of the earthly punishment will be deducted from the punishment to come: in it is glimpsed the promise of forgiveness. But, it might be said, are not such terrible sufferings a sign that God has abandoned the guilty man to the mercy of his fellow creatures? And, far from securing future absolution, do they not prefigure imminent damnation; so that, if the condemned man dies quickly, without a prolonged agony, is it not proof that God wishes to protect him and to prevent him falling into despair? There is, therefore, an ambiguity in this suffering that may signify equally well the truth of the crime or the error of the judges, the goodness or the evil of the criminal, the coincidence or the divergence between the judgment of men and that of God. Hence the insatiable curiosity that drove the spectators to the scaffold to witness the spectacle of sufferings truly endured; there one could decipher crime and innocence, the past and the future, the here below and the eternal. It was a moment of truth that all the spectators questioned: each word, each cry, the duration of the agony, the resisting body, the life that clung desperately to it, all this constituted a sign.[104]

Such potentially negative implications of biblical teaching on eschatological punishment need to be faced squarely at this point in our investigation. Yet the relevant exegetical data is so massive, the theological and philosophical issues entailed so profound, and current opinion on them so diverse, that there is no way to deal adequately with them in a few pages. What I intend to do is to clarify why the doctrine of eternal damnation is problematic for notions of restorative justice, then identify several reasons for questioning whether eschatological judgment really does amount to a scheme of strict retributive justice.

104. Foucault, *Discipline and Punish: The Birth of the Prison* (New York: Vintage Books, 1979), 46.

A Hell of a Problem

The idea that human history will climax in a definitive act of judgment, followed by the destruction of sinners or their consignment to hell,[105] cannot be regarded as a minor or incidental theme in Christian faith, for two main reasons. One is the sheer weight of biblical material that suggests otherwise. The theme is frequent in the teaching of Jesus,[106] particularly in Matthew's Gospel,[107] and widely attested elsewhere in the New Testament. The idea of eschatological condemnation explains what believers have been saved from, as well as what the wicked are destined for, and the threat of final loss is sometimes appealed to as a sanction for righteous behavior in the present.[108] The other reason has to do with theodicy. The biblical conception of God as all-powerful, all-knowing, and perfectly good requires ultimate vindication in the face of present sickness, sin, suffering, and death. The doctrine of the Last Judgment offers the hope that the results of human wrongdoing will be rectified, that people who have suffered un-

---

105. Considerable confusion is caused by the fact that the term "hell" has been used in English translations to render two different Greek terms in the New Testament with different referents. The term "Hades," which occurs eleven times (Matt. 16:18; 11:23; Luke 10:15; 16:23; Acts 2:27, 31; Rev. 1:18; 6:8; 20:13-14), usually designates the realm of the dead (roughly equivalent to Sheol in the Old Testament), whereas the term "Gehenna," which occurs twelve times (Mark 9:42-48; Matt. 5:22, 29-30; 8:11-12; 10:28; 13:41, 42, 50; 18:8-9; 22:13; 23:15, 33; 25:30; 24:51; Luke 12:4-5; 13:28-29; cf. James 3:6), designates the place of final punishment for the wicked (although Hades in Luke 16:23 includes torment). Furthermore, the popular notion of hell as the home of Satan is not linked directly in the New Testament with Hades (though cf. Rev. 20:10, 14) or Gehenna. It is linked, if at all, with the "abyss" (Luke 8:31; Rev. 9:1, 11; 20:1, 3; but cf. Rom. 10:7, an Old Testament quotation in which "abyss" is synonymous with "Hades/Sheol" — cf. Ps. 71:20; 107:26). The "gates of Hades" in Matthew 16:18 is probably better taken as a reference to death and destruction than to demonic powers, though this is disputed.

106. According to Reiser, more than 25 percent of the traditional discourse material of Jesus in the Synoptic tradition is concerned with the theme of final judgment. In the layers of the tradition, some 35 percent of the oral discourse in Q, 22 percent in Mark, 28 percent of the oral discourse material in Luke's special material, and a massive 64 percent of the discourse material in Matthew's special material is concerned with judgment (*Jesus and Judgment,* 303-4).

107. See B. Charette, *The Theme of Recompense in Matthew's Gospel* (Sheffield: Sheffield Academic Press, 1992), esp. 119-61.

108. On warrants and sanctions in New Testament ethics, see L. Keck, "Rethinking 'New Testament Ethics,'" *JBL* 115, no. 1 (1996): 11-14.

justly will be recompensed, and that the wicked who have escaped justice in this life will face it in the next. Intuitively most people know that without final judgment, there can be no ultimate justice.

So the notion of final judgment has fundamental importance to Christian belief. Yet it would be false to make it central. The heart of Christian proclamation is the good news of the dawning of God's kingdom, of Christ's conquest of sin and death, and of the renewing work of the Holy Spirit. References in the New Testament to the positive benefits of salvation here and now far outweigh references to the negative consequences of damnation in the future.[109] There are some graphic references to damnation in the Gospels, but Jesus was no hellfire preacher. As Küng points out, "Nowhere does he show any direct interest in hell. Nowhere does he reveal any special truths in regard to the hereafter. Nowhere does he describe the act of damnation or the torments of the damned. . . . The heart of his message, which is meant to be the *eu-angelion* — not a threatening but a joyous message — lies elsewhere."[110] In his careful historical study *Jesus and Judgment,* Marius Reiser demonstrates the pervasiveness of the theme of judgment in the preaching of Jesus, yet he finds the heart of Jesus' message in his announcement of salvation:

> Jesus' preaching was sustained by the conviction that the repentance of the individual and of the whole nation should not so much aim at avoiding catastrophe as at gaining God's salvation. . . . The central focus of his speech and action is not judgment and the way to avoid it, but the reign of God and how to gain it; it is not fear of judgment that should move Israel to repentance, but the fascination of the reign of God. Therefore his message could not be better summarized than in Mark 1:15. But when it met with rejection, Jesus had to point to the reverse side of the medal.[111]

That said, references to judgment and damnation still abound in the New Testament, and they pose profound problems, both philosophical and moral, for Christian belief. The problems are keenest for the traditional understanding of *hell as a place of everlasting, conscious tor-*

---

109. See I. H. Marshall, "The Nature of Christian Salvation," *EuroJTh* 4, no. 1 (1995): 29-43.

110. Küng, *Eternal Life?* 133-34.

111. Reiser, *Jesus and Judgment,* 255; cf. 315.

ment, which has long been considered the clear teaching of Scripture. Not only is its biblical basis highly questionable,[112] but the very idea of the damned being kept in a state of perpetual pain depends on two propositions that are, in the long run, insupportable.

The first proposition is that redemption can be considered complete even though sin and suffering continue forever in hell. If immortality is not a "natural" property of the human soul, if all life is a gift of God (1 Tim. 6:16; Acts 17:25-29; John 5:21), if nothing exists apart from the word of God (Rom. 11:36; Col. 1:17; Heb. 1:3), then the wicked who live forever in hell can do so only because God actively sustains them in existence, despite their predilection for corruption and even though there is no hope for their repentance and restoration. This results in the impossible scenario where, on the one hand, God's conquest of sin and death is deemed complete (1 Cor. 15:28), where all things have been reconciled to God (Col. 1:20), where every tear has been wiped from every eye, and mourning and pain have been ended

---

112. There is only one clear reference to eternal torment in the New Testament (Rev. 20:10). Not only does this refer to nonhuman figures (the devil, the beast, and the false prophet), which themselves represent evil systems rather than individuals, but it is highly symbolic language that is not intended to be taken literally. This is especially so since elsewhere we are told that God will destroy the devil (Heb. 2:14), and John himself decodes the symbol of the lake of fire as being "the second death" (20:6, 14; 21:8; cf. 2:11). In all other references to pain associated with judgment, such as wailing and gnashing of teeth (e.g., Matt. 13:42, 50; Luke 13:28) and torment (Luke 16:24; Rev. 14:10-11; 18:7, 10, 15), there is no clear indication that it is considered everlasting in nature. The texts may refer, for example, to a temporary experience of pain prior to final judgment, or to the reaction of the condemned to the passing of a verdict against them. (Note how in Revelation 14:10 the holy angels and the lamb are present during the torment.) Or they may simply be figurative depictions of the horror of final loss. Images of "unquenchable fire" (e.g., Matt. 3:12; Mark 9:43, 48) and "undying worms" (Mark 9:48; cf. Isa. 66:24) are also not meant to imply unending torture. Instead, they underline the fact that nothing can prevent the agents of destruction from completing their work, which is total obliteration (cf. Heb. 10:27; 12:29). In every case the evocative and metaphorical nature of apocalyptic and parabolic language must be allowed for. The overwhelming weight of biblical data favors annihilation or destruction as the fate of the wicked. Of the burgeoning literature on this, see E. W. Fudge, *The Fire that Consumes: A Biblical and Historical Study of Final Punishment* (Houston, Tex.: Providential Press, 1982); E. E. Ellis, "New Testament Teaching on Hell," in *The Reader Must Understand: Eschatology in Bible and Theology,* ed. K. E. Brower and M. W. Elliott (Leicester: IVP Apollos, 1997), 199-219; and W. Prestidge, *Life, Death, and Destiny* (Auckland, N.Z.: Resurrection Publishing, 1998).

forever (Rev. 21:4), and God has become "all in all" (1 Cor. 15:27), yet where, on the other hand, there is one corner of God's dominion where sin, suffering, and rebellion continue to exist, sustained by nothing less than the creative activity of God. The finality of God's victory over evil is fatally compromised by the notion of eternal existence in hell. One way around this objection is to propose that God's ultimate triumph depends not on the eradication of all evil but only on its definitive subjection to God's purposes. The continued existence of the wicked, now totally subservient to God's rule, serves positively to advertise God's final supremacy. But this will not do. The biblical writers never deny God's continuing sovereignty over evil, and their vivid pictures of ultimate redemption go well beyond the forcible subjection of evildoers to portray the total extinction of all evil. Indeed, it must be this way, for it is not God's power that needs vindicating but God's goodness, and God's sovereign goodness cannot be reconciled with the eternal persistence of evil. As Norman Krauss explains, "The power and right to punish evil cannot vindicate God's goodness. Vengeance and everlasting retribution do not undo or redress the wrong that has been done. Retribution is no substitute for restitution."[113]

The second insupportable proposition concerns the reason why the wicked are kept alive by God in hell. The traditional answer is that the residents of hell are sustained in existence in order to be punished retributively for their earthly sins, which is deemed necessary to vindicate God's justice. The problems with this explanation are manifold. One major problem relates to the matter of just deserts, the fit between the punishment and the crime. What human wrongdoing could possibly justify infinite punitive pain? Surely, on the principle of proportionality, for infinite punishment to be deserved, an infinite amount of harm must have been caused by sinners within the temporal limits of their earthly, finite existence. But is this the case? Is it even possible for a finite creature to cause infinite harm to God or to God's creation?

One common reply is to argue that human guilt is proportional to the *status* of the party offended against and to the amount of harm *intended*, not just to the severity of the actual harm done. Since God is an infinite being, and the intention of sinners is to reject in principle the rule of that being, sin against God is infinitely serious and merits infi-

113. Krauss, *God Our Saviour*, 213.

nite punishment.[114] Moreover, this calculation applies to every sin, even the smallest infraction (otherwise, some arbitrary measure of seriousness would be required) and to every sinner (even to atheists, who have no conscious intention of rejecting the rule of a God they do not believe exists). However, as J. L. Kvanvig shows, the "status argument" is philosophically flawed.[115] Certainly it does not apply in the earthly criminal realm. Killing an infant is no less serious than killing an adult; robbing a homeless street kid is no less immoral than robbing a wealthy person of high social status. Arguably it is morally more repugnant to harm a weaker party than a stronger one. That the situation is different with an ontologically superior being — namely, God — must simply be asserted as self-evident; it cannot be logically proven. Similar problems exist with regarding every sin as equally meriting infinite punishment and with viewing all human wrongdoing as an intentional rejection of God's rule.

Another solution to the problem of disproportionate punishment is to suggest that the impenitent in hell, by consistently refusing God, repeatedly sin and therefore merit ongoing punishment. D. A. Carson proposes that "at the end hell's inmates are full of sin. They hate and attract retribution, they still love only themselves and attract retribution, they are neither capable of nor desirous of repenting, and attract retribution."[116] This has been deemed "perhaps the strongest argument used by traditionalists."[117] But it is hardly satisfying. By rendering the activity of sinning an unending reality, this proposal seriously diminishes God's ultimate victory over evil and its effects, as mentioned above. Moreover, to suggest, as Carson and others do, that God wills the continuous punishment of sinners in order to glorify his holy justice is surely to remake divine justice in our own image, to view it as a tit-for-tat payback procedure that spirals on forever and ever.

114. For recent statements of this view, see R. A. Peterson, "A Traditionalist Response to John Stott's Arguments for Annihilationism," *JETS* 37, no. 4 (1994): 561-65; and L. Dixon, *The Other Side of the Good News: Confronting the Contemporary Challenges to Jesus' Teaching on Hell* (Wheaton, Ill.: Bridgepoint Books, 1992).

115. See especially Kvanvig, *The Problem of Hell* (Oxford: Oxford University Press, 1993), 25-66.

116. Carson, *The Gagging of God: Christianity Confronts Pluralism* (Grand Rapids: Zondervan, 1996), 534.

117. T. Gray, "Destroyed For Ever: An Examination of the Debates Concerning Annihilation and Conditional Immortality," *Themelios* 21, no. 1 (1996): 16.

As well as the problem of disproportionate deserts, there is also the problem of justifying eternal *suffering* as the penalty. What morally defensible motive can God have (and even God cannot be exempted from moral assessment)[118] for inflicting everlasting pain, least of all a God who "does not willingly afflict or grieve anyone" (Lam. 3:33), a God whose "anger is but for a moment; but [whose] favor is for a lifetime" (Ps. 30:5)? In the human realm the deliberate infliction of pain on another party is considered to be an intrinsic evil, unless it is deemed essential for the achievement of some greater good that will benefit the one who suffers. In the case of eternal torment, however, there is no greater good to be achieved; there is no future value that compensates for the pain of the present. "From God's side," says Walter Moberly, "there is no credible motive for inflicting retributive suffering on a really incorrigible sinner. . . . Deliberately to prolong a man's existence to all eternity in a condition of abject terror and demoralization, is unthinkable. To desire torture for torture's sake is admittedly diabolical and belongs only to the pathology of a diseased mind."[119] Because the pain of hell leads nowhere, because there is no benefit for those who endure it, Kvanvig aptly describes hell as "paradigmatic . . . of truly pointless, gratuitous evil."[120] Substituting mental anguish, such as remorse, frustration, and disappointment, for physical pain, as most contemporary advocates of eternal suffering do, does nothing to ease the problem. Pain is pain, whether suffered in mind or body, and the more that eternal torment is viewed as remorse and regret, the more it resembles the repentance which God seeks and which ought therefore to terminate the punishment! It has even been argued that the very notion of

118. Some argue that eternal suffering must simply be accepted as a theological fact despite its moral problems, and that it is wrong for a mere creature to subject God to moral scrutiny. However, if God is the author of morality, God's own actions must ultimately be shown to conform to the moral principles God imposes on humanity. If something must be called good because God does it, when by every criterion of morality such an action is evil, then all standards of morality collapse, and ultimately there becomes no way to differentiate between God and the Devil. Furthermore, if God is beyond all moral judgments, so that nothing God does could ever be said to be bad, then it should also be true that nothing God does can ever be said to be good or just or praiseworthy. It is true that God's ways are higher than ours (Isa. 55:9), but they are *higher* — not lower — than ours!

119. Moberly, *The Ethics of Punishment* (London: Faber & Faber, 1968), 343.

120. Kvanvig, *The Problem of Hell*, 9.

eternal remorse or regret is meaningless and impossible. Moberly suggests that a person who is so incurably wicked as to be consigned to hell would, by definition, lack the requisite conscience, moral insight, and self-awareness to feel guilt or remorse, or to recognize his or her suffering as deserved punishment. If any of those requisites existed, the person would be redeemable, and God would never abandon a potentially curable person to hell. Accordingly, "the notion of endless retributive and unredemptive punishment must be pronounced unthinkable. It is unthinkable because it combines elements that are really contradictory."[121]

What all this means is that it is impossible to justify morally the imposition of eternal suffering on human beings for their limited wrongdoings in this life. The argument that doing so is necessary to vindicate God's justice, and that this is the greater good that outweighs the sufferings of hell, is of no help. If to sustain someone in endless pain is immoral and unspeakably cruel, it cannot be a work of justice, and there is no logical reason why endless retribution is necessary to uphold God's justice. For this reason, and because a substantial body of exegetical evidence favors it, an increasing number of interpreters argue that the final judgment of the wicked consists of *their annihilation, not their endless suffering.* That is, to punish the wicked, God withdraws the gift of life, and they cease to exist; they are literally "destroyed."[122] Such punishment is still "eternal" (Matt. 25:46; 2 Thess. 1:9), but it is eternal in consequence or character, not in duration.[123] Annihilation-

---

121. Moberly, *The Ethics of Punishment*, 329-67 (quote from 339). See also E. R. Moberly, *Suffering, Innocent and Guilty* (London: SPCK, 1978), 102-21.

122. See, e.g., Matt. 10:28; Rom. 2:12; 9:22; Phil. 1:28; 3:19; 1 Thess. 5:3; 2 Thess. 1:9; 2 Pet. 3:7, 9; James 4:12.

123. The word "eternal" is used in both a qualitative and a quantitive sense in the Bible. It is sometimes urged that if eternal life in Matthew 25:46 is everlasting in duration, so too must be eternal punishment. But "eternal" in both phrases may simply designate that the realities in question pertain to the future age. Furthermore, inasmuch as life, by definition, is an ongoing state, "eternal life" includes the idea of everlasting existence. But punishment is a process rather than a state, and elsewhere when "eternal" describes an act or a process, it is the consequences rather than the process that are everlasting (e.g., Heb. 6:2, "eternal judgment"; Heb. 9:12, "eternal redemption"; Mark 3:29, "eternal sin"; 2 Thess. 1:9, "eternal destruction"; Jude 7, "eternal fire"). Eternal punishment is therefore something that is ultimate in significance and everlasting in effect, not in duration.

ism faces fewer moral difficulties than eternal suffering, but it still encounters the problem of how an eternal punishment can be regarded as a just and proportionate recompense for temporal, finite sins. An eternity of nothingness is as much an infinite penalty for finite sin as an eternity of pain. As Kvanvig puts it, "Nothing is to be gained in responding to objections to a penal theory by substituting metaphysical capital punishment for metaphysical life imprisonment."[124] Retributive punishment remains God's final word, whether it takes the form of eternal incarceration or irreversible execution, and God still suffers a staggering loss of the beings created in his own image.

Two other main options exist. One is to deny the outcome of damnation altogether, whatever its nature, in favor of *universal salvation.* Some critics reject the thought of hell entirely; others see it as a theoretical possibility that will never be realized; still others, like Jürgen Moltmann, suggest that Jesus' own sufferings exhausted and destroyed the torments of hell.[125] Certainly there is a clear theme in New Testament teaching that anticipates the reconciliation of all things to God (see further below). In light of this, and in view of what we know about the expansiveness of God's love, it is quite appropriate for Christians to hope fervently for the universal redemption of all humankind, especially since this is evidently something God personally desires (1 Tim. 2:4; 2 Pet. 3:9). But the repeated emphasis in Scripture on the possibility of eternal loss warns against superficial optimism, as does the stubborn reality of human freedom. We cannot glibly assume that, even given the choice, every person would freely choose union with God over final separation from God. Some people, through the practice of evil, may become so resistant to surrendering themselves in love to God that the very thought of eternal intimacy with God would seem excruciatingly painful.[126] The other, more promising option is to find *nonretributive categories* for explaining the doctrine of final judgment. For it is when hell is viewed as a matter of penal retribution that most of the moral and philosophical problems outlined above emerge.

124. Kvanvig, *The Problem of Hell,* 68. For a helpful summary of the debate between traditionalism and annihilationism, see Gray, "Destroyed For Ever," 14-18.

125. Moltmann, "The End of Everything Is God: Has Belief in Hell Had Its Day?" *ExpT* 108, no. 9 (1997): 263-64; Moltmann, *Jesus Christ for Today's World,* 142-45.

126. For a philosophical critique of universalism, see Kvanvig, *The Problem of Hell,* 73-96. For an exegetical and theological critique, see the references in note 143 below.

A Nonretributive Approach to Eschatological Judgment

The doctrine of final damnation is, as we have seen, usually explained in terms of God's retribution on human sin. Yet when measured against the retributive canon of just deserts, the punishment imposed is hard to justify, since it seems out of all proportion to the crime that occasions it. This is especially true if the punishment is understood as eternal torment, but is also the case if it is understood as destruction or annihilation. This calls into question whether the New Testament theme of eschatological judgment is best viewed as an exercise in strict retributive justice. Several considerations, I suggest, point in a different direction.

In the first place, it is important to affirm the priority of God's love in judgment as well as in redemption. The long-standing practice of appealing to heaven as proof of God's love and to hell as proof of God's justice is simplistic and misleading.[127] There is no contradiction between God's love and God's justice. Throughout the biblical story, God's basic orientation to humanity is one of self-giving love, with God conforming the demands of his holiness to those of his steadfast, redemptive love. "God's justice is his love in action," N. T. Wright explains. "God's love is the driving force of his justice."[128] While it may include punitive recompense for wrongdoing, God's justice is larger than retribution and is ultimately satisfied by healing and restoration, not by punishment. From this it follows that even the eschatological condemnation of the wicked at the Last Judgment must flow ultimately from the restorative love of God, not from the demands of retributive justice. It is out of undying love for every human being, not out of a need to exact retribution, that God declares eternal judgment on the impenitent.

This important — though paradoxical — insight serves to preserve

---

127. See Kvanvig, *The Problem of Hell*, 107-12. On the origins of this tradition, see J. Bonda, *The One Purpose of God: An Answer to the Doctrine of Eternal Punishment* (Grand Rapids: William B. Eerdmans, 1998), 1-44. W. Moberly aptly dismisses the doctrine of double predestination, in which most of the human race are created to be "vessels of wrath" to display God's justice, as "a moral monstrosity" and "a heresy more deadly than any other, because more dishonouring to God and striking more fatally at the root of the whole idea of God which Christ came to teach and to embody in action" (*The Ethics of Punishment*, 361).

128. Wright, *What Saint Paul Really Said* (Oxford: Lion, 1997), 110-11.

not only the unity of God's nature but also the initiative or sovereignty of God's action. For retributive justice is inherently reactive rather than proactive or creative in character; it is a response to something that has already happened. If final judgment is wholly retributive in character, it is compelled by something external to God: the existence of sin. If it is an expression of divine love, it issues from something within God's own being — namely, God's love for humanity and God's commitment to see human beings realize their potential. That potential is union with God. To enjoy such union, people must participate in God's perfection. This requires their full and free cooperation, a willing submission to God that cannot be coerced. Some may shrink from such surrender and choose instead radical separation from God. Out of love for them, God must honor their freedom of choice. It would be unloving and unjust to force them against their will to take up eternal residence in God's kingdom, which for the stubbornly impenitent would be an experience of hell.

It is true, however, that the idiom employed in the New Testament to depict final judgment includes notions of wrath, vengeance, and punishment, even of torment (Luke 16:23, 26; Matt. 18:34), beating (Luke 12:47-48), drowning (Mark 9:42), and being cut in pieces (Matt. 24:51/Luke 12:46). But it is crucial to recognize, in the second place, the figurative, parabolic nature of the language used to describe realities which, ex hypothesi, lie outside human experience. The diversity, grotesqueness, and mutually exclusive nature of the images used to depict hell (pitch darkness yet eternal fire, destroyed bodies yet ever-feeding maggots, and so on) corroborates the metaphorical, hyperbolic nature of such discourse. The same applies to images of reward and punishment. The basic thought is that earthly actions have eschatological significance and will receive appropriate recognition from God. But a wide range of images and metaphors from the world of human relations are used to express the process of assessment and its outcome. God has a treasury, keeps books, hires and fires, pays wages, harvests crops, herds animals, hands down sentences, scourges slaves, gives rewards, refines metal, confers prizes in athletic contests, holds feasts, bestows inheritances, and so on. Such language, says Jerome Quinn, is "figurative and connotative rather than denotative and literalistic."[129]

---

129. Quinn, "The Scriptures on Merit," in *Justification by Faith*, ed. H. G. Anderson, T. A. Murphy, and J. A. Burgess (Minneapolis: Augsburg, 1985), 88; cf. 84.

Notions of reward or repayment are simply commercial metaphors for the intensification of relationship with God granted to the redeemed. (What greater reward could there be?)[130] To envisage some kind of quantifiable material benefits is to miss the metaphorical reference of the language and to imply that something can be added to the bliss of knowing God. Conversely, the metaphors of judicially imposed punishments and torments for the condemned — wailing and gnashing of teeth — capture the loss and sheer horror involved in being excluded from relationship with God. (What greater punishment could there be?) To imagine some kind of cosmic torture-chamber where the lost suffer endless or prolonged retribution is to miss the figurative, apocalyptic nature of these utterances, as well as the paraenetic or pastoral intention behind them. While Jesus uses graphic imagery to visualize Gehenna, he does not relish or welcome the damnation of the wicked but portrays it precisely in order to avert it. In his careful study Reiser identifies "one important point" at which Jesus differs from the apocalyptic texts of Judaism:

> The depictions of judgment in early Jewish texts are quite often dictated by an unconcealed hatred and thirst for revenge: the hatred of the pious against the godless, of the righteous against the wicked, of the tortured against the torturers. In these texts, the eschatological judgment brings not only righteous punishment for sinners, but also serves for the final satisfaction of those who, against all obstacles, remained true to God and God's law.... Nothing of that can be found in the preaching of Jesus. His words about judgment are not inspired by hatred of sinners, but solely by love for them. In fact, he has come especially to call them to the eschatological banquet.[131]

So, although the metaphors of reward and punishment may suggest carefully calculated retribution, their intended referent is personal and relational, and, as Stephen Travis points out, "there cannot be genuine retribution in the context of personal relationships."[132] People's indi-

---

130. On sayings that seem to suggest degrees of reward in heaven, see C. L. Blomberg, "Degrees of Reward in the Kingdom of Heaven?" *JETS* 35, no. 2 (1991): 26-34; and Travis, *Christ and the Judgment of God*, 142-54.

131. Reiser, *Jesus and Judgment*, 321-22.

132. Travis, *Christ and the Judgment of God*, 44.

vidual destinies consist either of an intensification of their relationship with God or of an alienation from him. "To talk freely of punishment in the sense of retribution," Travis says, "is to distort the Christian message and encourage misunderstanding. To speak of relationship or lack of relationship with God is to get to the heart of the matter."[133]

Thirdly, while human works are subjected to divine assessment, the fundamental criterion of judgment is not external action but one's overall character and direction of life. Human works are evaluated inasmuch as they are the fruit of character and the essential manifestation of our relationship with God, however unconscious that may be (cf. Matt. 25:31-46; Rom. 2:12-16). Put otherwise, a person's basic orientation to the goodness that is God is displayed concretely in how one lives one's life, especially in how one treats other people. This in turn determines how one responds to a direct encounter with the manifestation of God's goodness in the person of Jesus, so that one's relationship to Jesus may serve as a measure of character, and vice versa.[134] This is why the New Testament divides humanity into only two groups, the saved and the lost, rather than into endless gradations based on varying merit.[135] The

---

133. Travis, *Christ and the Judgment of God,* 169.

134. There are at least four main criteria mentioned in the New Testament for a positive outcome at judgment: (1) one's treatment of others (e.g., Luke 10:25-37; Matt. 19:16-19; Matt. 5:22; 25:31-46); (2) one's good works in general (e.g., Matt. 7:15-23; 12:36; 25:14-30; Luke 19:11-27; John 8:51; Rom. 2:7-10; 2 Cor. 5:10; 2 Thess. 1:8; Eph. 5:6; 1 John 2:17; Heb. 5:9; Rev. 2:23; 22:12; 20:12); (3) one's intrinsic character (e.g., Matt. 18:3-4; 23:5-12; Gal. 5:19-21; Eph. 5:5); and (4) one's relationship to Christ (e.g., Mark 8:34-38; 10:21; Luke 13:34-35; 19:41-44; John 3:36; 6:40, 47, 51; 20:31; Acts 2:21; Rom. 10:10-13; 1 Cor. 15:22-23; 2 Tim. 2:10-11; Heb. 2:3; 10:29) or to God (Luke 10:27-28; James 1:12; 2:5; 2 Thess. 1:8). No contradiction exists between these four criteria. In several sayings, for example, "works" and "relationship to Jesus" are brought together as the basis for judgment (e.g., Luke 6:46-49/Matt. 7:24-27; Luke 12:8-9/Matt. 10:32-33; Luke 13:25-27; Matt. 7:21-23; Matt. 25:10-12). Like different facets of a diamond, each criterion gives expression to the same thing: a commitment and conformation of character to what is known of God's will.

135. Jesus sees two ways lying before people (Matt. 7:13-14; Luke 13:23-24), each with eternal significance. In the Gospels Jesus frequently divides people into two groups with two destinies: children of the kingdom and children of the evil one (Matt. 13:38); children of light and children of this world (Luke 16:8); the wise and the foolish (Matt. 7:24-27; 25:1-13); sheep and goats (Matt. 25:31-46); those who acknowledge him and those who deny him (Luke 12:8-9); those who enter life and those thrown into hell (Mark 9:42-48). Paul also sees only two destinies before people (e.g., Rom. 2:1-11; 1 Cor. 1:18).

fact that judgment is based on personal character and relationship to God undermines any notion of strict retribution. God is not some kind of heavenly certified accountant who carefully calculates appropriate repayment for each individual's deeds, but a God who does "not count their trespasses against them" (2 Cor. 5:18), a loving parent who "does not deal with us according to our sins, nor repay us according to our iniquities," but instead, remembering "that we are dust," a God who has "compassion for his children" (Ps. 103:6-14). Jesus' parables insist that God's will to redeem far outweighs his need to pay exact recompense for sins. In the parable of the workers in the vineyard, Jesus shows that those who think of God in terms of strict distributive or retributive justice fundamentally misunderstand God (Matt. 20:1-16; cf. Matt. 22:1-16; Luke 15:11-32; 18:9-14). Similarly, Paul, recognizing that a strictly retributional scheme would doom all humanity, insists that justification is a gift of pure grace (Rom. 3:23-24; cf. Eph. 2:8-10), not the outcome of a quid pro quo justice. For no matter how good our life or how many our good deeds, we can never merit or deserve the "reward" of salvation. The frequent use of the slave-master metaphor in the New Testament rules out all possibility of deserved reward, for any benefit that a first-century slave received from a master was never merited but was pure favor (Luke 17:7-10). Our relationship with God transcends all notions of just deserts, for it is transfused by unmerited grace.

In the fourth place, while the eschatological loss suffered by the impenitent may be regarded as the penalty of sin, and hence a punishment, it is not strictly retributive. Retributive punishment implies the external, secondary imposition of penalties in proportionate recompense for deeds done. But there is little hint of varying severities of punishment;[136] the lost are typically treated as a single category who suffer

---

136. In certain sayings Jesus speaks of "greater condemnation" or a "worse fate" awaiting those who have had greater knowledge and opportunity (Mark 12:40/Luke 20:47; Matt. 10:15/Luke 10:12-14; 11:22-24), and in Luke 12:47-48 he speaks of lesser and greater beatings. Some take this as indicating degrees of punishment in hell depending on merits (e.g., Carson, *The Gagging of God*, 533; C. L. Blomberg, "Eschatology and the Church: Some New Testament Perspectives," *Themelios* 23, no. 3 [1998]: 6). But these sayings are intended to underscore divine impartiality; God will take into account the opportunity and circumstances of people in determining judgment. This is not the same as teaching "grades of punishment." The reference in Luke 12:47-48 is part of the scenery of the parable and teaches, if anything, the principle that responsibility is com-

192

the same fate. As C. W. Emmet observes, "There are in the Gospels no 'poetic justice' parables, no limelight scenes of sensational punishments of evil-doers or dramatic vindication of virtue. There is no hint of any special doom on the Herods, Pilate, or the priests as individuals."[137] Furthermore, and crucially, the punishment in question — exclusion from relationship with God[138] — is not externally imposed by God but is the inherent, inevitable climax of the character of evil itself. Sin leads by inner necessity to death (Rom. 6:25; cf. 1:32), and ultimate salvation implies the final negation of sin and evil. God's respect for human freedom and personality means that God cannot force those who choose evil to become good. If the wicked freely resist God's healing grace offered in some definitive self-disclosure by God to them, then they will suffer the same negation of God's presence suffered by all else that is evil. But in truth the punishment suffered is self-inflicted, not retributively imposed; the impenitent "bring swift destruction upon themselves" (2 Pet. 2:1; cf. Luke 19:22; Acts 13:46). Since they choose to remain on "the road that leads to destruction" (Matt. 7:13), the only possible outcome is the complete eradication of their being ("their end is destruction," Phil. 3:19). That God allows this to occur has nothing to do with wreaking vengeance or retribution on sinners. As Miroslav Volf says, "God will judge, not because God gives people what they deserve, but because some people refuse to receive what no one deserves; if evildoers experience God's terror, it will not be because they have done evil, but because they have resisted to the end the powerful lure of the open arms of the crucified Messiah."[139] Judgment flows from the outworking of God's loving justice that works to make all things right for the benefit of sinners and to invite, but not coerce, their participation.

For this reason, we noted earlier that the notion of *everlasting existence* in hell separated from relationship with God is impossible to sus-

---

mensurate with endowment and opportunity. Moreover, can one meaningfully speak of degrees of unending pain? Does not the endless duration of the pain render any relative measures of severity both arbitrary and meaningless?

137. Emmet, "Retribution," *HDCG*, 2:518.

138. Matt. 25:46; 2 Thess. 1:9; cf. Phil. 1:23; 2 Cor. 5:8; 1 Thess. 4:17; 5:10.

139. Volf, *Exclusion and Embrace*, 298. Notwithstanding this quote, it should be noted that Volf refuses to shrink from affirming the essential violence of God's final judgment; see 275-306.

tain, since existence itself requires connection with God. Many thinkers still do argue for hell as a continuing state of self-incarceration, captured in C. S. Lewis's celebrated proposal that the doors of hell are locked from the inside, often combined with the thought that those in hell have become so devoid of moral consciousness that they have ceased to be personal beings. Kvanvig proposes a "composite view of hell" that combines the possibility of continued existence with the logical necessity of annihilation. He characterizes hell as "a journey beyond death toward annihilation, but with the possibility that the journey is never completed." Some people may be unfitted for heaven yet unready to make the kind of free, rational choice for annihilation that God, in his love, must honor, and they may therefore exist for an extended — perhaps an eternal — period in hell.[140] If such a scenario is to be envisaged, then God's attitude to those on the journey must be one of still seeking their reform and restoration, perhaps hoping their experience of pain will become penitential. Yet the proposal is deeply problematic, for God's endless patience becomes the cause of the endlessness of sin and suffering. The overwhelming evidence of the New Testament is that final judgment entails an irrevocable decision for life or death, for eternal union with God or definitive separation from God.

All this suggests that the retributive language and imagery of the New Testament do not a retributivist theology make. And yet — and this is the fifth point — retributional words and metaphors are still deliberately employed by the New Testament writers in discussing final judgment. This is partly because of the communicative power of such images, and partly because retributive terminology safeguards important theological truths. It attests, on the one hand, to human culpability and to the fact that human works are serious, consequential, and weighty matters. To choose between good and evil in this life has transcendent significance. On the other hand, it prevents the notion of self-imposed judgment degenerating into an impersonal, deistic cause-and-effect mechanism that operates apart from God's moral will. This cannot be so, for God is personal, sin is a personal affront to God, and the cause-and-effect process operates only because God personally enables it to

140. Kvanvig, *The Problem of Hell*, esp. 107-33, 136-61 (quote from 168). Cf. D. C. Spanner, "Is Hell for Ever?" *Churchman* 110, no. 2 (1996): 107-20; and D. Cheetham, "Hell as Potentially Temporal," *ExpT* 108, no. 9 (1997): 260-63.

operate. Retributivist categories safeguard God's personal and sovereign involvement in dealing with evil and the discriminating character of divine justice. Ultimately it is *God* who secures the triumph of righteousness and the destruction of sin, and God's dealings with human beings are never arbitrary or capricious. In practice, however, divine judgment works itself out nonretributively inasmuch as God "gives people up" to experience the consequences of their own free choices.

One final point remains to be made. I have argued so far that the idea of eschatological judgment does not operate on the basis of strict retributive justice, that the loss suffered by the impenitent is self-chosen, even if it entails God's active acceptance of their choice. But is all this enough to solve our problem? Does not biblical teaching on the definitive destruction of offenders at the Last Judgment, even if we view it more as a matter of metaphysical suicide than divinely imposed capital punishment, still remain an obstacle for a thoroughgoing, Christian philosophy of restorative justice? In one sense the answer is Yes. Hell is nothing if it is not a problem! But there are two good reasons not to exaggerate the dilemma unduly.

One has to do with the unique and truly definitive nature of final judgment. In all other situations where offenders are dealt with, an appeal can be made to some remaining goodness within them, however residual, to promote restoration. By contrast, anyone who is destroyed at the eschatological judgment will have become so totally identified with all that is evil that nothing remains of their personality to be restored. The utter uniqueness of this situation precludes using it to avoid a commitment to restoration in every other situation we face; if God works for restoration up until the very last moment, so too must we. It also precludes using the Last Judgment as a justification or paradigm for corresponding human action in present history, as happened during the Inquisition, for example. To the contrary, God's prerogative of final judgment challenges and critiques — rather than underwrites and validates — violent human retribution on wrongdoers (Rom. 12:19-21). "God is not needed to create guilt or to punish," Albert Camus once said. "Our fellow-men suffice, aided by ourselves. You were speaking of the Last Judgment. Allow me to laugh respectfully. I shall wait for it resolutely, for I have known what is worse, the judgment of men."[141]

---

141. Camus, *The Fall* (Harmondsworth: Penguin, 1957), 81.

As well as the issue of uniqueness, it is also crucial to recognize the limited, fragmentary nature of our knowledge about ultimate realities and resist dogmatic assertions about the inescapability of hell for all but a righteous minority. Certainly we must reckon with the possibility of eternal loss for some of God's creatures. It is affirmed throughout the New Testament, not least by Jesus himself, and it would be foolish to assume that he was making idle threats. The battle between good and evil is deadly serious, and habituating oneself to evil in this life is fraught with eschatological danger. But alongside warnings of eschatological separation lies a string of New Testament texts that proclaim the universal efficacy of Christ's atoning death (1 John 2:2; Heb. 2:9), the all-inclusive reach of God's mercy (John 12:32; Rom. 11:32-36; 1 Tim. 4:10; Titus 2:11; James 2:13), the eventual confession of Christ's lordship by every human tongue (Phil. 2:10-11; Rev. 7:9), and the final restoration of the entire created order to the divine intention (Rom. 8:18-27; 1 Cor. 15:22-28; Col. 1:19-20; Eph. 1:9-10 — cf. Acts 3:21). "Therefore, just as one man's trespass led to condemnation for all," Paul writes, "so one man's act of righteousness leads to justification and life for all" (Rom. 5:18; cf. 1 Cor. 15:28). How these two biblical themes — one that envisages two alternative, co-existing destinies, and the other that anticipates the uniting of all things in Christ — are to be reconciled is impossible to say.[142] Most interpreters weaken the universalist theme to mean not the reconciliation of literally all things to God but the reconciliation of all *remaining* things after the wicked have been removed from the scene. Salvation extends to all *kinds* of things and to all *classes* of people, but not to all individuals.[143] Others weaken the judgment theme, perhaps construing the depictions of hellfire as indicative of a painful but purgatorial encounter with God after death,[144] or perhaps, like Jan Bonda, envisaging a time beyond eternal destruction when God gives life and justification to the dead.[145] Maybe a humble agnosticism is the wisest option.

142. See M. E. Boring, "The Language of Universal Salvation in Paul," *JBL* 105, no. 2 (1986): 269-92.

143. See, e.g., N. T. Wright, "Towards a Biblical View of Universalism," *Themelios* 4, no. 2 (1979): 54-58; and Wright, "Universalism and the World-Wide Community," *Churchman* 89, no. 3 (1975): 197-212.

144. Küng, *Eternal Life?* 137-39 — cf. 211-13; Moberly, *The Ethics of Punishment,* 365-67.

145. "The judgment of the godless will not be the end," says Bonda. "All who are

How the destruction of all wickedness and the redemption of all things are both to be effected is known only to God. For our purposes, the point to notice is that God's final word is not retribution but restoration, the recreation of heaven and earth so that sin, suffering, sickness, and death are no more. "And the one who was seated on the throne said, 'See, I am making all things new'" (Rev. 21:3-5).

Summary

In the last two chapters I have traversed a huge amount of territory. My main goal has been to determine what role punishment has as a response to wrongdoing in light of the understanding of divine justice as God's redemptive or restorative action on behalf of people, which is paradigmatic for the exercise of human justice. We began by surveying the long-standing debate in legal and social theory over the purpose of and justification for criminal punishment, and outlined a way of understanding punishment as a potentially restorative mechanism. We also explored the extent to which different theories of punishment are reflected in Scripture. We found that while punishment in the Bible is sometimes justified in terms of deterrence, reprobation, and retribution, its overriding purpose is to promote repentance, reformation, and restoration, both of the covenant community and, where possible, of the individual offender.

We then turned to examine the discussion of divine and human punishment in the New Testament. Of the texts that speak of punishment administered by human agencies, some refer to punishment employed within the community of faith and some to punishments administered in wider society. In the first group we found that church discipline has a consistently restorative intent. No physical punishments, like flogging, stoning, or confiscation of property, were employed by the early church. Instead, offenders were rebuked for their actions, perhaps in progressive stages (Matt. 18:15-20), and if repentant were "restored gently" (Gal. 6:1). The ultimate penalty for recalcitrant

---

lost will one day come to conversion and return to the father, the God of love; *together with* the church they will kneel and join in their hymn of praise for the salvation he extends to all in the name of Jesus" (*The One Purpose of God,* 228).

offenders was excommunication or expulsion from the community. This was understood as both a cause of shame and a cause of danger since, separated from the protective fellowship, offenders become vulnerable to Satan's power. But even such a drastic step was intended to bring about contrition and restoration. Overall, the punishments employed as part of church discipline were inflicted out of equal concern for the integrity of the faith community and the spiritual welfare of the offender.

Most of the New Testament texts that describe punishments in wider society are merely descriptive of current penal practices. But in some cases, judicial authority is cast positively in the role of God's agent to reward good behavior and punish bad behavior (Rom. 13:1-7; 1 Pet. 2:14). This punitive action is described in Romans 13:4 as a historical outworking of God's wrath and vengeance. The best way to understand this, I suggested, was in keeping with the classical discussion on the present outworking of God's wrath in Romans 1:18-32. There divine wrath is not individually designed and personally administered retribution for sinful conduct but God's partial withdrawal of his protective hand to allow evil to run its course of self-destruction and to permit human beings to experience the woeful consequences of their wrong choices. It is not so much a retributive as an intrinsic punishment that has an ultimately redemptive or restorative intent.

Most references to divine punishment in the New Testament refer to final judgment. Here we found a clear affirmation that evil will not have the final word in human history but will be subjected to annihilating destruction. Those who refuse to appropriate the benefits of God's saving justice in the work of Christ also face the prospect of final destruction. This is not because in the final analysis retribution wins out over mercy but because their destiny remains determined by Adam's transgression rather than by the Second Adam's obedience (Rom. 5:12-21). Initial indications that the Last Judgment is entirely and wholly retributive, I suggested, need revising in light of the way judgment and its consequences are understood.

In sum, we must conclude that punishment has a significant place in the presentation of divine justice in the New Testament. But the purpose of this punishment is ultimately reparative or redemptive in design. It is intended to invite repentance and reformation from wrong-doers and/or to frustrate oppressors who seek to repress the gospel or persecute the weak. The ultimate display of divine punishment is reserved for the powers of evil themselves, thereby vouchsafing the enduring freedom of creation from corruption (Rom. 8:18-39). The way of escape has been provided by God. Those individuals who face destruction do so by their own choosing, not because God's retributive justice demands their demise. Restoration, not retribution, is the hallmark of God's justice and is God's final word in history.

CHAPTER 5

JUSTICE THAT KILLS

Is There a Place for Capital Punishment?

We have given considerable attention to the role of punishment in the administration of justice, both in criminological theory and in biblical teaching. Throughout human history the ultimate punishment for criminal offending has been death, and it usually has been afforded religious sanction.[1] This is true in biblical history as well. In fact, among the range of punishments currently employed in Western penal codes, the death penalty is unique in being able to claim direct biblical or divine sanction. (The same cannot be said, for example, about imprisonment.) Over the past fifty years, however, more and more countries have been abolishing the death penalty, although it still remains on the law books of around half the countries of the world. In these countries, offenses punishable by death range from violent crimes such as murder, rape, and armed robbery, to nonviolent crimes like black marketeering, drug smuggling, bribe-taking, counterfeiting, and prostitution. Not infrequently capital punishment is part of a larger apparatus of state-sponsored repression. According to Amnesty International, "The negative correlation between execution policy and governmental respect for human rights throughout the world can be demonstrated over and over again."[2] China is the strongest case in

---

1. See the massive historical survey by J. J. Megivern, *The Death Penalty: An Historical and Theological Survey* (Mahwah, N.J.: Paulist Press, 1997).

2. I. Gray and M. Stanley (for Amnesty International USA), *A Punishment in Search of a Crime: Americans Speak Out against the Death Penalty* (New York: Avon Books, 1989), 12.

point, with, on a conservative reckoning, up to ten thousand executions a year. Among Western democracies, the United States is virtually alone in retaining capital punishment for the crime of murder. It remains in force in about three-quarters of American states, with over three thousand inmates currently on death row. (New Zealand abolished the death penalty for murder in 1961, and for the remaining crimes of high treason and mutiny in the armed forces in 1989.) Yet at times of social upheaval or rising crime rates or in the aftermath of particularly brutal crimes, public clamor for the re-introduction or increased use of the death penalty usually grows louder. In 1966, only 42 percent of Americans favored the death penalty for murder; this had grown to 66 percent in 1981, and 79 percent by 1996.[3] The same pattern of rising support for capital punishment can be documented in many other Western countries as well.

Many Christians do not know how to respond to this situation. They feel caught in a tension between what they perceive to be the demands of justice on the one hand and the way of compassion and forgiveness taught by Jesus on the other. They might agree that Scripture should be the primary determinant of their ethical position, yet they can come to opposite conclusions about what Scripture requires on this matter. Even committed Christian pacifists are found on both sides of the fence.[4] This is the case because arriving at an informed and authentically Christian position on capital punishment is not easy. Many factors need to be weighed carefully. There is the *exegetical* question of what particular passages of Scripture mean, especially Genesis 9, John 8, and Romans 13; the *hermeneutical* question of whether New Testament teaching supersedes Old Testament teaching on this issue, or whether the Old Testament pattern continues unchanged; the *theological* question of whether a picture of God as Law-Giver or a picture of God as Liberator-Redeemer should serve as the controlling paradigm; and the *pragmatic* question of determining whether capital punishment is beneficial or harmful to society. There is also the *philosophical* question of how we are to understand the nature and function of justice. Justice is a relative concept; no absolute yardstick exists for determin-

3. These figures are from the Gallup Poll Archives 61, no. 4 (24 May 1996).

4. This is reflected in the debate between J. H. Redekop and E. A. Martens, *On Capital Punishment* (Hillsboro, Kans./Winnipeg, Man.: Kindred Press, 1987).

ing what constitutes a "just" penalty for a crime. Such judgments vary from culture to culture and age to age. In eighteenth-century England, up to 350 felonies carried the death penalty (with the approval of the established church);[5] in contemporary England, no criminal action is deemed worthy of execution. More fundamental still is whether criminal justice is conceptualized in retributive terms, with a leading concern being to "let the punishment fit the crime," or in restorative terms, with the key question being whether or not execution serves to restore the well-being of society and promote healing in the lives and relationships of those involved. Equally important is how we understand the relationship between justice and love, and the government's role in dispensing each.

Given these complexities, it is not surprising that Christians should be divided over the normative status of capital punishment. The support of churches for the elimination of the death penalty has often been a critical factor in countries that have abolished it. On the other hand, one of the significant factors in explaining America's retention of capital punishment is the punitive voice of fundamentalist Christianity,[6] while in New Zealand, the leading advocate for the reintroduction of the death penalty is the conservative Christian Heritage political party.[7] In this chapter, I will evaluate critically the biblical and moral arguments advanced by Christians who support capital punishment. Basically at issue is whether Scripture prescribes capital punishment as a universal, timeless principle of social life, or whether its sanction in biblical times is best understood as a temporary arrangement employed by the people of God under certain historical circumstances but now superseded by a fuller Christian ethic. How Christians answer this question has a major bearing on how they evaluate the use of execution by political authorities today. While it is possible to argue that on this issue, as on the issue of war, two completely different norms apply to church and state,[8] it is, in my view,

5. So T. J. Gorringe, *God's Just Vengeance: Crime, Violence, and the Rhetoric of Salvation* (Cambridge: Cambridge University Press, 1996), 158-60.

6. See K. H. Potter, "The Special Relationship: Anglo-American Attitudes to the Death Penalty," *ExpT* 106, no. 8 (1995): 231.

7. See G. Capill, "Political Initiatives in Response to Serious Violent Crime," *Stimulus* 2, no. 3 (1994): 63-68.

8. So E. A. Martens, "Capital Punishment and the Christian," in Redekop and Martens, *On Capital Punishment*, 27.

extremely problematic to do so. It is morally and theologically more defensible to assume that if we reach the conclusion that capital punishment is consistent with a biblical-Christian ethic, then Christians must be prepared to participate in its enforcement (as judges, prison officers, and executioners). Conversely, if we decide that capital punishment is contrary to such an ethic, then Christians should work toward its abolition in countries that still employ it and oppose all attempts to reintroduce it in countries that have dispensed with it.

Capital Punishment in the Bible

Differences among Christian ethicists on the validity of capital punishment center substantially on the interpretation of the biblical data. There is disagreement on the exegesis of crucial passages as well as on judgments about the overall direction of biblical teaching. In this section I will summarize the relevant biblical data and comment briefly on early Jewish practice. In the next section I will evaluate the implications of particular key texts for the death penalty debate.

The Death Penalty in the Old Testament

It is perhaps significant that the first interpersonal crime in the biblical story is murder and that the murderer does not receive capital justice. Although Abel's blood cried out from the ground for vengeance (Gen. 4:10), God imposes on Cain the punishment of exile, not death. Moreover, since Cain's exile would mean that anyone could kill him without fear of retribution (4:14), God acts to protect Cain's life by branding him and agreeing to become his surrogate avenger, warning that "whoever kills Cain will suffer a sevenfold vengeance" (4:15). A vicious cycle of revenge is thus forestalled by an act of clemency. But the damage is done. Violence has entered the human community, and it escalates horribly to the point where Lamech boasts, "I have killed a man for wounding me" (4:23). As John Goldingay observes, "The essence of sin East of Eden seems to lie in violence; it is for the pursuit of violence that Lamech adapts the first technology; and for the glorification of violence that he adapts the first art (Gen 4.23-24). It is because the world is filled with violence that God determines to destroy it (Gen 6.11-13)."[9] This state of affairs prompts divine regret at the creation of humanity (6:5-6) and a massive response of watery judgment. After the Flood, God makes a covenant with Noah, renewing the primeval command to have dominion over the earth and stipulating, for the first time, a "life for life" principle (Gen. 9:4-6).

When later in the biblical story the nation of Israel comes into existence, the death penalty becomes entrenched in complex legislation that no doubt grew and developed over a long period of time. With respect to the Decalogue, which is rightly regarded as the quintessence of biblical law, flagrant disregard of the first six commandments carries a mandatory death penalty, and it is optional for the seventh commandment.[10] In its extant form, Pentateuchal law prescribes the ultimate penalty for approximately twenty offenses of various kinds:

1. Unlawful Taking of Human Life
- murder (Exod. 21:12-14, 20; 22:2-3; Lev. 20:2; 24:17, 21; Num. 35:11-21; Deut. 19:11-13)
- accidentally causing the death of a pregnant woman (or her baby?) in the course of a fight (Exod. 21:22-25)
- owning an animal that has killed before and failing to keep it caged, so that it kills again (Exod. 21:28-30)
- avenging a death despite acquittal by the law (Deut. 17:12)
- perjury on a matter worthy of death (Deut. 19:16-19)

2. Other Interpersonal Offenses
- kidnapping (Exod. 21:16; Deut. 24:7)
- cursing one's parent (Exod. 21:17; Lev. 20:9)
- rebelling against one's parents (Deut. 21:18-21)
- striking a parent (Exod. 21:15)

3. Sexual Offenses
- adultery (Lev. 20:10; Deut. 22:22-24; Num. 5:12-30)

9. Goldingay, "Old Testament Sacrifice and the Death of Christ," in *Atonement Today*, ed. John Goldingay (London: SPCK, 1995), 15.

10. Cf. G. J. Wenham, "Law and the Legal System in the Old Testament," in *Law, Morality, and the Bible: A Symposium*, ed. B. N. Kaye and G. J. Wenham (Leicester: Inter-Varsity Press, 1978), 27-29.

- homosexual conduct (Lev. 20:13)
- bestiality (Lev. 20:15-16; Exod. 22:19)
- incest (Lev. 20:11-12)
- intercourse with both a woman and her mother (Lev. 20:14)
- rape of a married woman (but not of a virgin) (Deut. 22:25-29)
- prostitution by a priest's daughter (Lev. 21:9)
- fornication with a betrothed woman (Deut. 22:20-22; Gen. 38:24)

4. Religious Offenses
- blasphemy (Lev. 24:10-23)
- sorcery and witchcraft (Exod. 22:18; Lev. 20:27)
- child sacrifice (Lev. 20:2)
- idolatry and encouraging idolatry (Exod. 22:20; Deut. 13:1-16; 17:3-5; 18:20; cf. Num. 25:1-5)
- ignoring the decision of a priest or judge (Deut. 17:12)
- false claims to be a prophet (Deut. 13:5, 10)
- Sabbath-breaking (Exod. 31:14; Num. 15:32-34)
- intrusion of an alien into a sacred place or office (Num. 1:51; 3:10; 18:7)

Various modes of execution are recorded in the Old Testament. The most frequent is stoning (e.g., Lev. 20:2; Deut. 22:24; Josh. 7:25; 1 Kings 21:13). Prior to the execution of blasphemers, witnesses would place their hands on the head of the offender (Lev. 24:14), then pelt him or her with stones until dead. In certain cases, the first stone was to be thrown by the accusers, followed by the entire community.[11] The penalty of burning is prescribed for miscellaneous sexual offenses (Lev. 20:14; 21:9; Gen. 38:24 — cf. Dan. 3). Beheading is recorded as a royal

---

11. The Mishnah's description of stoning differs greatly from that of the Old Testament. The whole community is not involved, as in biblical times, and one stone (two if necessary) is dropped on the victim's heart from a height rather than many stones being thrown. This seems to be a humanitarian modification, since the bestiality of stoning as a method of execution is often noted by ancient authors. Cf. J. Blinzer, "The Jewish Punishment of Stoning in the New Testament Period," in *The Trial of Jesus,* ed. E. Bammel (London: SCM, 1970), 155n.23. Another reason may have been a concern to avoid disfigurement of the corpse in view of a popular belief that one's skeletal integrity at death affected one's resurrection state. Cf. D. Daube, *The New Testament and Rabbinic Judaism* (London: The Atholone Press, 1956), 301-21.

mode of execution of persons offensive to the king (2 Kings 6:31-32; 2 Sam. 16:9). Execution by sword (Exod. 32:27; Deut. 13:15), spear (Num. 25:7-8), arrow (Exod. 19:13), and impalement (Num. 25:4; 2 Sam. 21:6) are also mentioned. Sometimes following an execution, the corpse would be mutilated (2 Sam. 4:12) or hung in public as a deterrent (Deut. 21:22-23). Hanging and lethal torture, such as flaying alive, were not used as methods of execution in Israel or in ancient Near Eastern domestic justice generally (but cf. Esther 2:23; 7:10), though they were employed in warfare.

It is noteworthy that Pentateuchal law, as it stands, includes significant safeguards to prevent the accidental or deliberate miscarriage of capital justice, though how long these provisions co-existed in the law and whether they were ever fully applied are uncertain. For example, the standard of proof required amounted to virtual certainty (Deut. 17:4), with conviction usually requiring the testimony of more than one witness (Deut. 17:6; 19:15; Num. 35:30). Difficult cases were apparently deferred to judicial experts (Deut. 17:8-9). Stringent efforts were made to root out false witness, while perjury in capital cases was punishable by death (Deut. 19:16, 19). In cases of murder, substitute penalties were not permitted, preventing the wealthy and powerful from purchasing immunity from punishment and ruling out any discrimination on the basis of class or kin (Deut. 19:13; Lev. 27:29; Num. 35:31). In contrast to the Code of Hammurabi and the laws of European nations up until the eighteenth century, Pentateuchal law specified the death penalty only for crimes against persons and against God, not against property. A distinction was also drawn between murder and unpremeditated manslaughter, with cities of refuge being created to protect those guilty of manslaughter from avenging kin (Exod. 21:12-13; Num. 35:9-34; cf. Deut. 4:41-43; 19:1-10; Josh. 20:1-9). After comparing these provisions with those employed in the American legal system, David Llewellyn concludes that "in the areas of evidence, judgment, and sentencing the Mosaic law code functions more restrictedly than the American judicial system. Fewer people would be convicted under the Mosaic code than under the penal codes of any of our fifty states."[12]

---

12. Llewellyn, "Restoring the Death Penalty: Proceed with Caution," in L. Kehler et al., *Capital Punishment Study Guide* (Winnipeg: MCC Victim Offenders Ministries, 1980), 41. See also D. W. van Ness, "Punishable by Death," *Christianity Today* 31, no. 10 (1987):

Clearly, then, the Old Testament sanctions capital punishment for a wide range of offenses and reflects deeply on the legal provisions necessary for "just" executions. But caution is needed in assuming that the maximum penalty was invariably exacted, since the possibility existed in certain cases for lesser penalties or substitute ransoms to be paid. In the case of adultery, for example, Proverbs 6:32-35 implies that monetary compensation was acceptable to some husbands, while in the case of Sabbath-breaking, Nehemiah 13:15-21 and Isaiah 58:13-14 call for repentance rather than death. The fact that certain offenses were thought to merit death is therefore not to say that death was always imposed. The demand for at least two witnesses (Deut. 19:15) would also have practically limited application of the death penalty to only the most flagrant violations of the law. Furthermore, the legislative provisions of Pentateuchal law must be evaluated in connection with extralegal biblical narratives that record both compliance and noncompliance with capital prescriptions. Compliance is illustrated by such episodes as the execution of those involved with the golden calf (Exod. 32:27), Phineas's execution of two consenting adulterers (Num. 25:6-8), the death of Achan at Jericho (Josh. 7:24-26), and David's execution of Rechab and Baanah (2 Sam. 4:5-12). Noncompliance is shown by episodes where the death penalty was legally deserved but not enforced (e.g., Gen. 50:15-21; 1 Sam. 11:12-13; 14:43-45; 25:23-32; 2 Sam. 8:15; 12:13; 14:11; Hos. 3:1). Taken as a whole, then, while the Old Testament specifies death for certain infractions, it also allows — and often celebrates — clemency for specific offenders.

The Death Penalty in Early Judaism

In considering the place of capital punishment in the early Jewish community, we encounter a number of significant methodological difficulties. One perennial difficulty in the study of early Judaism concerns the dating of sources. It is often uncertain whether particular Jewish traditions recorded in the Mishnah or Talmud can be traced back to the Second Temple period or reflect later reality. It is also necessary to distin-

---

24-27. There are instances of the death penalty being carried out without due process (e.g., 2 Sam. 4:12; Num. 25:7-9), but the offenses in question were probably considered so obviously deserving of death that the penalty was considered incontestable.

guish between theory and practice, especially with respect to Jewish criminal (and even civil) law, since the actual practice of some laws required a political sovereignty that the Jews did not have at the time. G. F. Moore suspects, for example, that both the rigid procedures required in the Mishnah for convictions in capital offenses and the lengthy — often grisly — descriptions of modes of execution are largely academic and could have been devised only at a time when the administration of capital justice was in foreign hands.[13]

A particularly vexed question concerns the legal competence of Jewish authorities under Roman rule (roughly 6-66 C.E.) to deal with capital offenses against Jewish law.[14] The evidence is mixed. On the one hand, there are sources which claim that for forty years prior to the destruction of the Jerusalem temple, capital jurisdiction was taken away from Jewish courts.[15] On the other hand, there are several instances recorded of capital trials and executions by the Jews without the intervention of Roman authorities,[16] and an unusual privilege was given to the Jews to slay any foreigners, including even Roman citizens, who entered the temple precincts beyond a certain point.[17] Some historians think that the Sanhedrin only had the power to arrest the accused and hear evidence, with judgment and sentencing resting in the hands of the Roman procurator. Others claim that the Sanhedrin could pass judgment and sentence but that these decisions were subject to Roman ratification. Still others believe such ratification was unnecessary. On balance,

---

13. Moore, *Judaism in the First Centuries of the Christian Era: The Age of the Tannaim*, 2 vols. (Cambridge: Harvard University Press, 1927), 2:182-88. Four methods of execution are prescribed in the Mishnah (*m. Sanh*.7.1): stoning, burning (i.e., pouring molten lead down a person's throat), decapitation, and strangulation (prescribed in cases where the method of execution is not mentioned in the Bible). Other methods of securing death are sometimes mentioned, such as feeding a prisoner barley until his stomach explodes (*m. Sanh.* 9:5). Hanging was not permitted, except in terms of exposing a corpse after death in certain crimes.

14. See esp. E. Schürer, *The History of the Jewish People in the Age of Jesus Christ (175 BC–AD 135)*, rev. ed., 3 vols. (Edinburgh: T. & T. Clark, 1973), 1:378; 2:221-23; and R. E. Brown, *The Death of the Messiah: From Gethsemane to the Grave*, 2 vols. (New York: Doubleday, 1994), 1:363-72.

15. John 18:31; Josephus, *Antiquities*, XX:202; *b. Sanh.* 41a; *b. 'Abod. Zar.* 8b — cf. *Str-B*, 1:1026-27.

16. Cf. Acts 5:27-42 (note esp. v. 33); 7:57-60; 26:10; *m. Sanh.* 7:2; *t. Sanh.* 10:11.

17. Josephus, *War*, VI:124-26; cf. Acts 21:28-29.

it seems probable that Jewish courts could not inflict the death penalty without the permission of the Roman procurator,[18] except for certain religious offenses, such as when a Gentile transgressed the temple restriction, although it is possible the Romans turned a blind eye to local Jewish justice if no harm to Roman interests came of it.[19] Spontaneous lynching was apparently recognized as a legitimate mode of punishing gross religious offenses and was tolerated even in the Diaspora.[20] Accordingly, the plots to slay Paul in Damascus (Acts 9:23-24) and Jerusalem (23:12-15), as well as the stoning at Lystra (14:19) and perhaps the stoning of Stephen (7:57-60), may, from the Jewish point of view, have been legally justified (cf. also Luke 20:6; John 10:33; 11:8).

As well as recognizing the political constraints that Judaism labored under, we also need to take into account the complexities of Jewish law and the diversity that characterized Jewish interpretation of the Torah. Jewish law was enormously complex, comprising a mass of traditions and customs, written and unwritten provisions, inconsistencies and contradictions. Philip Alexander argues that, contrary to prevalent opinion, the Torah was not an undifferentiated, highly uniform and coherent body of law. "It is important to take a nuanced view of the Jewish law in the time of Jesus. In principle the Torah was uniformly divine. In practice all kinds of distinctions were recognized which cut across the seamless fabric of the Torah."[21] Among these was a distinction between enforced and unenforced capital offenses. In certain cases where transgressions of the law were considered to merit death, the

---

18. On the authority of Roman governors to exercise the *ius gladii*, see Schürer, *The History of the Jewish People in the Age of Jesus Christ*, 1:368-72; 2:219-220n.80.

19. So E. P. Sanders, "The Synoptic Jesus and the Law," in Sanders, *Jewish Law from Jesus to the Mishnah* (London: SCM, 1990), 17; and Brown, *The Death of the Messiah*, 1:371-72. G. Alon believes that the Sanhedrin continued to exercise capital punishment up until the destruction of Jerusalem, whether or not the Romans gave their approval, but that such jurisdiction came to a definitive end after the destruction. See *The Jews in Their Land in the Talmudic Era* (Cambridge: Harvard University Press, 1989), 206-12.

20. Philo, *Special Laws*, I:54-57; III:94-98; *m. Sanh.* 9:6; 3 Macc. 7:10-14. The capital crime of blasphemy for which Jesus and his followers were persecuted (e.g., Mark 2:7; 14:64; John 10:31-40; Acts 6:11; 26:19-23 — cf. Mark 3:20-30) probably covered a far greater area of insult to God and religion than the more restricted concept found in the Mishnah.

21. Alexander, "Jewish Law in the Time of Jesus: Towards a Clarification of the Problem," in *Law and Religion: Essays on the Place of Law in Israel and Early Christianity*, ed. B. Lindars (Cambridge: James Clarke, 1988), 57.

courts did not exact the penalty but left it to God to bring premature death upon the wrongdoer ("death at the hands of heaven"). Substitute penalties were also common, with the *lex talionis* being understood to furnish a basis for determining monetary compensation for the victim.

There was also great diversity in Jewish exegesis of the law. There was no single, universally acknowledged legal orthodoxy. Pinchas Lapide explains that when contemporary circumstances meant that a literal exegesis and application of a Torah passage threatened to run counter to what was believed to be its original intention, the rabbis were ready to use liberal norms in explaining them; "it is not the literal sense that is the final court of appeal for the teacher of Judaism, but rather the original intention, which is accessible only to those digging deeply."[22] Fundamental to the perceived intention of the law, Lapide insists, was the sanctity of human life. Noting that the statement "by these commandments you shall live" occurs seven times in Deuteronomy, the Talmudic fathers took the verb "live" as "a call for continual reinterpretation of scripture in order to promote and enhance human life, which is its central concern."[23] The Sabbath command — and indeed all commandments except those forbidding murder, incest, and idolatry — could and even should be broken in order to save one's own life or another's life.[24]

This same concern to preserve life expressed itself in a definite unwillingness to impose the death penalty. Since the institution is inscribed in Scripture, it could not be explicitly abrogated, and no doubt some first-century rabbis, like the second-century sage Shim'on ben Gamli'el II,[25] deemed its use essential to the maintenance of social order (cf. John 8:6). The reform of biblical methods of execution undertaken by the Pharisees between 100 B.C.E.–100 C.E., whether motivated by humanitarian or theological concerns,[26] suggests that capital punishment still oc-

---

22. Lapide, *The Sermon on the Mount: Utopia or Program for Action?* (Maryknoll, N.Y.: Orbis, 1986), 60-61.

23. Lapide, *The Sermon on the Mount*, 17.

24. Lapide, *The Sermon on the Mount*, 17, 62.

25. *m. Mak.* 1:10, cited in D. Novak, "Halakah," *ER*, 6:170.

26. Daube suggests that several biblical methods of execution came to be seen as problematic because they seriously disfigured or damaged the skeleton of the victim and might therefore adversely affect their resurrection state. Those stoned would receive bone fractures; those burned would be reduced to ashes; those beheaded would suffer skeletal dismemberment. To deal with this, methods of stoning and burning were modi-

curred frequently enough to warrant judicial reflection and reform. As a "zealous" Pharisee, Paul evidently regarded the death penalty as a legitimate tool to use in defense of the covenant.[27] Nevertheless, among many rabbis there seems to have been a pronounced tendency to oppose the death penalty in practice if not in principle. According to Josephus, the Pharisees were "not apt to be severe in punishments" and reluctant to see the death penalty employed.[28] This coheres with accounts in the New Testament of certain Pharisees acting to preserve Jesus from execution at the hands of Herod Antipas (Luke 13:31) and of Gamaliel advocating leniency toward the apostles (Acts 5:34-39). It is often observed, furthermore, that the Mishnah tractate "Sanhedrin" requires such strict rules of procedure and stringent standards of evidence, and such a large panel of judges (some twenty-three judges instead of the usual two- or three-judge panel, with the decison to acquit requiring a simple majority of one), that imposition of the death penalty would have been virtually impossible, and that this was clearly the intention of those who framed the rules.[29] The Mishnah itself brands a court that executes one person in seven years as "destructive," which R. Eleazer ben Azariah expands to "one in 70 years," while R. Tarfon and R. Akiba boasted that had they been members of the old Sanhedrin in Jerusalem (prior to 70 c.e.), no one would have ever been put to death.[30] According to the rabbinic institution of *hatra'ah*, a person could not be convicted of a capital offense unless he or she had been explicitly forewarned by the same two witnesses who actually saw the crime and the criminal had explicitly indicated that he or she was aware of both the status of the act to be committed and the exact type of

---

fied, some rabbis suggested substituting strangulation for decapitation, and a general preference was shown for strangulation where the Bible did not specify the form of execution. See further, Daube, *The New Testament and Rabbinic Judaism,* 302-8.

27. Acts 8:3; 9:1-2; 22:4; 26:9-11; Gal. 1:13-14; 1 Cor. 15:9-10; Phil. 3:6. On the violent implications of "zeal," see T. L. Donaldson, "Zealot and Convert: The Origin of Paul's Christ-Torah Antithesis," *CBQ* 51 (1989): 655-82; Donaldson, "Zealot," *ISBE,* 4:1175-79; and J. D. G. Dunn and A. M. Suggate, *The Justice of God: A Fresh Look at the Old Doctrine of Justification by Faith* (Carlisle: Paternoster, 1993), 23-25.

28. Josephus, *Antiquities,* XIII:294. Cf. B. H. Young, "'Save the Adultress!' Ancient Jewish *Responsa* in the Gospels?" *NTS* 41, no. 1 (1995): 63-65.

29. So most authorities — e.g., Sanders, "The Synoptic Jesus and the Law," 18; Moore, *Judaism in the First Centuries of the Christian Era,* 2:186-87; and *Dictionary of Judaism in the Biblical Period,* ed. J. Neusner and W. S. Green (Peabody, Mass.: Hendrickson, 1999), 510.

30. *m. Mak.* 1:10.

capital punishment it entailed — an almost impossible condition to meet![31] Even if this institution was not actually practiced, it manifests a general Jewish reluctance to take human life judicially.

The same reluctance is reflected in a willingness to interpret Torah passages prescribing the death penalty in ways that contradicted the letter of the text. Deuteronomy 13:13-17 commands the annihilation of an idolatrous city, but according to one Talmudic tradition, "There never was a condemned city, and never will be." Deuteronomy 21:18-21 prescribes execution for ill-mannered sons; to restrict its application, the Talmud states, "There never has been a stubborn and rebellious son, and never will be." It is suggested that such laws were written not to be applied literally but so that "you may study [them] and receive reward."[32] Infringement of the Sabbath law is a capital offense in Exodus 31:14 and in later Jewish law, but even the most unlikely excuses would be accepted by Jewish courts to avoid execution.[33] All this reflects a strong desire to avoid any possibility of executing an innocent person and thus exposing the judges before God to the crime of judicial murder (Exod. 23:7).[34] It also reflects a recognition of the sanctity of human life as an important hermeneutical axiom in biblical interpretation. For the rabbis, claims Lapide, "the sanctity of human life overrides almost all the rules of the Torah, whose life-promoting spirit is given priority over any individual regulation."[35] While executions, judicial and extrajudicial, did still take place, as the New Testament itself attests, the trend over time was for the death penalty in the Bible to be viewed more as an indication of the seriousness of a sin than as a desirable or obligatory literal penalty.[36]

The Death Penalty in the New Testament

There are several texts in the New Testament that either presuppose the existence of capital punishment or speak of people dying for their

---

31. *b. Sanh.* 40b-41a.

32. *b. Sanh.* 71a; *t. Sanh.* 11:6.

33. See Sanders, "The Synoptic Jesus and the Law," 18-19.

34. Moore, *Judaism in the First Centuries of the Christian Era,* 2:182-88.

35. Lapide, *The Sermon on the Mount,* 62.

36. *The Encyclopedia of the Jewish Religion,* ed. R. J. Z. Werblowsky and D. G. Wigoder (London: Masada Press, 1965), 80.

crimes (Matt. 26:52; Acts 25:11; Rom. 13:4) or for their faith (e.g., Acts 12:2; 26:10; Rev. 2:10, 13), without directly repudiating the practice itself. There is only one passage in the New Testament that refers directly to the question of the legitimacy of the death penalty (John 7:53–8:11), but both its exegesis and its authenticity are disputed. Other texts on nonviolence and love of enemy have a crucial bearing on the question of capital punishment, as we will see, but no unambiguous warrant is given in the New Testament for opposing the death penalty.

This fact, together with the sheer weight of biblical data sanctioning capital punishment, means that a prima facie case exists for regarding the death penalty as a divinely intended method of dealing with serious criminal offending. No wonder then that, according to opinion polls, the death penalty finds stronger endorsement among religious people than among atheists and agnostics, and more so among Jews than Christians. For many devout readers of Scripture, God and the gallows are perfectly compatible.[37] But just how strong is the biblical case for accepting capital punishment as a permanent, divinely intended feature of human affairs? And how persuasive are the moral and pragmatic arguments advanced in support of such a position?

A Critique of Biblical Arguments in Support of Capital Punishment

Supporters of capital punishment appeal to three main features of biblical teaching: the institution of the death penalty in Genesis 9, the endorsement of capital punishment in the stipulations of Mosaic law, and the lack of evidence in the New Testament for the rescinding of this provision of divine law. I want to respond to each of these in turn, suggesting that biblical texts ought *not* to be construed as furnishing divine approval for the practice of capital punishment today.

---

37. Referring to a 1976 poll in the United States, K. H. Potter observes, "It was more popular with men than with women, with whites than with blacks, with the rich than with the poor, with Republicans than with Democrats, with religious than with atheist or agnostic, with Jews than with Christians, with Catholics than with Protestants." Potter goes on to observe that "the most strident religious voice in recent years has been Bible belt and punitive." See "The Special Relationship," 230-31.

Genesis 9:4-6

This text is often taken as a clear-cut authorization for the taking of human life as an act of retributive justice.

> You shall not eat flesh with its life, that is, its blood. For your own life-blood I will surely require a reckoning: from every animal I will require it and from human beings, each one for the blood of another, I will require a reckoning for human life. Whoever sheds the blood of a human, by a human shall that person's blood be shed; for in his own image God made humankind.

Three features of this passage strengthen the case for seeing it as a crucial endorsement of capital punishment. First, inasmuch as the command is given to Noah, it is intended as a guideline for the whole human race, not just for the covenant community. It was commonplace in Jewish tradition to regard the covenant with Noah as binding on all humanity. Second, the rationale for capital punishment is that humankind is made in the image of God. Unjustified homicide is thus an affront to God's closest relative, and those responsible must forfeit the privilege of life in return. In this sense capital punishment may be understood as grounded in the creation order itself (cf. 9:6 and 1:27), and as such is permanently valid. Third, the text prescribes that the guilty party must be punished by retribution rather than rehabilitation. No substitute penalty is specified; a life in exchange for a life serves as the basic criterion of justice. Daryl Charles therefore insists,

> To extend mercy in exchange for justice at the level of premeditated murder . . . is to despise both the image of God in the victim as well as the death of the Lamb of God. The *imago Dei* exacts a life-for-a-life measure. Otherwise, human existence is not a sacred trust, but an expendable commodity. Stated differently, the deliberate extermination of a life by another individual is tantamount to killing God in effigy, for murder is the ultimate rebellion against divine authority.[38]

To deny that the ultimate human crime should be met with the ultimate punishment, Charles continues, "is a moral travesty that fails to

---

38. Charles, "Outrageous Atrocity or Moral Imperative? The Ethics of Capital Punishment," *StChEth* 6, no. 2 (1993): 12.

comprehend the *imago Dei* and a blatant contradiction of universally revealed canons of moral truth."[39]

What may be said in response? It is worth noting that some interpreters choose to read this text as a statement of fact rather than as a divine imperative. That is, instead of commanding or legitimating capital punishment, it simply affirms, in proverbial manner, that God's providence will catch up with murderers ("I will require"), without specifying how this will happen, though it will often be through some human agency such as avenging kin ("by a human shall that person's blood be shed"). To be fair, however, even if Genesis 9:4-6 is proverbial rather than legislative in form, it still entails some form of divine legitimation of the death penalty. But in assessing the significance of this legitimation for contemporary practice, several points need to be borne in mind.

To begin with, the primary intention of the text is to limit lethal violence, not to sanction it. Its enunciation of the life-for-a-life principle needs to be viewed against the background of pre-diluvian corruption, violence, and unrestrained vengeance. Lamech boasted, "I have killed a man for wounding me, a young man for striking me" (4:23), but here God states that a human life may be taken *only* in exchange for another human life. The injunction combines a reverence for human life (as bearer of God's image) with a strict limitation on the extinguishing of human life. Death cannot be exacted in repayment for lesser crimes than murder, like wounds or insults or dishonor or theft. Furthermore, the penalty must fall on the murderer alone; no sanction is given for blood feuds against the perpetrator's family or clan.

It also needs to be recognized that the Genesis text is not intended as an authorization for judicial authorities to employ execution in the running of society, least of all for governments in modern secular states. In the first instance, it is an assertion of the divine prerogative to act against sin — God declares, "*I* will require a reckoning for human life" (v. 5). In some sense the death of the offender serves as an act of atonement to God. The shedding of innocent blood creates a kind of moral pollution, even apparently in the animal kingdom (cf. v. 4), that can be removed only by the blood of the offender. This is *not* the purpose of capital punishment in secular criminal justice systems.

Most importantly, even if one accepts that the pre-Mosaic setting

39. Charles, "Outrageous Atrocity or Moral Imperative?" 14.

gives the commandment to Noah a potentially universal applicability, from a Christian perspective the text still stands under the ultimate scrutiny of New Testament teaching. The work of Christ affects even the covenant with Noah (cf. 1 Pet. 3:18-22; 2 Pet. 2:5). That the early Christians thought in such terms is shown by the way they deemed the food restrictions of the Noahic covenant (Gen. 9:4) to be voluntary for Gentile believers (Acts 15:29 — cf. 1 Cor. 8:8-9; 10:25; Rom. 14:14). If the provisions of Genesis 9:4 are modified in light of later developments in salvation history, the same could be true of 9:5. Before ascribing universal authority to Genesis 9:5, therefore, it needs to be asked what implications New Testament teaching has for its interpretation, both teaching that deals with Christian response to offending and teaching that relates to atonement for sin.

Pentateuchal Law

Some advocates of capital punishment argue that the death penalty ought to be exacted in contemporary society for the same list of crimes it is prescribed for in Mosaic law, using the same standards of evidence and perhaps even the same modes of execution! Most, however, accept that Mosaic law was intended primarily for the ancient covenant people of Israel and should not be carried over in all its detail into the Christian era unless there is strong reason for doing so. Among the score of capital offenses in Old Testament law, such a reason exists, it is argued, solely for the case of premeditated murder. The fact that the talionic "life for a life" principle is applied to homicide (Exod. 21:23-25; 21:12; Lev. 24:21; Deut. 19:19-21) is taken as powerful confirmation that this principle transcends its historical occasion in Pentateuchal law and extends its authority down to the present day. Deliberate murder, moreover, is unique among the capital offenses in Old Testament law, and in ancient Near Eastern law generally, in that substitute penalties are expressly forbidden (Num. 35:31; Deut. 19:13). Murderers must die.

This is a potent argument, but three hermeneutical considerations should be borne in mind. In the first place, the talionic "life for a life" principle needs to be evaluated in light of the larger purpose of *lex talionis*. As we saw in Chapter 2, the *lex* was intended to serve the twofold

217

purpose of limiting the destructive effect of penal consequences on the one hand, and providing an equitable basis for making restitution or reparation on the other. It was understood not to mandate specific in-kind punishments but to place limits on the kind and extent of recompense that wronged parties could seek. Now it is true that in the case of premeditated murder, a prohibition is placed on the substitution of alternative penalties. But the purpose of this prohibition is not so much to fix an immutable penalty for one particular crime as to underscore the unique seriousness of homicide within the range of capital offenses. This may explain why a similar prohibition is also specified in connection with crimes of enticement to idolatry (Deut. 13:8 — cf. 19:13) and perjury in capital trials (Deut. 19:19-21). Strictly speaking, the proscription of alternative penalties is not limited to murder; it is also used to mark certain other offenses as especially grave. This would support Christopher Wright's proposal that what we should take from the gradation of penalties in Israel's law is not a set of fixed punishments but a scale of values that gives priority to human life and relationships over property, possessions, and power.[40] James Megivern concurs:

> Law codes are not automatically to be understood as simple mirrors of practice. One function of the juridical death threat was to get people's attention, to lay down a solemn warning, to alert all to the extreme seriousness of certain misdeeds. This pedagogical function of the law is accomplished by the texts themselves. They articulate what the society's top values are and what is beyond the range of acceptable behavior in the ideal order. If they were ever implemented literally, however, the streets of the community would run red with blood, the populace would be slaughtered by its own courts. There is little evidence that Israel was ever such a sanguinary society.[41]

The second point confirms this judgment. Notwithstanding legislative prescriptions, there are narrative episodes where God does not require a life for a life in payment for murder, such as Cain's murder of

---

40. Wright, *Walking in the Ways of the Lord: The Ethical Authority of the Old Testament* (Leicester: Apollos, 1995), 104-5; Wright, *An Eye for an Eye: The Place of Old Testament Ethics Today* (Downers Grove, Ill.: InterVarsity Press, 1983), 163-68.

41. Megivern, *The Death Penalty: An Historical and Theological Survey* (Mahwah, N.J.: Paulist Press, 1997).

Abel (Gen. 4:8-16), Moses' killing of the Egyptian (Exod. 2:11-14), and David's murder of Uriah, even if in the latter case punitive consequences were believed to have been visited on David's own household (2 Sam. 11:14-17; 12:10-12). This demonstrates the importance of holding the prescriptions of biblical law in balance with the pragmatic realities reflected in biblical narratives. It also alerts us to the fact that ancient Near Eastern law codes are not legislation in the modern sense. They are primarily descriptions of classical legal problems rather than a set of hard-and-fast regulations to be applied to the letter in every case. Furthermore, the written codes we possess contain only a small proportion of the oral canon that would have been current and taken into account in adjudicating specific cases. Judges were guided by the Torah, but also by precedents and circumstances. As Wright points out, "The emphasis was on the imperative to do justice and act fairly without bribery or favouritism, but much was left to the discretion and judgment of those responsible (Deut 16:18-20; 17:8-13)."[42]

The third point is the most significant. According to Wayne House, "The biblical purpose of capital punishment is the promotion of retributive justice by civil government."[43] But this is not the most helpful or historically sensitive way to view the Mosaic prescriptions. In his discussion of punishments and crimes in the Old Testament and the ancient Near East, Raymond Westbrook stresses that the theoretical basis of these ancient legal systems was quite different from that of modern legal systems. Whereas modern law distinguishes between torts and crimes, in ancient Near Eastern law three main (but overlapping) categories can be distinguished: (1) acts causing personal damage where the level of moral culpability was low; here the initiative for redress rested in the hands of the victim, with the court's role being to award compensation; (2) acts that carried a high level of moral culpability, such as incest or blasphemy, and that were perceived to pollute the offender's environment like a contagious disease; here it was society through its official organs that took the initiative to protect itself by removing the pollution, usually by killing or exiling the offender, thereby appeasing divine wrath; and (3) acts such as homicide, rape, theft, wounding, and

---

42. Wright, *Walking in the Ways of the Lord*, 104.

43. House, "Crime and Punishment," in *The Death Penalty Debate*, ed. H. W. House and J. H. Yoder (Dallas: Word, 1991), 31.

adultery, which gave rise to a dual right for the victim or his family either to seek revenge or to accept a ransom in lieu of revenge; here the court's role was to set a limit on the level of revenge or ransom, with the *lex talionis* functioning as a limit to revenge and/or a guide to proportionate ransom.[44] The point to note is that in biblical law, murder belonged to both the second and the third categories. It was a private offense giving rise to the law of retaliation, but it was also a source of ritual pollution that needed to be purged.[45]

What this means is that the death penalty in biblical law is best understood not as an inalienable principle of state-administered retributive justice, nor even simply as a deterrent penalty, but as a cultic or religious requirement for "cleansing the land" of evil and safeguarding the holiness of the people of God (Num. 35:33). As Moshe Greenberg explains, "Capital crimes are a blot on the whole community. When the law decrees that the capital offender must die, it is not merely to punish him but to 'purge the evil from Israel' (Deut 17:12; cf. 13:5-11; 13:5; 17:7; 19:19; 21:21; 22:21-22, 24; 24:7; Judg 20:13; 2 Sam 19:13)."[46] The way in which stoning had to take place outside the camp or city[47] and involved the entire community[48] helped to dramatize the ritual pollution of sin and the community's expulsion of evil from its midst. The infliction of death, in other words, functioned as a ritual expiation or act of atonement for sin. This helps to explain the close parallel that exists between the scapegoat and sin-offering rituals in Leviticus 4:15 and 16:21, and the ritual associated with the execution of blasphemers in Leviticus 24:14. In both cases, hands are laid on the head of the victim, symbolically transferring the sin of the community to the condemned creature. It also explains why, when the identity of the murderer was unknown, the sacrifice of a heifer was required as a substitute act of purification at the city nearest the site of the murder (Deut. 21:1-9). This action would do nothing to undo the murder or deter similar crimes in the future, but it did somehow atone for the blood guilt that rested on the whole people and secured God's forgiveness.

44. Westbrook, "Punishments and Crimes," *ABD*, 5:548.
45. Westbrook, "Punishments and Crimes," 551; cf. 555.
46. Greenberg, "Crimes and Punishments," *IDB*, 1:734.
47. Lev. 24:14, 23; Num. 15:35-36; Deut. 17:5; 21:19; 1 Kings 21:10, 13.
48. Lev. 20:2; 24:14, 16, 23; Num. 15:35-36; Deut. 13:10; 17:7; 21:21; Josh. 7:25; 1 Kings 12:18; 2 Chron. 10:18.

Once again, death as an expiation of sin to avert divine wrath is *not* the function capital punishment is intended to fulfill in the modern world. Great caution is therefore needed in using prescriptions for capital punishment in the Mosaic system as justification for the use of capital punishment today in penal systems based on very different theoretical foundations. This is not to say that the notion of sacrificial expiation is totally foreign to the modern mind.[49] The way in which Bill Clinton during his term as governor of Arkansas allowed four men to be executed (including one mentally retarded black youth), each one in an election year, each one prior to an election,[50] carries disturbing overtones of ritual sacrifice to appease the electorate. More directly, Daryl Charles defends the necessity of capital punishment in expiatory terms:

> Guilt incurred by sin constitutes a debt in the present life that must be paid. Punitive dealings . . . provide the necessary atonement and restore the balance of justice and moral order that has been disturbed; they prepare man for eternity.[51]

> The Biblical witness is that murder cannot be atoned for [citing Gen. 9:6; Num. 35:31], inasmuch as it is the ultimate crime against God: effacing the *imago Dei*. Furthermore atonement for capital crimes is not pushed off into the *eschaton*. Rather criminal justice is to serve as a (present) shadow of eternal punishment.[52]

But from a Christian perspective, any such ascription of expiatory significance to capital punishment needs to be evaluated in light of the death of Christ, which is interpreted in sacrificial terms by several New Testament writers.[53] One dimension of the metaphor of sacrifice is the expiation of sin: Christ's death purges away definitively the pollution of sin. The writer to the Hebrews declares that Jesus "offered for all

---

49. See C. Gunton, *The Actuality of Atonement* (Grand Rapids: William B. Eerdmans, 1989), 120-28.

50. As observed in Potter, "The Special Relationship," 230. Worth noting here too is V. Redekop's suggestion that the criminal justice system in a secular society functions as a sacred institution that practices sacrifice! See "Scapegoats, the Bible, and Criminal Justice: Interacting with René Girard," *NPCJ* 13 (1993): 35-41.

51. Charles, "Outrageous Atrocity or Moral Imperative?" 6.

52. Charles, "Crime, the Christian, and Capital Justice," *JETS* 38, no. 3 (1995): 440.

53. See, e.g., Heb. 9:12-14, 22, 25-26; 12:24; 1 Pet. 1:2; 1 John 1:7; Rev. 7:14.

time a single sacrifice for sins" (10:12), thus setting aside all other modes of atonement. In Paul's judgment, Christ died "for the ungodly" (Rom. 5:6), absorbing their sinful, accursed state in his righteousness and rescuing them from the deadly consequences of their condition (2 Cor. 5:21; Gal. 3:13-14). In point of fact, Paul teaches that believers have *already* died, with Christ, the atoning death prescribed by divine law; "we are convinced that one has died for all," Paul declares; "therefore all have died" (2 Cor. 5:14; cf. Gal. 2:20). No further action is needed or possible to purge away sin. The atoning value of all Old Testament practices is thus fulfilled and superseded by the death of Christ. This means that the language of atonement cannot be used to defend capital punishment in the Christian era. By doing so, Charles ends up in a theological quagmire in which God requires dual atonement for murderers, once by their own death and once by Christ's: "Therefore the murderer can in fact stand forgiven in the sight of God, while he at the same time undergoes the capital sanction that God himself imposes through the civil authorities. Christ's mercy is not a mercy that erases penalties for human crimes."[54] But surely this renders divine forgiveness a dubious reality, for God apparently forgives a sin and punishes it at one and the same time or, worse, punishes it after allegedly forgiving it. It is one thing to see capital punishment as a debt owed to human society; it is another to see it as an atonement offered to God for a sin already atoned for at the cross and freely forgiven by God.

This does not mean that criminal sanctions of all kinds are rendered redundant, nor does it mean that the biblical case for capital punishment collapses entirely. But it *does* mean that Old Testament practice furnishes a dubious theoretical basis for insisting on capital justice in contemporary secular society. It also means that arguments which construe the offender's death as expiating his or her objective guilt before God must be rejected as inconsistent with New Testament teaching on atonement.[55] Some interpreters, of course, would contest the expiatory function of capital punishment in the Old Testament and insist that its capital laws are conceived as expressions of retribu-

54. Charles, "Crime, the Christian, and Capital Justice," 440.
55. Cf. W. C. Placher, "Christ Takes Our Place: Rethinking Atonement," *Interpretation* 53, no. 1 (1999): 14-15, 16.

tive justice more than — or as well as — ritual justice.[56] But even if this is so, Old Testament criminal law cannot be abstracted from its wider covenantal setting and translated without loss into the contemporary context, a context where criminal justice and social justice are kept strictly separate and where neither is rooted in a covenant relationship with God. Underscoring this difference is Howard Zehr's perceptive observation that the way in which administration of the death penalty in America falls most heavily on the poor and powerless and is inflicted for crimes without regard for the social inequalities that may have occasioned the offense fundamentally contradicts the holistic character of biblical justice and its concern to protect the disadvantaged.[57]

New Testament Material

Advocates of the death penalty insist that there is nothing in the New Testament which revokes the death penalty and that there are several indications which seem to endorse it. Implicit endorsements are found in Jesus' saying, "All who take the sword will perish by the sword" (Matt. 26:52), his depiction of royal slaughter in the Parable of the Ten Pounds (Luke 19:27), his instruction to his disciples to purchase swords (Luke 22:36), his acknowledgment of the legitimacy of courts (Matt. 5:25-26), and his quotation of the Mosaic prohibition on murder with no indication that he was rescinding the penalty (Matt. 5:21-22; cf. Exod. 21:12). Not only did Jesus reaffirm the law of Moses in general terms (Matt. 5:17-20/Luke 16:17), but he said or did nothing to countermand legislation relating to capital offenses. "If the Sermon on the Mount shows us anything about Jesus' attitude toward capital punishment," concludes Wayne House, "it shows us that he accepted it as a valid exercise of governmental authority and a proper part of the Mosaic Code."[58]

Further support is derived from Jesus' recognition of Pilate's God-given authority in John 19:11, which included the authority to crucify;

56. Martens, "Capital Punishment and the Christian," 28-29.

57. Zehr, *Death as a Penalty: A Moral, Practical and Theological Discussion* (Elkhart, Ind.: MCC, n.d.), 19.

58. House, "The New Testament and Capital Punishment," in H. W. House and J. H. Yoder, *The Death Penalty Debate* (Dallas: Word, 1991), 63.

from Jesus' apparent agreement with the dying thief's words that he was suffering justly for his crime (Luke 23:40-43); and from Paul's words to Festus, "If I am in the wrong and have committed something for which I deserve to die, I am not trying to escape death" (Acts 25:11), which presuppose that governmental authority has the right to put people to death. Paul's comment, after listing about thirty different sins, that "those who practice such things deserve to die" (Rom. 1:32), is also sometimes mentioned in this connection. Some writers cite the "execution" of Ananias and Sapphira (Acts 5:1-11) and even the death of Jesus himself as divine endorsement of the death penalty.[59] When Jesus refused to condone the execution of the woman taken in adultery (John 7:53–8:11) it was not because he opposed capital punishment per se, but because the legal grounds for conviction were lacking, or perhaps because he did not accept adultery as a capital offense alongside murder. The determinative passage in favor of capital punishment, however, is Romans 13:3-5:

> For rulers are not a terror to good conduct, but to bad. Do you wish to have no fear of the authority? Then do what is good, and you will receive its approval; for it is God's servant *[theou diakonos]* for your good. But if you do what is wrong, you should be afraid, for the authority does not bear the sword in vain *[ou gar eikē tēn machairan phorei]*. It is the servant of God to execute wrath on the wrongdoer *[ekdikos eis orgēn tō to kakon prassonti]*. Therefore one must be subject, not only because of wrath but also because of conscience.

Romans 13:1-7 is an exceedingly complex passage that has historically played a crucial role in Christian political ethics. Here we focus solely on the implications of the passage for penal justice concerns. There are three main features of the text that are taken to furnish principled support for the death penalty in domestic justice. First, what we might for convenience call "the state" (referred to in the text variously as "governing authorities" *[exousiais huperechousais, v. 1]*, "the rulers" *[hoi archontes, v. 3]*, and "the authority" *[hē exousia, v. 3 — cf. vv. 1, 2]*) is described as God's agent or servant to exercise wrath and vengeance on evildoers. When the state acts to punish evil and reward good, it does so not on its own authority but on behalf of God. While no private individual is enti-

59. N. L. Geisler, *Ethics: Alternatives and Issues* (Grand Rapids: Zondervan, 1971), 242.

tled to assume that his or her own vengeful feelings convey divine wrath (Rom. 12:17-21), it is incumbent upon the collective agency of the state to put into effect the wrath of God against wrongdoers. Such action further serves as a deterrent, for "if you do what is wrong, you should be afraid" (v. 4).

Second, the state's prerogative to punish evil includes the right to wield the sword *(tēn machairan phorei)*, which is taken as an explicit affirmation of the death penalty (v. 4). It perhaps echoes the technical term *ius gladii* or "law of the sword,"[60] which originally referred to military discipline but later embraced civil and criminal punishment as well. The sword in verse 4, says R. C. H. Lenski, is "not a mere symbol of power but the actual sword in the hands of the executioner who inflicts the death penalty on criminals."[61] Daryl Charles offers several observations in support of this: (1) The total absence of a military context in 12:17-13:7 argues against its being a reference to military discipline alone or to Rome's ability to wage war; the immediate context has to do with moral and civil behavior in the wider social order, with the sword being worn for the benefit of all citizens. (2) The reference to taxes in verse 6 is clearly literal; as part of the same hortatory teaching, the sword must also be literal. (3) The emphasis on the deterrence value of the sword implies that it inflicts actual death, and virtually every other reference to the sword in the New Testament relates in some manner to death.[62] (4) In the history of interpretation of Romans 13, the sword has been understood predominantly, though not exclusively, as giving divine authorization to the state to inflict the death penalty (even by the early Anabaptists). Accordingly, while the sword need not denote the death penalty exclusively, the plainest interpretive sense of Romans 13:4 includes it, and Paul's first readers would have almost certainly understood it to embrace capital punishment.[63]

Third, the whole tenor of the passage counsels Christian submission to civil authority, not unconditionally but at least when it acts to foster what is good and punish what is evil. Such submission is moti-

---

60. So G. Bornkamm, *Paul* (London: Hodder & Stoughton, 1971), 211.

61. Lenski, *St. Paul's Epistle to the Romans* (Minneapolis: Augsburg, 1936), 792.

62. Matt. 26:52; Luke 21:24; Acts 12:2; 16:27; Heb. 11:34, 37; Rev. 13:10.

63. Charles, "Pauline Ethics and Capital Justice: Proscription or Prescription (Rom. 12:17-13:7)?" unpublished paper presented at the SBL conference, November 1994, 13-15, 19-20.

vated partly by fear of retribution (or "wrath") and partly by "conscience" — that is, conscientious recognition that the authorities are servants of God and instruments in God's hands to maintain civil order (v. 5). Since such a role requires them to wield the sword, Christians have no right to agitate for abolition of the death penalty. To do so is to be more "Christian" than God and to confuse justice with love. "Maintaining justice and social order, not maintaining love, is the state's chief task," claims Charles.[64]

These then are the main New Testament texts cited in support of capital punishment. Since they all presuppose without objection — and none of them directly challenges — the institution of capital punishment in Jewish or Roman society, advocates of capital punishment insist that the burden of proof rests on its opponents to demonstrate where the New Testament repudiates Old Testament practice. As Charles puts it, "The abolitionist is constrained to demonstrate sufficiently that the death penalty for premeditated murder has been explicitly annulled. He must be able to answer the question of whether the Christian community, or society at large, has the right to declare null and void what is a universal moral imperative."[65] At first sight the evidence to the contrary seems compelling. But just how secure is this reading of the evidence?

Implicit Endorsements?

Certainly there are texts that presuppose capital punishment. But these texts no more condone the use of lethal violence by judicial authorities than texts that describe sin endorse sinning. Jesus' statement in Matthew 26:52 is an observation about human experience, not a legitimation of capital punishment. To construe elements of parabolic scenery (Luke 19:27) as support for the death penalty does violence to the parabolic genre. By the same logic we would have to condone torture (Matt. 18:34) and dishonest business practices (Luke 16:1-9). Jesus' word to his disciples about procuring swords (Luke 22:36) has nothing to do with capital punishment. (He was hardly appointing them as executioners!) By common agreement, the statement is best understood fig-

64. Charles, "Pauline Ethics and Capital Justice," 16.
65. Charles, "Outrageous Atrocity or Moral Imperative?" 14.

uratively.[66] Paul's comment to Festus (Acts 25:11) is an assertion of his legal innocence, not a validation of Roman execution practices. If the deaths of Ananias and Sapphira (Acts 5:1-11) are taken as support for capital punishment, then logically the episode supports execution for telling lies or embezzlement, and the list of capital offenses grows even longer if Romans 1:32 is also seen in such terms. To view the death of Jesus as ratification for capital punishment is to carry a theology of penal atonement to absurd lengths and to overlook the fact that his death is described elsewhere in the New Testament as an act of unjustifiable state violence.[67] Indeed, the fact that religious and state power combined to execute an innocent man in the interests of protecting an unjust status quo is perhaps the most eloquent testimony against capital punishment.

The claim that in Matthew 5 Jesus endorses Old Testament law in general and does nothing in particular to challenge the death penalty underestimates the radicalism of Jesus' stance with respect to prevail-

---

66. There are several reasons why this saying must be taken metaphorically, not literally. First, Jesus often uses dramatic figurative language (e.g., Matt. 5:29-30; 7:5; 23:24; Mark 10:25) that the disciples fail to understand (Mark 8:15-16; John 3:4; 6:42, 52). The term "sword" is used figuratively elsewhere in Luke (2:35) and in Matthew (10:34). Second, Jesus' language is general; the distinction he draws between the prosperous (those having purse and bag) and the destitute (those not having cloak or bag) hardly applied directly to the Twelve (who apparently lived out of a common purse). Instead, Jesus enunciates a principle applicable to his followers in general, and he was scarcely encouraging all his followers to arm themselves with weapons. Third, if Jesus was counseling his disciples henceforth to use physical force to defend themselves, he would be canceling out a major emphasis of his previous ethical teaching — love of enemy and nonretaliation (Luke 6:27-31; 9:55; 12:49-53; 17:3-4). Indeed, taken literally, Jesus would be saying that armed self-defense is an absolute priority, so much so that even the poor person ought to sell his cloak to buy a sword. (According to biblical law, a cloak is a person's most valued possession; not even a debtor could be deprived of it. See Exod. 22:26-27; Deut 24:12-13.) Fourth, verse 38 indicates that in taking Jesus' words literally, the disciples were misunderstanding him. The words *hikanon estin* ("It is enough," NSRV) could be translated "Enough of this!", which would help explain why Jesus later rebukes the disciple who strikes out with a sword in Gethsemane (22:49-50). Fifth, there is no indication that after these correctives, the disciples took Jesus' instructions literally; as R. Cassidy observes, "Within the whole of Acts, Luke never portrays the disciples possessing or utilizing swords or any other instrument of violence" (*Society and Politics in the Acts of the Apostles* [Maryknoll, N.Y.: Orbis, 1987], 38).

67. See, e.g., Acts 2:22-23; 3:13-18; 4:24-29; 7:51-53 — cf. 1 Cor. 2:8.

ing interpretations of the Torah. This again is enormously complex and controverted territory in current scholarship, and there is no space here to deal adequately with the question of Jesus' attitude toward Mosaic law. Suffice it to say that Jesus' relationship with the law is best conceptualized not in simple terms of continuity versus discontinuity, as is often done, but in terms of fulfillment versus nonfulfillment. Certainly Jesus remains fundamentally loyal to the Torah, confirming its divine origin and its continuing authority[68] and frequently using it to validate his own demands.[69] But at the same time, he brings the law to its eschatological fulfillment (Matt. 5:17-18), and in so doing transforms the meaning and application of the law in the messianic age.

This is how we should understand the so-called antitheses of Matthew 5:21-48. They represent the messianic *transfiguration* of the law that is simultaneously an endorsement of its true meaning. Jesus affirms the fundamental principles of the Torah but draws practical conclusions from them for his followers that sometimes run counter to the existing provisions of the law. It is not that Jesus overtly repeals biblical provisions for divorce, swearing oaths, or seeking recompense when wronged, not least because he had no institutional authority to do so and because Matthew 5:17-18 expressly denies that this was his intention (cf. 3:15). Rather, in bringing the law to its fulfillment and demanding an inward, heartfelt obedience to its true intentions, Jesus renders the literal application of these provisions redundant in the age of the kingdom. The category of "redundancy," I suggest, is a more useful one for understanding the antitheses than "abolition." The legal provisions remain in place, but they are no longer determinative, as currently understood, for the conduct of Jesus' followers, who now see something deeper in the law. Accordingly, as I argued in Chapter 2, the *lex talionis,* under which the death penalty functioned ("a life for a life"), is set aside by Jesus as a governing norm for conduct in the eschatological age. In its place he demands a self-giving love that seeks the welfare of the opponent and treasures the life even of the enemy (5:38-48). Dorothy Jean Weaver has argued that Jesus' instruction not to resist "the evil one" *(tō ponērō)* represents a conscious reversal of the purpose of the *lex talionis* in Deuteronomy 19, which was "to purge the evil [one] *[to ponēron]* from your midst" (Deut. 19:19-

68. See, e.g., Matt. 4:1-11/Luke 4:1-12; Mark 7:9-13/Matt. 15:1-9; Luke 16:17.
69. See, e.g., Mark 10:2-9, 17-22; 12:26, 29-31.

21). Insofar as it sanctions the execution of evildoers, the *lex talionis* legitimates violence and becomes death-dealing, but "Jesus repudiates the essential violence of the talionic principle and establishes the character of his own call to action, by contrast, as fundamentally life-affirming."[70] If that is the case, to construe Jesus' teaching in Matthew 5 as an endorsement of the state's inherent right to punish criminals by killing them runs directly counter to the central thrust of the passage.

It also runs counter to the pervasive emphasis on mercy in Jesus' teaching. The Sermon on the Mount opens with the declaration "Blessed are the merciful, for they will receive mercy" (Matt. 5:7), while elsewhere in Matthew's account of the teaching of Jesus, mercy and love serve as the hermeneutical keys for accessing the true meaning of the fulfilled law. Twice Jesus quotes Hosea 6:6, "I desire mercy, not sacrifice" (9:13; 12:7), thus underlining its importance for understanding God's will. In Matthew 22, Jesus tells the Pharisees that all the law and the prophets "depend" or "hang" on the "double love" commandment (22:40), while in Matthew 23 he attacks the scribes and Pharisees for majoring on minor details in the law and failing to see the law's fundamental purpose as fostering "the weightier matters of the law: justice and mercy and faith" (23:23). It is the primacy of love and compassion over the letter of the law that also explains Jesus' own conduct with respect to the law — his preparedness to eat with sinners, to neglect external purity stipulations, to heal and harvest on the Sabbath, and so on. Mercy is the true meaning of the law; mercy is the heart of God's justice; mercy "fulfills all righteousness" (3:15). Accordingly, as Richard Hays comments, "Those who are trained for the kingdom of heaven are trained to evaluate all norms, even the norms of the law itself, in terms of the criteria of love and mercy. In the community that lives this vision, acts of love and mercy should abound."[71] All attempts to justify

70. Weaver, "Transforming Nonresistance: From *Lex Talionis* to 'Do Not Resist the Evil One,'" in *The Love of Enemy and Nonretaliation in the New Testament*, ed. W. M. Swartley (Louisville: Westminster John Knox, 1992), 56. G. M. Zerbe considers Jesus' statement on the *lex talionis* "the only antithesis which rejects the law." See *Non-Retaliation in Early Jewish and New Testament Texts: Ethical Themes in Social Contexts* (Sheffield: Sheffield Academic Press, 1993), 205n.119.

71. Hays, *The Moral Vision of the New Testament: A Contemporary Introduction to New Testament Ethics* (Edinburgh: T. & T. Clark, 1996), 100-101. So also F. J. Matera, *New Testament Ethics: The Legacies of Jesus and Paul* (Louisville, Ky.: Westminster John Knox, 1996),

capital punishment from the law of Moses or the teaching of Jesus must come to grief on this profound truth.

John 7:53–8:11

Although not an original part of the Fourth Gospel, it is widely accepted that the story of the woman taken in adultery has "all the earmarks of historical veracity,"[72] and it has long been accorded canonical authority in Christian tradition. It is the only case in the New Testament where Jesus is expressly asked to adjudicate with respect to a capital offense (cf. Lev. 20:10; Deut. 22:23-24), and it is of enormous significance that he does so negatively. This applies even if it was unlikely that the penalty would have been carried out, though there is nothing in the story to suggest it would not have been.[73] It is sometimes urged that Jesus refused to condone the stoning of the woman because the two witnesses required by Mosaic law were not at hand, or because of the inherent inequity of executing only one of the offending parties when the law required both to die.[74] Some interpreters even speculate that every one of the woman's accusers were themselves guilty of committing adultery, so none were morally qualified to condemn her.[75] It follows

---

48; and K. P. Snodgrass, "Matthew's Understanding of the Law," *Interpretation* 46, no. 4 (1992): 369-78.

72. B. M. Metzger, *A Textual Commentary on the Greek New Testament* (London: United Bible Societies, 1971), 220. On the authenticity and textual status of this pericope, see also J. I. H. McDonald, "The So-Called *PERICOPE DE ADULTERA*," *NTS* 41, no. 3 (1995): 426; G. R. Beasley-Murray, *John* (Waco: Word, 1987), 143-44; J. Marsh, *The Gospel of Saint John* (Harmondsworth: Penguin, 1968), 681-84; and J. J. Rousseau & R. Arav, *Jesus and His World: An Archaeological and Cultural Dictionary* (London: SCM, 1995), 266.

73. Many scholars suspect that the death penalty for adultery was only rarely inflicted at the time, especially in urban areas; see L. Morris, *The Gospel According to John* (Grand Rapids: William B. Eerdmans, 1971), 887n.19; and D. A. Carson, *The Gospel According to John* (Leicester/Grand Rapids: Inter-Varsity Press/Eerdmans, 1991), 335. Yet the possibility of summary justice in such a highly charged situation cannot be ruled out. Morris suspects that if Jesus had refused to give a decision in the case, "the woman would certainly have been lynched" (888); so also J. D. M. Derrett, "The Woman Taken in Adultery," in Derrett, *Law in the New Testament* (London: Darton, Longman & Todd, 1970), 167; cf. 170-74.

74. See House, "The New Testament and Capital Punishment," 63-65; and Geisler, *Ethics*, 243-44.

75. R. Maclachlan, "Jesus and Judgment," *Stimulus* 2, no. 4 (1994): 48.

that had these statutory conditions been met, Jesus would have supported her execution.[76]

But this interpretation is entirely unconvincing. It casts Jesus in a rather unflattering light as a sharp legal attorney who secures the release of the guilty party by discrediting the witnesses for the prosecution and uses legal technicalities to subvert the just penalty of the law. Moreover, the details of the account suggest that all the conditions for lawful condemnation were in fact present. We are told twice that the woman had been "caught in the very act of committing adultery" (vv. 3-4), requiring the presence of witnesses. Jesus does not challenge the accuracy of the accusation; in fact, he himself acknowledges her legal guilt ("Go . . . and do not sin again," v. 11). Furthermore, it is the legal experts of the day, the scribes and Pharisees (v. 3), who bring the incident to Jesus. They were convinced they had a watertight case that would trap Jesus and secure "some charge to bring against him" (v. 6). They refer expressly to Mosaic legislation requiring her stoning (v. 5) and must have been confident of their legal position. They would scarcely have overlooked such an important matter as the availability and reliability of witnesses (cf. Deut. 19:16-21). Most importantly, the very fact that Jesus' opponents use a capital offense to test his adherence to Mosaic law implies they had already concluded from his other teaching that he would, as a matter of principle, oppose the infliction of death, even on a guilty person, and could thereby be shown to be setting himself in opposition to Moses.

Here I am assuming that the charge the scribes and Pharisees sought to bring against him (v. 6) was a charge before the Sanhedrin, not before the Roman courts. Some interpreters suggest that Jesus' enemies had him in a cleft stick. If he opposed the woman's execution, he could be charged with repudiating Mosaic law. If he condoned it, he could be accused of defying Rome's monopoly on legal execution (cf. John 18:31), as well as having blood on his own hands.[77] This interpre-

---

76. Derrett speculates that "had the accusers been sinless her stoning could have taken place with his approval" ("The Woman Taken in Adultery," 187).

77. So, e.g., A. Plummer, *The Gospel According to St. John* (1882; reprint, Grand Rapids: Baker, 1981), 184; J. H. Bernard, *A Critical and Exegetical Commentary on the Gospel According to St. John* (Edinburgh: T. & T. Clark, 1928), 2:718; J. Jeremias, "Zur Geschichtlichkeit des Verhors Jesu vor dem hohen Rat," *ZNW* 43 (1950-51): 148-50; C. K. Barrett, *The Gospel According to John: An Introduction with Commentary and Notes on the Greek Text* (London:

tation is certainly possible. But there is no hint in the details of the story of any intended deference to Rome, and it seems unlikely that the Roman authorities would have been any more troubled by the lynching of a Jewish adulteress than by the mob justice dished out to Stephen (cf. Acts 7:58). Nor would Jesus' mere condoning of a biblical principle have rendered him legally responsible for her death. Her accusers, who themselves obviously condone the biblical penalty, would have done the actual stoning. On balance it is more likely that the charge the scribes and Pharisees hoped to bring against Jesus was one of abrogating Mosaic law. Still, Jesus was in a difficult situation, as George Beasley-Murray points out: "If he upholds the Law, he contradicts his way of life and his preaching; if he maintains his outlook and preaching regarding sinners and denies Moses, he shows himself a lawless person and perverter of the people who must be brought to justice."[78]

All this means that it is with full cognizance of the legal justifiability of capital punishment in this specific case that Jesus refuses to condone the woman's execution. And he does so on several grounds. The first is that human life is sacred. Jesus' mysterious action of stooping "to draw with his finger on the ground" (vv. 6, 8) has teased readers of all time. Opinion differs on whether he drew pictures, wrote words, or doodled in the dust, and whether the author intends the emphasis to fall on his stooping posture, what he actually wrote, or the fact that he wrote on the ground. My guess is that the author intended Jesus' action on the ground *(eis tēn gēn)* to be a symbolic or parabolic reminder that human beings were created from "the dust of the ground" *(choun apo tēs gēs,* Gen. 2:7, LXX) as bearers of God's image. God gives life to earthly creatures, and only God should take it away.[79]

SPCK, 1978), 591-92; and R. E. Brown, *The Gospel According to John,* 2 vols. (London: Geoffrey Chapman, 1971), 1:337.

78. Beasley-Murray, *John,* 146.

79. The compound verb *kategraphen* in verse 6 can mean "draw" as well as "write," while the imperfect tense suggests a continuing activity, although the uncompounded *egraphen* in verse 8 means "write." Some exegetes suggest the emphasis falls on "the ground" (J. H. Bernard, *A Critical and Exegetical Commentary on the Gospel According to St. John,* 2 vols. [Edinburgh: T. & T. Clark, 1928), 2:719; Marsh, *The Gospel of Saint John,* 686), which permits an allusion to Genesis 2:7. Another possibility is that Jesus was seeking to remind the accusers of "the tablets of stone written with the finger of God" (Exod. 31:18; Deut. 9:10), which forbid killing as well as adultery (cf. Plummer, *The Gospel According to St. John,* 185). McDonald detects a prophetic dramatization of Jeremiah 17:13, where, in

The second reason for Jesus' stance is that all people are sinners, equally deserving of death and therefore equally disqualified from adjudicating in matters of life and death. "Let anyone among you who is without sin be the first to throw a stone at her" (v. 7). The suggestion that Jesus had the sin of adultery specifically in mind is implausible. The term "without sin" *(anamartētos)* is found only here in the New Testament, but in the Septuagint it denotes sins of various kinds, and it almost certainly has an inclusive meaning here. Nor is it true that the woman's accusers were, strictly speaking, false witnesses who risked becoming guilty of judicial murder if the woman died (Deut. 19:16-21).[80] Their testimony was true; after all, the woman had been caught *in coitu*. Jesus alone was "without sin" (John 8:21, 24, 46; cf. 2 Cor. 5:21; Heb. 4:15; 7:26-27) and therefore qualified to throw the first stone. But he refused to do so despite the woman's legal guilt. The case against her collapses as all her accusers withdraw. Jesus has rescued the woman without explicitly abrogating the law, as his enemies had hoped. The comment on "throwing the first stone" is not, as it is in proverbial use today, a general reference to hypocritical judgmentalism. Contextually it is a direct reference to the authority to execute. Jesus is not ruling out any right to exercise moral or legal discrimination, and he is not making moral perfection a prerequisite for exercising judicial authority. He is specifically challenging the right of the self-proclaimed "righteous" to kill other people in the name of defending the rule of law.

The third reason Jesus opposes execution of the woman is that his own presence on earth announces divine forgiveness for sins committed. "Jesus straightened up and said to her, 'Woman, where are they? Has no one condemned you?' She said, 'No one, sir.' And Jesus said, 'Neither do I condemn you. Go your way, and from now on do not sin again'" (vv. 10-11). Punitive measures are not taken in the interest of upholding some kind of mythical balance of justice. Instead, the offender is implicitly forgiven and placed on the path to spiritual and emotional restoration. Freed from condemnation, she is empowered to go forward and sin no more. The primary point of the story, J. I. H. McDonald suggests, is

---

the Greek text, those who reject and forsake God will be put to shame and "written in the dust" *(epi tēs gēs graphētōsan)*, thereby warning the accusers of divine judgment on them ("The So-Called *PERICOPE DE ADULTERA*," 421). For other suggestions, see the commentaries and Derrett, "The Woman Taken in Adultery," 175-86.

80. House, "The New Testament and Capital Punishment," 63-65.

that "in some situations, and perhaps with certain groups of people, the moral priority lies with the readiness to understand rather than condemn, with an unconditional acceptance of the sinner which looks to the future rather than the past (and who is without sin?), and with the liberation of the oppressed."[81] What better example is there of restorative justice overthrowing retributive justice in the Christian age?[82]

Romans 13:4

This brings us finally to Romans 13:1-7. The key issues here are whether the passage as a whole should be seen as conferring divine authority on the state to take human life and whether the power of the sword refers specifically to capital punishment. Admittedly, in light of the daily realities of life under the Roman imperium, it is hard to imagine Paul's readers not linking mention of the sword with the power of the Roman state to inflict death. There is, in my view, no good reason to exclude the connotation of death from the semantic range evoked by use of the word "sword" in connection with governing authority in Romans 13:4. Paul and his readers would have known from personal experience that Rome's possession of the sword often entailed death to those who resisted her will. But it is going much too far to read into this reference to the sword an enduring divine authorization for use of the death penalty by civil authorities.

To begin with, it must be recognized that Paul is not intending to elaborate a thoroughgoing political theology.[83] Paul's discussion reflects an interweaving of four main strands:[84] personal experience of the pragmatic realities of life under Rome, especially with regard to tax-

---

81. McDonald, "The So-Called *PERICOPE DE ADULTERA,*" 427.

82. R. E. Brown cautions of the story that "one should beware of attempts to make it a general norm forbidding enactments of capital punishment" (*The Gospel According to John,* 1:338). R. V. G. Tasker warns against seeing the woman's forgiveness as an evasion of the penalty she deserved, for Jesus himself would pay her penalty "by suffering in her place . . . a criminal's death" (*John: An Introduction and Commentary* [Leicester: Inter-Varsity Press, 1960], 112). But such warnings are themselves testimony to the story's inherent challenge to retributive justice.

83. See especially E. Käsemann, "Principles of Interpretation of Romans 13," in Käsemann, *New Testament Questions of Today* (London: SCM, 1969), 196-216.

84. Cf. P. Stuhlmacher, *Paul's Letter to the Romans: A Commentary* (Louisville, Ky.: Westminster John Knox, 1994), 199-200.

ation (v. 6); the technical language of Roman administrative practices; biblical-Jewish tradition concerning how God exercises providential control of the moral and social order through the agency of human rulers; and dominical tradition about rendering Caesar his due.[85] While it is true that Paul's discussion takes place at the level of general principles and is based on premises of general significance, most recent commentators agree that, contrary to classical interpretation, Paul does not set out in Romans 13 to develop a Christian "doctrine of the state" or to reflect hypothetically on the respective spheres of church and state. His primary intention is to give paraenetic teaching to Roman Christians who might be tempted to join in a popular campaign of tax resistance being fomented at the time. Tax avoidance and evasion were criminal offenses, and under the Julio-Claudian emperors, Thomas Coleman explains, even "failure to give due reverence and honour for benefactions attracted legal penalties."[86] Thus, as James Walters notes,

> The passage should be viewed as the communication of a missionary intervening in a crisis, not that of a theologian composing a systematic doctrine. Consequently, Romans 13:1-7 should not be interpreted as "Paul's Theology of Church and State," nor should it be utilized as subject matter for constructing such a theology without careful reflection on its function.[87]

Accordingly, while Paul affirms the God-given character of political au-

---

85. On the connection between Romans 13 and the tribute passage (Mark 12:13-17/Matt. 22:15-22/Luke 20:20-26), see M. Thompson, *Clothed with Christ: The Example and Teaching of Jesus in Romans 12:1–15:13* (Sheffield: Sheffield Academic Press, 1991), 111-20. The literary status of the unit is discussed by D. Kroger, "Paul and the Civil Authorities: An Exegesis of Romans 13:1-7," *AJT* 7, no. 2 (1993): 344-66. Many commentators now follow the historical analysis of J. Friedrich, W. Pohlmann, and P. Stuhlmacher, "Zur historischen Situation und Intention von Rom 13,1-7," *ZTK* 73 (1976): 131-66. More briefly, see Stuhlmacher, *Paul's Letter to the Romans,* 200-201, and, with differences, N. Elliott, *Liberating Paul: The Justice of God and the Politics of the Apostle* (Maryknoll, N.Y.: Orbis, 1994), 217-26. A radically different historical setting is proposed by M. Nanos, *The Mystery of Romans: The Jewish Context of Paul's Letter* (Minneapolis: Fortress Press, 1996), 289-336.

86. Coleman, "Binding Obligations in Romans 13:7: A Semantic Field and Social Context," *TynBul* 48, no. 2 (1997): 326.

87. Walters, *Ethnic Issues in Paul's Letter to the Romans: Changing Self-Definitions in Earliest Roman Christianity* (Valley Forge, Pa.: Trinity Press International, 1993), 65.

thority, it needs to be emphasized that he is not *addressing* the state or *authorizing* the state to do anything, least of all to kill people. Instead, he is addressing Christian believers and authorizing them to submit to the state's right to exist (vv. 1-2, 5); to recognize its God-given role under divine providence of protecting what is good and reprimanding what is bad, a commonplace in both Jewish and Greco-Roman moral tradition (vv. 3-4); and to render taxes, respect, and honor as they are due (vv. 6-7).[88] Therefore, to interpret the text as a direct authorization of the death penalty is to misunderstand authorial intention.

But is the reference to the sword a conscious allusion to the death penalty? Certainly this is possible.[89] But even if this is so, it is important to note that Paul stops short of entrenching the sword itself as a divine institution. It is not specifically the sword that serves as a servant of wrath and vengeance but "the authority" (*tēn exousian,* v. 3) or the state as a whole. Verse 4 has a carefully balanced structure. The phrase *theou gar diakonos estin* ("for it is God's servant") in verse 4d parallels the identical phrase in verse 4a, which in turn refers back to *tēn exousian* ("the authority") in verse 3. Paul's point is that when "the authority" is a terror to bad conduct, it serves as God's servant of wrath and vengeance. That it wears the sword, and not in vain (i.e., it is prepared to employ it), is a simple statement of fact, not an explicit endorsement of state-sponsored violence, any more than it is an implied endorsement of other aspects of the state's repertoire of enforcement, such as the oaths and sacrifices to pagan deities that magistrates offered in taking office. It is the punitive or protective *function* of the state that is affirmed, not the *methods* it uses. Note that this is the case even if we interpret "the sword" as a conscious reference to the death penalty or *ius gladii*.

Yet there is reason to doubt that Paul is echoing the *ius gladii* or thinking specifically of capital punishment. There is considerable doubt over whether, in Paul's day, "the law of the sword" extended to civil mag-

88. On the meaning of the obligations in verse 7, see Coleman, "Binding Obligations in Romans 13:7," 307-27; contrast Nanos, *The Mystery of Romans,* 314-21.

89. So Lenski, *St. Paul's Epistle to the Romans,* 791-92; C. K. Barrett, *The Epistle to the Romans* (London: A. & C. Black, 1962), 247; J. Murray, *The Epistle of Paul to the Romans,* 2 vols. (London: Marshall, Morgan & Scott, 1960), 2:152-53; and J. R. W. Stott, *The Message of Romans: Good News for the World* (Leicester: Inter-Varsity Press, 1994), 344-45. Cf. J. D. G. Dunn, *Romans 9–13,* 2 vols. (Waco: Word, 1988), 2:764; R. H. Stein, "The Argument of Romans 13:1-7," *NovT* 31, no. 4 (1989): 335-36.

istrates. Several scholars insist that for the first two centuries of the empire the *ius gladii* applied only to the power of execution that provincial governors had over troops under their command who were citizens. Since Paul and his readers were not soldiers, and few would have been Roman citizens, the "sword" in Romans 13:4 cannot therefore apply to the *ius gladii*.[90] In John Ziesler's judgment, all we can say with confidence is that the sword serves as "a reminder of the state's power of enforcement."[91] Similarly, Joseph Fitzmyer considers it to be "the symbol of penal authority, of the power legitimately possessed by a civil authority to coerce recalcitrant citizens to maintain order and strive for the common good by obeying the law of the society."[92] The close connection between Paul's phraseology "bearing the sword" *(tēn machairan phorei)* and the term "sword-bearers" *(machairphoroi)* found in papyrus documents to describe policemen who support the authorities in carrying out their duties, such as collecting taxes, suggests that sword-bearers would include civil guards and those who enforce taxation.[93]

Defenders of capital punishment usually object to taking "the sword" *(hē machaira)* in a symbolic or figurative rather than a literal sense. But some symbolic dimension is inescapable, for it is unlikely that Paul is thinking purely of decapitation, since beheading by sword was reserved for those with Roman citizenship, which few in the church possessed, and even then it was not as common a method of execution as strangulation. At the very least, then, *hē machaira* is a metonymy for the various modes of execution that Rome employed, including crucifixion, beheading, burial alive, burning, garroting, flaying alive, being thrown to wild

---

90. So A. N. Sherwin-White, *Roman Society and Roman Law in the New Testament* (Oxford: Clarendon, 1963), 8-11; C. E. B. Cranfield, *A Critical and Exegetical Commentary on the Epistle to the Romans*, 2 vols. (Edinburgh: T. & T. Clark, 1975, 1977), 2:666-67; J. A. Fitzmyer, *Romans* (New York: Doubleday, 1993), 668; and L. Morris, *The Epistle to the Romans* (Grand Rapids: William B. Eerdmans, 1988), 464. M. Borg rejects a link with capital punishment and sees the phrase as designating "the war-making ability of the Roman State." See "A New Context for Romans XIII," *NTS* 19, no. 2 (1973): 216-17.

91. Ziesler, *Paul's Letter to the Romans* (London/Philadelphia: SCM/Trinity, 1989), 312.

92. Fitzmyer, *Romans*, 668. So too W. Sanday and A. Headlam, who say that the sword is "the symbol of the executive and criminal jurisdiction of a magistrate" (*The Epistle to the Romans* [Edinburgh: T. & T. Clark, 1902], 367).

93. Friedrich et al., "Zur historischen Situation und Intention von Rom 13, 1-7," 144; Fitzmyer, *Romans*, 668.

beasts, and being thrown from a cliff. If it thus serves as a representative symbol for various forms of capital justice, it is hard to see why Paul could not have used it to embrace severe noncapital penalties as well[94] (such as corporal punishment, enslavement, life in the mines, banishment, fines, and confiscation of property), which might equally manifest "wrathful vengeance on evildoers" and would equally be a reason for criminals to fear. And if it is representative of this larger category of criminal punishments, then it seems natural to assume that Paul is employing *hē machaira* as a concrete symbol for the power of civil and criminal coercion in general rather than for capital punishment in particular, though the latter is not excluded. (Indeed, it could not be excluded if the text is to reflect historical realities.) The sword was known to have been a symbol of justice in Rome, and it is quite plausible that Paul uses it here as a concrete symbol of the state's judicial or police powers.[95] By the third century C.E., the term *ius gladii* was widely used to denote the power of civil coercion in general, and Paul seems to use "bearing the sword" in a similar vein. Significantly, E. Plümacher includes the usage in Romans 13:4 among the figurative uses of "sword" in the New Testament.[96]

Certain other textual details support this wider symbolic reference. The word used for sword *(hē machaira)* designates a "knife" or a "dagger" or "short sword" (cf. Gen. 22:6, 10; Josh. 5:2), not a long sword *(xiphos* or perhaps *rhomphaia)* more suitable for executions.[97] It is also said to be worn by the authorities or magistrates, not by an executioner. The use of the definite article ("the" sword) and the reference to "wearing" rather than wielding the sword *(phorein,* not *echein* or *pherein)* reinforce its symbolic associations.[98] It is perhaps significant that Paul's only other use of *machaira* is in Romans 8:35, where it might also serve

94. Cf. Charles, "Pauline Ethics and Capital Justice," 7, 20.

95. So J. H. Yoder, *The Politics of Jesus,* 2nd ed. (Grand Rapids/Carlisle: Eerdmans/Paternoster, 1994), 203-5; Yoder, "Jesus and the Civil Order," in *The Death Penalty Debate,* 146; J. Lasserre, *War and the Gospel* (London: James Clarke, 1962), 183-87; and G. H. C. MacGregor, *The New Testament Basis of Pacifism* (London: Fellowship of Reconciliation, 1953), 85.

96. Plümacher, "μάχαιρα," *EDNT,* 2:397-98.

97. See *TDNT,* 4:524-27; Yoder, *The Politics of Jesus,* 203-4; and P. B. Yoder, *From Word to Life: A Guide to the Art of Bible Study* (Scottdale, Pa.: Herald Press, 1982), 133-34. Cf. Friedrich et al., "Zur historischen Situation und Intention von Rom 13, 1-7," 141.

98. Cf. Cranfield, *A Critical and Exegetical Commentary on the Epistle to the Romans,* 2:667.

as a symbol of Roman penal authority, especially in view of Paul's own experience of imprisonment.[99] Jean Lasserre considers it doubtful that the Christians at Rome needed threatening with capital punishment, since they would hardly have been tempted to commit capital crimes.[100] More recent scholarship, however, proposes that Paul's specific intention is to dissuade Christians from joining in a tax revolt that was brewing at the time and that might prompt brutal suppression. If so, this again argues in favor of seeing the sword as a general symbol of Rome's coercive power rather than as a specific reference to the capital jurisdiction of Roman courts.

To draw these threads together: Even if Paul intends the sword to be a collective symbol of capital punishment, he cites it as a reason for fear when one does wrong, not as a divine institution. It is the state's general *function* of repressing evildoers that Paul links with its role as God's servant, not its use of the executioner's sword per se. Given that, even on this interpretation, Paul uses *machaira* as a metonymy, there is no reason to doubt that it is intended to represent a wide range of both capital and noncapital sanctions or, more generally still, that it serves as a concrete symbol of Rome's judicial and coercive authority as such. The choice is not between literal and figurative interpretations but between narrow and broader symbolic associations. To read the text as granting a divine authorization for the state's enduring right to kill wrongdoers disregards the hortatory character of the passage, the primary intention of Paul's instruction, and the symbolic nature of the language. Accordingly, Lasserre's conclusion remains valid: "No Christian justification of the death penalty can be deduced from Romans 13, so there is no single text in the New Testament which approves it."[101]

Summary of the Biblical Arguments

From the preceding discussion it is clear that Christian debate over the ethics of capital punishment is fundamentally a hermeneutical one. All

---

99. Cf. Zerbe, *Non-Retaliation in Early Jewish and New Testament Texts*, 229n.62.

100. Lasserre, *War and the Gospel*, 184.

101. Lasserre, *War and the Gospel*, 187; also MacGregor, *The New Testament Basis of Pacifism*, 85.

sides agree that the entirety of biblical teaching, both Old Testament and New Testament, must be taken into account. But key passages are exegeted differently, and the relationship between the testaments is construed differently.

On the one side, advocates of capital punishment such as Wayne House insist that the cumulative weight of biblical evidence confirms that, "whether or not we like it, the death penalty is compatible with the nature of God. . . . The concept of retribution supports it, and the biblical data permit it."[102] Capital punishment cannot be inherently immoral because God commanded it. It has been practiced since the beginning of recorded history, and the advent of the messianic era in no way lifts the ethical imperative for capital justice. According to Daryl Charles, "Jesus in no way sets aside civil-legal and moral stipulations that the Old Testament had stressed. The teaching recorded in Jesus' Sermon on the Mount is meant to address personal issues of the heart in the disciple's life, not the duties of the civil magistrates."[103] The principle of life-for-life represents a binding, unchanging ethical standard stemming from fundamental respect for human life as bearer of the *imago Dei*. Jesus' teaching may call us to new depths of love for neighbor, but, says J. R. Connery, "it does not contain prescriptions of magnanimity towards felons, murderers and other criminals; and any attempt to invoke such a 'law of love' in order to cover behaviour that is condemned ethically or morally in scripture is a theological perversion."[104]

On the other side, opponents of capital punishment concede that it is given divine sanction by Old Testament writers and that it played a significant role in the social order of ancient Israel. Its function, however, was not primarily to bolster notions of retributive justice but to express and preserve the holiness of God's people. Certain behaviors were seen as a source of contamination or pollution that could be removed only by ritual expiation. In some cases this involved the destruction of the agent of pollution through death. In the New Testament, it is the death of Christ that definitively destroys the uncleanness of sin. This renders redundant all other means of religious atonement and paves the way for the forgiveness and restoration of even the worst of offenders. To appeal

---

102. House, "Crime and Punishment," 24.

103. Charles, "Crime, the Christian, and Capital Justice," 436n.24.

104. Connery, "Capital Punishment," *EBCE*, 49.

to the death penalty in Old Testament times to justify its use in the penal systems of modern secular societies is therefore anachronistic. More importantly, the example, teaching, and saving work of Jesus Christ mark a significant shift in salvation history that summons a new way of responding to enemies. The New Testament presupposes the existence of capital punishment (like slavery and patriarchy) in the wider community and provides no unambiguous warrant for its abolition. But the underlying redemptive ethic of Christian revelation runs counter to it, and it does so even more clearly than it does with respect to slavery or patriarchy. The way of love taught and embodied by Jesus does not overturn all political and judicial organs of social control. But it does challenge the practice of lethal retribution against wrongdoers, especially when it is done in the name of a divine justice that has vindicated itself in the criminal execution of Jesus the Messiah, the Son of God.

A Critique of Other Arguments
for Capital Punishment

In addition to biblical arguments, a variety of other moral, theological, and pragmatic considerations enter the debate. In this section I will first summarize and then briefly evaluate the major ethical arguments used in defense of capital punishment.

The Need for Moral Boundaries

Scripture teaches — and society requires — that there be certain moral boundaries or limits that are more or less fixed. One such boundary is respect for human life. The prerogative to take life belongs to God alone (1 Sam. 2:6; 2 Kings 5:7; Job 1:20). Murder is thus an invasion of an area reserved for God. So serious is such an offense, Elmer Martens insists, that the ultimate penalty is appropriate: "Capital punishment stands therefore as a witness to the sacredness of life, and the seriousness of invading the realm reserved alone to God."[105] It expresses soci-

---

105. Martens, "Capital Punishment and the Christian," 24; so too Stott, *The Message of Romans,* 345.

ety's moral outrage at those who trespass beyond the frontier of decency and religion. The most serious punishment possible is to be reserved for those who casually take human life.

This is a compelling argument. It is true that murder is not only the most injurious of crimes, with irrevocable consequences, but is also the most profane. Life is sacred, and those who willfully destroy it commit sacrilege. It is also true that the best test for the morality of capital punishment is whether it expresses and enhances reverence for human life, since in the long run the only reliable protection for human life is deep belief in its sanctity in the collective consciousness of society. But seeking to uphold the sacredness of life by extinguishing the life of those who disregard it is a moral and a logical non sequitur. How does killing those who kill others demonstrate that it is wrong to kill? It does precisely the opposite, insofar as "the executioner pays the murderer the compliment of imitation," to use Walter Moberly's words.[106] The value of life is demeaned, not enhanced, by legal execution, for the criminal is treated not as a human person but as a thing, a malignant tumor to be removed in the interest of public health. To justify the judicial taking of life by an appeal to the sanctity of life is like defending war as an instrument of peace. In both cases the practice contradicts the precept. The means of achieving the end is so inconsistent with the end sought that the effort is doomed to failure. Significantly, John Howard Yoder uses an identical appeal to the sanctity of life to deny the right of the state to take life: "To sanctify means to set apart as belonging to God alone, and that is just what the Bible says about human life: it is not ours to take."[107] Only God has the right intentionally to terminate life (Rom 12:19).

Amnesty International uses the language of human rights to arrive at a similar conclusion. The most basic human right, as most international canons of human rights acknowledge, is the right to life. Capital punishment is a violation of that inalienable right:

> No matter what reason a government gives for executing prisoners or what method of execution is used, the death penalty cannot be defined purely as a criminal justice issue. The death penalty is a human rights

106. Moberly, *The Ethics of Punishment* (London: Faber & Faber, 1968), 45.

107. Yoder, *The Christian and Capital Punishment* (Newton, Kans.: Faith and Life Press, 1961), 4.

issue. The idea that a government can justify the punishment of death contradicts the very notion of human rights. The significance of human rights is precisely this: that some means may never be used to protect society because their use violates the values that make society worth protecting. The death penalty is wrong in all cases.[108]

Thus, whereas Martens claims that the death penalty guards the moral boundary of the sacredness of life, Amnesty International insists that such a boundary cannot be maintained if the government itself oversteps that boundary through the institutionalized, premeditated violence of execution. The argument that state-employed execution reinforces the value of life in the social consciousness should be reversed. The state enhances the value of human life more powerfully by setting the example of not taking life itself.

A Deterrent to Serious Crime

It is widely felt by people, largely on an intuitive basis, that capital punishment serves as a deterrent to crime, and there is some biblical support for such a view (Deut. 21:21; Rom. 13:4). "The entire criminal justice system," observes Daryl Charles, "historically has been based on the common sense notion that the more severe the penalty the greater is the deterrent effect in the would-be offender."[109] If capital punishment does not deter the murderer, then logically nor will any other kind of punishment. Charles appeals to studies based on economic models of supply-and-demand that have concluded that for every execution of a murderer, some eighteen murders would be deterred.[110] While research on the deterrent effects of capital punishment is ambiguous, he argues that it is better to err on the side of perhaps wrongly assuming its deterrence value than vice versa:

> If executing a convicted murderer is "barbaric," is it not all the more barbaric to make possible the sacrifice of additional lives in order to

108. *Amnesty International Handbook* (London: AI Publications, 1992), 34.

109. Charles, "Outrageous Atrocity or Moral Imperative?" 8-9.

110. For bibliographical details on these studies, see Charles, "Crime, the Christian, and Capital Justice," 439n.33.

save the life of the murderers? If, for the sake of the argument, capital punishment is implemented under the *mistaken* notion that it deters, the lives of convicted murderers are lost. If, on the other hand, capital punishment is abolished due to the *mistaken* belief that it does *not* deter, then *innocent lives* are lost. Social justice would therefore suggest — all things being equal — that the death penalty for premeditated murder should be retained, theological presuppositions aside.[111]

What undermines the deterrent effect of the death penalty in modern society, Charles argues, is the inconsistency with which it has been applied. In the United States, only a small percentage of those convicted of murder are sentenced to death, and a tiny percentage of those are actually executed. A more consistent application of the law would increase its deterrent value. "In truth," says Charles, "a law that is not enforced will not be feared, and a law that is not feared will not deter."[112] J. R. Connery is especially scathing of those who deny the deterrent value of execution: "The present writer can only say that he has still to hear of any executed murderer who committed yet another capital offense, which would indicate that capital punishment has some degree of success as a deterrent."[113]

Now there is no denying that, in general terms, punitive sanctions do have some deterrent effect, and there is a cold-blooded logic to Connery's position — interred criminals are permanently deterred! But the social and psychological variables that contribute to violent crime are too complex to be adequately controlled by external sanctions. The main weakness of the deterrence argument is its absurdly oversimplified conception of human nature. It assumes that crime is the result of conscious, rational choices and that before a person commits an offense, she or he undertakes a cost-benefit analysis to determine whether the possible costs — in this case, arrest and execution — outweigh the potential benefits. But most homicides are acts of passion committed in the heat of the moment, without thought of the personal consequences. Even those who commit premeditated murder do not usually expect to be caught, so the severity of the penalty does not enter into consideration. The most ferocious of punishments does little to deter crime if

111. Charles, "Outrageous Atrocity or Moral Imperative?" 9.
112. Charles, "Outrageous Atrocity or Moral Imperative?" 9.
113. Connery, "Capital Punishment," 50.

the criminal believes he or she has a sporting chance of getting away with it. The deterrence argument may have some relevance for crimes that require careful rational calculation, such as tax evasion, but it has limited cogency when it comes to crimes such as murder.

Research has never conclusively established that the death penalty deters crime or violence more effectively than other punishments.[114] It may even have the reverse effect. Some studies have detected a pattern of increased homicides immediately after a well-publicized execution. Potential killers may see the death penalty as evidence that lethal violence is legitimate. Instead of identifying with the offender who was caught and executed, and being suitably dissuaded from murder, they identify with the executioner. "They learn from these executions," Howard Zehr suggests, "that it is acceptable to eliminate someone who wrongs them, that violence is justified against the deserving."[115] If they have reached a state of readiness to kill, the atmosphere of violence surrounding execution may encourage them to translate this attitude into action.

Conversely, some of the lowest murder rates are found in countries where the death penalty has been abolished the longest. When Canada abolished the death penalty for murder in 1976, the murder rate declined by 5 percent. The same happened in Holland, the United Kingdom, and several American states.[116] The death penalty was abolished in New Zealand in 1941, then reintroduced in 1951 before being finally abolished in 1961. The period of reintroduction was not accompanied by any perceptible decrease in the homicide rate, as one might expect if capital punishment serves as a deterrent. One might also expect the United States — one of the few Western countries still to employ the death penalty, albeit sparingly — to have a lower crime rate than countries without the death penalty. In fact, its per-capita

114. Cf. Moberly, *The Ethics of Punishment*, 274-78, 291-96; and E. Gowers, *A Life for a Life? The Problem of Capital Punishment* (London: Chatto & Windus, 1956), 88-109. The methodology and results of studies employing economic models (cited on p. 243n.110) have been severely critiqued by other researchers; see the "Symposium on Current Death Penalty Issues 74," *Journal of Criminal Law and Criminology* (1983): 991.

115. Zehr, *Death as a Penalty*, 6; Redekop, "An Analysis of Capital Punishment," in *On Capital Punishment*, 12; *Amnesty International Handbook*, 34.

116. L. Kehler et al., *Capital Punishment Study Guide* (Winnipeg: MCC Victim Offenders Ministries, 1980), 36.

crime rate is five times higher than that of European countries without capital punishment.

The Demands of Justice

This argument asserts that justice *requires* a life for a life and that the salvific mercy of God in no way compromises God's demand for justice in the moral-legal sphere. Scripture attests to both the compassion and the justice of God. They are strikingly juxtaposed in Exodus 34:6-7 with no indication that God's compassion eclipses the need for retribution on wrongdoing. Accordingly, administration of the death penalty is to be seen not as revenge, violence, or cruelty but as the satisfaction of true justice that restores the moral balance. "A just order is disturbed by murder," declares Norman Geisler, "and *only* the death of the murderer can restore that justice."[117] On a psychological level, it also offers the family of the victim a sense of justice. They feel cheated of justice when their loved one has died but the perpetrator lives on. Former New York mayor Edward Koch once said, "When the killer lives, the victim dies twice."[118]

In the aftermath of murder, the desire for retribution against the offender — to see the murderer suffer what he or she has inflicted on the innocent victim — is understandable. But it provides no adequate moral justification for the taking of another human life, least of all for Christians. Killing the criminal will not restore life to the victim, nor does it create a just balance. The number of bereaved relatives is simply doubled. Certainly justice must be done, as best it can be in the circumstances, for only justice will promote healing. Justice requires that the offender be held accountable for his or her actions and that he or she accept responsibility for the pain caused. It also requires that the victim's loved ones have their anguish and loss acknowledged, their anger affirmed, and their questions answered, for these are essential conditions for their dealing with what has happened. Bitter, hateful revenge, by contrast, has no real therapeutic value in the treatment of grief, nor does it promote social well-being in the long run.

117. Geisler, *Ethics,* 247 (emphasis mine); also Charles, "Outrageous Atrocity or Moral Imperative?" 6, 12.

118. Quoted in Gray and Stanley, *A Punishment in Search of a Crime,* 16.

Capital punishment also permits a lethal form of scapegoating. It presupposes the total guilt of the offender and disregards society's share in the blame. It panders to the illusion that by killing criminals the problem of crime is being solved, when in reality it does nothing to remedy the social maladies that spawn crime. The General Synod of the Reformed Church in America made this observation in 1965:

> A society which teaches vice through permitting pornography, glorifies crime and violence through the entertainment industry, permits sub-standard schooling and housing through segregation has a share in the making of the offender. . . . Capital punishment is too cheap and easy a way of absolving the guilty conscience of mankind.[119]

This scapegoating is also not color-blind or gender-blind. Between 1930 and 1967, 50 percent of those executed in United States were black, although the black community makes up less than 10 percent of the total population. Carla Faye Tucker, who was put to death in February 1998, was the first woman to be executed in Texas since 1863, prompting the *Los Angeles Times* to ask, "Is Death Row a Sexist Alley?"[120] In America, women account for one in every eight people arrested for murder, but account for only one in every 50 sentenced to death, one in every 70 on death row, and only one of the 432 actually put to death in the last two decades. The fact that only a small percentage of those convicted of capital offenses are executed means that factors other than the guilt of the offender enter into the decision about whether the person dies. These factors often have less to do with mitigating circumstances surrounding the actual crime than with the defendant's ethnic and social background, his or her financial means, the quality of legal counsel, the makeup of the jury, the race or occupation or age or gender of the victim,[121] the particu-

119. From "Resolution on Capital Punishment," from the Reformed Church in America General Synod, 1965; reprinted in *Capital Punishment: What the Religious Community Says,* ed. J. P. Adams (New York: National Interreligious Task Force on Criminal Justice, n.d.), 24-27.

120. The *LA Times* article reappeared in the *New Zealand Sunday-Star Times,* 18 January 1998, C5.

121. According to Zehr, a black person convicted of killing a white person is forty times more likely to be sentenced to death than if the victim was another black. Over 50 percent of murder victims are black, but 87 percent of those on death row are there for killing whites. See *Death as a Penalty,* 9-11.

lar jurisdiction within which the crime is committed,[122] even the proximity of local or state elections.[123] In America, a shameful number of mentally retarded and disturbed people have faced the gallows. Administration of the death penalty, in other words, is inherently arbitrary and discriminatory. The only way to remove such discrimination is by mandatory sentences. But, as the U.S. Supreme Court has ruled, automatic sentences in capital cases are unacceptable because morality requires that individual circumstances be taken into account and that room be left for mercy. That justice requires different outcomes in different circumstances undermines the argument that justice *requires* the life of the killer in return for the life of the victim.

Protection of the Innocent

A fourth argument appeals to God's passionate concern for the protection of the innocent, which is widely attested in Scripture.[124] Killers have already shown callous disregard for innocent human life. If they are merely imprisoned, and at the expense of their victim's family as taxpayers, they will be back on the streets in a few years and once again threaten the safety of innocent people. Statistics show that between 95 and 98 percent of American prison inmates are eventually returned to society, and 68 percent of them will commit further crimes.[125] "Mur-

122. Between 1976 and 1997, there were 144 executions in Texas, compared with only four in California and one in Kentucky. By region, there were 345 executions in the American South, compared with 31 in the West, 42 in the Midwest, and only two in the Northeast.

123. K. H. Potter elaborates: "The extent of American democratic accountability — governors, congressmen and, in some states, even judges dependent on popular support to propel them into office, or keep them in it — with the concomitant reluctance of the legislature and the judiciary to lead rather than reflect popular opinion; the independent structure of local government with the concomitant fragmentation of criminal justice — each state being a law unto itself; the violence of its gun-toting culture; the persistence of its racism; and the emergence of an unofficial fundamentalist Christian establishment: these are the main reasons for the retention of the death penalty in the United States, a retention which makes it unique in the Western world" ("The Special Relationship," 229).

124. Cf. Exod. 23:7; Deut. 20:10, 14; Prov. 6:16-17, 1 Kings 20:31; 2 Kings 6:22; 24:4; Isa. 59:7.

125. So R. McQuilkin, *An Introduction to Biblical Ethics* (Wheaton: Tyndale, 1989), 359.

derers," Charles asserts, "generally do not rehabilitate."[126] To execute killers, therefore, is not only an act of justice but also an expression of neighbor-love for the criminal's potential victims in the future. "It can be a kind of mercy-killing," suggests Geisler, "that is, a kind of mercy to society to guarantee that this criminal will not repeat the crime he committed."[127] Conversely, to deny the death penalty is to guarantee life to the evil and jeopardy to the vulnerable.

Protection of the innocent is unquestionably a fundamental moral duty of society, but execution is not the only way to achieve it. In fact, the likelihood of a defendant facing death may even discourage juries from convicting a guilty person, perhaps heightening the risk of re-offending. Certainly there are some people who are so dangerous that they need to be removed indefinitely from society. But, contrary to Charles's unsubstantiated assertion, the vast majority of convicted murderers never kill a second time and pose no greater threat to the innocent than do other members of the community.[128] People convicted of murder are statistically the most unlikely to commit violent crimes again. Nor are they a special threat to innocent strangers. The vast majority of murder victims are spouses or friends of the murderer, not unsuspecting strangers. Nor is capital punishment a less costly form of protection than other forms, not even less costly than lifelong incarceration. Both the capital equipment required and the legal and political processes involved are extremely expensive. In a 1989 report, it was estimated that each execution costs Ohio $1 million, Florida $3.1 million, and Texas $6 million.[129] If such revenues were diverted into victim-support plans or crime-prevention policies, the impact would be considerable.

126. Charles, "Crime, the Christian, and Capital Justice," 437. Charles does not support this assertion with statistical evidence. Instead, he footnotes his personal opinion that death-row prisoners convert to faith in Christ because they are getting ready to meet their Maker, not because they have been rehabilitated.

127. Geisler, *Ethics*, 246.

128. This is not to say that paroled murderers never commit further crimes. Of the 136 murderers paroled in New Zealand since 1987, 60 have been convicted of further criminal offenses. However, only 18 have received further prison sentences of more than three months, and none of the 60 have killed again. These statistics were reported in *New Zealand Herald*, 28 November 1997, A12.

129. These statistics can be found in Gray and Stanley, *A Punishment in Search of a Crime*, 43.

Instead of guaranteeing protection for the innocent the practice of capital punishment itself poses a positive threat to the innocent in at least two ways. The first is by wrongful convictions. The law is fallible and is administered by fallible people. The miscarriage of justice in murder cases is frequent enough to make the use of capital punishment extremely troubling because, unlike all other judicial mistakes, it is irrevocable. To execute someone is to claim a God-like authority over human life but without the requisite God-like wisdom. Between 1893 and 1966, seventy-three wrongful executions are known to have occurred in the United States.[130] Robert McQuilkin downplays this consideration:

> [The problem of] mistaken execution of the innocent has been over-emphasised. The most liberal estimates of all varieties of crime in which innocent persons have been convicted is up to 5 percent. In capital cases, where no expense is spared and no avenue of defense unproved, such error is highly unlikely, but in the rare instance when it may occur, one is faced with the alternative of what the lack of this sanction may do in a society. As much as the naturalistic humanitarian might protest, extension of physical life is not the ultimate value.[131]

Gordon Clark, another Christian ethicist, expresses a similarly glib attitude toward the value of human life: "Do you prefer 10,000 murders to save one innocent man rather than one tragedy to save 5000 lives?"[132] Charles goes one step further: "Innocent deaths resulting from released or paroled criminals are *infinitely* more common than the potentially innocent person on death row."[133] But how often unjust executions occur is not the primary issue. That they occur at all is proof enough that human judgment is too uncertain to lay claim to absolute authority over life and death. The door should always be left open for judicial review and for new evidence.

Another way in which the innocent are harmed by the death penalty is through the brutalization of those required to supervise and

---

130. See Redekop, "An Analysis of Capital Punishment," 14-15.

131. McQuilkin, *An Introduction to Biblical Ethics,* 367.

132. Clark, "Capital Punishment," *BDCE,* 84. So too Charles, "Outrageous Atrocity or Moral Imperative?" 13.

133. Charles, "Crime, the Christian, and Capital Justice," 438n.30 (emphasis mine).

carry out executions. These people must forcibly suppress in themselves that very impulse toward the nurture and preservation of human life that criminals are put to death for having repressed in themselves. Those who cry out for the blood of murderers have usually never seen an execution, nor are they required to take part in its performance (unlike stoning in biblical times). When arguing about the rights and wrongs of capital punishment in abstract terms, it should never be forgotten that execution entails the deliberate, carefully planned, premeditated killing of another human being. It is the cold-blooded extinguishing of someone's life because that person is deemed to be no longer worthy of life — and that process dehumanizes all who take part.

To begin with, there are few "clean" methods of execution; the idea of a humane execution is a fantasy.[134] Hanging can easily be botched, with the victim slowly choking to death (in some recorded cases, taking up to fifteen minutes to die). Firing squads do not necessarily kill instantly. To avoid a sense of responsibility, the marksmen sometimes "cheat" by aiming away from the heart, with the result that the victim slowly bleeds to death. In 1977, Gary Gilmour was executed by firing squad. All four bullets pierced his heart. Yet it still took two minutes for him to die. Victims of the electric chair have been known to require several repeated charges of electricity to finally kill them. The gas chamber often results in slow, agonizing asphyxiation. Even use of lethal injections is not foolproof. In the execution of Stephen Morin in Texas on March 13, 1985, it took forty minutes for doctors to find a vein strong enough to take a catheter.[135]

Those who have had to supervise or carry out executions often speak of its devastating impact on them, and frequently come to oppose capital punishment in principle. One prison chaplain has said, "I would . . . invite anyone who talks about the death penalty as an abstraction, as something they'd like for society, to witness an execution. It is a horrific experience."[136] Preparations for execution sometimes have bizarre and chilling dimensions. Another chaplain tells of how one man was awakened at 3:30 A.M. by prison officers who shaved his head and spent an hour gently massaging conducting gel into his head

---

134. See Gray and Stanley, *A Punishment in Search of a Crime*, 19-46.
135. Gray and Stanley, *A Punishment in Search of a Crime*, 52-53.
136. Quoted in Gray and Stanley, *A Punishment in Search of a Crime*, 150.

and calf to prepare him for electrocution.[137] Of course, such stories could be countered by equally gruesome stories of the suffering mercilessly inflicted by murderers on their victims. But two wrongs do not make a right. The callousness of the crime is in no way altered by the callousness of execution; there is simply an increase in the amount of callousness that society suffers. And it reverses the direction of clear New Testament counsel: "Do not be overcome by evil, but overcome evil with good" (Rom. 12:21; cf. 1 Thess. 5:15; 1 Pet. 3:9).

Summary

In this chapter I have reviewed and critiqued the biblical and the moral arguments that are used by Christian advocates of the death penalty. Their case rests on a particular exegesis of key biblical texts describing capital punishment; it is reinforced by a hermeneutical stance that stresses the essential continuity of Old and New Testament teaching; it is informed significantly by the theological paradigm of God as Lawgiver and Enforcer; and it appeals to a range of ethical and pragmatic arguments that defend the essential justness of capital retribution and stress the beneficial effects on society, and even on the spiritual welfare of the condemned person,[138] of requiring a life for a life. Some of these writers are scathing toward opponents of the death penalty. "Contemporary efforts to abolish capital punishment," Clark insists, "proceed on a non-Christian view of man, a secular theory of criminal law, and a low estimate of the value of human life."[139] Charles similarly urges that opposition to the death penalty by all major Christian and Jewish groups in America "points to the near wholesale incorporation of secular ethical assumptions by American 'religious' into mainline American religious belief."[140] For Connery too, "the choice rests between the values represented by a secular theory of criminality and those enshrined

---

137. Gray and Stanley, *A Punishment in Search of a Crime*, 84-85.

138. McQuilkin comments, "How many people are privileged to know in advance the time of death and so to prepare? The criminal on death row has an uncommon opportunity to repent and prepare for his eternal dwelling place" (*An Introduction to Biblical Ethics*, 366).

139. Clark, "Capital Punishment," 84.

140. Charles, "Crime, the Christian, and Capital Justice," 432-33.

in biblical law." To oppose capital punishment is to claim that "the relevant biblical teaching is in fact fallacious" — an attitude that will soon lead to a denial of "the truth or validity of any or all parts of scripture at will."[141] In Charles's judgment, abolitionism rests on nothing less than "a fundamental misunderstanding of the holiness, righteousness and justice of God."[142]

Historically, and still so in America, it is such a mind-set among conservative Christians that has helped ensure the survival of capital punishment. It has always been those whose faith is most traditional, whose exegesis is most literal, whose reliance on the Old Testament is most pronounced, and whose identification with the political status quo is most obvious who have been most punitive in their understanding of justice. For such people, the Bible does not merely permit capital punishment; it enjoins it as a moral necessity.[143] But one wonders what has become in all of this of the redemptive concerns of the Christian gospel, a gospel that proclaims God's saving justice toward all, even the worst of criminal offenders, even those who murdered Jesus Christ (Luke 23:34), the image-bearer of God par excellence (2 Cor. 4:4; Col. 1:15; Heb. 1:3). Capital punishment is incompatible with a gospel of redemption and reconciliation. This is not to deny the seriousness of sin, or the moral repugnance of homicide, or the culpability of criminals, or the validity of penal sanctions as such. But, as John Redekop observes, the moral order of God's universe is grounded in and preserved by something more profound than the need to balance rewards and punishments on earth: "As recipients of boundless divine mercy Christians, of all people, should be 'the last ones' to clamor for justice, to press for a 'just death.'"[144]

Put positively, Christians should be the first to clamor for true justice, for redemptive justice, a justice that fosters healing and renewal, a justice informed by the spirit of Christ and not the letter of the law. Restorative justice cannot, of course, restore the life and relationships of murder victims. But nor can retributive capital justice, for only God can restore life to the dead. Restorative justice can, however, strive to

141. Connery, "Capital Punishment," 51.
142. Charles, "Crime, the Christian, and Capital Justice," 439n.36
143. So Potter, "The Special Relationship," 228.
144. Redekop, "An Analysis of Capital Punishment," 16-17.

bring as much good out of evil as possible. It can seek to bind up the brokenhearted and to work for the redemption of those who broke their hearts. It can seek to overcome evil with good.

CHAPTER 6

CONCLUSION

Forgiveness as the Consummation of Justice

O n December 14, 1993, two five-year-old Tongan children were killed by a hit-and-run driver on their way home from school in Mangere, South Auckland. It was several days before the unlicensed driver responsible, Filipo Tato, a young Samoan man, gave himself up to police. It was widely expected that the tragedy would provoke outbursts of violence between the Tongan and Samoan communities in the city, as had occurred in the past. But in an act that stunned the nation, the families of the two dead children chose the way of forgiveness and reconciliation. The offender appeared in court for sentencing wearing a red scarf. When a junior legal counsel suggested such attire was not appropriate, Tato responded, "It was given to me by the families of the two boys as a symbol of the blood of Christ representing his forgiveness." After his conviction, the families of the victims publicly forgave and embraced Tato in what one media commentator described as "an act of mercy and genuine Christian charity that dumbfounded revenge-seekers and upset conventional notions of justice and punishment."[1] The grandfather of one of the boys killed explained how the families came to choose forgiveness:

> Now it might seem to some people that the forgiveness we offered may indicate that we are not grieving. It's actually the very depth of our

---

1. F. McDonald, "When Forgiveness Is Not Enough," *New Zealand Listener,* 26 March 1994, 20.

grief that said to us, "Hey, listen, there's only one way out of this, and that's to offer forgiveness." In the very depth of our grief we couldn't see any other way out. To ask for revenge, to get the person responsible imprisoned for life, I don't think would have touched the heart of the matter.[2]

Conventional justice still ran its course, and the young Samoan was imprisoned. Forgiveness, the court deemed, was not enough. Justice had to be done, and seen to be done. But for all those directly involved, it was the act of forgiveness, not the punishment of imprisonment, that was the better justice in this tragic episode. It was forgiveness that brought good out of evil, that offered the hope of healing to the family of the victims and deliverance from the destructive power of guilt to the offender. In this concluding chapter I want to reflect further on the practical meaning and dynamics of forgiveness, since in the New Testament forgiveness, more than anything else, lies at the heart of what it means practically to imitate or be conformed to the way of Christ. Before doing so, however, I will summarize the results of the investigation thus far and comment briefly on the place of imitation in New Testament ethics.

Summary of Findings

Our investigation commenced with the observation that at first glance the New Testament has little to say about criminal justice issues. There is no corpus of criminal laws in the New Testament comparable to that of the Old Testament, and the New Testament authors seem more interested in questions of sin and salvation than crime and punishment. In the course of our study, however, that judgment has required modification in several respects. To begin with, we found a great deal of incidental material in the New Testament on all the major elements of the criminal justice system — laws, courts, crimes, criminals, police, prisons, and punishments. This material, notwithstanding its tangential nature, granted us fascinating insight into early Christian attitudes toward and experience of first-century Jewish and Roman penal justice systems (Chapter 1).

2. Cited in McDonald, "When Forgiveness Is Not Enough," 22.

We then turned to consider what the New Testament has to say about the justice of God, suggesting that this provides an important context for approaching criminal justice questions (Chapter 2). I argued that both Paul, who makes extensive use of justice/righteousness categories, especially in Romans, and Jesus, whose proclamation of the kingdom of God was essentially an announcement of the advent on earth of God's eschatological justice, stood firmly in the Old Testament-Jewish justice tradition. This tradition understood divine justice principally in terms of God's redemptive power intervening in situations of suffering and need to deliver the oppressed, thereby displaying the honor of God's name as a faithful, covenant-keeping God. The accent was on God's justice as a redemptive and reconstructive action more than a retributive or punitive one. Paul finds the supreme testimony to such justice in the death and resurrection of Christ; the Gospel writers find it also displayed in the life, ministry, and teaching of Jesus.

In light of these findings, the question arose of what place punishment has in the operation of restorative justice. Such a question cannot be avoided, not least because the same Scriptures that celebrate God's redeeming justice also record God's punitive intervention in response to human sin and wrongdoing. In attempting to answer this question, we first of all reviewed the extended debate in criminological thought over the purpose and morality of punishment (Chapter 3). We found that all the major theories of punishment which have enjoyed currency at some stage in recent history — the reformative, deterrent, and retributivist theories — have important insights to offer, but that the social institution of punishment is best understood and most readily justified in ethical terms when it serves the goal of restoration. Some of the insights of Walter Moberly's symbolic theory of punishment allowed us to penetrate more deeply into how criminal punishment can serve a restorative purpose. Punishment may be understood as a powerful symbol of the moral nature of crime and its entail, and of the need for annulment or renewal on the part of the offender.

We pursued the question further by next examining what the New Testament has to say about punishment (Chapter 4). It is impossible to escape the conclusion that punishment plays a significant role in the outworking of God's justice in the New Testament, even though the language of punishment is strikingly confined. There is evidence of disciplinary penalties being imposed on wrongdoers within the early

Christian communities, an endorsement of the role of the state in reprimanding criminal activities, a preparedness to discern the wrath of God at work in the misfortunes and calamities that accompany human sinfulness, and a repeated emphasis on the ultimate day of judgment, when "there will be anguish and distress for everyone who does evil" (Rom. 2:9). This body of material could easily be used to justify notions of retributive justice in human affairs. But we found, to the contrary, that the punishments imposed by God or by the community of faith nearly always have a redemptive intent, not always with respect to the individual punished, though this is common, but certainly with respect to the wider community, which is called to repentance and reformation in light of divine discipline. God's judgment on sin is everywhere affirmed, but this theme is not best understood in narrowly retributive terms. As part of the warp and woof of historical experience, divine wrath predominantly carries a remedial or reformative purpose; as part of the eschatological consummation, it is more a matter of recalcitrants choosing their own fate than of a secondary imposition of punitive retribution by God.

Finally, we considered the biblical, theological, and moral arguments commonly used to defend capital punishment as a divinely intended and inalienable feature of civil justice (Chapter 5). Christian interpreters who support the death penalty in the contemporary penal justice system point to the sheer weight of biblical data affirming its use, together with the alleged silence of the New Testament in challenging its legitimacy. In reply I argued that while the New Testament presupposes the use of capital punishment in its current social setting, and endorses the police powers of the state in controlling criminality, it also raises a fundamental challenge to the appropriateness of execution in the Christian era. The expiatory function of capital punishment in the Old Testament is fulfilled and superseded by the atoning death of Jesus; the judicial principle of the *lex talionis,* under which the death penalty functioned in Israel, is rendered redundant by the teaching of Jesus; and the legislative procedures that permitted execution of sinners are transcended by the example of Jesus, who refused to condemn to death the woman taken in adultery but instead forgave her and set her on the road to restoration.

In sum, there are powerful grounds for concluding that the New Testament does indeed offer us a vision of restorative justice. It deals not in the primary instance with an abstract cosmic order that needs to be upheld but with the world of persons in relation to one another and to God. In such a world, justice can be fully attained and God's righteousness vindicated not by the mere restraint and punishment of evil, which is the goal of retributive justice, but, as G. H. C. MacGregor puts it, they can be achieved "only by making evil persons see the sinfulness of their ways, through the employment of a redemptive method which will change the evil will, and restore right personal relationships, 'so making peace' (Col 1:20)."[3] In fact, we would arrive at the same conclusion even if we assumed that the purpose of justice is to affirm the moral order God has created. For according to the witness of the New Testament, the basic principle of the moral order is not the perfect balance of deed and desert but redeeming, merciful love. Consequently, only those social and criminal sanctions that are not merely punitive but redemptive or restorative in design are capable of demonstrating or affirming what actually is, what the world, from God's perspective, is really like.[4] Retributive justice seeks to check and punish evil; the justice commended in the New Testament is empowered with self-giving, long-suffering, redemptive love that seeks to overcome evil with good, to repair the damage done by sin, and to restore peace to human relationships.

Imitatio Christi — Imitatio Dei

At several points in our investigation, we have witnessed how at the root of biblical ethics lies the conviction that the standard for human

3. MacGregor, *The New Testament Basis of Pacifism* (London: Fellowship of Reconciliation, 1953), 68.

4. Stanley Hauerwas and William Willimon offer this perceptive insight. "We can only act within that world which we see. So the primary ethical question is not, What ought I now do? but rather, How does the world really look? The most interesting question about the Sermon [on the Mount] is not, Is this really a practical way to live in the world? but rather, Is this really the way the world is? What is 'practical' is related to what is real. If the world is a society in which only the strong, the independent, the detached, the liberated, and the successful are blessed, then we act accordingly. However, if the world is really a place where God blesses the poor, the hungry, and the persecuted for righteousness' sake, then we must act in accordance with reality or else appear bafflingly out of step with the way things are." See *Resident Aliens: Life in the Christian Colony* (Nashville: Abingdon Press, 1989), 88.

conduct is nothing less than the character and activity of God. "You shall be holy, for I am holy" (Lev. 11:45). It is God's own self who models and gives content to those qualities of character and conduct that are ethically most important for God's people, such as holiness, love, justice, mercy, and compassion (Mic. 6:8).[5] In Old Testament law, this finds expression in the so-called motive clause, wherein particular moral demands are predicated on a reminder of the gracious saving deeds of God.[6] In the New Testament, the imitation of God centers specifically on the imitation of Christ. The divine action we are called to mirror has already been mirrored for us in the person and actions of Jesus.[7] Because Jesus personally incarnates the moral and political message he proclaims about the inbreaking of God's justice, simply to hear the story of Jesus is already to receive moral instruction, while to emulate the example of Jesus is to imitate God.

The New Testament writers make this point in various ways. In Matthew's Gospel, for instance, there are only two verses where the word "perfect" occurs — once in a saying of Jesus calling his hearers to "be perfect . . . as your heavenly Father is perfect" (5:48), and once in a call to discipleship: "If you wish to be perfect, . . . come, follow me" (19:21). Matthew's point in this is obvious: *following Jesus is the way to become like God.* "Rather than leaving the imitation of God to the speculations of believers," John Haughey comments, "Jesus becomes the flesh and blood embodiment of the perfections of God, according to Matthew."[8] Paul too repeatedly summons his readers to imitate himself as he imitates the Lord,[9] while the author of 1 Peter reminds his audience that "Christ also suffered for you, leaving you an example, so that you should follow in his steps" (1 Pet. 2:21). For the New Testament writers,

5. See B. C. Birch, "Moral Agency, Community, and the Character of God in the Hebrew Bible," *Semeia* 66 (1995): 23-41 (esp. 29-33).

6. See especially Deuteronomy 12–28 and Leviticus 17–26. The Decalogue begins with a reminder of God's act of liberation (Deut. 5:15).

7. J. P. Meier, "Matthew 5:3-12," *Interpretation* 43, no. 3 (1990): 285; W. D. Davies and D. C. Allison, "Reflections on the Sermon on the Mount," *SJT* 44, no. 3 (1991): 309.

8. Haughey, "Jesus as the Justice of God," in *The Faith That Does Justice: Examining the Christian Sources for Social Change,* ed. J. C. Haughey (New York: Paulist Press, 1977), 279.

9. 1 Cor. 11:1; 2 Cor. 8:9; 1 Thess. 1:2-6; 2 Thess. 3:7-9; Phil. 2:5-11; 3:17 — cf. Eph. 4:32.

then, as James Gustafson points out, "the person of Jesus Christ is the paradigm for the life of the Christian community, and of individual members of the community."[10]

This *imitatio Christi — imitatio Dei* theme is not a simple mimicry of the externals of Jesus' life, nor is it an invitation to share in all the facets of divine activity in the world. As Stanley Hauerwas puts it, "We are called upon to be *like* Jesus, not to be Jesus."[11] Significantly for us, there is one dimension of God's action that believers are expressly *forbidden* to imitate — namely, God's role as avenger and judge.[12] While the New Testament affirms that God exercises wrath against evil and injustice in the world, and uses human agents to do so (Rom. 13:4; 1 Pet. 2:14), nowhere are Christians bidden to offer themselves as agents of divine punishment, even if the saints may exercise some ruling function after eschatological judgment (Matt. 19:28; 1 Cor. 6:2). In situations of intense suffering, the early Christians sometimes prayed, in apocalyptic idiom, for God to speed vindicating vengeance upon their oppressors.[13] But even here there is no hint of Christians ever believing that it was their role to take divine retribution into their own hands or that they considered God's coming judgment on evildoers to be paradigmatic for Christian action in prior history.[14] Definitive judgment on human evil is reserved for the returning Christ, for he alone has adequate knowledge and wisdom to do justice to sin.[15] Only his dealing with sinners can be sufficiently loving to qualify as true justice.[16]

On the other hand, believers are repeatedly called to imitate God's forgiving mercy and saving justice as manifested in Christ. They are to

10. Gustafson, "The Relation of the Gospels to the Moral Life," in *Jesus and Man's Hope,* ed. D. G. Miller and D. Y. Hadidan (Pittsburgh: Pittsburgh Theological Seminary, 1971), 2:110.

11. Hauerwas, *The Peaceable Kingdom* (London: SCM, 1983), 76.

12. Matt. 7:1; Luke 6:37; Rom. 14:3, 10, 13; 1 Cor. 4:3-5; Rom. 12:19; 1 Thess. 4:6; Heb. 10:30; Rev. 6:10; cf. Acts 7:24.

13. So, e.g., 2 Thess. 1:5-11; Rev. 6:10-11; 11:18; 18:6-10 etc. — cf. 2 Pet. 2:4-9; Jude 7.

14. A. Collins believes that the violent imagery of the book of Revelation "is apparently intended to release aggressive feelings in a harmless way," though she goes on to criticize John's strategy for dealing with violence, A. Collins, *Crisis and Catharsis: The Power of the Apocalypse* (Philadelphia: Westminster, 1984), 171.

15. On the inherent limitations of human justice, see W. Moberly, *The Ethics of Punishment* (London: Faber & Faber, 1968), 151-85.

16. Cf. MacGregor, *The New Testament Basis of Pacifism,* 62.

be merciful (Matt. 5:7), for God desires mercy, not sacrifice (Matt. 9:13; 12:7; Luke 10:37). They are to be peacemakers, for God is a peacemaker (Matt. 5:9; Rom. 5:8; 16:20; Eph. 2:14-22). They are to serve one another, "for the Son of Man came not to be served but to serve, and to give his life a ransom for many" (Mark 10:45). They are to love their enemies and pray for their persecutors, for their Father in heaven "is kind to the ungrateful and the wicked" (Luke 6:35) and "makes his sun rise on the evil and on the good and sends rain on the righteous and on the unrighteous" (Matt. 5:45). They are to forgive, as their heavenly father has forgiven them (Matt. 6:14), to be forbearing, kind, and tenderhearted to one another, as God in Christ has been toward them (Eph. 4:32; Col. 3:13). They are to be generous to the needy, just as Jesus Christ, though rich, became poor so that by his poverty others might become rich (2 Cor. 8:9; Phil. 2:5-11). They are to endure hostility without retaliation (1 Pet. 2:21; Heb. 12:3), to live as those who are "always being given up to death for Jesus' sake" (2 Cor. 4:10-11; Gal. 6:17). Christians are to "live in love, as Christ loved us and gave himself up for us" (Eph. 5:2; cf. John 13:34; 1 John 2:7; 3:11). In all these respects, they are to "grow up in every way into him who is the head, into Christ" (Eph. 4:15).

Such a concern to imitate and extend Christ's transformative, healing justice to those in need should shape and guide Christian involvement in and evaluation of the criminal justice system. Such concern should extend equally to the victims of crime, as the parable of the Good Samaritan illustrates (Luke 10:29-37), and to the perpetrators of crime, as Jesus' word of forgiveness to his executioners (Luke 23:34) and his fellow crucifixion victim (Luke 23:43) shows. Here, just as at the beginning of the human story, empathy is expressed for both victim (Gen. 4:10) and offender (Gen. 4:15). There are enough people in society calling for greater and greater punishment as the solution to rising crime. Followers of Jesus should be calling for more and more redemptive imagination on the part of the criminal justice system. Among other things, that means taking more seriously the role of forgiveness in the realization of justice. As we saw in Chapter 2, forgiveness belongs to the very character of Christian life and experience. It is decisively displayed and most fully known in the life, death, and resurrection of Jesus. Forgiveness is of the essence of life in God and a life patterned after God, and is therefore a matter about which Christians have something special to say. Yet forgiveness is also something common to human experience in general, accessible to different traditions and indispensable to the proper functioning of all human relationships, whether they are of a personal, social, or political nature.[17] To conclude this study, then, I want to offer some analytical and practical reflections on the hard work of forgiveness, which is the goal and culmination of the justice that heals.

The Nature and Task of Forgiveness

"To err is human, to forgive divine." This familiar proverb is often used by people to excuse themselves from the hard work of forgiveness. Only God can forgive, they reason; it is beyond the capacity of ordinary mortals to rise above their pain and bitterness to confer forgiveness on their abusers. But Christian commitment permits no such rationalization. The entire Christian message centers on forgiveness, which it views as both gift and demand. God's *offer* of forgiveness to sinners, and God's *demand* that those who receive this gift practice forgiveness in their relationships with others, are inseparably connected. Jesus articulates this forgiveness equation most succinctly: "Forgive, and you will be forgiven" (Luke 6:37). But, he cautions, "if you do not forgive others, neither will your Father forgive your trespasses" (Matt. 6:15; cf. Mark 11:25). It is because of this interdependence between God's gift of salvation and the activity of forgiveness, and also because of the sheer struggle involved to make it work in practice, that one can fairly say that forgiveness is "the demand of the Gospel that pinches the hardest."[18]

What Is Forgiveness?

Forgiveness is not a simple or univocal concept. There are many different expressions and degrees of forgiveness, depending on individual

17. On the relationship between Christian forgiveness and forgiveness found outside Christian contexts, see L. G. Jones, *Embodying Forgiveness: A Theological Analysis* (Grand Rapids: William B. Eerdmans, 1995), 210-25.

18. J. Peters, "The Function of Forgiveness in Social Relationships," in *Forgiveness,* ed. C. Floristán and C. Duquoc, Concilium 177 (Edinburgh: T. & T. Clark, 1986), 8.

circumstances and the nature of the harm suffered.[19] It is a very different matter, for example, to say "forgive me" when you belch at the dinner table than to say it to someone you have hurt in a very serious way. Forgiving a debt is different from forgiving a crime. Forgiving a child for being naughty is different from forgiving a nation for perpetrating genocide. Thus the force and implications of forgiveness vary significantly from situation to situation. Yet it is still possible to identify certain generic features of forgiveness, which the following definition seeks to capture:

> Forgiveness is what happens when the victim of some hurtful action freely chooses to release the perpetrator of that action from the bondage of guilt, gives up his or her own feelings of ill will, and surrenders any attempt to hurt or damage the perpetrator in return, thus clearing the way for reconciliation and restoration of relationship.

There are five key components to this definition. First, *forgiveness is the response of victims.* Only victims have the right to confer forgiveness on their abusers. I cannot forgive you for what you did to another person; only the person you hurt has that right. This applies even to divine forgiveness. God's "right" to forgive us stems from the fact that God is the ultimate victim of human wrongdoing, the one hurt by human unfaithfulness and sin. This is demonstrated supremely by the cross. In the crucifixion of Jesus, God becomes the innocent victim of human cruelty and abuse, yet chooses freely to forgive those who crushed him (Luke 23:4, 14, 22, 34, 47). Forgiveness, then, is "rooted in the truth of the victim," as Christian Duquoc puts it[20] — which is why offenders often find it so difficult to ask for forgiveness. It requires them to face the truth of what they have done to hurt someone else. Even the most hardened of offenders can find it deeply disturbing to confront their victim and witness firsthand the human consequences of their actions.

This is not to say that forgiveness is an entirely private exchange between two parties alone. Some aspects of forgiveness can be shown to offenders by nonvictims, even if the full experience of pardon cannot. As a nonvictim, I can choose not to allow your offense against someone

---

19. Cf. D. W. Augsburger, *Helping People Forgive* (Louisville, Ky.: Westminster John Knox, 1996), 17-24.

20. Duquoc, "The Forgiveness of God," in *Forgiveness,* 42-43.

else to affect your relationship with me or to make me think worse of you, and in that sense I exhibit a forgiving attitude toward you. But I cannot release you from the effects of your actions on your relationship with the victim. Only the victim can do that. It is also worth noting that there are different degrees of victimization. The most direct experience of forgiveness takes place in the interaction between the offender and the *primary victim,* the person who has actually suffered the injury directly. But those close to the victim, her friends and loved ones, also suffer hurt. They have their own feelings of betrayal, resentment, anger, hatred, and revenge. Insofar as these painful feelings have been forced on them by the offender, they too are victims. As *secondary victims,* they also have issues of forgiveness to confront. In addition, the suffering caused by an offense — especially an unresolved offense — can sometimes have an enduring intergenerational impact. The immediate victim and/or the actual offender may be long dead, but the injustice or bitterness created by the offense might still be felt by later generations. They are *subsequent victims* of the offender, who may also need to find a place of release from their pain through forgiving the absent offender (perhaps represented by his or her contemporary offspring). This has particular relevance to dealing with the legacy of military or political or ethnic grievances from the past.

Second, *forgiveness is something freely given to the perpetrator.* The derivation of "for-give" is revealing in this respect. Forgiveness is a "gift for" someone else, the guilty party, a gift of release from the burden of guilt and its destructive consequences in the offender's own life. The power of forgiveness comes from its gratuitous nature. It is freely given, an act of generosity. It is not deserved. It cannot be purchased or exchanged for some other benefit. It comes as a free offering on the part of the victim. If the wrongdoer is to benefit from this gift, he or she must know that it is being offered. Some audible word or visible action must come from the victim to "perform" the act of release. Of course, genuine forgiveness is more than a mere word that is spoken, a gesture that is made, or a feeling that is felt. It is an act of personal encounter, an affair of the heart, an enduring orientation of life.[21] But it frequently depends on words or actions (like weeping or embracing) to become effective. Usually the offender must confess his or her wrongful actions in words,

21. On forgiveness as a way of life, see Jones, *Embodying Forgiveness.*

and the victim must declare a word of release. Whether this statement of remission is uttered at the outset of the encounter between victim and victimizer as a statement of intention, at the end of the encounter as an act of closure, or is postponed indefinitely will depend on the circumstances of the offense, the balance of power between the parties, and the personalities of those involved.

Third, *forgiveness is also release for the victim.* It is not only for the good of the offender that forgiveness is necessary; it is also for the benefit of the person offended against. To suffer hurt, to be the victim of some conscious malice or violation by another person, can have a profound impact on the person's sense of self-worth and psychological well-being. The deeper the injury or the more violent the transgression, the greater the impact. Victims can feel debased, dishonored, disrespected, or shamed. They may become irritable or depressed, even suicidal. They may find their freedom constricted by fears and anxieties, by anger and bitterness, by hatred and resentment, not only for the offender but also for themselves. Self-loathing and self-blaming are a common legacy of victimization. The pain of the offense or the person of the offender thus comes to exercise power over the victim's entire life. As Virgil Elizondo puts it, "The greatest damage of an offence — often greater than the offence itself — is that it destroys my freedom to be me, for I will find myself involuntarily dominated by the inner rage and resentment — a type of spiritual poison which permeates throughout all my being — which will be a subconscious but very powerful influence in most of my life."[22] The act of forgiveness brings liberation from that power. As Howard Zehr explains,

> Forgiveness is letting go of the power the offense and the offender have over a person. It means no longer letting that offense and offender dominate. Without this experience of forgiveness, without this closure, the wound festers, the violation takes over our consciousness, our lives. It, and the offender, are in control. Real forgiveness, then, is an act of empowerment and healing. It allows one to move from victim to survivor.[23]

22. Elizondo, "I Forgive But I Do Not Forget," in *Forgiveness,* 70.
23. Zehr, *Changing Lenses: A New Focus for Crime and Justice* (Scottdale, Pa.: Herald Press, 1990), 47.

Forgiveness, in fact, is the *only* thing capable of releasing victims from the prison house of their pain, fear, and negative feelings. Forgiveness is therefore immensely powerful. Nothing else has the specific power of forgiveness to "free the future from the haunting legacies of the past."[24]

Forgiveness is also immensely creative. This leads to the fourth component of our definition: *forgiveness does not repay in kind.* In this sense forgiveness is not instinctive or "natural." When we are hurt, our immediate instinct is to hit back, to retaliate blow for blow, loss for loss, or to seek the legal punishment (i.e., the legitimate suffering) of the offender, pain for pain. We feel that the most effective way to appease the hurt of the offense is to inflict equal suffering in return. But in reality the "payback" instinct manifests the most terrifying characteristic of evil, its pernicious power to turn those who are sinned against into sinners in their own right, to suck the innocent into a pattern of imitative behavior that brings its own guilt. When an individual is hurt or abused, he or she is sinned against. The abuser perpetrates moral evil in robbing another of her peace and freedom, of his dignity or innocence; the victim suffers the physical evil of such loss.[25] But when, in response, the one sinned against dedicates his energies to securing the destruction or suffering of the offender, he too becomes a sinner. He emulates his abuser; he sins against another. As David Augsburger explains, "Rage responds to rage, evil demands repayment with evil, resentment replies to hostility, violence answers violence. All are locked into mimesis. The first blow is despicable, the second predictable as a counterblow, the third inescapable, and once the cycle of violence is established, the issue of who made the first move becomes moot."[26] Moreover, the payback mechanism ultimately cheats and deceives the victim (cf. Rom. 7:11). Retaliation promises satisfaction, a discharging of the burden of pain and resentment. But it fails to deliver real freedom, for even when the victim has hurt the offender, he or she is still cursed with the memory of the offense, which still brings feelings of anger and disgust. So evil multiplies. The victim is converted into an

---

24. G. Müller-Fahrenholz, *The Art of Forgiveness: Theological Reflections on Healing and Reconciliation* (Geneva: WCC Publications, 1997), 5.

25. For the distinction between moral and physical evil, see J. Sobrino, "Latin America: Place of Sin and Place of Forgiveness," in *Forgiveness*, 50.

26. Augsburger, *Helping People Forgive*, 141.

offender and the offender into a victim, a transposition often justified, ironically, in the name of doing justice.

To forgive is to transcend this instinct to hit back, to surrender one's right to exact payment in kind from the offender. It is a preparedness to absorb the pain of victimization without seeking to hurt in return as a way of getting even. This means that to forgive is a creative act of love. It is creative in that it acts in a way that is not dictated by the sinful action of another. Forgiveness is a response to pain that does not merely *re-act*, but *acts anew*. It acts unexpectedly, innovatively, creatively, unconditioned by the evil deed that provoked it. It breaks free from logic of equivalence; it interrupts the cycle of violence; it arrests the consequences of evil and starts afresh. As Duquoc puts it,

> Eye for eye is reassuring because the response is predetermined — but if we reject equivalence, if we decide that one particular eye is never worth another particular eye and that the damage inflicted on another never compensates for the loss suffered by the first, that there will be only an accumulation of evils, we have to create an attitude not determined by any rule, we have to be imaginative or creative. . . . The believer imitates the creative God when he exorcises the demands of legal justice and works at a new relationship with the one he has forgiven. This is the way in which forgiveness transforms human relationships and so possesses a capacity to reveal the original face of God.[27]

As well as being creative, forgiveness is a labor of love, a difficult form of love, a love even for one's enemy. It is motivated by a redemptive concern for the offender. In the belief that "love is as strong as death" (Song of Sol. 8:6), the victim offers the person who hurt her a chance to be free, to start again, to make amends, to escape the bondage of guilt. Such is the magnanimity — and the sheer magnitude — of forgiveness.

Finally, *forgiveness is fulfilled in reconciliation*. The goal of all love is to establish communion between persons, to bring people into open, trusting relationship. This is also true of forgiveness. The desire that leads to seeking or offering forgiveness is often a desire for the healing of the ruptured relationship. Even when there has been no conscious relationship between offender and victim prior to the offense, the crime itself has created a relationship, one that is ruptured at its very inception. This rela-

---

27. Duquoc, "The Forgiveness of God," 41.

tionship cannot be unmade by refusing to accept that it exists. It does exist, no matter how arbitary or uninvited its origins, and its distorted character needs to be addressed. Forgiveness deals with this distortion and clears the way for the recovery or repair of the relationship. Reconciliation thus represents the culmination of the forgiveness process.

Of course, sometimes reconciliation will not be possible. One such situation is that in which the offender refuses to acknowledge the harm he or she has done or seeks pardon. In the absence of repentance, the victim may still unilaterally choose to forgive the perpetrator, in the sense of letting go of his or her own feelings of resentment and renouncing the desire for revenge, perhaps even offering the offender a remission of guilt (cf. Luke 23:34). But reconciliation can occur only where both parties accept each other and commit themselves to a new relationship. One party may take the initiative and be more active in the cause, but ultimately both must cooperate if the relationship is to be renewed. Another instance is that in which the offender is dead or cannot be located. For example, one may unilaterally forgive an abusive parent after he or she has died, but full reconciliation with the person is not possible in this life. But where the potential for reconciliation does exist, forgiveness is the means to that end; it is a way of "regaining a brother or sister" (Matt. 5:23-24; 18:15) from their previous persona of offender or abuser or enemy.

At this point it is important to clarify that reconciliation never means going back to exactly the same relationship that existed before the offense, as though nothing has happened. The relationship between victim and offender is inevitably changed by what has transpired between them. Both parties have become different people through the experience of injury, guilt, shame, repentance, and forgiveness. Their relationship is not so much restored as renewed or renegotiated. It is not returned to its *original* condition but brought to a *healthier* condition. Sometimes the relationship will be stronger, closer, more fulfilling than before. New levels of intimacy and friendship may emerge. Often, however, the intimacy and trust of earlier times will not be recovered; the relationship will assume a more distant or formal character. But it will still be a healthier relationship than before because the bitterness and distrust or the imbalance of power that crippled the former relationship will have been dealt with and a more appropriate relationship between the parties established.

What Forgiveness Is Not

Another way to grasp the generic qualities of forgiveness is to clarify what it is not. One thing it is not, as we have seen, is instinctive or natural. It goes against the grain of human nature. This is why we find lots of reasons not to forgive. Often we do so by confusing forgiveness with other, more negative qualities, such as weakness or injustice.

But *forgiveness is not weakness*. It is not a sign of impotence.[28] It is not a refusal to stand up for one's legitimate rights, nor a passive acquiescence to abuse, nor a willingness to be walked all over for the sake of harmony. Forgiveness is not an act of cowardice. It is much easier to hate or retaliate than it is to forgive or be reconciled. Forgiveness requires immense strength and immense courage — strength to rise above the desire to strike back, and courage to expose oneself to the risk of further rejection and pain. Nor is forgiveness a supercilious gesture that aims to reduce the offender to a condition of weakness or dependence. Some have questioned the ethics of forgiveness on the grounds that it is a manipulative or subtle way of imposing a state of moral inferiority and indebtedness on another person. But this objection rests on the assumption that individuals ought to be autonomous and self-sufficient beings, never standing in need of charity, always able to deal with emotional injuries or guilt entirely on their own. But this is both alien to biblical anthropology and false to human experience.[29] As Augsburger observes, "We cannot heal ourselves; healing is either actualized, mediated, or surrogated within community. We are healed by the other; we heal each other."[30] When an injury has been done, both offender and offended *need* each other if such healing is to take place. The offender needs the offended to remit his or her guilt, accept repentance, and receive restitution. But the offended also needs the offender — to validate the injury suffered, to express her hurt and pain to, and to enable her to reclaim her dignity. True forgiveness creates not relationships of dominance and dependence but relationships of true equality, where both parties recognize their common humanity, their common

28. As Jones observes, "Forgiveness inevitably involves power and the dynamics of power relations. The granting or withholding of forgiveness entails an exercise in power" (*Embodying Forgiveness,* 148; cf. 190).

29. See further Peters, "The Function of Forgiveness in Social Relationships," 3-11.

30. Augsburger, *Helping People Forgive,* 97-98.

weakness and fallibility, their common participation in the brokenness of the human condition, where both affirm the equal value of the life and well-being of the other, where one party renounces his unjustified abuse of power over the other (expressed in the offense), and the other renounces his induced humiliation and has power restored to him. Forgiveness thus enables both parties to recover their true stature and to meet each other face to face. That is why genuine forgiveness leaves what Geiko Müller-Fahrenholz calls "an imprint of humility" on all who experience it.[31]

Second, *forgiveness is not an excusing of wrong.* To forgive wrongdoing is not the same thing as tolerating or minimizing evil, nor is it an evasion of moral responsibility or a denial of justice. The opposite is the case, for forgiveness requires mutual agreement that the deed done was morally wrong, as well as materially and emotionally hurtful, and that the wrongdoer is responsible for and remorseful about what has happened, and is committed to putting things right. Forgiveness, in other words, demands ethical seriousness. It enthrones rather than dethrones justice; it exposes rather than excuses wrong; it challenges rather than condones the actions of the perpetrator; it transforms rather than tolerates evil (Rom. 12:21).

For this reason, forgiveness need not stand in opposition to formal justice. They are different but related — and sometimes complementary — processes. Legal justice — the promulgation of laws and the prosecution and punishment of lawbreaking — operates largely at an impersonal level, as part of the social contract that binds society together. Forgiveness, on the other hand, operates at a personal, I-Thou level. It goes beyond matters of legal definition to address the relational and moral dimensions of offending. It is therefore possible for legal justice (entailing the vindication of law) and interpersonal forgiveness (entailing the remission of guilt and the healing of relationship) to work in parallel. There is much to be said for the legal system operating on an impersonal basis, not the least being its capacity to defend the innocent, control revenge, and prevent excessive punishment through carefully regulated judicial procedures. But from the perspective of restorative justice, the existing justice system can be faulted for giving too little attention to the relational dimensions of crime and its impact. Yet

31. Müller-Fahrenholz, *The Art of Forgiveness,* 37.

even the best system of restorative justice can never do the work of forgiveness. It can only seek to foster the conditions that are consistent with and supportive of the goal of relational healing. The actual work of forgiveness must remain voluntary and personal; it cannot be compelled by law or demanded by social expectation. If and when it happens, however, it represents the consummation of true justice, the putting right of what has gone wrong. Where it does not happen, justice cannot run its full course.

Third, *forgiveness is not denial.* One common strategy for dealing with profound emotional pain is to repress it, to deny that one is feeling it, to pretend that nothing serious has happened. Extended forms of denial or repression can lead to illnesses and character distortions of various kinds. But forgiveness is not a matter of denying one's pain or of redefining the offense as a nonoffense. As Zehr explains, "It does not mean saying, 'It wasn't so bad, it doesn't matter.' It was bad, it does matter, and to deny that is to devalue both the experience of suffering and the very humanity of the person responsible."[32] To forgive, by contrast, requires an honest acknowledgment that one has suffered real loss because of the action of another, and typically requires a time of grieving or mourning over what has been lost. It also means admitting the rage — even the hatred — one may feel toward the offender. In the short term, such feelings are not only understandable and excusable but reflect morally significant values about justice and accountability and one's inherent dignity and right to respect. Feelings of anger and hatred must not be denied. Taking a hint from the imprecatory psalms, Miroslav Volf suggests that articulating such feelings to God can help facilitate the emergence of forgiveness, for in doing so the victim confronts the depths of his or her own desire to injure and exclude:

> This is no mere cathartic discharge of pent up aggression before the Almighty who ought to care. Much more significantly, by placing unattended rage before God we place both our unjust enemy and our own vengeful self face to face with a God who loves and does justice. Hidden in the dark chambers of our hearts and nourished by a system of darkness, hate grows and seeks to infest everything with its hellish will to exclusion. In the light of the justice and love of God, however,

32. Zehr, *Changing Lenses*, 46-47.

hate recedes and the seed is planted for the miracle of forgiveness. Forgiveness flounders because I exclude the enemy from the community of humans even as I exclude myself from the community of sinners. But no one can be in the presence of the God of the crucified Messiah for long without overcoming this double exclusion — without transposing the enemy from the sphere of monstrous inhumanity into the sphere of shared humanity and herself from the sphere of proud innocence into the sphere of common sinfulness.[33]

At its heart, then, forgiveness is a form of "speaking the truth in love" (Eph. 4:15), not of denying the truth for fear of the pain.

Most importantly, *forgiveness is not forgetfulness.* The common advice given to squabbling children to "forgive and forget" may be viable for minor irritations. But with serious injuries it is wrong to equate forgiveness with forgetfulness or to treat them as mutually dependent. On the one hand, it is quite possible to forget without forgiving, to repress the memory of an offense as a coping strategy but not to have dealt with it properly. Perpetrators can learn to forget the wrongs they have done; victims can teach themselves not to bring traumatic events to consciousness. But forgetfulness in these cases is not a sign of forgiveness but a sign of unforgiveness. On the other hand, it is impossible to forgive while forgetting. It is precisely because an abuse is remembered, not forgotten, that forgiveness is possible. The very process of forgiveness is a kind of "memorial activity," a conscious recalling of a past hurtful event, in all its concreteness, in order to deal with it.

After forgiveness has occurred, it is true that a sort of forgetting does, and should, occur. It is a forgetting in the sense that the offense no longer dominates waking consciousness or continues to feed a festering sense of rage or bitterness. The hurt recedes into the background; its sting is drawn, and it assumes different proportions. In other words, forgiveness enables a healing of memories, which is experienced as a type of forgetting. But even here, the memory of the offense does not vanish magically into oblivion but rather is integrated into one's life experience. The memory of the violation remains, but its character changes. It no longer serves a negative, destructive purpose but comes to play a more constructive role. It becomes part of one's per-

33. Volf, *Exclusion and Embrace: A Theological Exploration of Identity, Otherness, and Reconciliation* (Nashville: Abingdon Press, 1996), 124.

sonal biography. Like a physical scar, it bears witness to one's past healing, and perhaps even to pain's ultimate defeat.[34] Such memories can also serve to sensitize victims to the sufferings of others and to keep them alert to their own capacity to hurt others as they have been hurt themselves. So it is remembering, not forgetting, that is intrinsic to forgiveness. To forgive is not to forget but to be liberated from the painful and damaging effects of the memory and to be opened to a different future than the one imposed by the injury and its impact.

Finally, *forgiveness is not automatic.* It usually does not just happen of its own accord. It is a discipline to be mastered. It is a craft to be acquired, a lifelong learning process into which we are initiated as novices and at which we improve with practice.[35] Furthermore, each situation where forgiveness operates is unique, so there is nothing mechanical or stereotyped about how forgiveness occurs. It begins with a volitional decision to choose the path of healing, but arriving at the place of forgiveness does not come quickly or easily. Forgiveness cannot simply be willed or forced or rushed into existence. It takes time for intentions, words, and feelings to converge. How much time it takes will depend on many factors, such as the magnitude of the injury, the character of the prior relationship between the parties, the level of the wrongdoer's culpability, and whether the offense was an isolated act or a recurrent phenomenon. Like grief, forgiveness is best thought of as a process more than an event, a process through which people move at their own pace and in their own way. It is therefore not possible to prescribe a single "how to" procedure that everyone should follow. There are, however,

---

34. In a powerful discussion, Volf argues that final redemption must involve not just a forgiveness of our sins but also a forgetting of them (Isa. 43:18-19, 25 — cf. 65:17; Jer. 31:34) and of the suffering and brutalities that human beings have endured (Rev. 21:4), since no theodicy is adequate to deal with the problem of evil: "For if heaven cannot rectify Auschwitz, then the memory of Auschwitz must undo the experience of heaven. Redemption will be complete only when the creation of 'all things new' is coupled with the passage of 'all things old' into the double *nihil* of nonexistence and nonremembrance" (136). The present healing of memories that flows from forgiveness can thus be seen as a limited anticipation of eschatological nonremembrance, although before the final day we must also keep alive the memory of the suffering of victims of injustice. See further *Exclusion and Embrace*, 131-40. But cf. S. Hauerwas, "Why Time Cannot and Should Not Heal the Wounds of History, but Time Has Been and Can Be Redeemed," *SJT* 53, no. 1 (2000), esp. 40-46.

35. On this, see Jones, *Embodying Forgiveness*, 225-39.

common phases or components of the forgiveness process, like the grief process, that can be named and described, even if they do not occur in a standard sequence and are not experienced in precisely the same way by everyone. Understanding these components can be helpful for people struggling to experience forgiveness.

The Dynamics of Forgiveness

In outlining the dynamics of the forgiveness process, I will assume a situation where a clear wrong has been done and where both wrongdoer and victim wish to address the resulting moral and relational damage. Of course, matters become much more complex where facts are disputed, where responsibility is ambiguous, or where the personalities involved vary in maturity or moral sensitivity (as they often do). But here I will envisage a simple scenario and adopt the victim's perspective on it because this will allow the major components of the forgiveness cycle to stand out more clearly. Let me stress again that although I present it as a linear sequence, in practice people often circle back and forth between different components of the process.

(1) *Acknowledging the situation needing forgiveness.* To forgive requires, at the outset, an honest acknowledgment that one has suffered — and is still suffering — pain because of the actions of another. There is a need to name the specific incident or incidents that have created this pain, to identify the person or persons held responsible for it, and to acknowledge the emotional withdrawal that has occurred as a consequence of it. There is also the need to be clear that the situation in question has not yet been adequately dealt with, even if previous attempts have been made to do so.

(2) *Deciding to enter the forgiveness cycle.* Forgiveness initially is an act of the will; it does not happen unless we intend it to happen. So after acknowledging the abuse suffered, we are confronted with a choice between two kinds of pain. We can choose either to continue to live with the pain of the injury and its consequences or to embrace the pain of entering the forgiveness process. It is not a choice between accepting or evading suffering but a matter of which form of suffering to embrace. The decision to choose the pain of forgiveness may be motivated by a desire to obey God, or by a longing to be free of the destructive conse-

275

quences of unforgiveness, or by a concern for reconciliation with the person who hurt us. Conversely, it may be hindered by such things as fear of the unknown, self-righteousness, pride, a strong sense of justice, or simple selfishness. But where a person overcomes such hindrances and opts for forgiveness, it begins with a commitment of the will rather than with feelings. Both head and heart must ultimately be involved, but head precedes heart. The head sets the goal; the heart brings the experienced reality.[36]

(3) *Giving voice to the pain and anger.* Forgiveness may begin with our heads, but it cannot usually transpire entirely within our minds. Because the injury suffered is not just rational or moral or material but also emotional, forgiveness requires a healing of the emotions, a releasing of pent-up negative emotional energy. For this to occur, the injured party must recall, in some detail, what victims would rather forget — the experience of violation or betrayal or disappointment — and name the emotions felt. Deliberately choosing to relive traumatic events in this way requires considerable courage. It also often requires the companionship of someone willing to listen without expressing disapproval or judgment or quibbling over details. Perseverance is also necessary, for it can take many retellings of painful experiences before the victim reaches a point where he or she is able to discharge the feelings of victimization. Like grief, forgiveness, as Augsburger points out, may entail "multiple journeys into memory to tell and retell the past," until the pain recedes, and we are ready to integrate the loss into our lives.[37]

(4) *Being open to the offender.* As well as giving expression to feelings of pain and anger, victims must also deal with and eventually change their feelings toward the person who harmed them. When we are deeply hurt by another person, we tend to view that person in a way that is shaped, if not entirely controlled, by his or her action of injuring us. Little else enters into our picture of the person responsible. Consequently, it becomes easy to hate, despise, even demonize the offender. To be ready to forgive, we need to change the way we perceive the offender, to disengage the injurer from her behavior, to change her identity from abuser to

36. On this, see R. Kraybill, "From Head to Heart: The Cycle of Reconciliation," *MCC Conciliation Quarterly,* Fall 1988, 13-15.
37. Augsburger, *Helping People Forgive,* 68-72.

valuable human being, loved by God, despite the wrong she has done, a fellow human being whom we resemble in more ways than we differ from. Two things can help this change to take place. One is humility, a recognition of our own fallibility and sinfulness, our own capacity to injure others, our own guilt for doing so many times, and our own constant need of forgiveness. This is not to excuse the offender by saying, "We all make mistakes"; it is to recognize that we are all offenders and we are all victims. We all belong to the same stream of broken humanity. We all do wrong, as Scripture reminds us: "There is no one who is righteous, not even one" (Rom. 3:10). Acknowledgment of our own human frailty and sinfulness can help us to accept (not condone) the weakness and sin of the one who has injured us. The other thing that helps is sincere repentance by the injurer. When the wrongdoer expresses genuine remorse for her action, she asserts an identity that is distinct from the identity of the one who committed the deed. This makes it much easier for the victim to forgive her, because he sees before him a different person from the one who hurt him. By repenting, she has disavowed her previous behavior and pledged to follow a different course. The gift of forgiveness affirms this new identity as one that no longer merits the victim's resentment or revenge.

(5) *Being willing to experience "the fellowship of sufferings."* When one person intentionally injures another, both victim and perpetrator are unavoidably bound together by their common experience. Both are chained to the same transgression and its aftermath. One is bound by guilt and shame, the other by bitterness and pain. Forgiveness is a process of unlocking the chains of this mutual bondage. Because they are bound together to the event, both victim and offender need each other to experience liberation and healing from the continuing thrall of the offense. The offender needs the victim to trigger or sharpen his contrition, to hear his confession, remit his guilt, and to affirm his ability to start fresh. The victim needs the offender to hear her pain, answer her questions, absorb her resentment, and affirm her dignity. Each holds the key to the other's liberation. For this "mutual unbinding" to happen, both parties must return together to the original act to talk about what happened and to face squarely all the destructive and shameful implications that ensued. This is an immensely threatening and painful experience for both parties. It requires exposing one's deepest vulnerabilities and feelings to the one who has become an enemy.

But it is out of this shared pain that the miracle of forgiveness is born. As the perpetrator confesses the guilt of his deed to the face of the party who suffered it, he experiences shame and humiliation. He is stripped of his defenses and appears naked before her. The victim witnesses this pain at the same time that she is brought back to the origin of her own pain and experiences once again the abasement or betrayal suffered at his hands. Witnessing her pain in turn deepens the perpetrator's shame and sorrow. Forgiveness occurs as a compassionate exchange of pain.[38] Each party enters into the pain of the other, and a miraculous liberation occurs. The dignity of both is restored. The perpetrator renounces his abuse of power, the victim rises from her induced powerlessness, and their relationship is transformed by the fellowship of their sufferings.[39]

(6) *Forgiving other parties.* Sometimes a victim becomes aware that, besides blaming the actual offender, he also blames other parties for what has happened. He may blame other people for failing to protect him from harm. He may blame himself for being "stupid enough" to allow the injury to have occurred. He may blame God for the terrible things that happen in the world. Such blaming may be a projection on to self and others of resentment due the offender. If that is the case, it will dissipate after the major work of forgiveness is accomplished. If not, the victim may have to work through a forgiveness process with each of these other parties he believes is blameworthy.

(7) *Becoming reconciled with the past.* The traditional Christian concept of repentance includes the "three Rs" — remorse (for the hurt caused), renewal (of life direction), and material restitution (to the victim). Restitution is often an important component in the forgiveness process, but it is important to understand its proper role. It is not payment for forgiveness. The offender does not purchase pardon from the victim by paying compensation for the pain suffered, for forgiveness is by definition gratuitous in nature. Restitution is also not a way of repairing the past, of restoring the status quo ante. It is an illusion to think that the wheel of history can ever be turned back or the past uncreated. It is simply not possible to restore the life of murder victims, the innocence of abused children, the damaged limbs of torture vic-

---

38. Müller-Fahrenholz, *The Art of Forgiveness,* 26.
39. Cf. Phil. 3:10-11; Rom. 6:5; 2 Cor. 1:5; 4:10; Gal. 2:19-20; 6:14; Col. 1:24.

tims. Stolen property can be replaced, but the experience of forced deprivation cannot be expunged. So if restitution is neither payment for forgiveness nor repayment for damage done, what role does it play?

At one level, it serves as a tangible expression of the genuineness of the offender's repentance, an external symbol that an internal change has occurred. (By contrast, mere restitution without confession and repentance — a common governmental strategy for dealing with past wrongs — does not have the same effect, for victims may feel that the wrongs they have endured are minimized or trivialized by being given a cash value for purposes of settlement.) At another level, restitution affirms the victim's significance as a person of worth and value. In place of having used the victim for his or her own ends, the offender now honors the victim as an independent subject with whom he shares his resources and power. In doing so, the offender also empowers and equips the victim for a better future. Restitution, then, is not about repaying the past or purchasing pardon in the present but about affirming the victim's significance and helping provide for her future. Yet, at the same time, this enables the victim to be reconciled with the negative realities of the past so that they no longer control the present and the future.

(8) *Becoming reconciled with the persons involved in the episode.* We have already seen how the goal and culmination of the forgiveness process is a renewed relationship between the injurer and the injured. This may not always be possible. But when both parties can accept that a rupture to their relationship has occurred, and when they have together walked the demanding road of confession and forgiveness, the way is cleared for reconciliation. Whether the new relationship is closer or more distant than before will depend upon multiple factors. But the relationship will always be healthier than it was in the aftermath of the offense.

Forgiveness and the Justice System

So far I have described the nature of forgiveness largely from an individual or personal perspective. This is understandable because, at the end of the day, forgiveness is something that individual personalities offer and receive. At the same time, it is important not to wholly psychologize and privatize forgiveness, for it can also have collective and political applications. This may be harder to grasp for Westerners shaped by liberal individualism than it is for those who belong to more collective cultures. But ultimately the only answer to deep-seated ethnic and political hatreds — such as those that exist in Northern Ireland and the Middle East and the Balkans — is for hostile communities to find a place of mutual forgiveness and release. In a similar way, arguably the only hope for improving the plight of the poorest countries in the world is for Western nations to remit or forgive their burgeoning debts and allow them a fresh start. Forgiveness, then, has a social as well as an individual dimension.

It is here that forgiveness intersects with criminal justice concerns. I proposed earlier that interpersonal forgiveness and legal justice are different processes that can run in parallel rather than in opposition. Because forgiveness is an affair of the heart and wholly gratuitous, it cannot be compelled by the courts or enshrined in the law. Yet it should not be entirely left out of the equation, as it usually is in the current penal system. The practice of restorative justice strives to address the relational dimensions of criminal offending and to employ procedures, such as Family Group Conferencing in the New Zealand youth court system, that are conducive to — rather than indifferent or resistant toward — the possibility of forgiveness occurring. Perhaps the most compelling recent example of a state-sponsored institutional procedure for dealing with serious criminal offending that seeks to be open to the occurrence of forgiveness and healing is the Truth and Reconciliation Commission (TRC) in South Africa.

Established by an act of parliament in 1995, the TRC sat for some two-and-a-half years under the chairmanship of Archbishop Desmond Tutu. During this time it listened to thousands of cases of human rights abuses perpetrated under the apartheid regime, including the abduction, torture, maiming, and murder of innocent people. To deal with those guilty of such gross violations, the new South African government adopted a middle path between the punitive approach of the Nuremberg and Tokyo war-crimes tribunals on the one hand and the blanket amnesties conferred by the fledgling democracies of several Latin American countries on the other.[40] It was willing to grant amnes-

---

40. For a comparison between the TRC and Nuremberg, see R. Gerloff, "Truth, a New Society, and Reconciliation: The Truth and Reconciliation Commission in South Africa

ties to perpetrators but only in return for a full disclosure of their activities and the naming of superiors whose orders they were following. Those who failed to apply for amnesty or to meet its conditions adequately could be pursued by the criminal courts. At the same time, it aimed to give victims the opportunity to tell their stories, to learn the names of those responsible for their suffering, and, if possible, to be compensated for their losses.

The TRC has not been without its critics and detractors, and definite limitations existed in its terms of reference and mode of operation. Some critics claimed the TRC favored offenders more than victims. Whereas the Commission was empowered to grant amnesty to offenders in return for their simply telling the truth, not necessarily with any sense of contrition or apology, it could only recommend to the government that compensation be paid to victims. This gave rise to the feeling that it was easier for the guilty to get amnesty than it was for the victims to get justice. This feeling has been compounded by the tardiness of the government in making reparation payments. According to a memorandum sent to the South African Minister of Justice on 29 October 1999 by the Khulumani Support Group, even "urgent interim reparations have not been realized for the majority of victims who made a submission." This, together with lack of action against perpetrators who did not apply for amnesty, is threatening to undermine the TRC process. The memorandum concludes by demanding that the government act to ensure that victims and survivors of apartheid atrocities receive urgent interim and adequate final reparations, as well as appropriate public recognition, through such things as the renaming of public facilities after them.[41]

Another criticism of the TRC is that those who sought amnesty tended to be the "foot soldiers" who carried out the gruesome and bloody atrocities rather than those who planned and ordered them, or the official defenders, architects, and legitimizers of apartheid as a whole.[42] Even if individual police officers or security agents disclosed

---

from a German Perspective," *Missionalia* 26, no. 1 (1998): 24-33. On the problem of granting impunity to perpetrators of human rights abuses, see G. Jacques, *Beyond Impunity: An Ecumenical Approach to Truth, Justice, and Reconciliation* (Geneva: WCC Publications, 2000).

41. Memorandum to the Minister of Justice, Mr. Punuell Maduna, from the Khulumani Support Group, 29 October 1999 (available at bhamber@csvr.org.za).

42. T. S. Maluleke, "Truth, National Unity, and Reconciliation in South Africa: Aspects of the Emerging Theological Agenda," *Missionalia* 25, no. 1 (1997): 64-65.

all they knew of their deeds, "full disclosure" could not occur because most of those involved behind the scenes remained invisible. In addition, the TRC could not meet the needs of all victims. The sheer scale of the problem meant that only a tiny percentage of the actual victims of apartheid could appear before the commission. It has been estimated that 16.5 million people were charged with offenses under the laws of apartheid after 1960, and around 80 percent of those arrested suffered physical assault,[43] so that even the thousands of testimonies heard by the TRC constituted only the tip of the iceberg of actual victimization. The Commission had a brief to deal only with "gross violations of human rights," but even then some victims felt they were not given sufficient opportunity to tell of their sufferings or the sufferings of their community. Many critics of the TRC have also pointed to the discrepancy between the benevolence of the Commission toward white offenders and the continuing and intensifying poverty of the black underclass in South Africa.

But none of this should blind us to the remarkable achievements of the TRC. Certainly it was not a perfect model, and it is best seen as a catalyst for social change and a step along the road to reconciliation and racial justice rather than the definitive attainment of such goals. But it represents a historically unique attempt to deploy the resources and authority of the collective state in the service of relational healing with respect to crimes of unimaginable brutality. Although chaired by an archbishop and counting four Christian ministers among its seventeen commissioners, the TRC was not a religious body but a judicial entity with legal authority and a political agenda. Yet given the personal influence of Desmond Tutu, the deep spirituality of many of the black victims,[44] the deliberate focus on issues of healing and reconciliation, and the concern to allow room for affective or emotional involvement in the proceedings, the Commission's public hearings, as one observer noted, "often resembled something of a cross between a court room and a religious ceremony."[45] Some have scoffed at the imposition of a

43. "South Africa's Truth and Reconciliation Commission," ed. S. Lind, *MCC Peace Office Newsletter* 28, no. 3 (1998): 2.

44. On this, see Müller-Fahrenholz, *The Art of Forgiveness,* 93.

45. Maluleke, "Truth, National Unity, and Reconciliation," 83. On the symbolic and ritual dimension of the process, see A. Krog, "The Truth and Reconciliation Commission — A National Ritual?" *Missionalia* 26, no. 1 (1998): 5-16.

Christian mentality of forgiveness on the judicial process. But the TRC had no power to offer or compel forgiveness or to manufacture repentance on the part of the criminals. It could only provide a platform for victims to remember and retell the offenses committed against them and an opportunity for offenders to own up to their deeds and tell the truth about them. Perpetrators were not required to demonstrate remorse or offer restitution, but often did so spontaneously when confronted with the human devastation they had caused. Victims were not encouraged to forgive, but miracles of grace often took place. Some victims spoke of their readiness to forgive those who had killed or maimed their loved ones as long as they could know who they were forgiving, what they had done, and why. Desmond Tutu commented on the readiness, even eagerness, of some victims to forgive: "It has been almost breathtaking, this willingness to forgive, this magnanimity, this nobility of spirit."[46] Other observers have been similarly moved. One writes, "I have been sometimes almost overwhelmed by expressions of remarkable magnanimity and generosity shown by those who have suffered so horrendously."[47]

Such forgiveness — which offers release to both victim and offender and furnishes a better foundation for national reconciliation than simple retribution — was forthcoming because the TRC pursued what Müller-Fahrenholz terms "justice with a restoring face."[48] It sought to restore dignity and personhood to victims and to offer a fresh start to offenders by making room for truth in place of silence, repentance in place of denial, mercy instead of retribution, and forgiveness instead of hatred. Even after listening personally to more than a thousand eyewitness accounts of criminal atrocities, sometimes overcome with weeping at the pain of the victims as he did so, Desmond Tutu could still say, "I have come to believe fervently that forgiveness is not just a spiritual thing that is ethereal and unrelated to the real world, the harsh world out there. I have come to believe very fervently that without forgiveness, there is no future."[49]

46. Tutu, "Truth and Reconciliation and Healing," *MCC Peace Office Newsletter* 28, no. 3 (1998): 2.

47. A. Boraine, "Can Truthtelling Promote Reconciliation?" *MCC Peace Office Newsletter* 28, no. 3 (1998): 10.

48. Müller-Fahrenholz, *The Art of Forgiveness,* 95.

49. On a Radio New Zealand interview, 7 June 1998, quoted by J. Consedine, "Twin

Restorative justice cannot manufacture repentance and forgiveness. But by placing a concern for the healing of hurts, the renewal of relationships, and the re-creation of community at the heart of its agenda, it makes room for the miracle of forgiveness to occur and for a new future to dawn. Nothing could be more compatible with the message of the New Testament than this. For without diminishing the reality of evil, without denying the culpability of those who commit crime or minimizing the pain of those who suffer at their hands, and without dispensing with punishment as a mechanism for constraining evil and promoting change, the New Testament looks *beyond retribution* to a vision of justice that is finally satisfied only by the defeat of evil and the healing of its victims, by the repentance of sinners and the forgiveness of their sins, by the restoration of peace and the renewal of hope — a justice that manifests God's redemptive work of making all things new.

Pillars of Justice: Morality and the Law," in *Restorative Justice: Contemporary Themes and Practice,* ed. H. Bowen and J. Consedine (Lyttelton, N.Z.: Ploughshares Publications, 1999), 43.

BIBLIOGRAPHY

Achtemeier, E. R. "Mercy, Merciful; Compassion; Pity." *IDB*, 3:352-54.

———. "Righteousness in the Old Testament." *IDB*, 4:80-85.

Achtemeier, P. J. "Finding the Way to Paul's Theology: A Response to J. Christiaan Beker and J. Paul Sampley." In *Pauline Theology Volume I: Thessalonians, Philippians, Galatians, Philemon*, ed. J. M. Bassler, 25-36. Minneapolis: Fortress Press, 1991.

———. *Romans*. Atlanta: John Knox, 1985.

Adams, J. P., ed. *Capital Punishment: What the Religious Community Says*. New York: National Interreligious Task Force on Criminal Justice, n.d.

Alexander, P. S. "Jewish Law in the Time of Jesus: Towards a Clarification of the Problem." In *Law and Religion: Essays on the Place of Law in Israel and Early Christianity*, ed. B. Lindars, 44-58. Cambridge: James Clarke, 1988.

Alon, G. *The Jews in Their Land in the Talmudic Era*. Cambridge/London: Harvard University Press, 1989.

Amnesty International. *Amnesty International Handbook*. London: AI Publications, 1992.

Anderson, H. G., T. A. Murphy, and J. A. Burgess, eds. *Justification by Faith*. Minneapolis: Augsburg, 1985.

Anderson, J. S. "The Social Function of Curses in the Hebrew Bible." *ZAW* 110, no. 2 (1998): 223-37.

Atkin, B., and K. Evans, eds. *Human Rights and the Common Good: Christian Perspectives*. Wellington, N.Z.: Victoria University Press, 1999.

Augsburger, D. W. *Helping People Forgive*. Louisville, Ky.: Westminster John Knox, 1996.

Austad, T. "Attitudes towards the State in Western Theological Thinking." *Themelios* 16, no. 1 (1990): 18-22.

Baker, N. "Mediation, Reparation, and Justice." In *Relational Justice: Repairing the Breach*, ed. J. Burnside and N. Baker, 71-81. Winchester, U.K.: Waterside Press, 1994.

Balch, D. L., E. Ferguson, and W. A. Meeks, eds. *Greeks, Romans, and Christians*. Minneapolis: Fortress Press, 1990.

Bammel, E., ed. *The Trial of Jesus*. London: SCM, 1970.

Banks, R., ed. *Reconciliation and Hope*. Grand Rapids: William B. Eerdmans, 1974.

Barclay, J. M. G. "Jesus and Paul." *DPL*, 492-503.

———. *Jews in the Mediterranean Diaspora from Alexander to Trajan (323 BCE–117 CE)*. Edinburgh: T. & T. Clark, 1996.

———. "Paul and the Law: Observations on Some Recent Debates." *Themelios* 12, no. 1 (1986): 5-15.

———. "Thessalonica and Corinth: Social Contrasts in Pauline Christianity." *JSNT* 47 (1992): 49-74.

Barclay, O. "The Nature of Christian Morality." In *Law, Morality, and the Bible: A Symposium*, ed. B. N. Kaye and G. J. Wenham, 125-50. Leicester: Inter-Varsity Press, 1978.

———. "The Theology of Social Ethics: A Survey of Current Positions." *Interchange* 36 (1985): 6-23.

Barclay, O., and C. Sugden. "Biblical Social Ethics in a Mixed Society." *EvQ* 62, no. 1 (1990): 5-18.

Barclay, W. *The Letter to the Romans*. Edinburgh: St. Andrews, 1957.

Barnett, W. A. "The Scripture and Capital Punishment." In *Essays on the Death Penalty*, ed. T. R. Ingram, 73-80. Houston: St. Thomas Press, 1963.

Barr, J. "Ancient Biblical Laws and Modern Human Rights." In *Justice and the Holy: Essays in Honour of Walter Harrelson*, ed. D. A. Knight and P. J. Peters, 21-33. Atlanta: Scholars Press, 1989.

Barrett, C. K. *The Epistle to the Romans*. London: A. & C. Black, 1962.

———. "The First Christian Moral Legislation." In *The Bible in Human Society: Essays in Honour of John Rogerson*, ed. M. D. R. Carroll, D. J. A. Clines, and P. R. Davies, 58-66. Sheffield: Sheffield Academic Press, 1995.

———. *The Gospel According to John: An Introduction with Commentary and Notes on the Greek Text*. 2d ed. London: SPCK, 1978.

Barth, K. *A Shorter Commentary on Romans*. London: SCM, 1959.

Barth, M. "Jews and Gentiles: The Social Character of Justification in Paul." *JES* 5 (1968): 241-67.

Bassett, W., and P. Huizing, eds. *Judgment in the Church*. New York: Seabury Press, 1977.

Bassler, J. M., ed. *Pauline Theology*. Minneapolis: Fortress Press, 1991.

Bauckham, R. J. *Jude, 2 Peter*. Waco: Word, 1983.

———. "Universalism." *Themelios* 4, no. 2 (1979): 48-52.

Baxter, C. A. "The Cursed Beloved: A Reconsideration of Penal Substitution." In *Atonement Today*, ed. J. Goldingay, 54-72. London: SPCK, 1995.

Beare, F. W. *The Gospel According to Matthew*. Oxford: Blackwell, 1981.

Beasley-Murray, G. R. *John*. WBC 36. Waco: Word, 1987.

———. "Matthew 6:33: The Kingdom of God and the Ethics of Jesus." In *Neues Testament und Ethik*, ed. H. Merklein, 84-98. Freiburg/Basel/Wein: Herder, 1989.

Beaton, R. "Messiah and Justice: A Key to Matthew's Use of Isaiah 42:1-4?" *JSNT* 75 (1999): 5-23.

Behm, J. "ἀνάθεμα κτλ." *TDNT,* 1:354-56.

Beisner, E. C. "Justice and Poverty: Two Views Contrasted." *Transformation* 10, no. 1 (1993): 16-22.

Beker, J. C. "The Relationship between Sin and Death in Romans." In *The Conversation Continues,* ed. R. T. Fortna and B. R. Gaventa, 55-61. Nashville: Abingdon Press, 1990.

Berman, H. J. "Law and Religion: An Overview." *ER,* 8:463-64.

Berman, H. J. "Law and Religion in the West." *ER,* 8:472-75.

Bernard, J. H. *A Critical and Exegetical Commentary on the Gospel According to St. John.* 2 vols. Edinburgh: T. & T. Clark, 1928.

Best, E. *The First and Second Epistle to the Thessalonians.* London: A. & C. Black, 1977.

Bianchi, H. "The Biblical Vision of Justice." *NPCJ,* 2 (1984), 1-9.

Birch, B. C. "Moral Agency, Community, and the Character of God in the Hebrew Bible." *Semeia* 66 (1995): 23-41.

Birch, B. C., and L. L. Rasmussen. *Bible and Ethics in the Christian Life.* (Minneapolis: Augsburg, 1989).

Bisseker, H. "Punishment." *HDCG,* 2:456-57.

Black, M. *Romans.* London/Grand Rapids: Marshall, Morgan & Scott/William B. Eerdmans, 1973.

Blackman, P. "The Hell of Non-Being." *Churchman* 110, no. 2 (1996): 121-30.

Blinzer, J. "The Jewish Punishment of Stoning in the New Testament Period." In *The Trial of Jesus,* ed. E. Bammel, 147-65. London: SCM, 1970.

Blomberg, C. L. "Degrees of Reward in the Kingdom of Heaven?" *JETS* 35, no. 2 (1991): 26-34.

———. "Eschatology and the Church: Some New Testament Perspectives." *Themelios* 23, no. 3 (1998): 3-26.

Blum, E. A. "Shall You Surely Not Die?" *Themelios* 4, no. 2 (1979): 58-62.

Boers, A. P. *Justice that Heals: A Biblical Vision for Victims and Offenders.* Newton, Kans.: Faith & Life Press, 1992.

Boers, H. *The Justification of the Gentiles: Paul's Letters to the Galatians and Romans.* Peabody, Mass.: Hendrickson, 1994.

Bonda, J. *The One Purpose of God: An Answer to the Doctrine of Eternal Punishment.* Grand Rapids: William B. Eerdmans, 1998.

Boraine, A. "Can Truthtelling Promote Reconciliation?" *MCC Peace Office Newsletter* 28, no. 3 (1998): 9-11.

Borchert, G. L. "Wrath, Destruction." *DPL,* 991-93.

Borg, M. "A New Context for Romans XIII." *NTS* 19, no. 2 (1973): 205-18.

Boring, M. E. "The Language of Universal Salvation in Paul." *JBL* 105, no. 2 (1986): 269-92.

Bornkamm, G. *Paul.* London: Hodder & Stoughton, 1971.

———. "The Revelation of God's Wrath (Romans 1-3)." In Bornkamm, *Early Christian Experience,* 47-70. London: SCM, 1969.

Boston, J. "Christianity in the Public Square: The Churches and Social Justice." In *Voices for Justice: Church, Law, and State in New Zealand,* ed. J. Boston and A. Cameron, 11-35. Palmerston North, N.Z.: Dunmore Press, 1994.

BIBLIOGRAPHY

————. "Love, Justice, and the State." In *Voices for Justice: Church, Law, and State in New Zealand*, ed. J. Boston and A. Cameron, 69-105. Palmerston North, N.Z.: Dunmore Press, 1994.

Boston, J., and A. Cameron, eds. *Voices for Justice: Church, Law, and State in New Zealand.* Palmerston North, N.Z.: Dunmore Press, 1994.

Bottoms, A. "Avoiding Injustice, Promoting Legitimacy and Relationships." In *Relational Justice: Repairing the Breach*, ed. J. Burnside and N. Baker, 53-68. Winchester, U.K.: Waterside Press, 1994.

Bowen, H. "Making Justice Work." In *Restorative Justice: Contemporary Themes and Practice*, ed. H. Bowen and J. Consedine, 17-24. Lyttelton, N.Z.: Ploughshares Publications, 1999.

Bowen, H., and J. Boyack. *The New Zealand Restorative Justice Practice Manual.* Auckland, N.Z.: Restorative Justice Trust, 2000.

Bowen, H., and J. Consedine, eds. *Restorative Justice: Contemporary Themes and Practice.* Lyttelton, N.Z.: Ploughshares Publications, 1999.

Boyack, J. "How Sayest the Court of Appeal?" In *Restorative Justice: Contemporary Themes and Practice*, ed. H. Bowen and J. Consedine, 67-71. Lyttelton, N.Z.: Ploughshares Publications, 1999.

Bradley, I. *The Power of Sacrifice.* London: Darton, Longman & Todd, 1995.

Braithwaite, J. *Crime, Shame, and Reintegration.* Cambridge: Cambridge University Press, 1989.

Brauch, M. T. "Perspectives on 'God's Righteousness' in Recent German Discussion." In *Paul and Palestinian Judaism*, ed. E. P. Sanders, 523-42. London: SCM, 1977.

Bray, G. "Hell: Eternal Punishment or Total Annihilation?" *Evangel*, Summer 1992, 19-24.

————. "Justification: The Reformers and Recent New Testament Scholarship." *Churchman* 109, no. 2 (1995): 102-26.

Brinsmead, R. D. "The Heart of New Testament Ethics." *CV* 5, no. 1 (1982): 12-24.

————. "Justification by Faith and Human Rights." *CV* 9 (1983): 1-6.

————. "Justification by Faith Re-Examined." *CV*, Special Issue, no. 1 (1983).

————. "Notes on Justification in the Book of Romans." *CV* 9 (1983): 1-10.

————. "The Scandal of God's Justice," Parts 1-3. *CV* 6, 7, 8 (1983).

Broer, I. "Das Ius Talionis im Neuen Testament." *NTS* 40, no. 1 (1994): 1-21.

Brower, K. E., and M. W. Elliott, eds. *The Reader Must Understand: Eschatology in Bible and Theology.* Leicester: Inter-Varsity Press — Apollos, 1997.

Brown, C. E. "The Atonement: Healing in a Postmodern Society." *Interpretation* 53, no. 1 (1999): 34-43.

————. "'The Last Enemy Is Death': Paul and the Pastoral Task." *Interpretation* 43, no. 4 (1989): 380-92.

Brown, M. J. A. "Empowering the Victim in the New Zealand Youth Justice Process — A Strategy for Healing." Unpublished paper presented to the Eighth International Symposium on Victimology, Adelaide, Australia, 23 August 1994.

Brown, R. E. *The Death of the Messiah: From Gethsemane to the Grave.* 2 vols. New York: Doubleday, 1994.

————. *The Gospel According to John,* Anchor Bible Series. 2 vols. London: Geoffrey Chapman, 1971.

Bruce, F. F. *The Epistle of Paul to the Romans.* Leicester: Inter-Varsity Press, 1963.

————. *The Epistle to the Galatians: A Commentary on the Greek Text.* Exeter: Paternoster, 1982.

————. *1 & 2 Thessalonians.* Waco, Tex.: Word, 1982.

————. "Paul and the Law in Recent Research." In *Law and Religion: Essays on the Place of Law in Israel and Early Christianity,* ed. B. Lindars, 115-25. Cambridge: James Clarke, 1988.

Bultmann, R. "δικαοισύνη Θεοῦ." *JBL* 83 (1964): 12-16.

————. "ἔλεος κτλ." *TDNT,* 2:477-87.

————. *Theology of the New Testament.* 2 vols. London: SCM, 1956.

Burgess, J. A. "Rewards, but in a Very Different Sense." In *Justification by Faith,* ed. H. G. Anderson, T. A. Murphy, and J. A. Burgess, 94-110. Minneapolis: Augsburg, 1985.

Burkholder, J. R. "Mennonite Peace Theology: Reconnaissance and Exploration." Unpublished paper presented at the Peace Theology Colloquium VI, June 1991.

————. *Mennonites in Ecumenical Dialogue on Peace and Justice.* Akron, Pa.: MCC Occasional Paper 7, 1988.

————. "Nonresistance." *ME,* 5:637-38.

Burkholder, J. R., and B. N. Gingerich, eds. *Mennonite Peace Theology: A Panorama of Types.* Akron, Pa: MCC, 1991.

Burnside, J. "Tension and Tradition in the Pursuit of Justice." In *Relational Justice: Repairing the Breach,* ed. J. Burnside and N. Baker, 42-52. Winchester, U.K.: Waterside Press, 1994.

Burnside, J., and N. Baker, eds. *Relational Justice: Repairing the Breach.* Winchester, U.K.: Waterside Press, 1994.

Byrne, B. J. "How Can We Interpret Romans Theologically Today?" *ABR* 47 (1999): 29-42.

————. "Living Out the Righteousness of God: The Contribution of Rom 6:1–8:13 to an Understanding of Paul's Ethical Presuppositions." *CBQ* 43, no. 4 (1981): 557-81.

Cahill, L. Sowle. *Between the Sexes: Foundations for a Christian Ethics of Sexuality.* Philadelphia: Fortress Press, 1985.

Campbell, B. "Flesh and Spirit in 1 Cor 5:5: An Exercise in Rhetorical Criticism." *JETS* 36, no. 3 (1993): 331-42.

Campbell, D. A. "The Atonement in Paul." *Anvil* 11, no. 3 (1994): 237-50.

————. "False Presuppositions in the ΠΙΣΤΙΣ ΧΡΙΣΤΟΥ Debate: A Response to Brian Dodd." *JBL* 119, no. 4 (1997): 713-19.

————. "Romans 1:17 — A *Crux Interpretum* for the ΠΙΣΤΙΣ ΧΡΙΣΤΟΥ Debate." *JBL* 113, no. 2 (1994): 265-85.

————, ed. *The Call to Serve: Biblical and Theological Perspectives on Ministry.* Sheffield: Sheffield Academic Press, 1996.

Camus, A. *The Fall.* Harmondsworth: Penguin, 1957.

Capill, G. "Political Initiatives in Response to Serious Violent Crime." *Stimulus* 2, no. 3 (1994): 63-68.

Carey, G. A. "A Bible Study." In *Essays on the Death Penalty,* ed. T. R. Ingram, 103-38. Houston: St. Thomas Press, 1963.

Carroll, J. T., and J. B. Green. *The Death of Jesus in Early Christianity.* Peabody, Mass.: Hendrickson, 1995.

Carroll, M. D. R., D. J. A. Clines, and P. R. Davies, eds. *The Bible in Human Society: Essays in Honour of John Rogerson.* Sheffield: Sheffield Academic Press, 1995.

Carson, D. A. *The Gagging of God: Christianity Confronts Pluralism.* Grand Rapids: William B. Eerdmans, 1996.

———. *The Gospel According to John.* Leicester/Grand Rapids: Inter-Varsity Press/William B. Eerdmans, 1991.

———, ed. *Right with God: Justification in the Bible and the World.* Exeter/Grand Rapids: Paternoster/Baker, 1992.

Cassidy, R. J. *Society and Politics in Acts of the Apostles.* Maryknoll, N.Y.: Orbis, 1987.

Cayley, D. *The Expanding Prison: The Crisis in Crime and Punishment and the Search for Alternatives.* Toronto: Anansi Press, 1998.

Chan, S. "The Logic of Hell: A Response to Annihilationism." *ERT* 18, no. 1 (1994): 20-32.

Chapman, S. "Maori and the Justice System." *Stimulus* 2, no. 3 (1994): 23-28.

Charette, B. *The Theme of Recompense in Matthew's Gospel.* Sheffield: Sheffield Academic Press, 1992.

Charles, J. D. "Crime, the Christian, and Capital Justice." *JETS* 38, no. 3 (1995): 429-41.

———. "Outrageous Atrocity or Moral Imperative? The Ethics of Capital Punishment." *StChEth* 6, no. 2 (1993): 1-14.

———. "Pauline Ethics and Capital Justice: Proscription or Prescription? (Rom. 12:17–13:7)." Unpublished paper presented at the SBL Conference, November 1994.

Charlesworth, J. *Jesus within Judaism.* New York: Doubleday, 1988.

Cheetham, D. "Hell as Potentially Temporal." *ExpT* 108, no. 9 (1997): 260-63.

Chilton, B. D. "The Hungry Knife: Towards a Sense of Sacrifice." In *The Bible in Human Society: Essays in Honour of John Rogerson,* ed. M. D. R. Carroll, D. J. A. Clines, and P. R. Davies, 122-38. Sheffield: Sheffield Academic Press, 1995.

———. *Pure Kingdom: Jesus' Vision of God.* Grand Rapids: William B. Eerdmans, 1996.

Chilton, B. D., and J. I. H. McDonald. *Jesus and the Ethics of the Kingdom.* London: SPCK, 1987.

Christie, N. "Crime, Pain, and Death." *NPCJ* 1 (1984), 1-14.

The Church Council on Justice and Corrections. *Satisfying Justice: A Compendium of Initiatives, Programs, and Legislative Measures.* Ottawa, Ont.: The Church Council on Justice and Corrections, 1996.

Clark, G. H. "Capital Punishment." *BDCE,* 84.

Clarke, A. D. "The Good and the Just in Romans 5:7." *TynBul* 41, no. 1 (1990): 128-42.

Cohen, A. *Everyman's Talmud.* London: J. M. Dent & Sons, 1932.

Cole, G. A. "Justice: Retributive or Reformative?" *RTR* 45, no. 1 (1986): 5-12.

Coleman, T. M. "Binding Obligations in Romans 13:7: A Semantic Field and Social Context." *TynBul* 48, no. 2 (1997): 307-27.

Collins, A. Y. *Crisis and Catharsis: The Power of the Apocalypse.* Philadelphia: Westminster Press, 1984.

————. "The Function of 'Excommunication' in Paul." *HTR* 73, nos. 1-2 (1980): 251-63.

Compston, C. "Local Justice: A Personal View." In *Relational Justice: Repairing the Breach,* ed. J. Burnside and N. Baker, 483-92. Winchester, U.K.: Waterside Press, 1994.

Connery, J. R. "Capital Punishment." *EBCE,* 48-51.

Consedine, J. "New Zealand Criminal Justice — A Moment of Truth." *Stimulus* 2, no. 3 (1994): 12-15.

————. *A Poison in the Bloodstream.* Queen Charlotte Sound, N.Z.: Cape Catley Ltd., 1990.

————. *Restorative Justice: Healing the Effects of Crime.* Lyttelton, N.Z.: Ploughshares Publications, 1995.

————. "Towards a Theology of Restorative Justice." *Stimulus* 8, no. 1 (2000): 20-26.

————. "Twin Pillars of Justice: Morality and the Law." In *Restorative Justice: Contemporary Themes and Practice,* ed. H. Bowen and J. Consedine, 36-44. Lyttelton, N.Z.: Ploughshares Publications, 1999.

————, ed. "Penal Abolition: Is It a Christian Option?" *The Common Good* 4 (1997): 1-19.

Conzelmann, H. *A Commentary on the First Epistle to the Corinthians.* Philadelphia: Fortress Press, 1975.

Cosgrove, C. H. "Justification in Paul: A Linguistic and Theological Reflection." *JBL* 106, no. 4 (1987): 653-70.

————. "The Justification of the Other: An Interpretation of Rom 1:18–4:25." In *SBL Seminar Papers,* 613-34. Chico, Calif.: Scholars Press, 1992.

Cotham, P. C., ed. *Christian Social Ethics: Perspectives and Problems.* Grand Rapids: Baker, 1979.

Cousar, C. B. "Paul and the Death of Jesus." *Interpretation* 52, no. 1 (1998): 38-52.

Coyle, A. "My Brother's Keeper: Relationships in Prison." In *Relational Justice: Repairing the Breach,* ed. J. Burnside and N. Baker, 122-30. Winchester, U.K.: Waterside Press, 1994.

Cranfield, C. E. B. "The Christian's Political Responsibility According to the New Testament." *SJT* 15 (1962): 176-92.

————. *A Critical and Exegetical Commentary on the Epistle to the Romans.* 2 vols. Edinburgh: T. & T. Clark, 1975, 1977.

Crockett, W. V. "The Metaphorical View." In *Four Views on Hell,* ed. W. V. Crockett, 43-76. Grand Rapids: Zondervan, 1992.

————, ed. *Four Views on Hell.* Grand Rapids: Zondervan, 1992.

Cronbach, A. "Righteousness in Jewish Literature 200 BC-AD 100." *IDB,* 4:85-91.

Culbertson, R. G. "Perspectives on Punishment and Sentencing." In *Christian Social Ethics: Perspectives and Problems,* ed. P. C. Cotham, 217-45. Grand Rapids: Baker, 1979.

Cullmann, O. *The State in the New Testament.* London: SCM, 1957.

Dahms, J. V. "Dying with Christ." *JETS* 36, no. 1 (1993): 15-23.

Daube, D. *The New Testament and Rabbinic Judaism.* London: The Athlone Press, 1956.

Davies, C. "Crime and the Rise and Decline of a Relational Society." In *Relational Justice: Repairing the Breach,* ed. J. Burnside and N. Baker, 31-41. Winchester, U.K.: Waterside Press, 1994.

Davies, W. D. *Paul and Rabbinic Judaism.* London: SPCK, 1958.

――――. "Paul and the Law: Pitfalls in Interpretation." In *Paul and Paulinism,* ed. M. D. Hooker and S. G. Wilson, 4-16. London: SPCK, 1982.

――――. "The Relevance of the Moral Teaching of the Early Church." In *Neotestamentica et Semitica: Studies in Honour of Matthew Black,* ed. E. E. Ellis and M. Wilcox, 30-49. Edinburgh: T. & T. Clark, 1969.

Davies, W. D., and D. C. Allison Jr. *A Critical and Exegetical Commentary on the Gospel According to Saint Matthew.* 3 vols. Edinburgh: T. & T. Clark, 1991.

――――. "Reflections on the Sermon on the Mount." *SJT* 44, no. 3 (1991): 283-309.

De Vos, C. S. "Stepmothers, Concubines, and the Case of ΠΟΡΝΕΙΑ in 1 Corinthians 5." *NTS* 44, no. 1 (1998): 104-14.

Delcor, M. "The Courts of the Church of Corinth and the Courts of Qumran." In *Paul and the Dead Sea Scrolls,* ed. J. Murphy-O'Connor and J. H. Charlesworth, 69-84. New York: Crossroad Publishing, 1990.

Den Heyer, C. J. *Jesus and the Doctrine of Atonement.* London: SCM, 1998.

Denison, K. "Restorative Justice in Ourselves." *NPCJ* 11 (1991), 1-13.

Derrett, J. D. M. "Judgment and 1 Corinthians 6." *NTS* 37, no. 1 (1991): 22-36.

――――. "The Woman Taken in Adultery." In J. D. M. Derrett, *Law in the New Testament,* 156-88. London: Darton, Longman & Todd, 1970.

Dickey Young, P. "Beyond Moral Influence to an Atoning Life." *Theology Today* 52, no. 3 (1995): 344-55.

Dixon, L. *The Other Side of the Good News: Confronting the Contemporary Challenges to Jesus' Teaching on Hell.* Wheaton, Ill.: Bridgepoint Books, 1992.

Dodd, B. "Romans 1:17 — A *Crux Interpretum* for the ΠΙΣΤΙΣ ΧΡΙΣΤΟΥ Debate?" *JBL* 114, no. 3 (1995): 470-73.

Dodd, C. H. *The Epistle of Paul to the Romans.* London: Hodder & Stoughton, 1932.

Dolinko, D. "Some Thoughts about Retributivism." *Ethics* 101 (1991): 537-59.

Donahue, J. R. "Biblical Perspectives on Justice." In *The Faith that Does Justice: Examining the Christian Sources for Social Change,* ed. J. C. Haughey, 68-112. New York: Paulist Press, 1977.

Donaldson, T. L. "Zealot." *ISBE,* 4:1175-79.

――――. "Zealot and Convert: The Origin of Paul's Christ-Torah Antithesis." *CBQ* 51 (1989): 655-82.

Donfried, K. P. "Justification and the Last Judgement in Paul." *ZNW,* 67 (1976): 90-110.

Douglas, B. "Crime and Punishment." *Christianity and Crisis,* 13 May 1991, 145-47.

Douglas, M. "Justice as the Cornerstone: An Interpretation of Leviticus 18–20." *Interpretation* 53, no. 4 (1999): 341-50.

Duff, N. J. "Atonement and the Christian Life: Reformed Doctrine from a Feminist Perspective." *Interpretation* 53, no. 1 (1999): 21-33.

Dumbrell, B. "Justification and the New Covenant." *Churchman* 112, no. 1 (1998): 17-29.

Dunn, J. D. G. *Christian Liberty: A New Testament Perspective.* Carlisle: Paternoster, 1993.

————. *The Epistle to the Galatians.* Peabody, Mass.: Hendrickson, 1993.

————. *The Living Word.* London: SCM, 1987.

————. "Once More, ΠΙΣΤΙΣ ΧΡΙΣΤΟΥ." *SBL Seminar Papers,* 730-44. Chico, Calif.: Scholars Press, 1991.

————. *The Parting of the Ways between Christianity and Judaism and Their Significance for the Character of Christianity.* London/Philadelphia: SCM/Trinity, 1991.

————. "Paul's Epistle to the Romans: An Analysis of the Structure and Argument." *ANRW* 2.25.4 (1988): 2842-90.

————. "Paul's Understanding of the Death of Jesus." In *Reconciliation and Hope,* ed. R. Banks, 125-41. Grand Rapids: William B. Eerdmans, 1974.

————. *Romans,* WBC 38. 2 vols. Dallas: Word, 1988.

————. *The Theology of Paul the Apostle.* Edinburgh: T. & T. Clark, 1998.

Dunn, J. D. G., and A. M. Suggate. *The Justice of God: A Fresh Look at the Old Doctrine of Justification by Faith.* Carlisle: Paternoster, 1993.

Dunnill, J. "Is the Bible a Handbook for Ethics?" *F&F* 3, no. 2 (1994): 3-7.

Duquoc, C. "The Forgiveness of God." In *Forgiveness,* Concilium 177, ed. C. Floristán and C. Duquoc, 35-44. Edinburgh: T. & T. Clark, 1986.

Durie Hall, D. "Restorative Justice: A Maori Perspective." In *Restorative Justice: Contemporary Themes and Practice,* ed. H. Bowen and J. Consedine, 25-35. Lyttelton, N.Z.: Ploughshares Publications, 1999.

Durken, D., ed. *Sin, Salvation, and the Spirit.* Collegeville: Liturgical Press, 1979.

Edwards, D. L., and J. R. W. Stott. *Essentials: A Liberal-Evangelical Dialogue.* London: Hodder & Stoughton, 1988.

Elizondo, V. "I Forgive but I Do Not Forget," in *Forgiveness,* Concilium 177, ed. C. Floristán and C. Duquoc, 69-79. Edinburgh: T. & T. Clark, 1986.

Elliott, N. *Liberating Paul: The Justice of God and the Politics of the Apostle.* Maryknoll, N.Y.: Orbis, 1994.

Ellis, E. E. "New Testament Teaching on Hell." In *The Reader Must Understand: Eschatology in Bible and Theology,* ed. K. E. Brower and M. W. Elliott, 199-219. Leicester: Inter-Varsity Press — Apollos, 1997.

Ellis, E. E., and M. Wilcox, eds. *Neotestamentica et Semitica: Studies in Honour of Matthew Black.* Edinburgh: T. & T. Clark, 1969.

Emmet, C. W. "Retribution." *HDCG,* 2:518-20.

Epstein, L. *Social Justice in the Ancient Near East and the People of the Bible.* London: SCM, 1986.

Esser, H.-H. "Mercy and Compassion." *NIDNTT,* 2:593-601.

Evans, C. A., and J. A. Sanders. *Paul and the Scriptures of Israel.* Sheffield: Sheffield Academic Press, 1993.

Falkenroth, U., and C. Brown. "Punishment, Vengeance." *NIDNTT,* 3:92-100.

Faulkner, D. "Relational Justice: A Dynamic for Reform." In *Relational Justice: Repairing the Breach,* ed. J. Burnside and N. Baker, 159-74. Winchester, U.K.: Waterside Press, 1994.

Fee, G. D. *The First Epistle to the Corinthians*. Grand Rapids: William B. Eerdmans, 1987.

———. *God's Empowering Presence*. Peabody, Mass.: Hendrickson, 1994.

Fiddes, P. S. *Past Event and Present Salvation: The Christian Idea of Atonement*. London/Louisville, Ky.: Darton, Longman & Todd/Westminster John Knox, 1989.

Finger, T. N. *Christian Theology: An Eschatological Approach*. 2 vols. Scottdale, Pa.: Herald Press, 1989.

Fiore, B. "Passion in Paul and Plutarch: 1 Corinthians 5-6 and the Polemic against Epicureans." In *Greeks, Romans, and Christians*, ed. D. L. Balch, E. Ferguson, and W. A. Meeks, 135-43. Minneapolis: Fortress Press, 1990.

Fisher, E. J. "Explorations and Responses: *LEX TALIONIS* in the Bible and Rabbinic Tradition." *JES* 19, no. 3 (1982): 582-87.

Fitzgerald, J. T. "The Problem of Perjury in Greek Context: Prolegomena to an Exegesis of Matthew 5:33; 1 Timothy 1:10; and *Didache* 2:3." In *The Social World of the First Christians*, ed. L. M. White and O. L. Yarbrough, 156-77. Minneapolis: Augsburg Fortress, 1995.

Fitzmyer, J. A. "The Consecutive Meaning of EΦ' Ω in Romans 5:12." *NTS* 39 (1993): 321-39.

———. *Romans*. Anchor Bible Series. New York: Doubleday, 1993.

Floristán, C., and C. Duquoc, eds. *Forgiveness*, Concilium 177. Edinburgh: T. & T. Clark, 1986.

Ford, J. Massyngbaerde. "Cursing and Blessing as Vehicles of Violence and Peace in Scripture." In *Peace in a Nuclear Age: The Bishops' Pastoral Letter in Perspective*, ed. C. J. Reid Jr., 20-33. Washington: Catholic University of America Press, 1986.

Forrester, D. B. *Christian Justice and Public Policy*. Cambridge: Cambridge University Press, 1997.

———. "Political Justice and Christian Theology." *StChEth* 3, no. 1 (1990): 1-13.

Forster, G. *"To Live Good": The Police and the Community*. Bramcote: Grove Booklet on Ethics 47, 1982.

Fortna, R. T., and B. R. Gaventa. *The Conversation Continues*. Nashville: Abingdon Press, 1990.

Foucault, M. *Discipline and Punish: The Birth of the Prison*. New York: Vintage Books, 1979.

Frey, C. "The Impact of the Biblical Idea of Justice on Present Discussions of Social Justice." In *Justice and Righteousness: Biblical Themes and Their Influence*, ed. H. G. Reventlow and Y. Hoffman, 91-130. Sheffield: Sheffield Academic Press, 1992.

Friedrich, J., W. Pohlmann, and P. Stuhlmacher. "Zur historischen Situation und Intention von Rom 13,1-7." *ZTK* 73 (1976): 131-66.

Fryer, N. S. L. "The Meaning and Translation of *Hilasterion* in Romans 3:25." *EvQ* 59, no. 2 (1987): 99-106.

Fudge, E. W. *The Fire that Consumes: A Biblical and Historical Study of Final Punishment*. Houston: Providential Press, 1982.

Fudge, E. W., and R. A. Peterson. *Two Views of Hell: A Biblical and Theological Dialogue*. Downers Grove, Ill.: InterVarsity Press, 2000.

Fung, R. Y. K. *The Epistle to the Galatians*. Grand Rapids: William B. Eerdmans, 1988.

———. "The Forensic Character of Justification." *Themelios* 16, no. 1 (1977): 16-20.

————. "The Status of Justification by Faith in Paul's Thought: A Brief Survey of the Modern Debate." *Themelios* 6, no. 3 (1981): 4-10.

Furnish, V. P. *II Corinthians.* New York: Doubleday, 1984.

Gallardo, J. *The Biblical Way of Justice.* Scottdale, Pa.: Herald Press, 1983.

Garlington, D. B. "The Obedience of Faith in the Letter to the Romans, Part 1: The Meaning of ὑπακοὴ πίστεως (Rom 1:5; 16:26)." *WTJ* 52, no. 2 (1990): 201-24.

————. "The Obedience of Faith in the Letter to the Romans, Part 2: The Obedience of Faith and Judgment by Works." *WTJ* 53, no. 1 (1991): 47-72.

————. "The Obedience of Faith in the Letter to the Romans, Part 3: The Obedience of Christ and the Obedience of the Christian." *WTJ* 55, no. 1 (1993): 87-112; 55, no. 2 (1993): 281-97.

Garrett, S. R. "The God of This World and the Affliction of Paul." In *Greeks, Romans, and Christians,* ed. D. L. Balch, E. Ferguson, and W. A. Meeks, 99-117. Minneapolis: Fortress Press, 1990.

Geisler, N. L. *Ethics: Alternatives and Issues.* Grand Rapids: Zondervan, 1971.

Georgi, D. *Theocracy in Paul's Praxis and Theology.* Minneapolis: Fortress Press, 1991.

Gerloff, R. "Truth, a New Society, and Reconciliation: The Truth and Reconciliation Commission in South Africa from a German Perspective." *Missionalia* 26, no. 1 (1998): 17-53.

Gill, A. *Life on the Road: The Gospel Basis for a Messianic Lifestyle.* Homebush West, N.S.W.: Anzea, 1989.

Gill, R. *Moral Communities.* Exeter: University of Exeter Press, 1992.

Goldingay, J. "Old Testament Sacrifice and the Death of Christ." In *Atonement Today,* ed. J. Goldingay, 3-20. London: SPCK, 1995.

————. "Your Iniquities Have Made a Separation between You and Your God." In *Atonement Today,* ed. J. Goldingay, 39-53. London: SPCK, 1995.

————, ed. *Atonement Today.* London: SPCK, 1995.

Gorringe, T. J. "Community, Imprisonment, and Social Justice: Punishment – The Need for Roots." In *The State of Imprisonment,* Occasional Paper No. 38, ed. A. R. Morton, 47-55. Edinburgh: Centre for Theology and Public Issues, University of Edinburgh, 1997.

————. *God's Just Vengeance: Crime, Violence, and the Rhetoric of Salvation.* Cambridge: Cambridge University Press, 1996.

Goulder, M. D. "Libertines? (1 Cor 5-6)." *NovT* 41, no. 4 (1999): 334-48.

Gowers, E. *A Life for a Life? The Problem of Capital Punishment.* London: Chatto & Windus, 1956.

Gray, I., and M. Stanley. *A Punishment in Search of a Crime: Americans Speak Out against the Death Penalty* (for Amnesty International USA). New York: Avon Books, 1989.

Gray, T. "Destroyed for Ever: An Examination of the Debates Concerning Annihilation and Conditional Immortality." *Themelios* 21, no. 1 (1996): 14-18.

————. "The Nature of Hell: Reflections on the Debate between Conditionalism and the Traditional View of Hell." In *The Reader Must Understand: Eschatology in Bible and Theology,* ed. K. E. Brower and M. W. Elliott, 231-41. Leicester: Inter-Varsity Press – Apollos, 1997.

Green, J. B., and M. Turner, eds. *Jesus of Nazareth: Lord and Christ.* Grand Rapids/ Carlisle: William B. Eerdmans/Paternoster, 1994.

Greenberg, M. "Crimes and Punishments." *IDB,* 1:733-44.

Grey, M. "Falling into Freedom: Searching for New Interpretations of Sin in a Secular Society." *SJT* 47, no. 2 (1994): 223-43.

Grider, J. K., and G. L. Knapp. "Punish." *ISBE,* 3:1051-54.

Griffith, L. *The Fall of the Prison: Biblical Perspectives on Prison Abolition.* Grand Rapids: William B. Eerdmans, 1993.

Grimsrud, T. "Healing Justice: The Prophet Amos and a 'New' Theology of Justice." In *Peace and Justice Shall Embrace: Power and Theopolitics in the Bible: Essays in Honour of M. Lind,* ed. T. Grimsrud and L. L. Johns, 64-85. Telford, Pa.: Pandora Press, 1999.

————, and H. Zehr. "Rethinking God, Justice, and Treatment of Offenders." *Journal of Offender Rehabilitation,* vol. 31, no. 3. Forthcoming.

Guelich, R. A. *The Sermon on the Mount.* Waco, Tex.: Word, 1982.

Gundry, R. H. "Grace, Works, and Staying Saved in Paul." *Biblica* 66 (1985): 1-38.

————. *Matthew: A Commentary on His Literary and Theological Art.* Grand Rapids: William B. Eerdmans, 1982.

Gunton, C. *The Actuality of Atonement.* Grand Rapids: William B. Eerdmans, 1989.

Gustafson, J. M. "The Relation of the Gospels to the Moral Life." In D. G. Miller and D. Y. Hadidian, *Jesus and Man's Hope,* 2:103-17. Pittsburgh: Pittsburgh Theological Seminary, 1971.

Haenchen, E. *The Acts of the Apostles: A Commentary.* Philadelphia: Westminster Press, 1971.

Hagner, D. A. *The Jewish Reclamation of Jesus.* Grand Rapids: Zondervan, 1984.

————. "Paul and Judaism: The Jewish Matrix of Early Christianity: Issues in the Current Debate." *BBR* 3 (1993): 111-130.

Hakiaha, M. "Resolving Conflict from a Maori Perspective." In *Restorative Justice: Contemporary Themes and Practice,* ed. H. Bowen and J. Consedine, 90-94. Lyttelton, N. Z.: Ploughshares Publications, 1999.

Hamerton-Kelly, R. G. "Sacred Violence and the Curse of the Law (Galatians 3:13): The Sacrifice of Christ as Sacrificial Travesty." *NTS* 36, no. 1 (1990): 98-118.

Hanson, A. T. *The Wrath of the Lamb.* London: SPCK, 1957.

Harding, J. "Youth Crime: A Relational Perspective." In *Relational Justice: Repairing the Breach,* ed. J. Burnside and N. Baker, 104-13. Winchester, U.K.: Waterside Press, 1994.

Harrelson, W. *The Ten Commandments and Human Rights.* Philadelphia: Fortress Press, 1980.

Harrington, D. J. "The Jewishness of Jesus: Facing Some Problems." *CBQ* 49, no. 1 (1987): 13.

————. "Paul and Judaism: 5 Puzzles." *BR* 9, no. 2 (1993): 19-25, 52.

Harris, G. "The Beginnings of Church Discipline: 1 Corinthians 5." *NTS* 37, no. 4 (1991): 1-21.

Harrison, R. K., ed. "Punishment," "Restitution," "Retribution," "Revenge." *EBCE,* 340, 352-53.

Harrisville, R. A. "ΠΙΣΤΙΣ ΧΡΙΣΤΟΥ: Witness of the Fathers." *NovT* 36, no. 3 (1994): 233-41.

Harvey, A. E. *Strenuous Commands: The Ethic of Jesus.* London: SCM, 1990.

Harvey, J. D. "The 'With Christ' Motif in Paul's Thought." *JETS* 35, no. 3 (1992): 329-40.

Hauerwas, S. *The Peaceable Kingdom.* London: SCM, 1983.

————. "Why Time Cannot and Should Not Heal the Wounds of History, but Time Has Been and Can Be Redeemed." *SJT* 53, no. 1 (2000): 33-49.

————, and W. Willimon. *Resident Aliens: Life in the Christian Colony.* Nashville: Abingdon Press, 1989.

Haugen, G. A. *Good News about Injustice: A Witness of Courage in a Hurting World.* Leicester/Downers Grove, Ill.: InterVarsity Press, 1999.

Haughey, J. C. "Jesus as the Justice of God." In *The Faith that Does Justice: Examining the Christian Sources for Social Change,* ed. J. C. Haughey, 264-90. New York: Paulist Press, 1977.

————, ed. *The Faith that Does Justice: Examining the Christian Sources for Social Change.* New York: Paulist Press, 1977.

Havelaar, H. "Hellenistic Parallels to Acts 5:1-11 and the Problem of Conflicting Interpretations." *JSNT* 67 (1997): 63-82.

Havener, I. "A Curse for Salvation — 1 Corinthians 5:1-5." In *Sin, Salvation, and the Spirit,* ed. D. Durken, 334-44. Collegeville: Liturgical Press, 1979.

Hawthorne, G. F., and O. Betz, eds. *Tradition and Interpretation in the New Testament.* Grand Rapids/Tübingen: William B. Eerdmans/J. C. B. Mohr, 1987.

Hay, D. M. "*Pistis* as 'Ground for Faith' in Hellenized Judaism and Paul." *JBL* 108, no. 3 (1989): 461-76.

————, ed. *Pauline Theology, Volume II: 1 & 2 Corinthians.* Minneapolis: Fortress Press, 1993.

Hay, D. M., and E. E. Johnson, eds. *Pauline Theology, Volume III: Romans.* Minneapolis: Augsburg, 1995.

Hayden, A., and P. Henderson. "Victims: The Invisible People." In *Restorative Justice: Contemporary Themes and Practice,* ed. H. Bowen and J. Consedine, 78-82. Lyttelton, N.Z.: Ploughshares Publications, 1999.

Hayes, J. H. "Atonement in the Book of Leviticus." *Interpretation* 52, no. 1 (1998): 5-15.

Hayes, Z. J. "The Purgatorial View." In *Four Views on Hell,* ed. W. V. Crockett, 91-118. Grand Rapids: Zondervan, 1992.

Hays, R. B. "Adam, Israel, Christ: The Question of Covenant in the Theology of Romans: A Response to Leander E. Keck and N. T. Wright." In *Pauline Theology, Volume III: Romans,* ed. D. M. Hay and E. E. Johnson, 68-86. Minneapolis: Fortress Press, 1995.

————. *Echoes of Scripture in the Letters of Paul.* New Haven: Yale University Press, 1989.

————. *The Faith of Jesus Christ,* SBLDS 56. Chico, Calif.: Scholars Press, 1983.

————. "Justification." *ABD*, 3:1129-33.

————. "ΠΙΣΤΙΣ and Pauline Christology: What Is at Stake?" In *SBL Seminar Papers,* 714-29. Chico, Calif.: Scholars Press, 1991.

————. *The Moral Vision of the New Testament: A Contemporary Introduction to New Testament Ethics*. Edinburgh: T. & T. Clark, 1996.

————. "Psalm 3 and the Logic of Romans 3." *JBL* 99 (1980): 107-15.

Head, P. M. "The Duration of Divine Judgment in the New Testament." In *The Reader Must Understand: Eschatology in Bible and Theology*, ed. K. E. Brower and M. W. Elliott, 221-27. Leicester: Inter-Varsity Press — Apollos, 1997.

Henry, C. F. "Justification: A Doctrine in Crisis." *JETS* 38, no. 1 (1995): 57-65.

————. "Prison Reform." *BDCE*, 532-34.

Herion, G. A. "Retribution." *ISBE*, 4:154-59.

————. "Wrath of God (OT)." *ABD*, 6:986-96.

Herzog II, W. R. *Jesus: Justice and the Reign of God: A Ministry of Liberation*. Louisville, Ky.: Westminster John Knox, 2000.

Heschel, A. J. *The Prophets*. New York: Jewish Publication Society of America, 1962.

Hick, J. *Death and Eternal Life*. London: Collins, 1976.

Hickey, C. "Alternative Dispute Resolution within Criminal Justice." In *Restorative Justice: Contemporary Themes and Practice*, ed. H. Bowen and J. Consedine, 83-89. Lyttelton, N.Z.: Ploughshares Publications, 1999.

Hill, M. "The Victory of Personal Relationships: Paul and Social Ethics." In *Christians in Society*, Explorations 3, ed. B. G. Webb, 131-44. Homebush West, N.S.W.: Lancer, 1988.

Hirsch, F. E., and J. K. Grider. "Crime." *ISBE*, 1:815-17.

Hoffman, Y. "The Creativity of Theodicy." In *Justice and Righteousness: Biblical Themes and Their Influence*, ed. H. G. Reventlow and Y. Hoffman, 117-30. Sheffield: Sheffield Academic Press, 1992.

Hook, H. P. "Punishment." *BDCE*, 556-57.

Hooker, M. D. "Adam in Romans." *NTS* 6 (1959/60): 297-306.

————. *From Adam to Christ: Essays on Paul*. Cambridge: Cambridge University Press, 1990.

————. *Not Ashamed of the Gospel: New Testament Interpretations of the Death of Christ*. Carlisle: Paternoster, 1994.

————. "ΠΙΣΤΙΣ ΧΡΙΣΤΟΥ." *NTS* 35 (1989): 321-42.

Hooker, M. D., and S. G. Wilson, eds. *Paul and Paulinism*. London: SPCK, 1982.

Horrell, D. G. *The Social Ethos of the Corinthian Correspondence: Interests and Ideology from 1 Corinthians to 1 Clement*. Edinburgh: T. & T. Clark, 1996.

Horsely, R. A. "Ethics and Exegesis: 'Love Your Enemies' and the Doctrine of Nonviolence." In *The Love of Enemy and Nonretaliation in the New Testament*, ed. W. M. Swartley, 72-101, 126-32. Louisville, Ky.: Westminster John Knox, 1992.

House, H. W. "Crime and Punishment." In H. W. House and J. H. Yoder, *The Death Penalty Debate*, 13-33. Dallas: Word, 1991.

————. "The New Testament and Capital Punishment." In H. W. House and J. H. Yoder, *The Death Penalty Debate*, 59-69. Dallas: Word, 1991.

House, H. W., and J. H. Yoder. *The Death Penalty Debate*. Dallas: Word, 1991.

Howell Jr., D. N. "The Center of Pauline Theology." *BS* 151 (1994): 50-70.

Hoyles, J. A. *Punishment in the Bible*. London: Epworth, 1986.

Hudson, B. A. *Understanding Justice: An Introduction to Ideas, Perspectives, and Controversies in Modern Penal Theory.* Buckingham: Open University Press, 1996.

Hughes, P. E. "Conditional Immortality." *Evangel,* Summer 1992, 10-12.

Hultgren, A. "The *Pistis Christou* Formulation in Paul." *NovT* 22 (1980): 248-63.

Ignatieff, M. "Imprisonment and the Need for Justice." *Theology* 45, no. 764 (1992): 97-101.

Ingram, T. R. "The Keystone of Our Penal System." In *Essays on the Death Penalty,* ed. T. R. Ingram, 55-62. Houston: St. Thomas Press, 1963.

Ingram T. R., ed. *Essays on the Death Penalty.* Houston: St. Thomas Press, 1963.

Isasi-Díaz, A. M. "Justice and Social Change." *DFTh,* 150-62.

Jacques, G. *Beyond Impunity: An Ecumenical Approach to Truth, Justice, and Reconciliation.* Geneva: WCC Publications, 2000.

Jennings, W. J. "The Criminal Among Us." *The Other Side,* September-October 1995, 43-47, 62.

Jeremias, J. *The Central Message of the New Testament.* London: SCM, 1965.

———. "Zur Geschichtlichkeit des Verhors Jesu vor dem hohen Rat." *ZNW* 43 (1950-51): 148-50.

Jeschke, M. *Discipling the Brother: Congregational Discipline According to the Gospel.* Scottdale, Pa.: Herald Press, 1972.

Johnson Jr., S. L. "'God Gave Them Up': A Study in Divine Retribution." *BS* 129, no. 514 (1972): 124-33.

Johnson, L. T. "Rom 3:21-26 and the Faith of Jesus." *CBQ* 44 (1982): 77-90.

Jones, L. G. *Embodying Forgiveness: A Theological Analysis.* Grand Rapids: William B. Eerdmans, 1995.

Jones, R. G. "How Christians Actually Arrive at Ethical Decisions." *ExpT* 105, no. 10 (1994): 292-96.

Käsemann, E. *Commentary on Romans.* London: SCM, 1980.

———. "Justification and Salvation History in the Epistle to the Romans." In E. Käsemann, *Perspectives on Paul,* 60-78. London: SCM, 1969.

———. *New Testament Questions of Today.* London: SCM, 1969.

———. "Principles of Interpretation of Romans 13." In E. Käsemann, *New Testament Questions of Today,* 196-216. London: SCM, 1969.

———. "The Righteousness of God in Paul." In *New Testament Questions of Today,* 168-82. London: SCM, 1969.

———. "The Saving Significance of the Death of Jesus in Paul." In E. Käsemann, *Perspectives on Paul,* 32-59. London: SCM, 1969.

———. "Sentences of Holy Law in the New Testament." In E. Käsemann, *New Testament Questions of Today,* 66-81. London: SCM, 1969.

Kay, J. K. "The Word of the Cross at the Turn of the Ages." *Interpretation* 53, no. 1 (1999): 44-56.

Kaye, B. N. "Law and Morality in the Epistles of the New Testament." In *Law, Morality, and the Bible: A Symposium,* ed. B. N. Kaye and G. J. Wenham, 72-97. Leicester: Inter-Varsity Press, 1978.

———. "The New Testament and the Social Order." In *Law, Morality, and the Bible: A*

Symposium, ed. B. N. Kaye and G. J. Wenham, 98-113. Leicester: Inter-Varsity Press, 1978.

Kaye, B. N., and G. J. Wenham. *Law, Morality, and the Bible: A Symposium.* Leicester: Inter-Varsity Press, 1978.

Kaylor, R. D. *Jesus the Prophet: His Vision of the Kingdom on Earth.* Louisville, Ky.: Westminster John Knox, 1994.

Keck, L. E. "Jesus' Faith in Romans." *JBL* 108, no. 3 (1989): 443-60.

———. "Rethinking 'New Testament Ethics.'" *JBL* 115, no. 1 (1996): 3-16.

———. "What Makes Romans Tick?" In *Pauline Theology, Volume III: Romans,* ed. D. M. Hay and E. E. Johnson, 3-29. Minneapolis: Fortress Press, 1995.

Kehler, L., et al. *Capital Punishment Study Guide.* Winnipeg: MCC Victim Offenders Ministries, 1980.

Kelly, D. M. "Religion and Justice: The Volcano and the Terrace." *Review of Religious Research* 26 (1984): 3-14.

Kelsey, D. H. "Whatever Happened to the Doctrine of Sin?" *ThTo* 50, no. 2 (1993): 169-78.

Kidner, D. A. *The Death Penalty: An Ethical and Biblical Exposition.* London: Falcon Booklets, 1963.

———. "Retribution and Punishment in the Old Testament in Light of the New Testament." *SBET* 1 (1983): 3-9.

Kilgallen, J. J. "Forgiveness of Sins (Luke 7:36-50)." *NovT* 40, no. 2 (1998): 105-16.

———. "Luke 7:41-42 and Forgiveness of Sins." *ExpT* 111, no. 2 (1999): 46-47.

Kilner, J. F. "A Pauline Approach to Ethical Decision-Making." *Interpretation* 43, no. 4 (1989): 366-79.

Kinman, B. "'Appoint the Despised as Judges!' (1 Corinthians 6:4)." *TynBul* 48, no. 2 (1997): 345-54.

Kissane, K. "Punish and Be Damned." *Time Magazine,* 28 June 1993, 28-33.

Klassen, W. "Coals of Fire: Sign of Repentance or Revenge?" *NTS* 9, no. 4 (1962/1963): 337-50.

———. "'Love Your Enemies': Some Reflections on the Current Status of Research." In *The Love of Enemy and Nonretaliation in the New Testament,* ed. W. M. Swartley, 1-31. Louisville, Ky.: Westminster John Knox, 1992.

Knierim, R. P. *The Task of Old Testament Theology: Substance, Method, and Cases.* Grand Rapids: William B. Eerdmans, 1995.

Knight, D. A. "The Ethics of Human Life in the Hebrew Bible." In *Justice and the Holy: Essays in Honour of Walter Harrelson,* ed. D. A. Knight and P. J. Peters, 65-88. Atlanta: Scholars Press, 1989.

Knight, D. A., and P. J. Peters, eds. *Justice and the Holy: Essays in Honour of Walter Harrelson.* Atlanta: Scholars Press, 1989.

Knight, G. A. F. "Is 'Righteous' Right?" *SJT* 41 (1988): 1-10.

Knight III, G. W. *The Pastoral Epistles: A Commentary on the Greek Text.* Carlisle/Grand Rapids: Paternoster/William B. Eerdmans, 1992.

Koch, K. "Is There a Doctrine of Retribution in the Old Testament?" In *Theodicy in the Old Testament,* ed. J. L. Crenshaw, 57-87. Philadelphia/London: Fortress Press/SPCK, 1983.

Koontz, T. "Mennonites and the State: Preliminary Reflections." In *Essays on Peace Theology and Witness,* ed. W. M. Swartley, 35-60. Elkhart, Ind.: Institute of Mennonite Studies, 1988.

Krauss, C. N. *God Our Saviour: Theology in a Christological Mode.* Scottdale, Pa.: Herald Press, 1991.

————. *Jesus Christ Our Lord: Christology from a Disciple's Perspective.* Scottdale, Pa.: Herald Press, 1987.

Kraybill, R. "From Head to Heart: The Cycle of Reconciliation." *MCC Conciliation Quarterly,* Fall 1988, 13-15.

Krog, A. "The Truth and Reconciliation Commission — A National Ritual?" *Missionalia* 26, no. 1 (1998): 5-16.

Kroger, D. "Paul and the Civil Authorities: An Exegesis of Romans 13:1-7." *AJT* 7, no. 2 (1993): 344-66.

Kruse, C. G. "The Offender and the Offence in 2 Corinthians 2:5 and 7:12." *EvQ* 88, no. 2 (1988): 129-39.

Küng, H. *Eternal Life? Life after Death as a Medical, Philosophical, and Theological Problem.* Garden City, N.Y.: Doubleday, 1984.

Kvanvig, J. L. *The Problem of Hell.* Oxford: Oxford University Press, 1993.

Ladd, G. E. "Righteousness in Romans." *SWJT* 19, no. 1 (1976): 6-17.

Lambrecht, J., and R. W. Thompson. *Justification by Faith.* Wilmington, Del.: Michael Glazier, 1989.

Lapide, P. *The Sermon on the Mount: Utopia or Program for Action?* Maryknoll, N.Y.: Orbis, 1986.

Lapsley, M. "The Heart of Justice: Truth, Mercy, Healing, Forgiveness." In *Restorative Justice: Contemporary Themes and Practice,* ed. H. Bowen and J. Consedine, 45-50. Lyttelton, N.Z.: Ploughshares Publications, 1999.

Lasserre, J. *War and the Gospel.* London: James Clarke, 1962.

Lebacqz, K. "Justice." *DFTh,* 158-59.

Leech, K. *True God: An Exploration in Spiritual Theology.* London: Sheldon Press, 1985.

Lenski, R. C. H. *St. Paul's Epistle to the Romans.* Minneapolis: Augsburg, 1936.

Leuba, J.-L. "Reward." In *Vocabulary of the Bible,* ed. J.-J. Von Allmen, 369-71. London: Lutterworth, 1958.

Lewis, C. S. "The Humanitarian Theory of Punishment." In *Essays on the Death Penalty,* ed. T. R. Ingram, 1-12. Houston: St. Thomas Press, 1963.

Lewis, J. P. "'The Gates of Hell Shall Not Prevail against It' (Matt 16:18): A Study of the History of Interpretation." *JETS* 38, no. 3 (1995): 349-67.

Lieu, J. M. "Reading in Canon and Community: Deuteronomy 21:22-23, a Test Case for Dialogue." In *The Bible in Human Society: Essays in Honour of John Rogerson,* ed. M. D. R. Carroll, D. J. A. Clines, and P. R. Davies, 317-34. Sheffield: Sheffield Academic Press, 1995.

Lilley, J. P. U. "The Judgment of God: The Problem of the Canaanites." *Themelios* 22, no. 2 (1997): 3-12.

Limburg, J. "Human Rights in the Old Testament." *Concilium* 124 (1979): 20-26.

Lind, M. C. "Law in the Old Testament." In *The Bible and Law,* ed. W. M. Swartley, 9-41. Elkhart, Ind.: Institute of Mennonite Studies, 1982.

————. "Transformation of Justice: From Moses to Jesus." *NPCJ* 5 (1986): 1-22.

Lind, S., ed. "South Africa's Truth and Reconciliation Commission." *MCC Peace Office Newsletter* 28, no. 3 (1998): 1-12.

Lindars, B. *The Gospel of John*. Grand Rapids/London: William B. Eerdmans/Marshall, Morgan & Scott, 1972.

————, ed. *Law and Religion: Essays on the Place of Law in Israel and Early Christianity*. Cambridge: James Clarke, 1988.

Lindsay, D. R. "The Roots and Development of the πιστ- Word Group as Faith Terminology." *JSNT* 49 (1993): 103-18.

Llewellyn, D. "Restoring the Death Penalty: Proceed with Caution." In L. Kehler et al., *Capital Punishment Study Guide, 39-43*. Winnipeg: MCC Victim Offenders Ministries, 1980.

Lohfink, G. *Jesus and Community: The Social Dimension of the Christian Faith*. London: SPCK, 1985.

Lohse, E. "*Emuna* und *Pistis* — Jüdisches und urchristliches Verständnis des Glaubens." *ZNW* 64 (1977): 147-63.

Longenecker, B. "ΠΙΣΤΙΣ in Romans 3.25: Neglected Evidence for the Faithfulness of Christ?" *NTS* 39 (1993): 478-80.

Longenecker, R. N. "The Foundational Conviction of New Testament Christology: The Obedience/Faithfulness/Sonship of Christ." In *Jesus of Nazareth: Lord and Christ*, ed. J. B. Green and M. Turner, 473-88. Grand Rapids/Carlisle: William B. Eerdmans/Paternoster, 1994.

Lorton, D. "The Treatment of Criminals in Ancient Egypt: Through the New Kingdom." *JESHO* 20, no. 1 (1977): 1-64.

Luc, A. "Interpreting the Curses in the Psalms." *JETS* 42, no. 3 (1999): 396-410.

Lührmann, D. *Glaube im frühen Christentum*. Gütersloh: Gütersloher Verlaghaus Gerd Mohn, 1976.

Macalpine, C. S. "Vengeance." *HDCG*, 2:791-92.

MacGregor, G. H. C. *The New Testament Basis of Pacifism*. London: Fellowship of Reconciliation, 1953.

MacGuire, D. G. *The Moral Core of Judaism and Christianity: Reclaiming the Revolution*. Minneapolis: Fortress Press, 1993.

Maclachlan, R. "Jesus and Judgment." *Stimulus* 2, no. 4 (1994): 48.

————. "A Response to Crime and Punishment." *Stimulus* 1, no. 3 (1993): 47-48.

————. "What of Biblical Law?" *Stimulus* 2, no. 3 (1994): 58.

MacLean, B. H. "The Absence of an Atoning Sacrifice in Paul's Soteriology." *NTS* 38, no. 4 (1992): 531-53.

Mafico, T. L. J. "Just, Justice." *ABD*, 3:1127-29.

Malina, B. J., and R. L. Rohrbaugh. *Social Science Commentary on the Synoptic Gospels*. Minneapolis: Fortress Press, 1992.

Maluleke, T. S. "Truth, National Unity, and Reconciliation in South Africa: Aspects of the Emerging Theological Agenda." *Missionalia* 25, no. 1 (1997): 59-86.

Manson, T. W. *On Paul and John: Some Selected Theological Themes*. London: SCM, 1963.

Marcus, J. "The Gates of Hades and the Keys of the Kingdom (Matt 16:18-19)." *CBQ* 50 (1988): 443-55.

Marrow, S. B. "Principles for Interpreting the New Testament Soteriological Terms." *NTS* 36, no. 2 (1990): 268-80.

Marsh, J. *The Gospel of Saint John*. Harmondsworth: Penguin, 1968.

Marshall, C. D. "The Atonement as a Work of Justice." *Stimulus* 5, no. 3 (1997): 2-7.

———. "Bearing the Sword in Vain? Romans 13:4, John Howard Yoder, and the Death Penalty Debate." *F&F* 5, nos. 1-2 (1996): 60-65.

———. "The Challenge of the Beatitudes (Part One)." *F&F* 4, no. 2 (1995): 5-11.

———. "The Challenge of the Beatitudes (Part Two)." *F&F* 4, no. 3 (1995): 4-9.

———. "Crime and Punishment." *Stimulus* 1, no. 2 (1993): 37-42.

———. *Faith as a Theme in Mark's Narrative*, SNTSMS 68. Cambridge: Cambridge University Press, 1989.

———. "'For Me to Live Is Christ': Pauline Spirituality as a Basis for Ministry." In *The Call to Serve: Biblical and Theological Perspectives on Ministry*, ed. D. A. Campbell, 96-116. Sheffield: Sheffield Academic Press, 1996.

———. "Jesus and the Death Penalty." *Stimulus* 3, no. 1 (1995): 45-46.

———. *Kingdom Come: The Kingdom of God in the Teaching of Jesus*. Auckland, N.Z.: Impetus, 1993.

———. "'Made a Little Lower than the Angels': Human Rights in the Biblical Tradition." In *Human Rights and the Common Good: Christian Perspectives*, ed. B. Atkin and K. Evans, 14-76. Wellington, N.Z.: Victoria University Press, 1999.

———. "New Testament Reflections on Crime and Punishment." *Stimulus* 2, no. 3 (1994): 43-55.

———. "Paul and Christian Social Responsibility." *Anvil* 17, no. 1 (2000): 7-18.

———. "Paul and Jesus: Continuity or Discontinuity?" *Stimulus* 5, no. 4 (1997): 32-42.

———. "Paul's Gospel of Divine Justice." In *The Vision New Zealand Congress*, ed. B. Patrick, 106-15. Auckland, N.Z.: Vision New Zealand, 1993.

———. "Through the Eye of the Needle: Faith and Discipleship." *F&F* 3, no. 4 (1994): 8-12.

———. "The Use of the Bible in Ethics: Scripture, Ethics, and the Social Justice Statement." In *Voices for Justice: Church, Law, and State in New Zealand*, ed. J. Boston and A. Cameron, 107-46. Palmerston North, N.Z.: Dunmore Press, 1994.

Marshall, I. H. "The Nature of Christian Salvation." *EuroJTh* 4, no. 1 (1995): 29-43.

Martens, E. A. "Capital Punishment and the Christian." In *On Capital Punishment*, ed. J. H. Redekop and E. A. Martens, 19-29. Hillsboro, Kans./Winnipeg, Man.: Kindred Press, 1987.

Martin, R. P. *2 Corinthians*. Waco: Word, 1986.

Matera, F. J. *New Testament Ethics: The Legacies of Jesus and Paul*. Louisville, Ky.: Westminster John Knox, 1996.

Matlock, R. B. "Demythologizing the PISTIS CRISTOU Debate: Cautionary Remarks from a Lexical Semantic Prespective." *NovT* 42, no. 1 (2000): 1-23.

McClister, D. "'Where Two or Three Are Gathered Together': Literary Structure as a Key to Meaning in Matt 17:22–20:19." *JETS* 39, no. 4 (1996): 549-58.

McDonald, F. "When Forgiveness Is Not Enough." *New Zealand Listener*, 26 March 1994, 20-27.

BIBLIOGRAPHY

McDonald, J. I. H. "Romans 13:1-7 and Christian Social Ethics Today." *The Modern Churchman* 29, no. 2 (1987): 19-25.

———. "The So-Called *PERICOPE DE ADULTERA.*" *NTS* 41, no. 3 (1995): 415-27.

McElrea, F. W. M. "Justice in the Community: The New Zealand Experience." In *Relational Justice: Repairing the Breach,* ed. J. Burnside and N. Baker, 93-103. Winchester, U.K.: Waterside Press, 1994.

———. "The New Zealand Model of Family Group Conferences." *European Journal of Criminal Policy and Research* 6 (1998): 527-43.

———. "Restorative Justice: The New Zealand Youth Court: A Model for Development in Other Courts?" Unpublished paper presented at the National Conference of District Court Judges, Rotorua, N.Z., 6-9 April 1994.

———. "Taking Responsibility in Being Accountable." In *Restorative Justice: Contemporary Themes and Practice,* ed. H. Bowen and J. Consedine, 56-63. Lyttelton, N.Z.: Ploughshares Publications, 1999.

———. "Why Relational Justice Works." *Relational Justice Bulletin* 2 (April 1999): 6-7.

McGrath, A. E. "Doctrine and Ethics." *JETS* 34, no. 2 (1991): 145-56.

———. "Justice and Justification: Semantic and Juristic Aspects of the Christian Doctrine of Justification." *SJT* 35 (1982): 403-18.

———. "Justification: The New Ecumenical Debate." *Themelios* 13, no. 2 (1987): 43-48.

———. "'The Righteousness of God' from Augustine to Luther." *StTh* 36 (1982): 63-78.

McKenzie, M. "Christian Norms in the Ethical Square: An Impossible Dream?" *JETS* 38, no. 3 (1995): 413-27.

McKenzie, P. "Crime and Punishment in the Old Testament." *Stimulus* 2, no. 3 (1994): 16-22.

McQuilkin, R. *An Introduction to Biblical Ethics.* Wheaton: Tyndale, 1989.

Meeks, W. *The Moral World of the First Christians.* London: SPCK, 1987.

Megivern, J. J. *The Death Penalty: An Historical and Theological Survey.* Mahwah, N.J.: Paulist Press, 1997.

Meier, J. P. "Matthew 5:3-12." *Interpretation* 43, no. 3 (1990): 281-85.

Mendez, G. W. "Justification and Social Justice." In *Right with God: Justification in the Bible and the World,* ed. D. A. Carson, 178-96. Exeter/Grand Rapids: Paternoster/Baker, 1992.

Merklein, H., ed. *Neues Testament und Ethik.* Freiburg/Basel/Wein: Herder, 1989.

Metzger, B. M. *A Textual Commentary on the Greek New Testament.* London: United Bible Societies, 1971.

Milavec, A. "The Social Setting of 'Turning the Other Cheek' and 'Loving One's Enemies' in Light of the *Didache.*" *BTB* 25, no. 3 (1995): 131-43.

Miles, M. R. "Imitation of Christ: Is It Possible in the Twentieth Century?" *Princeton Seminary Bulletin* 10, no. 1 (1989): 7-22.

Milgrom, J. "*Lex Talionis* and the Rabbis." *BR* 12, no. 2 (1996): 16, 48.

Milikowsky, C. "Which Gehenna? Retribution and Eschatology in the Synoptic Gospels and in Early Jewish Texts." *NTS* 34, no. 2 (1988): 238-49.

Mitchell, A. C. "Rich and Poor in the Courts of Corinth: Litigiousness and Status in 1 Corinthians 6:1-11." *NTS* 39, no. 4 (1993): 562-86.

Moberly, E. R. "Penology." *NDCE,* 462-64.

———. "Retribution." *NDCE,* 549-50.

———. *Suffering, Innocent and Guilty.* London: SPCK, 1978.

Moberly, W. *The Ethics of Punishment.* London: Faber & Faber, 1968.

Moltmann, J. "The End of Everything Is God: Has Belief in Hell Had Its Day?" *ExpT* 108, no. 9 (1997): 263-64.

———. *Jesus Christ for Today's World.* London: SCM, 1994.

Moltmann-Wendel, E. "Is There a Feminist Theology of the Cross?" In *The Scandal of a Crucified World: Perspectives on the Cross and Suffering,* ed. J. Tesfai, 87-98. Maryknoll, N.Y.: Orbis, 1994.

Moo, D. J. "Jesus and the Authority of the Mosaic Law." *JSNT* 20 (1984): 3-49.

———. "Paul and the Law in the Last Ten Years." *SJT* 40 (1987): 287-307.

———. *The Wycliffe Exegetical Commentary on Romans 1–8.* Chicago: Moody, 1991.

Moore, G. F. *Judaism in the First Centuries of the Christian Era: The Age of the Tannaim* (Cambridge: Harvard University Press, 1927), 2 Vols.

Morgan, R. *Romans.* New Testament Guides. Sheffield: Sheffield Academic Press, 1995.

Morris, L. *The Apostolic Preaching of the Cross.* Grand Rapids: William B. Eerdmans, 1965.

———. *Commentary on the Gospel of John.* Grand Rapids: William B. Eerdmans, 1971.

———. *The Cross in the New Testament.* Exeter: Paternoster, 1966.

———. *The Epistle to the Romans.* Grand Rapids: William B. Eerdmans, 1988.

Morris, R. "From Misery Justice to Transformative Justice." *The Common Good* 4 (1997): 7-9.

Morton, A. R., ed. *The State of Imprisonment,* Occasional Paper No. 38. Edinburgh: Centre for Theology and Public Issues, University of Edinburgh, 1997.

Mosedale, S. *Heaven and Hell: The Final Divergence?* Birmingham: Association of Conservative Evangelicals in Methodism, 1985.

Mott, S. C. *A Christian Perspective on Political Thought.* New York/Oxford: Oxford University Press, 1993.

———. "Civil Authority." *DPL,* 141-43.

———. "The Partiality of Biblical Justice." *Transformation* 10, no. 1 (1993): 23-29.

———. "The Use of the Bible in Social Ethics II: The Use of the New Testament," Part I, *Transformation* 1, no. 2 (1984): 11-20; "The Use of the Bible in Social Ethics II: The Use of the New Testament: Part II, Objections to the Enterprise," *Transformation* 1, no. 3 (1984): 19-26.

Motyer, S. "Justification in the New Testament Outside the Pauline Corpus." *Vox Evangelica* 22 (1992): 71-89.

Moulder, J. "Romans 13 and Conscientious Disobedience." *JTSA* 21 (1977): 13-23.

Moule, C. F. D. "Jesus, Judaism, and Paul." In *Tradition and Interpretation in the New Testament,* ed. G. F. Hawthorne with O. Betz, 43-52. Grand Rapids/Tübingen: William B. Eerdmans/J. C. B. Mohr, 1987.

———. "Punishment and Retribution: An Attempt to Delimit Their Scope in New

Testament Thought." *NPCJ* 10 (1990): 1-21. (This article was originally published in *Svensk exegetisk årsbok* 30 [1965], 21-36.)

Moxnes, H. "Honor and Shame." *BTB* 23, no. 4 (1993): 167-76.

———. "Honour and Righteousness in Romans." *JSNT* 32 (1988): 61-77.

Müller-Fahrenholz, G. *The Art of Forgiveness: Theological Reflections on Healing and Reconciliation.* Geneva: WCC Publications, 1997.

Munro, W. "Romans 13:1-7: Apartheid's Last Biblical Refuge." *BTB* 20, no. 4 (1990): 161-68.

Murphy-O'Connor, J., and J. H. Charlesworth, eds. *Paul and the Dead Sea Scrolls.* New York: Crossroad Publishing, 1990.

Murray, J. *The Epistle of Paul to the Romans.* 2 vols. London: Marshall, Morgan & Scott, 1960.

Myers, C. D. "Romans, Epistle to the." *ABD,* 5:816-30.

Nanos, M. D. *The Mystery of Romans: The Jewish Context of Paul's Letter.* Minneapolis: Fortress Press, 1996.

Nebe, G. "Righteousness in Paul." In *Justice and Righteousness: Biblical Themes and Their Influence,* ed. H. G. Reventlow and Y. Hoffman, 131-53. Sheffield: Sheffield Academic Press, 1992.

Netland, H. "Exclusivism, Tolerance, and Truth." *ERT* 12, no. 3 (1988): 240-60.

Neusner, J., and W. S. Green, eds. *Dictionary of Judaism in the Biblical Period.* Peabody, Mass.: Hendrickson, 1999.

Newman, C. C., ed. *Jesus and the Restoration of Israel: A Critical Assessment of N. T. Wright's "Jesus and the Victory of God."* Downers Grove, Ill./Carlisle: InterVarsity Press/Paternoster, 1999.

Nicholls, B. J. "The Salvation and Lostness of Mankind." *ERT* 15, no. 1 (1991): 4-21.

Nixon, R. "Fulfilling the Law: Gospels and Acts." In *Law, Morality, and the Bible: A Symposium,* ed. B. N. Kaye and G. J. Wenham, 53-71. Leicester: Inter-Varsity Press, 1978.

———. "The Universality of the Concept of Law." In *Law, Morality, and the Bible: A Symposium,* ed. B. N. Kaye and G. J. Wenham, 114-21. Leicester: Inter-Varsity Press, 1978.

Northey, Wayne. "Justice Is Peacemaking: A Biblical Theology of Peacemaking in Response to Criminal Conflict." *NPCJ* 12 (1992), 1-74.

———. "Rediscovering Spiritual Roots: The Judeo-Christian Tradition and Criminal Justice." *The Justice Professional* 11 (1998): 47-70.

———. "Restorative Justice: Rebirth of an Ancient Practice." *NPCJ* 14 (1994), 1-39.

Novak, D. "Halakah." *ER,* 6:158-73.

O'Brien, P. T. "Justification in Paul and Some Crucial Issues of the Last Two Decades." In *Right with God: Justification in the Bible and the World,* ed. D. A. Carson, 69-95. Exeter: Paternoster, 1992.

Olley, J. W. "Righteousness — Some Issues in Old Testament Translation into English." *TBT* 38 (1987): 309-13.

Olson, M. "The God Who Dared." *The Other Side* 26, no. 3 (1990): 11-15.

———. "Gospel Justice: Responding to Heaven's Whispers." *The Other Side* 24, no. 3 (1989): 20-24.

Bibliography

————. "No More Prisons, No Not One." *The Other Side* 25, no. 3 (1989): 24-25.

Olu Igenoza, A. "Universalism and New Testament Christianity." *ERT* 12, no. 3 (1988): 261-75.

Orlinsky, H. M. "The Forensic Character of the Hebrew Bible." In *Justice and the Holy: Essays in Honour of Walter Harrelson,* ed. D. A. Knight and P. J. Peters, 89-97. Atlanta: Scholars Press, 1989.

Otto, R. E. "Justification and Justice: An Edwardsean Proposal." *EvQ* 65, no. 2 (1993): 131-45.

Packer, J. I. "Justification." *EDT,* 593-97.

————. "The Problem of Eternal Punishment." *Crux* 26, no. 3 (1990): 18-25.

————. *What Did the Cross Achieve? The Logic of Penal Substitution.* Leicester: Tyndale Press, TSF Monograph, 1974.

Patrick, B., ed. *The Vision New Zealand Congress.* Auckland, N.Z.: Vision New Zealand, 1993.

Patrick, M. W. "Understanding the 'Understanding Distance' Today: The Love Command of Jesus." In *Interpreting Disciples: Practical Theology in the Disciples of Christ,* ed. L. D. Richesin and L. D. Bouchard, 101-29. Fort Worth: Texas University Press, 1987.

Patte, D. *The Ethics of Biblical Interpretation: A Reevaluation.* Louisville, Ky.: Westminster John Knox, 1995.

Pavlich, G. C. *Justice Fragmented: Mediating Community Disputes under Postmodern Conditions.* London: Routledge, 1996.

Pedersen, A. "Forensic Justification: A Process Feminist Critique." *Process Studies* 22, no. 2 (1993): 84-92.

Peels, H. G. L. *The Vengeance of God: The Meaning of the Root NQM and the Function of the NQM-Texts in the Context of Divine Revelation in the Old Testament.* Leiden/New York/Köln: E. J. Brill, 1995.

Perkins, P. "Apocalyptic Sectarianism and Love Commands: The Johannine Epistles and Revelation." In *The Love of Enemy and Nonretaliation in the New Testament,* ed. W. M. Swartley, 287-96. Louisville, Ky.: Westminster John Knox, 1992.

Peters, J. "The Function of Forgiveness in Social Relationships." In *Forgiveness,* Concilium 177, ed. C. Floristán and C. Duquoc, 3-11. Edinburgh: T. & T. Clark, 1986.

Peterson, R. A. "A Traditionalist Response to John Stott's Arguments for Annihilationism." *JETS* 37, no. 4 (1994): 553-68.

Pilch, J. J., and B. J. Malina, eds. *Biblical Social Values and Their Meaning: A Handbook.* Peabody, Mass.: Hendrickson, 1993.

Pinnock, C. H. "The Conditional View." In *Four Views on Hell,* ed. W. V. Crockett, 135-66. Grand Rapids: Zondervan, 1992.

Piper, J. "The Demonstration of the Righteousness of God in Romans 3:25, 26." *JSNT* 7 (1980): 2-32.

Placher, W. C. "Christ Takes Our Place: Rethinking Atonement." *Interpretation* 53, no. 1 (1999): 5-20.

Plevnik, J. "The Center of Paul's Theology." *CBQ* 51 (1989): 461-78.

Plümacher, E. "μάχαιρα." *EDNT,* 2:397-98.

307

Plummer, A. *The Gospel According to St. John.* 1882; reprint, Grand Rapids: Baker, 1981.

Porter, S. E. "A Newer Perspective on Paul: Romans 1-8 through the Eyes of Literary Analysis." In *The Bible in Human Society: Essays in Honour of John Rogerson,* ed. M. D. R. Carroll, D. J. A. Clines, and P. R. Davies, 366-92. Sheffield: Sheffield Academic Press, 1995.

———. "The Pauline Concept of Original Sin, in Light of Rabbinic Background." *TynBul* 41, no. 1 (1990): 3-30.

Potter, K. H. "The Special Relationship: Anglo-American Attitudes to the Death Penalty." *ExpT* 106, no. 8 (1995): 228-31.

Poucher, J. "Crimes and Punishments." *HDB,* 1:520-27.

Prestidge, W. *Life, Death, and Destiny.* Auckland, N.Z.: Resurrection Publishing, 1998.

Preston, R. "Capital Punishment." *NDCE,* 75-76.

Pritchard, J. B., ed. *Ancient Near Eastern Texts Relating to the Old Testament.* Princeton: Princeton University Press, 1955.

Quast, K. *Reading the Corinthian Correspondence: An Introduction.* /Mahwah, N.J.: Paulist Press, 1994.

Quinn, J. D. "The Scriptures on Merit." In *Justification by Faith,* ed. H. G. Anderson, T. A. Murphy, and J. A. Burgess, 82-93. Minneapolis: Augsburg, 1985.

Ramsey, P. M. "The Biblical Norm of Righteousness." *Interpretation* 24, no. 4 (1970): 419-29.

Rangihaka, R. "Restorative Justice: A Police View." In *Restorative Justice: Contemporary Themes and Practice,* ed. H. Bowen and J. Consedine, 72-77. Lyttelton, N.Z.: Ploughshares Publications, 1999.

Rapske, B. M. "The Importance of Helpers to the Imprisoned Paul in the Book of Acts." *TynBul* 42, no. 1 (1991): 3-30.

Redekop, J. H. "An Analysis of Capital Punishment." In *On Capital Punishment,* ed. J. H. Redekop and E. A. Martens, 1-18. Hillsboro, Kans./Winnipeg, Man.: Kindred Press, 1987.

Redekop, V. "Scapegoats, the Bible, and Criminal Justice: Interacting with René Girard." *NPCJ* 13 (1993) 1-50.

Reid Jr., C. J., ed. *Peace in a Nuclear Age: The Bishops' Pastoral Letter in Perspective.* Washington: Catholic University of America Press, 1986.

Reid, G., ed. *The Great Acquittal: Justification by Faith and Current Christian Thought.* London: Fount, 1980.

Reiser, M. *Jesus and Judgment: The Eschatological Proclamation in Its Jewish Context.* Minneapolis: Fortress Press, 1997.

Renger, J. "Wrongdoing and Its Sanctions: On 'Criminal' and 'Civil' Law in the Old Babylonian Period." *JESHO* 20, no. 1 (1977): 65-77.

Renner, J. T. E., and V. C. Pfitzner. "Justice and Human Rights: Some Biblical Perspectives." *LTJ* 24, no. 1 (1990): 3-10.

Reumann, J. "Righteousness (Early Judaism, Greco-Roman World, New Testament)." *ABD,* 5:736-73.

———. *Righteousness in the New Testament.* Philadelphia: Fortress Press, 1982.

Reventlow, H. G. "Righteousness as Order of the World: Some Remarks Towards a

Programme," H. G. Reventlow & Y. Hoffman (eds.), *Justice and Righteousness: Biblical Themes and Their Influence.* Sheffield: Sheffield Academic Press, 1992, 163-72.

Reventlow, H. G., and Y. Hoffman, eds. *Justice and Righteousness: Biblical Themes and Their Influence.* Sheffield: Sheffield Academic Press, 1992.

Ricoeur, P. "The Golden Rule: Exegetical and Theological Perplexities." *NTS* 36 (1990): 392-97.

Ridderbos, H. *Paul: An Outline of His Theology.* Grand Rapids: William B. Eerdmans, 1975.

Riemschneider, K. K. "Prison and Punishment in Early Anatolia." *JESHO* 20, no. 1 (1977): 114-26.

Robinson, J. A. T. *Wrestling with Romans.* London: SCM, 1979.

Roetzal, C. J. "Paul and the Law: Whence and Whither?" *Currents in Biblical Research* 3 (1995): 249-75.

Rosner, B. S. "Temple and Holiness in 1 Corinthians 5." *TynBul* 42, no. 1 (1991): 137-45.

———. "'Οὐχὶ μᾶλλον ἐπενθήσατε': Corporate Responsibility in 1 Corinthians 5." *NTS* 38, no. 3 (1992): 470-73.

Rousseau, J. J., and R. Arav. *Jesus and His World: An Archaeological and Cultural Dictionary.* London: SCM, 1995.

Rubio, M. "The Christian Virtue of Forgiveness." In *Forgiveness,* Concilium 177, ed. C. Floristán and C. Duquoc, 80-94. Edinburgh: T. & T. Clark, 1986.

Ruprecht, A. A. "Legal System, Roman." *DPL,* 546-50.

Ryan, E. "Creative Criminal Justice." In *Restorative Justice: Contemporary Themes and Practice,* ed. H. Bowen and J. Consedine, 51-55. Lyttelton, N.Z.: Ploughshares Publications, 1999.

Sampley, J. P. "From Text to Thought World: The Route to Paul's Ways." In *Pauline Theology,* ed. J. M. Bassler, 1:3-14. Minneapolis: Fortress Press, 1991.

Sanday, W., and A. C. Headlam. *A Critical and Exegetical Commentary on the Epistle to the Romans.* 5th ed. Edinburgh: T. & T. Clark, 1902.

Sanders, E. P. *Paul and Palestinian Judaism.* London: SCM, 1977.

———. "The Synoptic Jesus and the Law." In E. P. Sanders, *Jewish Law from Jesus to the Mishnah: Five Studies,* 1-96. London: SCM, 1990.

Sasson, J. M. "Treatment of Criminals at Mari: A Survey." *JESHO* 20, no. 1 (1977): 90-113.

Schlatter, A. *Romans: The Righteousness of God.* Peabody, Mass.: Hendrickson, 1995.

Schluter, M. "What Is Relational Justice?" In *Relational Justice: Repairing the Breach,* ed. J. Burnside and N. Baker, 17-27. Winchester, U.K.: Waterside Press, 1994.

Schluter, M., and D. Lee. *The R Factor.* London: Hodder & Stoughton, 1993.

Schluter, M., and R. Clements. "Jubilee Institutional Norms: A Middle Way between Creation Ethics and Kingdom Ethics as the Basis for Christian Political Action." *EvQ* 62, no. 1 (1990): 37-62.

Schmidt, D. "1 Thess 2:13-16: Linguistic Evidence for an Interpolation." *JBL* 102, no. 2 (1983): 269-79.

Schreiner, T. R. "Reading Romans Theologically: A Review Article." *JETS* 41, no. 4 (1998): 641-48.

BIBLIOGRAPHY

Schrenk, G. "δίκη κτλ." *TDNT,* 2:174-225.

Schroeder, C. "'Standing in the Breach': Turning Away the Wrath of God." *Interpretation* 52, no. 1 (1998): 16-23.

Schürer, E. *The History of the Jewish People in the Age of Jesus Christ (175 BC–AD 135).* Revised by G. Vermes and F. Millar. 3 vols. Edinburgh: T. & T. Clark, 1973.

Schüssler Fiorenza, E. "The Ethics of Biblical Interpretation: Decentering Biblical Scholarship." *JBL* 107, no. 1 (1988): 3-17.

———. "Judging and Judgment in the New Testament Communities." In *Judgment in the Church,* Concilium no. 107, ed. W. Bassett and P. Huizing. New York: Seabury Press, 1977, 1-8.

Scriven, C. *The Transformation of Culture: Christian Social Ethics after H. Richard Niebuhr.* Scottdale, Pa.: Herald Press, 1988.

Scullion, J. J. "Righteousness (OT)." *ABD,* 5:724-36.

Searle, D. "The Cross of Christ." *EuroJTh* 8, no. 1 (1999): 3-22.

Searle, K. M. "Is There a Case for Capital Punishment?" *Stimulus* 1, no. 3 (1993): 45-47.

Seebass, H. "Righteousness, Justification." *NIDNTT,* 3:352-77.

Seifrid, M. A. *Justification by Faith: The Origin and Development of a Central Pauline Theme.* Leiden: E. J. Brill, 1992.

———. "The 'New Perspective on Paul' and Its Problems." *Themelios* 25, no. 2 (2000): 4-18.

Shaw, G. B. *The Crime of Imprisonment.* New York: Citadel Press, 1961.

Shaw, R. "Prisoners' Children: Symptom of a Failing Justice System." In *Relational Justice: Repairing the Breach,* ed. J. Burnside and N. Baker, 114-21. Winchester, U.K.: Waterside Press, 1994.

Sherwin-White, A. N. *Roman Society and Roman Law in the New Testament.* Oxford: Clarendon, 1963.

Simon, U. "Rewards and Punishments." *NDCE* 553-55.

Singer, P., ed. *A Companion to Ethics.* Oxford: Blackwell Publishers, 1991.

Smail, T. "Can One Man Die for the People?" In *Atonement Today,* ed. J. Goldingay, 73-92. London: SPCK, 1995.

Snodgrass, K. P. "Justification by Grace — To the Doers: An Analysis of the Place of Romans 2 in the Theology of Paul." *NTS* 32 (1986): 72-93.

———. "Matthew's Understanding of the Law." *Interpretation* 46, no. 4 (1992): 369-78.

Soards, M. C. "Käsemann's 'Righteousness' Re-examined." *CBQ* 49, no. 2 (1987): 264-67.

Soares-Prabhu, G. "'As We Forgive': Interhuman Forgiveness in the Teaching of Jesus." In *Forgiveness,* Concilium 177, ed. C. Floristán and C. Duquoc, 57-66. Edinburgh: T. & T. Clark, 1986.

Sobrino, J. "Latin America: Place of Sin and Place of Forgiveness." In *Forgiveness,* Concilium 177, ed. C. Floristán and C. Duquoc, 45-56. Edinburgh: T. & T. Clark, 1986.

South, J. T. "A Critique of the 'Curse/Death' Interpretation of 1 Corinthians 5:1-8." *NTS* 39, no. 4 (1993): 539-61.

Spanner, D. C. "Is Hell for Ever?" *Churchman* 110, no. 2 (1996): 107-20.

Stambaugh, J., and D. Balch. *The Social World of the First Christians.* London: SPCK, 1986.

Stayer, J. M. *Anabaptists and the Sword,* 2d rev. ed. Lawrence, Kans.: Coronado Press, 1976.

Stein, R. H. "The Argument of Romans 13:1-7." *NovT* 31, no. 4 (1989): 325-43.

Stendahl, K. *Final Account: Paul's Letter to the Romans.* Minneapolis: Fortress Press, 1995.

————. *Paul among Jews and Gentiles.* Philadelphia: Fortress Press, 1976.

Steussy, M. "Righteousness." *DFTh,* 245-46.

Stigers, H. G. "Sedeq." *TWOT,* 2:752-55.

Stott, J., and N. Miller, eds. *Crime and the Responsible Community.* London: Hodder & Stoughton, 1980.

Stott, J. R. W. *The Message of Romans: Good News for the World.* Leicester: Inter-Varsity Press, 1994.

Streater, D. "Justification by Faith Yesterday and Today." *Churchman* 113, no. 2 (1999): 147-57.

Studzinski, R. "Remember and Forgive: Psychological Dimensions of Forgiveness." In *Forgiveness, Concilium* 177, ed. C. Floristán and C. Duquoc, 12-21. Edinburgh: T. & T. Clark, 1986.

Stuhlmacher, P. *Paul's Letter to the Romans: A Commentary.* Louisville, Ky.: Westminster John Knox, 1994.

————. "The Theme of Romans." *ABR* 36 (1988): 31-44.

Sturm, D. "Natural Law." *ER,* 10:318-24.

Swartley, W. M. *Israel's Scripture Traditions and the Synoptic Gospels: Story Shaping Story.* Peabody, Mass.: Hendrickson, 1994.

————, ed. *The Bible and Law.* Elkhart, Ind.: Institute of Mennonite Studies, 1982.

————, ed. *Essays on Peace Theology and Witness.* Elkhart, Ind.: Institute of Mennonite Studies, 1988.

————, ed. *The Love of Enemy and Nonretaliation in the New Testament.* Louisville, Ky.: Westminster John Knox, 1992.

Talbot, T. "Punishment, Forgiveness, and Divine Justice." *RelSt* 29 (1993): 151-68.

Tamez, E. "Justification by Faith." *DFTh,* 162-63.

Tannehill, R. C. "The 'Focal Instance' as a Form of New Testament Speech: A Study in Matthew 5:39b-42." *JR* 50 (1970): 372-85.

Tasker, R. V. G. *John: An Introduction and Commentary.* Leicester: Inter-Varsity Press, 1960.

Taylor, E. L. H. "The Death Penalty." In *Essays on the Death Penalty,* ed. T. R. Ingram, 13-44. Houston: St. Thomas Press, 1963.

————. "Medicine or Morals as the Basis of Justice and Law?" In *Essays on the Death Penalty,* ed. T. R. Ingram, 81-102. Houston: St. Thomas Press, 1963.

Taylor, G. A. "Capital Punishment . . . Right and Necessary." In *Essays on the Death Penalty,* ed. T. R. Ingram, 45-54. Houston: St. Thomas Press, 1963.

Taylor, R. B. "Retaliation." *HDCG,* 2:517-18.

Ten, C. L. "Crime and Punishment." In *A Companion to Ethics,* ed. P. Singer, 366-72. Oxford: Blackwell Publishers, 1991.

Tesfai, J., ed. *The Scandal of a Crucified World: Perspectives on the Cross and Suffering.* Mary-knoll, N.Y.: Orbis, 1994.

Theissen, G. "Nonviolence and Love of Our Enemies (Matthew 5:38-48; Luke 6:27-38)." In G. Thiessen, *Social Reality and the Early Christians: Theology, Ethics, and the World of the New Testament,* 115-56. Edinburgh: T. & T. Clark, 1992.

Thielman, F. *From Plight to Solution: A Jewish Framework for Understanding Paul's View of the Law in Galatians and Romans.* Leiden: E. J. Brill, 1989.

———. "Law." *DPL,* 529-42.

Thompson, B. P., ed. *Scripture: Meaning and Method.* Hull, U.K.: Hull University Press, 1987.

Thompson, M. *Clothed with Christ: The Example and Teaching of Jesus in Romans 12:1–15:13.* Sheffield: Sheffield Academic Press, 1991.

Thorburn, S. "Restoration: A Better Way." In *Restorative Justice: Contemporary Themes and Practice,* ed. H. Bowen and J. Consedine, 64-66. Lyttelton, N.Z.: Ploughshares Publications, 1999.

Thrall, M. E. "The Offender and the Offence: A Problem of Detection in 2 Corinthians." In *Scripture: Meaning and Method,* ed. B. P. Thompson. Hull, U.K.: Hull University Press, 1987.

Tobin, T. H. "Controversy and Continuity in Romans 1:18–3:20." *CBQ* 55, no. 3 (1993): 298-318.

———. *The Spirituality of Paul.* Wilmington, Del.: Michael Glazier, 1987.

Toews, J. E. "Some Theses toward a Theology of Law in the New Testament." In *The Bible and Law,* ed. W. M. Swartley, 43-64. Elkhart, Ind.: Institute of Mennonite Studies, 1982.

Tolstoy, L. *The Kingdom of God and Peace Essays.* London: Oxford University Press, 1936.

———. *The Law of Love and the Law of Violence.* New York: Holt, Rinehart & Winston, 1970.

Towner, W. S. "Retribution." *IDB Supp,* 742-44.

Townsend, C. "Believing in Justice." In *Relational Justice: Repairing the Breach,* ed. J. Burnside and N. Baker, 133-46. Winchester, U.K.: Waterside Press, 1994.

Townsend, C., et al. *Political Christians in a Plural Society: A New Strategy for a Biblical Contribution.* Cambridge: Jubilee Policy Group, 1994.

Travis, S. H. *Christ and the Judgment of God: Divine Retribution in the New Testament.* London: Marshall & Pickering, 1986.

———. "Christ as Bearer of Divine Judgement in Paul's Thought about the Atonement." In *Jesus of Nazareth: Lord and Christ,* ed. J. B. Green and M. Turner, 332-45. Grand Rapids/Carlisle: William B. Eerdmans/Paternoster, 1994.

———. "The Problem of Judgement." *Themelios* 11, no. 2 (1986): 52-57.

———. "Wrath of God (NT)." *ABD,* 6: 996-98.

Troeltsch, E. *The Social Teaching of the Christian Churches.* 2 vols. London/New York: George Allen & Unwin/MacMillan, 1931.

Turner, K. "Justification and Justice in a Theology of Grace." *Theology Today* 55 (1999): 510-23.

Tutu, D. "Truth and Reconciliation and Healing." *MCC Peace Office Newsletter* 28, no. 3 (1998): 2-4.

Bibliography

Ucko, H., ed. *The Jubilee Challenge: Utopia or Possibility?* Geneva: WCC Publications, 1997.

Umbreit, M. *Crime and Reconciliation: Creative Options for Victims and Offenders.* Nashville: Abingdon, 1985.

van der Merwe, H. "The TRC: A Foundation for Community Reconciliation?" *MCC Peace Office Newsletter* 28, no. 3 (1998): 4-6.

van Ness, D. W. "Punishable by Death." *Christianity Today* 31, no. 10 (1987): 24-27.

van Schalkwyk, A. "A Gendered Truth: Women's Testimonies at the TRC and Reconciliation." *Missionalia* 27, no. 2 (1999): 165-88.

Vellenga, J. T. "Is Capital Punishment Wrong?" In *Essays on the Death Penalty,* ed. T. R. Ingram, 63-72. Houston: St. Thomas Press, 1963.

Vencer, J. "The Christian and the Death Penalty." Supplement to *The Evangelicals Today,* August/September 1992, 1-8.

Vermes, G. *The Dead Sea Scrolls in English,* 3d ed. Sheffield: Sheffield Academic Press, 1987.

Volf, M. *Exclusion and Embrace: A Theological Exploration of Identity, Otherness, and Reconciliation.* Nashville: Abingdon Press, 1996.

————, ed. *A Passion for God's Reign: Theology, Christian Learning, and the Christian Self.* Essays by J. Moltmann, N. Wolterstorff, and E. T. Charry. Grand Rapids: William B. Eerdmans, 1998.

von Rad, G. *Old Testament Theology.* 2 vols. London: SCM, 1962.

Walker, P. "Repairing the Breach: A Personal Motivation." In *Relational Justice: Repairing the Breach,* ed. J. Burnside and N. Baker, 147-55. Winchester, U.K.: Waterside Press, 1994.

Walters, J. C. *Ethnic Issues in Paul's Letter to the Romans: Changing Self-Definitions in Earliest Roman Christianity.* Valley Forge, Pa.: Trinity Press International, 1993.

Walvoord, J. F. "The Literal View." In *Four Views on Hell,* ed. W. V. Crockett, 11-28. Grand Rapids: Zondervan, 1992.

Wansink, C. S. *Chained in Christ: The Experience and Rhetoric of Paul's Imprisonments.* Sheffield: Sheffield Academic Press, 1996.

Ward, T. "Sin 'Not unto Death' and Sin 'unto Death' in 1 John 5:16." *Churchman* 109, no. 3 (1995): 226-37.

Watson, N. "Justification — A New Look." *ABR* 18 (1970): 41-43.

Weaver, D. J. "Transforming Nonresistance: From *Lex Talionis* to 'Do Not Resist the Evil One.'" In *The Love of Enemy and Nonretaliation in the New Testament,* ed. W. M. Swartley, 32-71. Louisville, Ky.: Westminster John Knox, 1992.

Webb, B. G., ed. *Christians in Society,* Explorations 3. Homebush West, N.S.W.: Lancer, 1988.

Weber, K. "The Image of the Sheep and the Goats in Matthew 25:1-46." *CBQ* 59, no. 4 (1997): 657-78.

Weinfeld, M. *Social Justice in Ancient Israel and in the Ancient Near East.* Minneapolis: Fortress Press, 1995.

Wengst, K. *Pax Romana and the Peace of Christ.* London: SCM, 1987.

Wenham, D. *Paul: Follower of Jesus or Founder of Christianity?* Grand Rapids: William B. Eerdmans, 1995.

BIBLIOGRAPHY

Wenham, G. J. "Grace and Law in the Old Testament." In *Law, Morality, and the Bible: A Symposium*, ed. B. N. Kaye and G. J. Wenham, 3-23. Leicester: Inter-Varsity Press, 1978.

———. "Law and the Legal System in the Old Testament." In *Law, Morality, and the Bible: A Symposium*, ed. B. N. Kaye and G. J. Wenham, 24-52. Leicester: Inter-Varsity Press, 1978.

———. "Original Sin in Genesis 1-11." *Churchman* 104, no. 4 (1990): 309-28.

Werblowsky, R. J. Z., and D. G. Wigoder, eds. *The Encyclopedia of the Jewish Religion*. London: Masada Press, 1965.

Westbrook, R. "Punishments and Crimes." *ABD*, 5:546-56.

Westerholm, S. *Israel's Law and the Church's Faith: Paul and His Recent Interpreters*. Grand Rapids: William B. Eerdmans, 1988.

———. *Preface to the Study of Paul*. Grand Rapids: William B. Eerdmans, 1997.

White, R. E. O. *Biblical Ethics: The Changing Continuity of Christian Ethics*. 2 vols. Exeter: Paternoster, 1979.

Wiebe, B. "Messianic Ethics." *Interpretation* 45, no. 1 (1991): 29-42.

———. *Messianic Ethics: Jesus' Proclamation of the Kingdom of God and the Church in Response*. Waterloo, Ont.: Herald Press, 1992.

Williams, D. J. *Paul's Metaphors: Their Context and Character*. Peabody, Mass.: Hendrickson, 1999.

Williams, R. "Penance in the Penitentiary." *Theology* 45, no. 764 (1992): 88-96.

Williams, S. K. "Again *Pistis Christou*." *CBQ* 49, no. 3 (1987): 431-47.

———. "The Righteousness of God in Romans." *JBL* 99 (1980): 241-98.

Wink, W. "Neither Passivity nor Violence: Jesus' Third Way (Matt 5:38-42 par)." In *The Love of Enemy and Nonretaliation in the New Testament*, ed. W. M. Swartley, 102-25, 133-36. Louisville, Ky.: Westminster John Knox, 1992.

———. *Violence and Non-Violence in South Africa: Jesus' Third Way*. Phildelphia/Santa Cruz: New Society Publishers, 1987.

Winter, B. "Civil Litigation in Secular Corinth and the Church: The Forensic Background to 1 Corinthians 6:1-8." *NTS* 37, no. 4 (1991): 557-72.

Wintle, B. C. "Justification in Pauline Thought." In *Right with God: Justification in the Bible and the World*, ed. D. A. Carson, 53-64. Exeter: Paternoster, 1992.

Witherington III, B. *Conflict and Community in Corinth: A Socio-Rhetorical Commentary on 1 and 2 Corinthians*. Exeter/Grand Rapids: Paternoster/William B. Eerdmans, 1995.

Wogaman, J. P. "Toward a Christian Definition of Justice." *Transformation* 7, no. 2 (1990): 18-23.

Wood, C. *The End of Punishment: Christian Perspectives on the Crisis in Criminal Justice*. Edinburgh: Saint Andrew Press, 1991.

Woodhead, L. "Love and Justice." *StChEth* 5, no. 1 (1992): 44-63.

Woods, L. "Opposition to a Man and His Message: Paul's 'Thorn in the Flesh' (2 Cor 12:7)." *ABR* 39 (1991): 44-53.

Wortham, R. A. "The Problem of Anti-Judaism in 1 Thess 2:14-16 and Related Pauline Texts." *BTB* 25, no. 1 (1995): 37-44.

Wray, D. E. "Biblical Church Discipline." *Churchman* 110, no. 4 (1996): 330-49.

Wright, C. J. H. *An Eye for an Eye: The Place of Old Testament Ethics Today.* Downers Grove, Ill.: InterVarsity Press, 1983.

———. *Human Rights: A Study in Biblical Themes.* Bramcote: Grove Books, 1979.

———. "Universalism and the World-Wide Community." *Churchman* 89, no. 3 (1975): 197-212.

———. *Walking in the Ways of the Lord: The Ethical Authority of the Old Testament.* Leicester: Apollos, 1995.

Wright, N. T. *The Climax of the Covenant: Christ and the Law in Pauline Theology.* Edinburgh: T. & T. Clark, 1991.

———. *Jesus and the Victory of God.* London: SPCK, 1996.

———. "Justification: The Biblical Basis and Its Relevance for Contemporary Evangelicalism." In *The Great Acquittal: Justification by Faith and Current Christian Thought,* ed. G. Reid, 13-37. London: Fount, 1980.

———. *The New Testament and the People of God.* London/Minneapolis: SPCK/Fortress Press, 1992.

———. "The New Testament and the 'State.'" *Themelios* 16, no. 1 (1990): 11-17.

———. "On Becoming the Righteousness of God: 2 Corinthians 5:21." In *Pauline Theology, Volume II: 1 and 2 Corinthians,* ed. D. M. Hay, 200-208. Minneapolis: Fortress Press, 1993.

———. "Paul and Submission to the State: Four Expositions on Romans 13:1-7." *Third Way* 2, no. 9 (1978): 6-7; 2, no. 10 (1978): 9; 2, no. 11 (1978): 7; 2, no. 12 (1978): 16.

———. "Romans and the Theology of Paul." In *Pauline Theology, Volume III: Romans,* ed. D. M. Hay and E. E. Johnson, 30-67. Minneapolis: Augsburg, 1995.

———. "Towards a Biblical View of Universalism." *Themelios* 4, no. 2 (1979): 54-58.

———. "Universalism and the World-Wide Community." *Churchman* 89, no. 3 (1975): 197–212.

———. *What Saint Paul Really Said.* Oxford: Lion, 1997.

Yinger, K. L. "Romans 12:14-21 and Nonretaliation in Second Temple Judaism: Addressing Persecution within the Community." *CBQ* 60 (1998): 74-96.

Yoder, J. H. "Anabaptists and the Sword Revisited: Systematic Historiography and Undogmatic Nonresistants." *Sonderdruck aus 'Zeitschrift für Kirchengeschichte,'* 2:270-83.

———. *The Christian and Capital Punishment.* Newton, Kans.: Faith and Life Press, 1961.

———. *Christian Attitudes to War, Peace, and Revolution: A Companion to Bainton.* Elkhart, Ind.: Goshen Biblical Seminary, 1983.

———. *The Christian Witness to the State.* Newton, Kans.: Faith and Life Press, 1964.

———. "The Death Penalty: A Christian Perspective." In *Capital Punishment Study Guide,* ed. L. Kehler et al., 44-50. Winnipeg: MCC Victim Offenders Ministries, 1980.

———. "Jesus and the Civil Order." In H. W. House and J. H. Yoder, *The Death Penalty Debate,* 139-47. Dallas: Word, 1991.

———. *The Politics of Jesus.* 2d ed. Grand Rapids/Carlisle: William B. Eerdmans/Paternoster, 1994.

Yoder, P. B. *From Word to Life: A Guide to the Art of Bible Study.* Scottdale, Pa.: Herald Press, 1982.

―――. *Shalom: The Bible's Word for Salvation, Justice, and Peace.* Newton, Kans.: Faith and Life Press, 1987.

Young, B. H. "'Save the Adulteress!' Ancient Jewish *Responsa* in the Gospels?" *NTS* 41, no. 1 (1995): 59-70.

Zehr, H. *Changing Lenses: A New Focus for Crime and Justice.* Scottdale, Pa.: Herald Press, 1990.

―――. *Death as a Penalty: A Moral, Practical, and Theological Discussion.* Elkhart, Ind.: MCC, n.d.

―――. "Justice that Heals: The Practice." *Stimulus* 2, no. 3 (1994): 69-74.

―――. "Justice that Heals: The Vision." *Stimulus* 2, no. 3 (1994): 5-11.

―――. "Retributive Justice, Restorative Justice." *NPCJ* 4 (1985).

Zerbe, G. M. *Non-Retaliation in Early Jewish and New Testament Texts: Ethical Themes in Social Contexts.* Sheffield: Sheffield Academic Press, 1993.

―――. "Paul's Ethic of Nonretaliation." In *The Love of Enemy and Nonretaliation in the New Testament,* ed. W. M. Swartley, 177-222. Louisville, Ky.: Westminster John Knox, 1992.

Ziesler, J. A. *The Meaning of Righteousness in Paul.* Cambridge: Cambridge University Press, 1971.

―――. *Paul's Letter to the Romans.* London/Philadelphia: SCM/Trinity, 1989.

―――. "Justification by Faith in the Light of the 'New Perspective' on Paul." *Theology* 759 (May/June, 1991): 188-93.

INDEX OF SCRIPTURE REFERENCES

INDEX OF SCRIPTURE REFERENCES

318

INDEX OF MODERN AUTHORS

INDEX OF SUBJECTS

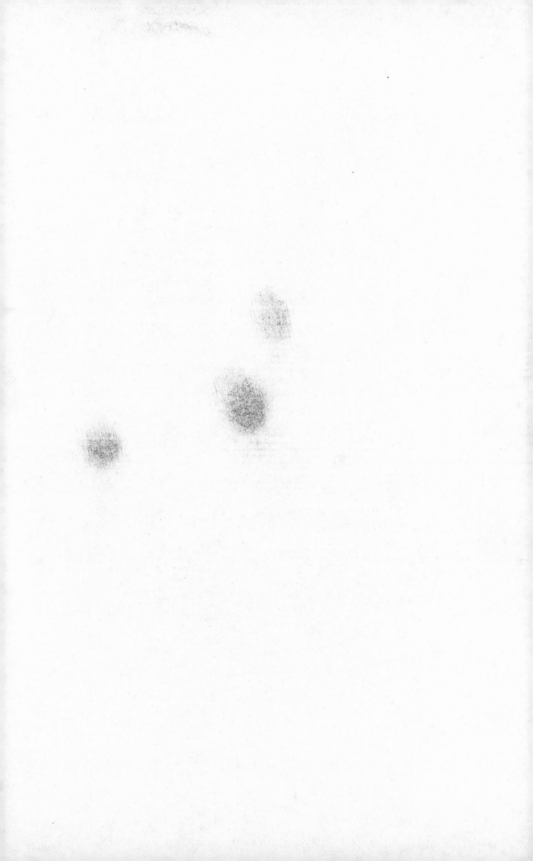